Jürg Kohlas   Bertrand Meyer
André Schiper (Eds.)

Dependable Systems: Software, Computing, Networks

Research Results of the DICS Program

 Springer

Volume Editors

Jürg Kohlas
University of Fribourg
Department of Informatics
Bd. de Pérolles 90, CH-1700 Fribourg, Switzerland
E-mail: juerg.kohlas@unifr.ch

Bertrand Meyer
ETH Zurich
Department of Computer Science
Clausiusstrasse 59, CH-8092 Zurich, Switzerland
E-mail: Bertrand.Meyer@inf.ethz.ch

André Schiper
EPFL, Faculté IC, Station 14
CH-1015 Lausanne, Switzerland
E-mail: andre.schiper@epfl.ch

Library of Congress Control Number: 2006929805

CR Subject Classification (1998): D.2, D.4, C.4, B.8

LNCS Sublibrary: SL 2 – Programming and Software Engineering

ISSN   0302-9743
ISBN-10   3-540-36821-3 Springer Berlin Heidelberg New York
ISBN-13   978-3-540-36821-2 Springer Berlin Heidelberg New York

Springer is a part of Springer Science+Business Media

springer.com

© Springer-Verlag Berlin Heidelberg 2006

Typesetting: Camera-ready by author, data conversion by Scientific Publishing Services, Chennai, India
Printed on acid-free paper   SPIN: 11808107   06/3142   5 4 3 2 1 0

Preface

Civilization relies on a functioning infrastructure, which is more and more enabled through information and communication technologies (ICT). A dependable information infrastructure is thus crucial for the modern society. On the other hand, information and communication systems belong to the most complex artifacts ever built by mankind. The design and operation of these systems are challenging tasks. Theories, methods and tools which help to master the problems encountered in the design process and the management of operations are therefore of utmost importance for the future of information and communication technology.

In view of the relevance of this topic in computer science, the Hasler Foundation launched in 2002 a research program on "Dependable Information and Communication Systems" (DICS). The call for projects was addressed to all Swiss universities. More than 40 short project proposals were submitted. Of these, 18 were selected for a hearing, in which a subset of these projects were selected and invited to submit complete project proposals. Finally, nine projects were selected for funding by the Hasler Foundation. All these projects were also partially supported by the universities involved as well as by other third parties, in particular by the Swiss National Foundation for Research.

The DICS projects started at the end of 2002 and the beginning of 2003. The members of the project teams met twice at workshops organized by the Hasler Foundation. The first one took place in Münchenwiler on March 16 and 17, 2004, the second workshop, which marked the conclusion of the projects, in Löwenberg on October 13 and 14, 2005. Each time more than 40 scientists participated in the workshop. The present volume documents the results of the DICS research program. Of course, the subject of dependable information and communication systems is not exhausted by this program. Much research is still needed. Therefore at the end of 2005, the Hasler Foundation launched a new program on "Managing Complexity of Information and Communication Systems" (MICS), which is intended as a follow-up and an extension of DICS.

The Hasler Foundation's existing endowments derive from the former Hasler AG (1852-1986), a pioneer of the Swiss telecommunications industry. The foundation is committed to promoting high-level research and education in the field of information and telecommunication systems. DICS is one of the research programs launched and supported by the foundation. We refer readers to the website www.haslerfoundation.ch for further information.

The Hasler Foundation thanks the editors and the authors of the present volume for their contributions. The editors also thank C. Schneuwly for assistance in editing. Finally, we thank Springer for accepting this volume in the prestigious *Lecture Notes in Computer Science*. It is our hope that this volume helps

to encourage further research in the crucial field of dependability of information
and communication systems.

May 2006   Jürg Kohlas
          Chairman of the Scientific Committee of the Hasler Foundation

Final DICS workshop, 13 October 2005: The participants at the training center of the
Swiss Federal Railways in Löwenberg (Photo: B. Meyer)

Introduction

For all the marvels that information technology delivers, we should never forget — and the users of our systems should never let us forget — that as the results we produce become ever more impressive, the burden on us to make them perform reliably grows ever heavier, simply because the more people rely on them the more critical any failure can be. This is the whole topic of dependability, a central issue in all disciplines of systems engineering.

No single publication could by itself do justice to this rich and vibrant field of research; the present volume presents a snapshot of some of the most interesting work being performed on this theme by teams in top Swiss universities. It covers three key aspects of dependability:

- Dependable software
- Dependable computing
- Dependable networks

Following this triple focus, the book consists of three surveys in Part I, one on each of these topics, then a collection of research contributions in Parts II, III and IV; each of these parts is devoted again to one of the topics, in the same order.

As the surveys in Part I will show, merely *defining* dependability is already a significant task. Each survey identifies major issues of dependability and presents the state of the art in providing solutions. Meyer's survey on dependable *software* uses a broad brush to explore the various techniques available for increasing the reliability of software systems, from management standards such as CMMI all the way down to static analysis, proofs and tests. Schiper's survey on the general topic of dependable *systems* introduces the fundamental, application-independent techniques in the field, with a special emphasis on replication techniques and the associated communication issues. The last survey, by Kurant, Nguyen and Thiran, addresses the specific area of IP over fiber networks, clearly essential in the future growth of the Internet and other networks; it focuses on techniques for failure location, protection and restoration.

Part II explores some aspects of *dependable software*. In the first chapter of this part, Arslan, Eugster, Meyer and Vaucouleur describe the current state of the SCOOP method — Simple Concurrent Object-Oriented Programming — and its implementation, designed to bring concurrent programming in its various incarnations (from multithreading to Internet programming) to the same level of abstraction and dependability as its sequential counterpart. The result is integrated in the object-oriented framework of the Eiffel language and fundamentally relies on notions of Design by Contract.

For a related set of applications of increasing importance, and in particular Web services, XML has emerged as the communication vehicle of choice, but in today's practice remains dissociated from programming languages, introducing a detrimental gap. Emir, Maneth and Odersky present the Scala language and framework which combine XML, Web Services and, again, concurrency in the framework of an object-oriented programming language, allowing a seamless integration of these different aspects under a single notational framework. As the reader will undoubtedly note, the design is based on decisions very different from those of SCOOP, providing the opportunity for interesting comparisons of viewpoints.

It is often difficult in a single step to arrive at a correct software solution for a complex problem; hence the idea of development by successive *refinements*. Baar, Marković, Fondement and Strohmeier explore its application to the stepwise development of object-oriented software by introducing the notion of contract refinement and applying it to an extended example. Unlike the previous two contributions this one uses, as its underlying technology, not a programming language but the UML modeling notation.

UML also underlies the final contribution to Part II, by Buchs, Pedro and Lúcio, devoted to the generation of test directly from specifications, expressed in the Fondue subset of UML; subsetting is indeed necessary for defining a precise semantics.

Part III is devoted to *dependable computing*, i.e., dependability at the middleware or system level. The first paper by Bünzli et al. presents recent advances in the context of group communication. Group communication is an abstraction that allows a distributed group of processes to provide a reliable service in spite of possible failures within the group. Reliability is achieved by replication: group communication provides the adequate communication abstraction among the replicas. The paper addresses various aspects of group communication: protocol frameworks used to build group communication stacks, new architectures for group communication stacks, specification of group communication, verification of distributed algorithms related to group communication and verification of group communication stacks.

The second paper, by Gerlach, Schaeli and Hersch, is devoted to dependability in the context of parallel applications. The authors have built a framework called *DPS (Dynamic Parallel Schedules)*, based on a flow graph, for the development of parallel applications on a cluster of workstations. The paper describes how fault tolerance has been added to the DPS framework using two techniques: backup threads (stateless and stateful) and checkpoints. A backup thread is mapped on a different node than its primary thread, allowing the computation to proceed in case of failures. Checkpointing allows a long-running computation to be restarted from a state different from its initial state.

The last paper of Part III, by Pautasso, Bausch and Alonso, addresses a similar problem in the context of a virtual laboratory, characterized by long-running and large-scale computations on a cluster. Virtual experiments are typically modelled as workflows. The paper describes the *JOpera* workflow system and focusses on its fault tolerant features. The system is able to adapt to processor failures by rescheduling jobs. The system also tolerates failures within its kernel, by ensuring that process execution resumes in a consistent state after a failure. Moreover, the kernel is able to automatically adapt its configuration to optimally use the available resources.

Part IV is devoted to *dependable networks*. The paper by Ducatelle et al. addresses the problem of failure location and traffic rerouting in large IP-over-fiber and wireless ad hoc networks. Traffic rerouting takes place once the failure has been located. Two algorithms for failure location are presented, one for IP/WDM (Wave-length Division Multiplexing), the other for wireless sensor networks. In a second part, failure restoration by rerouting is addressed. In the context of wireless sensor networks, failure restoration is done by a routing algorithm inspired from ant colonies.

The paper by Erlebach et al. addresses the robustness of the Internet. The authors point out that the traditional model of the Internet as a graph of autonomous system does not capture accurately the way traffic is routed, an important factor of robustness. Traffic routing mainly depends on economic relationships between autonomic systems. Traffic routing can be incorporated using the *valley-free path model*. However, this model makes the evaluation of the robustness computationally more difficult. Complexity and approximation results for disjoint paths and minimum cuts in that model are discussed. Experimental findings concerning the number of vertex-disjoint valid paths and the sizes of minimal cuts are also summarized.

The last paper, by Albrecht, Kuhn and Wattenhofer, is devoted to peer-to-peer (*P2P*) overlay networks. P2P systems are based on common desktop machines ("peers") distributed over a large-scale network such as the Internet. The focus of most research in P2P systems is the development of an efficient lookup operation: given a key, locate the peer responsible for the key. P2P systems are characterized by a high rate of peers joining and leaving the system (called *churns*). The paper describes a robust P2P system that can cope with such a highly dynamic situation. The idea is to maintain a simulated hypercube, and to adapt to churns by rearranging peers or by adjusting the dimension of the hypercube to the number of peers in the system.

May 2006   Bertrand Meyer, André Schiper

Table of Contents

Part IV: Dependable Networks

Dependable Software

Bertrand Meyer

ETH Zurich
http://se.ethz.ch

Abstract. Achieving software reliability takes many complementary techniques, directed at the process or at the products. This survey summarizes some of the most fruitful ideas.

1 Overview

Everyone who uses software or relies on devices or processes that use software — in other words, everyone — has a natural interest in guarantees that programs will perform properly. The following pages provide a review of techniques to improve software quality.

There are many subcultures of software quality research, often seemingly sealed off from each other; mentioning process-based approaches such as CMMI to programming language technologists, or tests to people working on proofs, can be as incongruous as bringing up Balanchine among baseball fans. This survey disregards such established cultural fences and instead attempts to include as many as possible of the relevant areas, on the assumption that producing good software is hard enough that "every little bit counts" [60]. As a result we will encounter techniques of very diverse kinds.

A note of warning to the reader seeking objectivity: I have not shied away from including references — easy to spot — to my own work, with the expectation (if a justification is needed) that it makes the result more lively than a cold inspection limited to other people's products and publications.

2 Scope and Terminology

The first task is to define some of the fundamental terms. Even the first word of this article's title, determined by the Hasler Foundation's "Dependable Information and Communication Systems" project, requires clarification.

2.1 Reliability and Dependability

In the software engineering literature the more familiar term is not "dependable" but "reliable", as in "software reliability". A check through general-purpose and technical dictionaries confirms that the two have similar definitions and are usually translated identically into foreign languages.

There does exist a definition of dependability [1] from the eponymous IFIP Working Group 10.4 [39] that treats reliability as only one among dependability

J. Kohlas, B. Meyer, and A. Schiper (Eds.): Dependable Systems, LNCS 4028, pp. 1 – 33, 2006.

attributes, along with availability, safety, confidentiality, integrity and maintainability. While possibly applicable to a computing system as a whole, this classification does not seem right for their software part, as some attributes such as availability are not properties of the software per se, others such as confidentiality are included in reliability (through one of its components, security), and the remaining ones such as maintainability are of dubious meaning for software, being better covered by other quality factors such as extendibility and reusability [57].

As a consequence of these observations the present survey interprets dependability as meaning the same thing, for software, as reliability.

2.2 Defining Reliability

The term "software reliability" itself lacks a universally accepted definition. One could argue for taking it to cover all "external quality factors" such as ease of use, efficiency and extendibility, and even "internal quality factors" such as modularity. (The distinction, detailed in [57], is that external factors are the properties, immediate or longterm, that affect companies and people purchasing and using the software, whereas internal factors are perceptible only to software developers although in the end they determine the attainment of external factors.)

It is reasonable to retain a more restricted view in which reliability only covers three external factors: *correctness*, *robustness* and *security*. This doesn't imply that others are irrelevant; for example even the most correct, robust and secure system can hardly be considered dependable if in practice it takes ages to react to inputs, an *efficiency* problem. The same goes for *ease of use*: many software disasters on record happened with systems that implemented the right functions but made them available through error-prone user interfaces. The reasons for limiting ourselves to the three factors listed are, first, that including all others would turn this discussion into a survey of essentially the whole of software engineering (see [33]); second, that the techniques to achieve these three factors, although already very diverse, have a certain kindred spirit, not shared by those for enhancing efficiency (like performance optimization techniques), ease of use (like ergonomic design) and other external and internal factor.

2.3 Correctness, Robustness, Security

For the three factors retained, we may rely on the following definitions:

- Correctness is a system's ability to perform according to its specification in cases of use within that specification.
- Robustness is a system's ability to prevent damage in cases of erroneous use outside of its specification.
- Security is a system's ability to prevent damage in cases of hostile use outside of its specification.

They correspond to levels of increasing departure from the specification. The specification of any realistic system makes assumptions, explicit or implicit, about the conditions of its use: a C compiler's specification doesn't define a generated program if the input is payroll data, any more than a payroll program defines a pay check if the input is a C program; and a building's access control software specification cannot define what happens if the building has burned. By nature, the requirements defined by robustness and security are different from those of correctness: outside of the specification, we can no longer talk of "performing" according to that specification, but only seek the more modest goal of "preventing damage"; note that this implies the ability to *detect* attempts at erroneous or hostile use.

Security deserves a special mention as in recent years it has assumed a highly visible place in software concerns. This is a phenomenon to be both lamented, as it signals the end of a golden age of software development when we could concentrate on devising the best possible functionality without too much concern about the world's nastiness, and at the same time taken to advantage, since it has finally brought home to corporations the seriousness of software quality issues, a result that decades of hectoring by advocates of modern software engineering practices had failed to achieve. One of the most visible signs of this phenomenon is Bill Gates's edict famously halting all development in February of 2001 in favor of code reviews for hunting down security flaws. Many of these flaws, such as the most obnoxious, buffer overflow, are simply the result of poor software engineering practices. Even if focusing on security means looking at the symptom rather than the cause, fixing security implies taking a coherent look at software tools and techniques and requires, in the end, ensuring reliability as a whole.

2.4 Product and Process

Any comprehensive discussion of software issues must consider two complementary aspects: *product* and *process*.

The products are the software elements whose reliability we are trying to assess; the process includes the mechanisms and procedures whereby people and their organizations build these products.

2.5 The Products of Software

The products themselves are diverse. In the end the most important one, for which we may assess correctness, robustness and security, is code. But even that simple term covers several kinds of product: source code as programmers see it, machine code as the computer executes it, and any intermediate versions as exist on modern platforms, such as the bytecode of virtual machines.

Beyond code, we should consider many other products, which in their own ways are all "software": requirements, specifications, design diagrams and other design documents, test data — but also test plans —, user documentation, teaching aids...

To realize why it is important in the search for quality to pay attention to products other than code, it suffices to consider the results of numerous studies, some already decades old [10], showing the steep progression of the cost of correcting an error the later it is identified in the lifecycle.

2.6 Deficiencies

In trying to ascertain the reliability of a software product or process we must often — like a detective or a fire prevention engineer — adopt a negative mindset and look for sources of *violation* of reliability properties. The accepted terminology here distinguishes three levels:

- A *failure* is a malfunction of the software. Note that this term does not directly apply to products other than executable code.
- A *fault* is a departure of the software product from the properties it should have satisfied. A failure always comes from a fault, although not necessarily a fault in the code: it could be in the specification, in the documentation, or in a nonsoftware product such as the hardware on which the system runs.
- An *error* is a wrong human decision made during the construction of the system. "Wrong" is a subjective term, but for this discussion it's clear what it means: a decision is wrong if it can lead to a fault (which can in turn cause failures).

In a discussion limited to *software* reliability, all faults and hence all failures result from errors, since software is an intellectual product not subject to the slings and arrows of the physical world.

The more familiar term for "error" is *bug*. The upper crust of the software engineering literature shuns it for its animist connotations. "Error" has the benefit of admitting that our mistakes don't creep into our software: we insert them ourselves. In practice, as may be expected, everyone says "bug".

2.7 Verification and Validation

Even with subjectivity removed from the definition of "error", definitions for the other two levels above remains relative: what constitutes a "malfunction" (for the definition of failures) or a "departure" from desirable properties (for faults) can only be assessed with respect to some description of the expected characteristics.

While such reference descriptions exist for some categories of software product — an element of code is relative to a design, the design is relative to a specification, the specification is relative to an analysis of the requirements — the chain always stops somewhere; for example one cannot in the end certify that the requirements have no fault, as this would mean assessing them against some higher-level description, and would only push the problem further to assessing the value of the description itself. Turtles all the way up.

Even in the absence of another reference (another turtle) against which to assess a particular product, we can often obtain some evaluation of its quality by performing *internal* checks. For example:

- A program that does not initialize one of its variables along a particular path is suspicious, independently of any of its properties vis-à-vis the fulfillment of its specification.
- A poorly written user manual may not explicitly violate the prescriptions of another project document, but is problematic all the same.

This observation leads to distinguishing two complementary kinds of reliability assessment, *verification* and *validation*, often combined in the abbreviation "V&V":

- Verification is *internal* assessment of the consistency of the product, considered just by itself. The last two examples illustrated properties that are subject to verification: for code; for documentation. Type checking is another example.

- Validation is *relative* assessment of a product vis-à-vis another that defines some of the properties that it should satisfy: code against design, design against specification, specification against requirements, documentation against standards, observed practices against company rules, delivery dates against project milestones, observed defect rates against defined goals, test suites against coverage metrics.

A popular version of this distinction [10] is that verification is about ascertaining that the product is "doing things right" and validation that it is "doing the right thing". It only applies to code, however, since a specification, a project plan or a test plan do not "do" anything.

3 Classifying Approaches

One of the reasons for the diversity of approaches to software quality is the multiplicity of problems they address. The following table shows a list of criteria, essentially orthogonal, for classifying them.

Criteria for classifying approaches to software reliability

A priori (*build*)		A posteriori (*assess and correct*)
Process		Product
Manual		Tool-supported
Technology-neutral		Technology-specific
Product- and phase-neutral	*vs*	Product- or phase-specific
Static (uses software text)		Dynamic (requires execution)
Informal		Mathematical
Complete (guarantee)		Partial (some progress)
Free		Commercial

The first distinction is cultural almost as much as it is technical. With *a priori* techniques the emphasis is methodological: telling development teams to apply certain rules to produce a better product. With *a posteriori* techniques, the goal is to examine a proposed software product or process element for possible deficiencies, with the aim of correcting them. While it is natural to state that the two are complementary rather than contradictory — a defense often used by proponents of "a posteriori" approaches such as testing when criticized for accepting software technology as it is rather than helping to improve it — they correspond to different views of the software world, one hopeful of prevention and the other willing to settle down for cure.

The second distinction corresponds to the two dimensions of software engineering cited above: are we working on the *products*, or on the *processes* leading to them?

Some approaches are of a methodological nature and just require applying some practices; we may call them *manual*, in contrast with techniques that are *tool-supported* and hence at least partially automated.

An idea can be applicable regardless of technology choices; for example processbased techniques such as CMMI, discussed below, explicitly stay away from prescribing specific technologies. At the other extreme, certain techniques may be applicable only if you accept a certain programming language, specification method, tool or other technology choice. We may talk of *technology-neutral* and *technology-specific* approaches; this is more a spectrum of possibilities than a black-and-white distinction, since many approaches assume a certain class of technologies—such as object-oriented development — encompassing many variants.

Some techniques apply to a specific product or phase of the lifecycle: specification (a specification language), implementation (a static analyzer of code)... They are *product-specific*, or *phase-specific*. Others, such as configuration management tools, apply to many or all product kinds; they are *product-neutral*. "Product" is used here to denote one of the types of outcome of the software construction process.

For techniques directed at program quality, an important division exists between *dynamic* approaches such as testing, which rely on executing the program, and purely *static* ones, such as static analysis and program proofs, which only need to analyze the program text. Here too some nuances exist: a simulation technique requires execution and hence can be classified as dynamic even though the execution doesn't use the normal run-time environment; model-checking is classified as static even though in some respect it is close to testing.

Some methods are based on *mathematical* techniques; this is obviously the case with program proofs and formal specification in general. Many are more *informal*.

A technique intended to assess quality properties can give you a *complete* guarantee that they are satisfied, or—more commonly—some *partial* reassurance to this effect.

The final distinction is economic: between techniques in the public domain — usable for free, in the ordinary sense of the term — and commercial ones.

4 Process-Based Approaches

We start with the least technical approaches, emphasizing management procedures and organizational techniques.

4.1 Lifecycle Models

One of the defining acts of software engineering was the recognition of the separate activities involved, in the form of "lifecycle models" that prescribe a certain order of tasks (see the figure on the adjacent page). The initial model is the so-called "waterfall" [11], still used as a reference for discussions of the software process although no longer recommended for literal application. Variants include:

- The "V model" which retains the sequential approach of the waterfall but divides the process into two parts, the branches of the "V"; activities along the first branch are for development, those in the second branch are for verification and validation, each applied to the results of one of the steps along the first branch.

Lifecycle models, illustrated

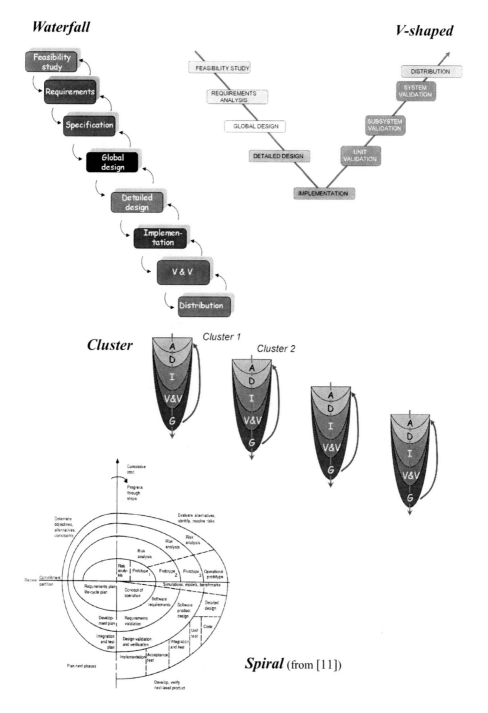

Spiral (from [11])

- The "Spiral model" [11] which focuses on reducing risk in project management, in particular the risk caused by the all-or-nothing attitude of the Waterfall approach. The spiral model suggests isolating subsets of the system's functionality that are small enough to be implemented quickly, and when they have been implemented taking advantage of the experience to proceed to other parts of the system. The idea is connected with the notion of rapid prototyping.
- The "Rational Unified Process", distinguishing four phases, inception, elaboration, construction and transition, with a spiral-like iterative style of development and a set of recommended "best practices" such as configuration management.
- The "Cluster model" [51] [57], emphasizing a different form of incrementality— building a system by layers, from the most fundamental to the most user-oriented — and a *seamless* process treating successive activities, from analysis to design, implementation and maintenance, as a continuum. This model also introduces, as part of the individual lifecycle of every cluster, a *generalization* step to prepare for future reuse of some of the developed elements.

The figure shows pictorial representations of some of these models.

Whatever their effect on how people actually develop software, the contribution of lifecycle models has been a classification and definition of the activities involved in software development, even when these activities are not executed as *phases* in the precise order mandated by, for example, the waterfall model. Software quality benefits in particular from:

- A distinction between *requirements*, the recording of user requirements, and *specification*, their translation into a systematic form suitable for software development, where rigor and precision are essential.
- Recognition of the importance of Verification and Validation tasks.
- Recognition of post-delivery activities such as maintenance, although they still do not occupy a visible enough place. Many software troubles result from evolutions posterior to the initial release.
- In the Cluster model, the presence, for each cluster, of the generalization task to prepare for reuse.
- Also in the Cluster model, the use of a *seamless* and *reversible* approach which unifies the methods, tools, techniques and notations that help throughout the software process, rather than exaggerate them. (The textbook counter-example here is the use of UML for analysis and design [56].)
- The growing emphasis on *incrementality* in the development process, even if this concept is understood differently in, for example, the spiral, cluster and RUP models.

4.2 Organizational Standards

Another process-related set of developments has had a major effect, largely beneficial, on some segments of the industry. In the early 1990s the US Department of Defense, concerned with the need to assess its suppliers' software capabilities and to establish consistent standards, entrusted the Software Engineering Institute with the task of developing a "Capability Maturity Model", whose current incarnation, CMMI [74] (the I is for Integration) provides a collection of standards applicable to various disciplines, rather than a single model for software. Largely independently, the International Standard Organization has produced a set of software-oriented variants of its 9000-series quality standards, which share a number of properties with CMMI. The present discussion is based on CMMI.

Beyond its original target community, CMM and CMMI have been the catalyst for one of the major phenomena of the IT industry starting in the mid-nineties: the development of offshore software production, especially in India [63]. CMMI qualification provides suppliers of outsourcing development services with quality standards and the associated possibility of independent certification, without which customers would not be have known how to trust distant, initially unknown contractors.

CMMI is (in the earlier classification) product-neutral, phase-neutral and technology-neutral. In its application to software it is intended only to determine how well an organization controls its development process by defining and documenting it, recording and assessing how it is applied in practice, and working to improve it. It doesn't prescribe what the process should be, only how much you are on top of it. You could presumably be developing in PL/I on IBM 370 and get CMMI qualification.

CMMI assesses both the *capability* level of individual "process areas" in (such as software) in an organization, and the *maturity* of an organization as a whole. It distinguishes five levels of increasing maturity:

- *Performed*: projects happen and results get produced, but there is little control and no reproducibility; the process is essentially reactive.
- *Managed*: processes are clearly defined for individual projects, but not for the organization as a whole. They remain largely reactive.
- *Defined*: proactive process defined for the organization.
- *Quantitatively managed*: the control mechanisms do not limit themselves to qualitative techniques, but add well-defined numerical measurements.
- *Optimizing*: the mechanisms for controlling processes are sufficiently well established that the focus can shift on improving the organization and its processes.

Through their emphasis on the process and its repeatability, CMMI and ISO standards help improve the quality of software development. One may expect such improvements of the process to have a positive effect on the resulting products as well; but they are only part of the solution. After a software error—one module of the software was expecting measures in the metric system, another was providing them in English units — was identified as the cause of the failure of the NASA Mars Orbiter Vehicle mission [82], an engineer from the project noted that the organization was heavily into ISO and other process standards. Process models and process-focused practices are not a substitute for using the best technological solutions. Tailored versions of CMMI that would not shy away from integrating specific technologies such as object technology could be extremely useful. In the meantime, the technology-neutral requirements of CMMI can be applied by organizations to get a better hold on their software processes.

4.3 Extreme Programming

The Extreme Programming movement [6] is a reaction against precisely the kinds of lifecycle models and process-oriented approaches just reviewed. XP (as it is also called) emphasizes instead the primacy of code. Some of the principal ideas include:

- Short release cycles to get frequent feedback.
- Pair programming (two people at a keyboard and terminal).
- Test-driven development.
- A general distrust of specification and design: *testing* is the preferred guide of development.
- Emphasis on programmers' welfare.

Some of these practices are clearly beneficial to quality but were developed prior to XP, in particular short release cycles (Microsoft's "daily build" as described in 1995 by Cusumano and Shelby [19], see also [54]) and the use of frequent testing as part of development (see e.g. "quality first" [55]). Those really specific to XP are of limited interest (while sometimes a good practice, pair programming cannot be imposed indiscriminately, both because it doesn't work for some people and because those who find it useful may not find it useful all the time) or, in the case of tests viewed as a *replacement* for specifications, downright detrimental. See [75] and [64] for critiques of the approach.

4.4 Code Inspections

A long-established quality practice is the inspection, also known as *review*: a session designed to examine a certain software element with the aim of finding flaws. The most common form is *code* inspection, but the process can be applied to any kind of software engineering product. Rules include:

- Small meeting: at most 8 people or so, including the developer of the element under review.
- The elements under review and any supporting documents must be circulated in advance; the participants should have read them and identified possible criticisms before the meeting. The allotted time should be bounded, for example 2 or 3 hours.
- The meeting must have a moderator to guide discussions and a secretary to record results.
- The moderator should not be the developer's manager. The intent is to evaluate products, not people.
- The sole goal is to identify deficiencies and confirm that they are indeed deficiencies; correction is not part of the process and should not be attempted during the meeting.

Code inspections can help avoid errors, but to assess their usefulness one must compare the costs with those of running automated *tools* that can catch some of the same problems without human intervention; static analyzers, discussed below, are an example.

Some companies have institutionalized the rule that no developer may check in code (integrate it into the repository for a current or future product) without approval by one other developer, a limited form of code inspection that has a clearly beneficial effect by forcing the original developer to convince at least one other team member of the suitability of the contribution.

4.5 Open-Source Processes

A generalization of the idea of code inspection is the frequent assertion, by members of the open-source community, that the open-source process dramatically improves quality by enabling many people to take a critical look at the software text; some have gone so far as to state that *"given enough eyes, all bugs are shallow"* [73].

As with many of the other techniques reviewed, we may see in this idea a beneficial contribution, but not a panacea. John Viega gives [78] the example of a widely used security program in which *"in the past two years, several very subtle buffer overflow problems have been found... Almost all had been in the code for years, even though it had been examined many times by both hackers and security auditors One tool was able to identify one of the problems as potentially exploitable, but researchers examined the code thoroughly and came to the conclusion that there was no way the problem could be exploited."* (The last observation is anecdotal evidence for the above observation that tools such as static analyzers are potentially superior to human analysis.)

While is no evidence that open-source software as a whole is better (or worse) than commercial software, and no absolute rule should be expected if only because of the wide variety of products and processes on both sides, it is clear that more eyes potentially see *more* bugs.

4.6 Requirements Engineering

In areas such as embedded systems, many serious software failures have been traced [45] to inadequate requirements rather than to deficiencies introduced in later phases. Systematic techniques for requirements analysis are available [76] [40] to improve this critical task of collecting customer wishes and translating them into a form that can serve as a basis for a software project.

4.7 Design Patterns

A process-related advance that has had a strong beneficial effect on software development is the emergence of design patterns [32]. A pattern is an architectural scheme that has been recognized as fruitful through frequent use in applications, and for which a precise description exists according to a standard format. Patterns provide a common vocabulary to developers, hence simplifying design discussions, and enable them to benefit from the collective wisdom of their predecessors.

A (minority) view of patterns [62] [65] understands them as a first step towards the technique discussed next, reusable components. Patterns, in this interpretation, suffer from the limitation that each developer must manually insert the corresponding solutions into the architecture of every applicable system. If instead it is possible to turn the pattern into a reusable component, developers can directly reuse the corresponding solution through an API (Abstract Program Interface). The observation here is that *it is better to reuse than to redo*. Investigations [65] suggest that with the help of appropriate programming language constructs up to two thirds of common design patterns can be thus **componentized**.

4.8 Trusted Components

Quality improvement techniques, whether they emphasize the process or the product, are only as good as their actual application by programmers. The magnitude of the necessary education effort is enough to temper any hope of major short-term improvements, especially given that many programmers have not had the benefit of a formal computer science education to start with.

Another practical impediment to continued quality improvement comes from market forces. The short-term commercial interest of a company is generally to release software that is "good enough" [83]: software that has barely passed the threshold under which the market would reject it because of bad quality; not excellent software. The extra time and expense to go from the first to the second stage may mean, for the company, losing the market to a less scrupulous competitor, and possibly going out of business. For the industry as a whole, software quality has indeed improved regularly over time but tends to peak below the optimum.

An approach that can overcome these obstacles is increased reliance on reusable components, providing pre-built solutions to problems that arise in many different applications, either regardless of the technical domain (*general-purpose* component libraries) or in particular fields (*specialized* libraries). Components have already changed the nature of software development by providing conveniently packaged implementations, accessible through abstract interfaces, of common aspects such as graphical user interfaces, database manipulation, basic numerical algorithms, fundamental data structures and others, thereby elevating the level at which programmers write their applications. When the components themselves are of good quality, such reuse has highly beneficial effects since developers can direct their efforts to the quality of the application-specific part of their programs.

Examining more closely the relationship of components to quality actually highlights two separate effects: it is comforting to know that the quality of a system will benefit from the quality of its components; but we must note that reuse magnifies the bad as well as the good: *imperfections* can be even more damaging in components than in "one-ofa-kind" developments, since they affect every application that relies on a component.

The notion of *trusted component* [58] [61] follows from this analysis that one of the most pressing and promising tasks for improving software quality is the industrial production of reusable components equipped with a guarantee of quality. Producing such trusted components may involve most of the techniques discussed elsewhere in this article. For some of the more difficult ones, such as program proving, application to components may be the best way to justify the cost and effort and recoup the investment thanks to the scaling effect of component reuse: once a component has reached the level of quality at which it can really be trusted, it will benefit every application that relies on it.

5 Tools and Environments

Transitioning now to product-oriented solutions, we examine some of the progress in tools available to software developers — to the extent that it is relevant for software quality.

5.1 Configuration Management

Configuration management is a both practice (for the software developer) and a service (from the supporting tools), so it could in principle be classified under "process" as well as under "product". It belongs more properly to the latter category since it's tools that make configuration management realistic; applied as a pure organizational practice without good tool support, it quickly becomes tedious and ceases being applied.

Configuration management may be defined as the systematic collecting and registering of project elements, including in particular the ability to:

- Register a new version of any project element.
- Retrieve *any* previously registered version of any project element
- Register dependencies, both between project elements and between registered *versions* of project elements (e.g. A relies on B, and version 10 of A requires version 7, 8 or 9 of B).
- Construct composite products from their constituents — for example, build an executable version of a program from its modules — or reconstruct earlier versions, in accordance with registered dependencies.

A significant number of software disasters on record followed from configuration management errors, typically due to reintroducing an obsolete version of a module when compiling a new release of a program, or using an obsolete version of some data file. Excuses no longer exist for such errors, as acceptable configuration management tools, both commercial and open-source, are widely available. These tools, while still far from what one could hope for, have made configuration management one of the most important practices of modern software development.

Source code is not the only beneficiary of configuration management. Any product that evolves, has dependencies on other elements and may need restoring to an earlier state should be considered for inclusion in the configuration management repository. Besides code this may include project plans, specification and design documents, user manuals, training documents such as PowerPoint slides, test data files.

5.2 Metrics and Models

If we believe Lord Kelvin's (approximate) maxim that all serious study is quantitative, then software and software development should be susceptible to measurement, tempered of course by Einstein's equally famous quote that not everything measurable is worth measuring. A few software properties, process or product, are at the same time measurable, worth measuring and relevant to software reliability.

On the process side, **cost** in its various dimensions is a prime concern. While it is important to record costs, if only for CMMI-style traceability, what most project managers want at a particular time is a *model* to estimate the cost of a future project or of the remainder of a current project. Such models do exist and can be useful, at least if the development process is stable and the project is comparable to previous ones: then by estimating a number of project parameters and relying on historical data for comparison one can predict costs—essentially, person-months—within reasonable average accuracy. A well-known cost model, for which free and commercial tools are available, is COCOMO II [12].

During the development of a system, **faults** will be reported. In principle they shouldn't be comparable to the faults of a material product, since software is an intellectual product and doesn't erode, wear out or collapse under attack from the weather. In practice, however, statistical analysis shows that faults in large projects can follow patterns that resemble those of hardware systems and are susceptible to similar statistical prediction techniques. That such patterns can exist is in fact consistent with intuition: if the tests on the last five builds of a product under development have each uncovered one hundred new bugs each, it is unlikely that the next iteration will have zero bugs, or a thousand. *Software reliability engineering* [69][46] elaborates on these ideas to develop models for assessing and predicting failures, faults and errors. As with cost models, a requirement for meaningful predictions is the ability to rely on historical data for calibration. Reliability models are not widely known, but could help software projects understand, predict and manage anomalies better.

More generally, numerous **metrics** have been proposed to provide quantitative assessments of software properties. Measures of complexity, for example, include: "source lines of code" (SLOC), the most primitive, but useful all the same; "function points" [25], which count the number of elementary mechanisms implemented by the software; measures of the complexity of the control graph, such as "cyclomatic complexity" [48][49]; and measures specifically adapted to object-oriented software [35][59]. The EiffelStudio environment [30] makes it possible to compute many metrics applied to a project under development, including measures regarding the use of contracts (section 8), and to compare them with values on record. While not necessarily meaningful in isolation, such measures elements are a useful control tool for the manager; they are in line with the CMMI's insistence that an organization can only reach the higher levels of process maturity (4 and 5) by moving from the qualitative to the quantitative, and should be part of the data collected for such an effort.

5.3 Static Analyzers

Static analyzers are another important category of tools, increasingly integrated in development environments, whose purpose is to examine the software text for deficiencies. They lie somewhere between type checkers (themselves integrated in compilers) and full program provers, and will be studied below (7.2) after the discussion of proofs.

5.4 Integrated Development Environments

Beyond individual tools the evolution of software development has led to the widespread of integrated tool suites known as IDEs for Integrated (originally: Interactive) Development Environments. Among the best known are Microsoft's Visual Studio [66] and IBM's Eclipse [27]; EiffelStudio [30] is another example. These environments, equipped with increasingly sophisticated graphical user interfaces, provide under a single roof a whole battery of mechanisms to write software (editors), manage its evolution (configuration management), compile it (compilers, interpreters, optimizers), examine it effectively (browsers), run it and elucidate the sources of faults (debuggers, testers), analyze it for possible inconsistencies and errors (static analysis), generate code from design and analysis diagrams or the other way around (diagramming, "Computer-Aided Software

Engineering" or CASE, reverse engineering), change architecture in a safe way through tool-controlled transformations (refactoring), perform measurements as noted above (metric tools), and other tasks.

This is one of the most active areas in software engineering; programmers, for whom IDEs are the basic daily tools, are directly interested in their quality, so that open-source projects such as Eclipse and EiffelStudio benefit from active community participation. The effect of these advanced frameworks on software reliability, while diffuse, is undeniable, as their increasing cleverness supports quality in several ways: finding bugs through static and dynamic techniques; avoiding new bugs through mechanisms such as refactoring; generating some of the code without manual intervention; and, more generally, providing a level of comfort that frees programmers from distractions and lets them apply their best skills to the hardest issues of software construction.

6 Programming Languages

The evolution of programming languages plays its part in the search for more reliable software. High-level languages contribute both positively, by providing higher levels of expression through advanced constructs freeing the programmer (in the same spirit as modern IDEs) from mundane, repetitive or irrelevant tasks, and negatively, by ruling out certain potentially unsafe constructs and, as a result, eradicate entire classes of bugs at the source.

The realization that programming language constructs could exert a major influence on software quality both through what they offer and what they forbid dates back to *structured* programming [22] [20] which, in the early seventies, led to rejecting the **goto** as a control structure in favor of more expressive constructs — sequence, conditional, loop, recursion. The next major step was *object-oriented* programming, introducing a full new set of abstractions, in particular the notion of class, providing decomposition based on object types rather than individual operations, and techniques of inheritance and genericity.

In both cases the benefit comes largely from being able to reason *less operationally* about software. A software text represents many possible executions, so many in fact that it is hard to understand the program — and hence to get it right — by thinking in terms of what happens at execution [22]. Both structured and object-oriented techniques make it possible to limit such operational thinking and instead understand the abstract properties of future run-time behaviors by applying the usual rules of logical reasoning.

In drawing the list of programming languages' most important contributions to quality, we must indeed put at the top all the mechanisms that have to do with **structure**. With ever larger programs addressing ever more ambitious goals, the production and maintenance of reliable software requires safe and powerful modular decomposition facilities. Particularly noteworthy are:

- As pointed out, the **class** mechanism, which provides a general basis for stable modules with a clear role in the overall architecture.
- Techniques for **information hiding**, which protect modules against details of other modules, and permit independent evolution of the various parts of a system.

- **Inheritance**, allowing the classification and systematic organization of classes into structured collections, especially with *multiple* inheritance.
- **Genericity**, allowing the construction of type-parameterized modules.

Another benefit of modern languages is **static typing** which requires programmers to declare types for all the variables and other entities in their programs, then takes advantage of this information to detect possible inconsistencies in their use and reject programs, at compilation time, until all types fit. Static typing is particularly interesting in object-oriented languages since inheritance supports a flexible type system in which types can be compatible even if they are not identical, as long as one describes a specialization of the other.

Another key advance is **garbage collection**, which frees programmers from having to worry about the details of memory management and removes an entire class of errors —such as attempts to access a previously freed memory cell—which can otherwise be particularly hard to detect and to correct, in particular because the resulting failures are often intermittent rather than deterministic. Strictly speaking, garbage collection is a property of the language implementation, but it's the language definition that makes it possible, as with modern object-oriented languages, or not, as in languages such as C that permit arbitrary pointer arithmetic and type conversions.

Exception handling, as present in modern programming languages, helps improve software robustness by allowing developers to include recovery code for run-time faults that would otherwise be fatal, such as arithmetic overflow or running out of memory.

A mechanism that is equally far-reaching in its abstraction benefits is the "closure", "delegate" or "**agent**" [62]. Such constructs wrap operations in objects that can then be passed around anonymously across modules of a system, making it possible to treat routines as first-class values. They drastically simplify certain kinds of software such as numerical applications, GUI programming and other event-driven (or "publishsubscribe") schemes.

The application of programming language techniques to improving software quality is limited by the continued reliance of significant parts of the software industry on older languages. In particular:

- Operating systems and low-level system-related tend to be written in C, which retains its attractions for such applications in spite of widely known deficiencies, such as the possibility of buffer overflow.
- The embedded and mission-critical community sometimes prefers to use lowlevel languages, including assembly, for fear of the risks potentially introduced by compilers and other supporting tools.

The "Verifying Compiler Grand Challenge" [38] [77] is an attempt to support the development of tools that—even with such programming languages—will guarantee, during the process of compiling and thanks to techniques described in the following sections, the reliability of the programs they process.

7 Static Verification Techniques

Static techniques work solely from the analysis of the software text: unlike dynamic techniques such as tests they do not require any execution to verify software or report errors.

7.1 Proofs

Perhaps the principal difference between mathematics and engineering is that only mathematics allows providing absolute guarantees. Given the proper axioms, I can assert with total confidence that two plus two equals four. But if I want to drive to Berne the best assurance I can get that my car will not break down is a probability. I know it's higher than if I just drive it to the suburbs, and lower than if my goal were Prague, Alma-Ata, Peking or Bombay; I can make it higher by buying a new, better car; but it will never be one. Even with the highest attention to quality and maintenance, physical products will occasionally fail.

Under appropriate assumptions, a program is like a mathematical proposition rather than a material device: any general property of the program—stating that *all* executions of the program will achieve a certain goal, or that *at least one* possible execution will— is either true or false, and whether it is true or not is entirely determined by the text of the program, at least if we assume correct functioning of the hardware and of other software elements needed to carry out program execution (compiler, run-time system, operating system). Another way of expressing this observation is that a programming language is similar to a mathematical theory, in which certain propositions are true and others false, as determined by the axioms and inference rules.

In principle, then, it should be possible to prove or disprove properties of programs, in particular correctness, robustness and security properties, using the same rigorous techniques as in the proofs of any mathematical theorem. This assumes overcoming a number of technical difficulties:

- Programming languages are generally *not* defined as mathematical theories but through natural-language documents possessing a varying degree of precision. To make formal reasoning possible requires describing them in mathematical form; this is known as providing a *mathematical semantics* (or "formal semantics") to a programming language and is a huge task, especially when it comes to modeling advanced mechanisms such as exception handling and concurrency, as well as the details of computer arithmetic since the computer's view of integers and reals strays from their standard mathematical properties.
- The theorems to be proved involve specific properties of programs, such as the value of a certain variable not exceeding a certain threshold at a certain state of the execution. Any proof process requires the ability to express such properties; this means extending the programming language with boolean-valued expressions, called *assertions*. Common languages other than Eiffel do not include an assertion mechanism; this means that programmers will have to resort to special extensions such as JML for Java [43] (see also Spec#, an extension of the C# language [5]) and annotate programs with the appropriate assertions. Some tools such as Daikon help in this process by extracting tentative assertions from the program itself [31].
- In practice the software's actual operation depends, as noted, on those of a supporting hardware and software environment; proofs of the software must be complemented by guarantees about that environment.
- Not all properties lend themselves to easy enunciation. In particular, "nonfunctional" properties such as performance (response time, bandwidth, memory occupation) are hard to model.

- More generally, a proof is only as useful as the program properties being proven. What is being proved is not the perfection of the program in any absolute sense, nor even its quality, but only that it satisfies the assertions stated. It is never possible to know that *all* properties of interest have been included. This is not just a theoretical problem: security attacks often take advantage of auxiliary aspects of the program's behavior, which its design and verification did not take into account.
- Even if the language, the context and the properties of interest are fully specified semantically and the properties relevant, the proof process remains a challenge. It cannot in any case be performed manually, since even the proof of a few properties of a moderately sized programs quickly reaches into the thousands of proof steps. Fully automated proofs are, on the other hand, generally not possible. Despite considerable advances in computer-assisted proof technology (for programs as well as other applications) significant proofs still require considerable user interaction and expert knowledge.

Of course the effort may well be worthwhile, especially in two cases: life-critical systems in transportation and defense to which, indeed, much proof work has been directed; and reusable components, for which the effort is justified—as explained in the discussion of Trusted Components above — by the scaling-up effect of reuse.

Here are some of the basic ideas about how proofs work. A typical program element to prove would be, in Eiffel notation.

```
decrement
          -- Decrease counter by one.
    require
          counter > 0
    do
          counter := counter - 1
    ensure
          counter = old counter - 1
          counter >= 0
    end
```

This has a program body, the **do** clause, and two assertions, a "precondition" introduced by **require** and a "postcondition" introduced by **ensure** and consisting of two subclauses implicitly connected by an **and**. Assertions are essentially Boolean expressions of the language with the possibility, in a postcondition, of using the **old** notation to refer to values on entry: here the first subclause of the postcondition states that the value of counter will have been decreased by one after execution of the **do** clause.

Program proofs deal with such annotated programs, also called *contracted* programs (see section 8 below). The annotations remind us that proofs and other software quality assurance technique can never give us absolute guarantees of quality: we can never say that a program is "correct", only assess it — whether through rigorous techniques like proofs or using more partial ones such as those reviewed next—*relatively to* explicitly stated properties, expressed here through assertions integrated in the program text.

From a programmer's viewpoint the above extract is simply the text of a routine to be executed, with some extra annotations, the precondition and postcondition, expressing properties to be satisfied before and after. But for proof purposes this text is a *theorem*, asserting that whenever the body (the **do** clause with its assignment instruction) is executed with the precondition satisfied it will terminate in such a way that the postcondition is satisfied.

This theorem appears to hold trivially but — even before addressing the concern noted above that computer integers are not quite the same as mathematical integers — proving it requires the proper mathematical framework. The basic rule of *axiomatic semantics* (or "Hoare semantics" [37]) covering such cases is the assignment axiom, which for any variable x and expression e states that the following holds

> **require** $Q(e)$ **do** $x := e$ **ensure** $Q(x)$

where $Q(x)$ is an assertion which may depend on x; then $Q(e)$ is the same assertion with every mention of x replaced by e, except for **old** x which must be replaced by x.

This very general axiom captures the properties of assignment (in the absence of side effect in the evaluation of e); its remarkable feature is that it is applicable even if the source expression e contains occurrences of the target variable x, as in the example (where x is counter).

We may indeed apply the axiom to prove the example's correctness. Let $Q1(x)$ be $x =$ **old** $x - 1$, corresponding to the first subclause of the postcondition, and $Q2(x)$ be $x >= 0$. Applying the rule to $Q1$ (counter), we replace counter by counter + 1 and **old** counter by counter; this gives counter − 1 = counter − 1, which trivially holds. Applying now the same transformations to $Q2$ (counter), we get *counter* − 1 >= 0, which is equivalent to the precondition counter > 0. This proves the correctness of our little assertion-equipped example.

From there the theory moves to more complex constructions. An inference rule states that if you have proved

> **require** P **do** *Instruction_1* **ensure** Q

and

> **require** Q **do** *Instruction_2* **ensure** R

(note the postcondition of the first part matching the precondition of the second part) you are entitled to deduce

> **require** P **do** *Instruction_1* ; *Instruction_2* **ensure** Rt

and so on for more instructions. A rule in the same style enables you to deduce properties of **if** c **then** I1 **else** I2 **end** from properties of I1 and I2. More advanced is the case of loops: to prove the properties of

> **from**
>   *Initialization*
> **until**
>   *Exit*
> **loop**
>   *Body*
> **end**

you need, in this general approach, to introduce a new assertion called the **loop invariant** and an integer expression called the **loop variant**. The invariant is a weakened form of the desired postcondition, which serves as approximation of the final goal; for example if the goal is to compute the maximum of a set of values, the invariant will be "Result is the maximum of the values processed so far". The advantage of the invariant is that it is possible both to:

- Ensure the invariant through initialization (the **from** clause in the above notation); in the example the invariant will be trivially true if we start with just one value and set Result to that value.
- Preserve the invariant through one iteration of the loop body (the **loop** clause); in the example it suffices to extend the set of processed values by one element v and execute **if** v > Result **then** Result := v **end**.

If indeed a loop possesses such an invariant and its execution terminates, then on exit the invariant will still hold (since it was ensured by the initialization and preserved by all the loop iterations), together with the Exit condition. The combination of these two assertions gives the postcondition of the loop. Seen the other way around, if we started from a desired postcondition and weakened it to get an invariant, we will obtain a correct program. In the example, if the exit condition states that we have processed all values of interest, combining this property with the invariant "Result is the maximum of the values processed so far" tells us that Result is the maximum of all values.

Such reasoning is only interesting if the loop execution actually terminates; this is where the loop variant comes in. It is an integer expression which must have a nonnegative value after the Initialization and decrease, while remaining non-negative, whenever the Body is executed with the Exit condition not satisfied. The existence of such an expression is enough to guarantee termination since a non-negative integer value cannot decrease forever. In the example a variant is $N - i$ where N is the total number of values being considered for the maximum (the proof assumes a finite set) and i the number of values processed.

Axioms and inference rules similarly exist for other constructs of programming languages, becoming, as noted, more intricate as one moves on to more advanced mechanisms.

For concurrent, reactive and real-time systems, boolean assertions of the kind illustrated above may not be sufficient; it is often convenient to rely on properties of **temporal logic** [47], which given a set of successive observations of a program's execution, can express, for a boolean property Q:

- **forever** Q: from now on, Q will always hold.
- **eventually** Q: at some point in the future (where "future" includes now), Q will hold.
- P **until** Q: Q will hold at some point in the future, and until then P will hold.

Regardless of the kind of programs and properties being targeted, there are two approaches to producing program proofs. The **analytic** method takes programs as they exist, then after equipping them with assertions, either manually or with some automated aid as noted above, attempts the proof. The **constructive** method [24] [2] [68] integrates the proof process in the software construction process, often using successive *refinements* to go from specification to implementation through a sequence of transformations, each proved to preserve correctness, and integrating more practical constraints at every step. Proof technology has had some notable successes, including in industrial systems (and in hardware design), but until recently has remained beyond the reach of most software projects.

7.2 Static Analysis

If hoping for a proof covering all the correctness, reliability and security properties of potential interest is often too ambitious, the problem becomes more approachable if we settle for a subset of these properties — a subset that may be very partial but very interesting. For example being able to determine that no buffer overflow can ever arise in a certain program—in other words, to provide a firm guarantee, through analysis of the program text, that every index used at run time to access an item in an array or a character in a string will be within the defined bounds—is of great practical value since this rules out a whole class of security attacks.

Static analysis is the tool-supported analysis of software texts for the purpose of assessing specific quality properties. Being "static", it requires no execution and hence can in principle be applied to software products other than code. Proofs are a special case, the most far-reaching, but other static analysis techniques are available.

At the other extreme, a well-established form of elementary static analysis is *type checking*, which benefits programs written in a statically typed programming language. Type checking, usually performed by the compiler rather than by a separate tool, ascertains the type consistency of assignments, routine calls and expressions, and rejects any program that contains a type incompatibility.

More generally, techniques usually characterized as static analysis lie somewhere between such basic compiler checks and full program proofs. Violations that can typically be detected by static analysis include:

- Variables that, on some control paths, would be accessed before being initialized (in languages such as C that do not guarantee initialization).
- Improper array and string access (buffer overflow).
- Memory properties: attempt to access a freed location, double freeing, memory leak…
- Pointer management (again in low-level languages such as C): attempts to follow void or otherwise invalid pointers.
- Concurrency control: deadlocks, data races.
- Miscellaneous: certain cases of arithmetic overflow or underflow, changes to supposedly constant strings…

Static analysis tools such as PREfix [72] have been regularly applied for several years to new versions of the Windows code base and have avoided many potential errors.

One of the issues of static analysis is the occurrence of *false alarms*: inconsistency reports that, on inspection, do not reveal any actual error. This was the weak point of older static analyzers, such as the widely known *Lint* tool which complements the type checking of C compilers: for a large program they can easily swamp their users under thousand of messages, most of them spurious, but requiring a manual walkthrough to sort out the good from the bad. (In the search for errors, of course, the "good" is what otherwise would be considered the bad: evidence of wrongdoing.) Progress in static analysis has been successful in considerably reducing the occurrence of false alarms.

The popularity of static analysis is growing; the current trend is to extend the reach of static analysis tools ever further towards program proofs. Two examples are:

- Techniques of *abstract interpretation* [18] with the supporting ASTRÉE tool [9], which has been used to prove the absence of run-time errors in the primary flight control software, written in C, for the Airbus A340 fly-by-wire system.
- ESC-Java [21] and, more recently, the Boogie analyzer [4] make program proving less obtrusive by incrementally extending the kind of diagnostics with which programmers are familiar, for example type errors, to more advanced checks such as the impossibility to guarantee that an invariant is preserved.

7.3 Model Checking

The **model checking** approach to verification [36] [17] [3] is static, like proofs and static analysis, but provides a natural link to the dynamic techniques (testing) studied below. The inherent limitation of tests is that they can never be exhaustive; for any significant system—in fact, even for toy examples—the number of possible cases skyrockets into the combinatorial stratosphere, where the orders of magnitude invite lyrical comparisons with the number of particles in the universe.

The useful measure is the number of possible *states* of a program. The notion of state was implicit in the earlier discussion of assertions. A state is simply a snapshot of the program execution, as could be observed, if we stop that execution, by looking up the contents of the program's memory, or more realistically by using the debugger to examine the values of the program's variables. Indeed it is the combination of all the variables' values that determines the state. With every 64-bit integer variable potentially having 2^{64} values, it is not surprising that the estimates quickly go galactic.

Model checking attempts exhaustive analysis of program states anyway by performing *predicate abstraction*. The idea is to simplify the program by replacing all expressions by boolean expressions (predicates), with only two possible values, so that the size of the state space decreases dramatically; it will still be large, but the power of modern computers, together with smart algorithms, can make its exploration tractable. Then to determine that a desired property holds — for example, a security property such as the absence of buffer overflows, or a timing property such as the absence of deadlock — it suffices to evaluate the corresponding assertion in all of the abstract states and, if a violation of that assertion (or *counter-example*) is found, to check that it also arises in the original program.

For example, predicate abstraction will reduce a conditional instruction **if** a > b **then**... to **if** p **then**..., where p is a boolean. This immediately cuts down the number of cases from 2128 to 2. The drawback is that the resulting program is only a caricature of the original; it loses the relation of p to other predicates involving a and b. But it has an interesting property: *if the original violates the assertion, then the abstracted version also does*. So the next task is to look for any such violation in the abstracted version. This may be possible through exhaustive examination of its reduced state space, and if so is *guaranteed* to find any violation in the original program, but even so is not the end of the story, since the reverse proposition does not hold: a counter-example in the abstracted program does not necessarily signal a counter-example in the original. It could result from the artificial merging of several cases, for example if it occurs on a path — impossible in an execution of the original program — obtained by selecting both p and q as true where q is the abstraction of $b > a + 1$. Then examining the state space of the abstracted program will either:

- Not find any violations, in which case it *proves* there was none in the original program.
- Report violations, each of which might be an error in the original or simply a false alarm generated by the abstraction process.

So the remaining task, if counter-examples have been found, is to ascertain whether they arise in the original. This involves defining the path predicate that leads to each counter-example, expressing it in terms of the original program variables (that is to say, removing the predicate abstraction, giving, in the example, a > b **and** b > a + 1) and determining if any combination of values for the program variables can satisfy the predicate: if such a combination, or *variable assignment*, exists, then the counter example is a real one; if not, as in the case given, it is spurious.

This problem of *predicate satisfiability* is computationally hard; finding efficient algorithms is one of the central areas of research in model checking.

The focus on counter-examples gives model checking a practical advantage over traditional proof techniques. Unless a software element was built with verification in mind (through a "constructive method" as defined above), the first attempt to verify it will often fail. With proofs, this failure doesn't tell us the source of the problem—and could actually signal a limitation of the proof procedure rather than an error in the program. With model checking, you get a counter-example which directly shows what's wrong.

Model checking has captured considerable attention in recent years, first in hardware design and then in reactive and real-time systems, for which the assertions of interest are often expressed in temporal logic.

8 Design by Contract

The goal of developing software to support full proofs of correctness properties is, as noted, desirable but still unrealistic for most projects. Even a short brush with program proving methods suggests, however, that more rigor can be highly beneficial to software quality. The techniques of *Design by Contract* go in this direction and deliver part of the corresponding benefits without requiring the full formality of proof-directed development.

The discussion of proofs introduced Eiffel notations such as
- **require** assertion   -- A routine precondition
- **ensure** assertion   -- A routine postcondition

associated with individual routines. They are examples of **contract** elements which specify abstract semantic properties of program constructs. Contracts apply in particular to:

- Individual routines: **precondition**, stating the condition under which a routine is applicable; **postcondition**, stating what condition it will guarantee in return when it terminates.
- In object-oriented programming, classes: **class invariant**, stating consistency conditions that must hold whenever an object is in a stable state. For example, the invariant for a "paragraph" class in a text processing system may state that the total length of letters and spaces is equal to the paragraph width. Every routine that can modify an instance of the class may assume the class invariant on entry (in addition to its precondition) and must restore it on exit (in addition to ensuring its postcondition).
- Loops: **invariant** and (integer) **variant** as discussed above.
- Individual instructions: "assert" or "check" constructs.

The discipline of Design by Contract [53] [57] [67] gives a central role to these mechanisms in software development. It views the overall process of building a system as defining a multitude of relationships between "client" and "supplier" modules, each specified through a contract in the same manner as relationships between companies in the commercial world.

The benefits of such a method, if carried systematically, extend throughout the lifecycle, supporting the goal of *seamlessness* discussed earlier:

- Contracts can be used to express *requirements* and *specifications* in a precise yet understandable way, preferable to pure "bubbles and arrows" notations, although of course they can be displayed graphically too.
- The method is also a powerful guide to *design* and *implementation*, helping developers to understand better the precise reason and context for every module they produce, and as a consequence to get the module right.
- Contracts serve as a *documentation* mechanism: the "**contract view**" of a class, which discards implementation-dependent elements but retains externally relevant elements and in particular preconditions, postconditions and class invariants, often provides just the right form of documentation for software elements, especially reusable components: precise enough thanks to the contracts; abstract enough thanks to the removal of implementation properties; extracted from the program text, and hence having a better chance of being up to date (at least one major software disaster was traced [41] to a software element whose specification had changed, unbeknownst to the developers who reused it); cheap to produce, since this form of documentation can be generated by tools from the source text, rather than written separately; and multi-purpose, since the output can be tuned to any appropriate format such as HTML. Eiffel environments such as EiffelStudio produce such views [30], which serve as the basic form of software documentation.
- Contracts are also useful for *managers* to understand the software at a high level of abstraction, and as a tool to control *maintenance*.
- In object-oriented programming, contracts provide a framework for the proper use of *inheritance*, by allowing developers to specify the semantic framework within which routines may be further refined in descendant classes. This is connected with the preceding comment about management, since a consequence is to allowa manager to check that refinements to an design are consistent with its original

intent, which may have been defined by the top designers in the organization and expressed in the form of contracts.

- Most visibly, contracts are a **testing** and **debugging** mechanism. Since an execution that violates an assertion always signals a bug, turning on contract monitoring during development provides a remarkable technique for identifying bugs. This idea is pursued further by some of the tools cited in the discussion of testing below.

Design by Contract mechanisms are integrated in the design of the Eiffel language [52] [28] and a key part of the practice of the associated method. Dozens of contract extensions have been proposed for other programming languages (as well as UML [80]), including many designs such as JML [43] for Java and the Spec# extension of C# [5].

9 Testing

Testing [70] [8] is the most widely used form of program verification, and still for many teams essentially the only one. In academic circles testing has long suffered from a famous comment [23] that (because of the astronomical number of possible states) "testing can only show the presence of bugs, but never to show their absence". In retrospect it's hard to find a rational explanation for why this comment ever detracted anyone from the importance of tests, since it in no way disproves the usefulness of testing: finding bugs is a very important task of software development. All it indicates is that we should understand that finding bugs is indeed the sole purpose of testing, and not delude ourselves that test results directly reflect the level of quality of a product under development.

9.1 Components of a Test

Successful testing relies on a **test plan**: a strategy, expressed in a document, describing choices for the tasks of the testing process. These tasks include:

- Determining which parts to test.
- Finding the appropriate input values to exercise.
- Determining the expected properties of the results (known as *oracles*). Input values and the associated oracles together make up *test cases*, the collection of which constitutes a *test suite*.
- Instrumenting the software to run the tests (rather than perform its normal operation, or in addition to it); this is known as building a **test harness**, which may involve *test drivers* to solicit specific parts to be tested, and *stubs* to stand for parts of the system that will not be tested but need a placeholder when other parts call them.
- Running the software on the selected inputs.
- Comparing the outputs and behavior to the oracles.
- Recording the test data (test cases, oracles, outputs) for future re-testing of the system, in particular *regression testing*, the task of verifying that previously corrected errors have not reappeared.

In addition there will be a phase of *correction* of the errors uncovered by the test, but in line with the above observations this is not part of testing in the strict sense.

9.2 Kinds of Test

One may classify tests with respect to their **scope** (this was used in the earlier description of the V model of the lifecycle):

- A*unit test* covers a module of the software.
- *Integration test* covers a complete cluster or subsystem.
- A*system test* covers the complete delivery.
- *User Acceptance Testing* involves the participation of the recipients of the system (in addition to the developers, responsible for the preceding variants) to determine whether they are satisfied with the delivery.
- *Business Confidence Testing* is further testing with the users, in conditions as close as possible to the real operating environment.

An orthogonal classification addresses **what** is being tested:

- *Functional* testing: whether the system fulfills the functions defined in the specification.
- *Performance* testing: its use of resources.
- *Stress* testing: its behavior under extreme conditions, such as heavy user load.

Yet another dimension is **intent**: testing can be *fault-directed* to find deficiencies but also (despite the above warnings), *conformance-directed* to estimate satisfaction of desired properties, or *acceptance testing* for users to decide whether to approve the product. *Regression testing*, as noted, re-runs tests corresponding to previously identified errors; surprisingly to the layman, errors have a knack for surging back into the software, sometimes repeatedly, long after they were thought corrected.

The testing technique, in particular the construction of test suites, can be:

- *Black-box*: based on knowledge of the system's specification only.
- *White-box*: based on knowledge of the code, which makes it possible for example to try to exercise as much of that code as possible.

Observing the state of the art in software testing suggests that four issues are critical: managing the test process; estimating the quality of test suites; devising oracles; and— the toughest — generating test cases automatically.

9.3 Managing the Testing Process

Test management has been made easier through the appearance of **testing frameworks** such as JUnit [42] and Gobo Eiffel Test [7] which record test harnesses to allow running the tests automatically. This removes a considerable part of the burden of testing and is important for regression testing.

An example of a framework for regression testing of a compiler, incorporating every bug ever found since 1991, is EiffelWeasel [29]. Such automated testing require a solid multi-process infrastructure, to ensure for example that if a test run causes a crash the testing process doesn't also crash but records the problem and moves on to the next test.

9.4 Estimating Test Quality

Being able to estimate the quality of a test suite is essential in particular to know when to stop testing. The techniques are different for white-box and black-box testing.

With white-box testing it is possible to define various levels of **coverage**, each assuming the preceding ones: *instruction* coverage, ensuring that through the execution of the selected test cases every instruction is executed at least once; *branch* coverage, where every boolean condition tests at least once to true and once to false; *condition* coverage, where this is also the case for boolean sub-expressions; *path* coverage, for which every path has been taken; *loop* coverage, where each loop body has been executed at least *n* times for set *n*.

Another technique for measuring test suite quality in white-box approaches is **mutation testing** [79]. Starting with a program that passes its test suite, this consists of making modifications — similar, if possible, to the kind of errors that programmers would make — to the program, and running the tests again. If a "mutant" program still passes the tests, this indicates (once you have made sure the mutant is not *equivalent* to the original, in other words, the changes are meaningful) that the tests were not sufficient. Mutation testing is an active area of research [71]; one of the challenges is to use appropriate mutation operators, to ensure diversity of the mutants.

With black-box testing the previous techniques are not available since they assume access to the source code to set up the test plan. It is possible to define notions of *specification coverage* to estimate whether the tests have exercised the various cases listed in the specification; if contracts are present, this will mean analyzing the various cases listed in the preconditions. *Partition testing* [81] is the general name for techniques (black- or white-box) that split the input domain into representative subsets, with the implication that any test suite must cover all the subsets.

9.5 Defining Oracles

An oracle, allowing interpretation of testing results, provides a decision criterion for accepting or rejecting the result of a test. The preparation of oracles can be as much work as the rest of the test plan. The best solution that can be recommended is to rely on contracts: any functional property of a software system (with the possible exception of some user-interface properties for which human assessment may be required) can be expressed as a routine postcondition or a class invariant.

These assertions can be included in the test harness, but it is of course best, as noted in the discussion of Design by Contract, to make them an integral part of the software to be tested as it is developed; they will then provide the other benefits cited, such as aid to design and built-in documentation, and will facilitate regression testing.

9.6 Test Case Generation

The last of the four critical issues listed, test case generation, is probably the toughest; *automatic* generation in particular. Even though we can't ever get close to exhaustive testing, we want the test process to cover as many cases as possible, and especially to make sure they are representative of the various potential program executions—as can be assessed in white-box testing by coverage measures and mutation, but needs to be sought in any form of testing.

For any realistic program, manually prepared tests will never cover enough cases; in addition, they are tedious to prepare. Hence the work on automatic test case generation, which tries to produce as many representative test cases as possible, typically working from specifications only (black-box). Two tools in this area are Korat for JML [13] and AutoTest for Eiffel [15] (which draws on the advantage that—contracts being native to Eiffel—existing Eiffel software is typically equipped with large numbers of assertions, so that AutoTest can be run on software *as is*, and indeed has already uncovered a significant number of problems in existing programs and libraries).

Manual tests, which benefit from human insight, remain indispensable. The two kinds are complementary: manual tests are good at depth, automatically generated tests at breadth. In particular, any run that ever uncovered a bug, whether through manual or automatic techniques, should become part of the regression test suite. AutoTest integrates manual tests and regression tests within the automatic test case generation and execution framework [44].

Automatic test case generation needs a strategy for selecting inputs. Contrary to intuition, *random* testing [34], which selects test data randomly from the input domain, can be an effective strategy if tuned to ensure a reasonably even distribution over that domain, a policy known as *adaptive random testing* [14] which has so far been applied to integers and other simple values (for which a clear notion of distance exists, so that "even distribution" is immediately meaningful). Recent work [16] extends the idea to object-oriented programming by defining a notion of object distance.

10   Conclusion

This survey has taken a broad sweep across many techniques that all have something to contribute to the aim of software reliability. While it has stayed away from the gloomy picture of the state of the industry which seems to be de rigueur in discussions of this topic, and is not justified given the considerable amount of quality-enhancing ideas, techniques and tools that are available today and the considerable amount of good work currently in progress, it cannot fail to note as a conclusion that the industry could do much more to take advantage of all these efforts and results.

There is not enough of a reliability culture in the software world; too often, the order of concerns is cost, then deadlines, then quality. It is time to reassess priorities.

Acknowledgments

The material in this chapter derives in part from the slides for an ETH industry course on Testing and Software Quality Assurance prepared with the help of Ilinca Ciupa, Andreas Leitner and Bernd Schoeller. The discussion of CMMI benefited from the work of Peter Kolb in the preparation of another ETH course, "Software Engineering for Outsourced and Offshored Development". Bernd Schoeller and Ilinca Ciupa provided important comments on the draft.

"Design by Contract" is a trademark of Eiffel Software.

The context for this survey was provided by the Hasler Foundation's grant for our SCOOP work in the DICS project. We are very grateful for the opportunities that the grant and the project have provided, in particular for the experience gained in the two DICS workshops in 2004 and 2005.

References

Note: All URLs listed were active in April 2006.

[1] Algirdas Avizienis, Jean-Claude Laprie and Brian Randell: *Fundamental Concepts of Dependability*, in *Proceedings of Third Information Survivability Report*, October 2000, pages 7-12, available among other places at citeseer.ist.psu.edu/article/avizienis01 fundamental.html.

[2] Ralph Back: *A Calculus of Refinements for Program Derivations*, in *Acta Informatica*, vol. 25, 1988, pages 593-624, available at crest.cs.abo.fi/publications/public/1988/ ACalculusOfRefinementsForProgramDerivationsA.pdf.

[3] Thomas Ball and Sriram K. Rajamani: *Automatically Validating Temporal Safety Properties of Interfaces*, in *SPIN 2001*, Proceedings of Workshop on Model Checking of Software, Lecture Notes in Computer Science 2057, Springer-Verlag, May 2001, pages 103-122, available at tinyurl.com/qrm9m.

[4] Mike Barnett, Robert DeLine, Manuel Fähndrich, K. Rustan M. Leino, Wolfram Schulte: *Verification of object-oriented programs with invariants*, in *Journal of Object Technology*, vol. 3, no. 6, Special issue: ECOOP 2003 workshop on Formal Techniques for Java-like Programs, June 2004, pages 27-56, available at www.jot.fm/issues/issue_2004_06/article2.

[5] Mike Barnett, K. Rustan M. Leino and Wolfram Schulte: *The Spec# Programming System: An Overview*, in *CASSIS 2004: Construction and Analysis of Safe, Secure Interoperable Smart devices*, Lecture Notes in Computer Science 3362, Springer-Verlag, 2004, available at research.microsoft.com/specsharp/papers/krml136.pdf; see also other Spec# papers at research.microsoft.com/specsharp/.

[6] Kent Beck and Cynthia Andres: *Extreme Programming Explained: Embrace Change.* 2ⁿᵈ edition, Addison-Wesley, 2004.

[7] Éric Bezault: Gobo Eiffel Test, online documentation at www.gobosoft.com/eiffel/gobo/ getest/index.html.

[8] Robert Binder: Testing *Object-Oriented Systems: Models, Patterns, and Tools*, Addison-Wesley, 1999.

[9] Bruno Blanchet, Patrick Cousot, Radhia Cousot, Jérôme Feret, Laurent Mauborgne, Antoine Miné, David Monniaux and Xavier Rival: *ASTRÉE: A Static Analyzer for Large Safety-Critical Software*, in *Applied Deductive Verification*, Dagstuhl Seminar 3451, November 2003, available at www.di.ens.fr/~cousot/COUSOTtalks/Dagstuhl-3451-2003.shtml. See also ASTRÉE page at www.astree.ens.fr.

[10] Barry W. Boehm: *Software Engineering Economics*, Prentice Hall, 1981.

[11] Barry W. Boehm: *A Spiral Model of Software Development and Enhancement*, in Computer (IEEE), vol. 21, no. 5, May 1988, pages 61-72.

[12] Barry W. Boehm et al.: *Software Cost Estimation with COCOMO II*, Prentice Hall, 2000.

[13] Chandrasekhar Boyapati, Sarfraz Khurshid and Darko Marinov: *Korat: Automated Testing Based on Java Predicates*, in Proceedings of the 2002 International Symposium on Software Testing and Analysis (ISSTA), Rome, July 22--24, 2002, available at tinyurl.com/qwwd3.

[14] T.Y. Chen, H. Leung and I.K. Mak: *Adaptive random testing*, in *Advances in Science - ASIAN 2004: Higher-Level Decision Making*, 9th Asian Computing Science Conference, ed. Michael J. Maher, Lecture Notes in Computer Science 3321, Springer-Verlag, 2004, available at tinyurl.com/lpxn5.

[15] Ilinca Ciupa and Andreas Leitner: *Automated Testing Based on Design by Contract*, in Proceedings of Net.ObjectsDays 2005, 6th Annual Conference on Object-Oriented and Internet-Based Technologies, Concepts and Applications for a Networked World, 2005, pages 545-557, available at se.ethz.ch/people/ciupa/papers/soqua05.pdf. See also AutoTest page at se.ethz.ch/research/autotest.

[16] Ilinca Ciupa, Andreas Leitner, Manuel Oriol and BertrandMeyer: *Object Distance and its Application to Adaptive Random testing of Object-Oriented Programs*, submitted for publication, 2006, available at se.ethz.ch/~meyer/publications/testing/object_distance.pdf.

[17] Edmund M. Clarke Jr., Orna Grumberg and Doron A. Peled: *Model Checking*, MIT Press, 1999.

[18] Patrick Cousot: *Verification by Abstract Interpretation*, in *International Symposium on Verification Theory & Practice Honoring Zohar Manna's 64th Birthday*, ed. Nachum Dershowitz, Lecture Notes in Computer Science 2772, Springer-Verlag, 2003, pages 243-268.

[19] Michael Cusumano and Richard Selby: *Microsoft Secrets*, The Free Press, 1995.

[20] Ole-Johan Dahl, Edsger W. Dijkstra and C.A.R. Hoare: *Structured Programming*, Academic Press, 1971.

[21] David L. Detlefs, K. Rustan, M. Leino, Greg Nelson, and James B. Saxe: *Extended Static Checking*, Research Report 159, Compaq Systems Research Center, December 1998, available at ftp://gatekeeper.research.compaq.com/pub/DEC/SRC/researchreports/SRC-159.pdf.

[22] Edsger W. Dijkstra: *Go To Statement Considered Harmful*, in *Communications of the ACM*, Vol. 11, No. 3, March 1968, pages 147-148, available at www.acm.org/classics/oct95/.

[23] Edsger W. Dijkstra: *Notes on Structured Programming*, in [20]; original typescript available at www.cs.utexas.edu/users/EWD/ewd02xx/EWD249.PDF.

[24] Edsger W. Dijkstra: *A Discipline of Programming*, Prentice Hall, 1978.

[25] Brian J. Dreger: *Function Point Analysis*, Prentice Hall, 1989.

[26] Paul Dubois, Mark Howard, Bertrand Meyer, Michael Schweitzer and Emmanuel Stapf: *From Calls to Agents*, in *Journal of Object-Oriented Programming* (JOOP), vol. 12, no. 6, September 1999, available at se.ethz.ch/~meyer/publications/joop/agent.pdf.

[27] Eclipse pages at www.eclipse.org.

[28] ECMA/ISO: *Eiffel: Analysis, Design and Programming Language*, standard ECMA 367, accepted in April 2006 as ISO standard, available at www.ecmainternational.org/publications/standards/Ecma-367.htm.

[29] Eiffel open-source development site at eiffelsoftware.origo.ethz.ch/index.php/Main_Page.

[30] Eiffel Software: EiffelStudio documentation, online at eiffel.com.

[31] Michael D. Ernst, J. Cockrell,William G. Griswold and David Notkin: *Dynamically Discovering Likely Program Invariants to Support Program Evolution*, in *IEEE Transactions on Software Engineering*, vol. 27, no. 2, February 2001, pages 1-25, available at pag.csail.mit.edu/~mernst/pubs/invariants-tse2001.pdf.

[32] Erich Gamma, Richard Helms, Ralph Johnson and John Vlissides: *Design Patterns*, Addison-Wesley, 1994.

[33] Carlo Ghezzi, Mehdi Jazayeri, Dino Mandrioli, *Software Engineering*, 2nd edition, Prentice Hall, 2003.

[34] Richard Hamlet: *Random Testing*, in Encyclopedia of Software Engineering, ed. J. J. Marciniak, 1994, available at tinyurl.com/rcjxg.

[35] Brian Henderson-Sellers: *Object-Oriented Metrics: Measures of Complexity*, Prentice Hall, 1995.

[36] Thomas A. Henzinger, Xavier Nicollin, Joseph Sifakis and Sergio Yovine: *Symbolic Model Checking for Real-Time Systems*, in *Logic in Computer Science*, Proceedings of 7th Symposium in Logics for Computer Science, Santa Cruz, California, 1992, pages 394-406, available at tinyurl.com/lb5fm.

[37] C.A.R. Hoare: *An axiomatic basis for computer programming*, in *Communications of the ACM*, Vol. 12, no. 10, October 1969, pages 576 - 580, available at tinyurl.com/ory2s.

[38] C.A.R. Hoare and Jayadev Misra: *Verified Software: Theories, Tools, Experiments, Vision of a Grand Challenge Project*, October 2005, foundation paper for the VSTTE conference [77], available at vstte.ethz.ch/pdfs/vstte-hoare-misra.pdf.

[39] IFIPWorking Group 10.4 on dependable computing and fault tolerance: home page at www.dependability.org.

[40] Michael Jackson: *Problem Frames: Analysing and Structuring Software Development Problems*, Addison-Wesley, 2001.

[41] Jean-Marc Jézéquel and Bertrand Meyer: *Design by Contract: The Lessons of Ariane*, in *Computer* (IEEE), vol. 30, no. 1, January 1997, pages 129-130, available at archive.eiffel.com/doc/manuals/technology/contract/ariane/page.html.

[42] JUnit pages at SourceForge: junit.sourceforge.net.

[43] Gary T. Leavens and Yoonsik Cheon: *Design by Contract with JML* (Draft), at ftp://ftp.cs.iastate.edu/pub/leavens/JML/jmldbc.pdf; see also other JML papers at www.cs.iastate.edu/~leavens/JML/.

[44] Andreas Leitner, Ilinca Ciupa, Bertrand Meyer and Mark Howard: *Reconciling Manual and Automated Testing: The AutoTest Experience*, submitted for publication, 2006.

[45] Nancy G. Leveson: *System Safety in Computer-Controlled Automotive Systems*, SAE Congress, March 2000, available at sunnyday.mit.edu/papers/sae.pdf.

[46] Michael R. Lyu (ed.): Handbook of Software Reliability Engineering, IEEE Computer Society Press and McGraw-Hill, 1995; also available online at www.cse.cuhk.edu.hk/~lyu/book/reliability/.

[47] Zohar Manna and Amir Pnueli: *The temporal logic of reactive and concurrent systems*, Springer-Verlag, 1992.

[48] Thomas J. McCabe: *A Complexity Measure*, in *IEEE Transactions on Software Engineering*, vol. 2, no. 4, December 1976, pages 308-320.

[49] Thomas J. McCabe and Charles W. Butler: *Design Complexity Measurement and Testing*, in *Communications of the ACM*, vol. 32, no. 12, December 1989, pages 1415-1425.

[50] Bertrand Meyer: *Introduction to the Theory of Programming Languages*, Prentice Hall, 1990.

[51] Bertrand Meyer, *The New Culture of Software Development: Reflections on the Practice of Object-Oriented Design*, in *Advances in Object-Oriented Software Engineering*, eds. D. Mandrioli, B. Meyer, Prentice Hall, 1991.

[52] Bertrand Meyer: *Eiffel: The Language*, 2nd printing, Prentice Hall, 1992.

[53] Bertrand Meyer: *Applying "Design by Contract"*, in *Computer* (IEEE), 25, 10, October 1992, pages 40-51.

[54] Bertrand Meyer: *Object Success*, Prentice Hall, 1995.

[55] Bertrand Meyer: *Practice to Perfect: The Quality First Model,* in *Computer (IEEE)*, May 1997, pages 102-106, available at se.ethz.ch/~meyer/publications/computer/quality_first.pdf.

[56] Bertrand Meyer: *UML: The Positive Spin*, in *American Programmer*, 1997, available at archive.eiffel.com/doc/manuals/technology/bmarticles/uml/page.html.

[57] Bertrand Meyer: *Object-Oriented Software Construction*, 2ⁿᵈ edition, Prentice Hall, 1997.

[58] Bertrand Meyer, Christine Mingins and Heinz Schmidt: *Providing Trusted Components to the Industry*, in *Computer* (IEEE), vol. 31, no. 5, May 1998, pages 104-105, available at se.ethz.ch/~meyer/publications/computer/trusted.pdf.

[59] Bertrand Meyer: *The Role of Object-Oriented Metrics*, in Computer (IEEE), vol. 31, no. 11, November 1998, pages 123-125, available at se.ethz.ch/~meyer/publications/computer/metrics.

[60] Bertrand Meyer, *Every Little Bit Counts: Towards Reliable Software*, in *Computer* (IEEE_, vol. 32, no. 11, November 1999, pages 131-133, available at se.ethz.ch/~meyer/publications/computer/reliable.pdf.

[61] Bertrand Meyer: *The Grand Challenge of Trusted Components*, in *ICSE 25* (International Conference on Software Engineering, Portland, Oregon, May 2003), IEEE Computer Press, 2003.

[62] Bertrand Meyer: *The Power of Abstraction, Reuse and Simplicity: An Object- Oriented Library for Event-Driven Design,* in *From Object-Orientation to Formal Methods: Essays in Memory of Ole-Johan Dahl*, eds. Olaf Owe, Stein Krogdahl, Tom Lyche, Lecture Notes in Computer Science 2635, Springer-Verlag, 2004, pages 236-271, available at se.ethz.ch/~meyer/publications/lncs/events.pdf.

[63] Bertrand Meyer: *Offshore Development: The Unspoken Revolution in Software Engineering*, in *Computer* (IEEE), January 2006, pages 122-124, available at se.ethz.ch/~meyer/publications/computer/outsourcing.pdf.

[64] Bertrand Meyer: *What will remain of Extreme Programming?*, in *EiffelWorld*, Vol. 5, no. 2, February 2006, available at www.eiffel.com/general/monthly_column/2006/February.html.

[65] Bertrand Meyer and Karine Arnout: *Componentization: the Visitor Example*, to appear in *Computer* (IEEE), 2006, draft available at se.ethz.ch/~meyer/publications/computer/visitor.pdf.

[66] Microsoft: Visual Studio pages at msdn.microsoft.com/vstudio.

[67] Richard Mitchell and Jim McKim: *Design by Contract by Example*, Addison-Wesley, 2001.

[68] Carroll Morgan: *Programming from Specifications*, 2ⁿᵈ edition, Prentice Hall, 1994, available at web.comlab.ox.ac.uk/oucl/publications/books/PfS/.

[69] John Musa: *Software Reliability Engineering*, 2ⁿᵈ edition, McGraw-Hill, 1998.

[70] Glenford J. Myers, Corey Sandler, Tom Badgett and Todd M. Thomas: *The Art of Software Testing*, 2ⁿᵈ edition, Wiley, 2004.

[71] Jeff Offutt: Mutation testing papers at www.ise.gmu.edu/~ofut/rsrch/mut.html.

[72] John Pincus: presentations (mostly PowerPoint slides) on PREfix and PREfast at research.microsoft.com/users/jpincus/.

[73] Eric Raymond: *The Cathedral and the Bazaar: Musings on Linux and Open Source by an Accidental Revolutionary*, O' Reilly, 1999; earlier version available at www.firstmonday.org/issues/issue3_3/raymond/.

[74] Software Engineering Institute, CMMI site, available at www.sei.cmu.edu/cmmi.

[75] Matt Stephens and Doug Rosenberg: *Extreme Programming Refactored: The Case Against XP*, aPress, 2003.

[76] Axel van Lamsweerde: *Goal-Oriented Requirements Engineering: A Guided Tour*, in Proceedings of the 5th IEEE International Symposium on Requirements Engineering, August 2001, available at tinyurl.com/mscpj.

[77] Verified Software: Theories, Tools, Experiments: International IFIP conference, ETH Zurich, October 2005, see VSTTE conference site at vstte.ethz.ch.

[78] John Viega: *The Myth of Open-Source Security*, 2000, available at www. developer.com/tech/article.php/626641; follow-up article, *Open-Source Security: Still at Myth*, September 2004, available at www.onlamp.com/pub/a/security/2004/09/16/ open_source_security_myths.html.

[79] Jeffrey M. Voas and Gary McGraw: *Software Fault Injection: Inoculating Programs Against Errors*, Wiley, 1998.

[80] Jos Warmer and Anneke Kleppe: *The Object Constraint Language: Getting Your Models Ready for MDA*, 2nd edition, Addison-Wesley, 2003.

[81] Elaine J. Weyuker and Bingchiang Jeng: *Analyzing Partition Testing Strategies*, in IEEE *Transactions on Software Engineering*, vol. 17, no. 9, July 1991, pp. 97-108.

[82] Wikipedia: entry "Mars Climate Orbiter", available at en.wikipedia.org/wiki/ Mars_Climate_Orbiter.

[83] Edward Yourdon: *When Good Enough Software Is Best*, in *Software* (IEEE), vol. 12, no. 3, May 1995, pages 79-81.

Dependable Systems*

André Schiper

Ecole Polytechnique Fédérale de Lausanne (EPFL)
1015 Lausanne, Switzerland
Andre.Schiper@epfl.ch

Abstract. Improving the dependability of computer systems is a critical and essential task. In this context, the paper surveys techniques that allow to achieve fault tolerance in distributed systems by *replication*. The main replication techniques are first explained. Then *group communication* is introduced as the communication infrastructure that allows the implementation of the different replication techniques. Finally the difficulty of implementing group communication is discussed, and the most important algorithms are presented.

1 Introduction

Computer systems become every day more and more complex. As a consequence the probability of problems in these systems increases over the years. To avoid this from becoming a major issue, researchers have since many years worked on improving the dependability of these systems. The methods involved are traditionally classified as *fault prevention, fault tolerance, fault removal* and *fault forecasting* [23]. *Fault prevention* refers to methods for preventing the occurrence or the introduction of faults in the system. *Fault tolerance* refers to methods allowing the system to provide a service complying with the specification in spite of faults. *Fault removal* refers to methods for reducing the number and the severity of faults. *Fault forecasting* refers to methods for estimating the presence of faults (with the goal to locate and remove them). We concentrate here on fault tolerance.

Several techniques to achieve fault tolerance have been developed over the years. The different techniques are related to the specificity of applications. For example, a centralized application differs from a distributed application involving several computing systems. We consider here distributed applications. Fault tolerance for distributed applications can be achieved with different techniques: *transactions, checkpointing* and *replication*.

Transactions have been introduced many years ago in the context of database systems [3]. A transaction allows us to group a sequence of operations while ensuring some properties on these operations, called *ACID* properties [3]: *Atomicity, Consistency, Isolation* and *Durability*. *Atomicity* requires that either all

---

* Almost the same paper appears under the title *Group Communication: from practice to theory* in *Proceedings SOFSEM 2006: Theory and Practice of Computer Science, Merin, Czech Republic, January 2006*, Springer, LNCS 383, pages 117-137, 2006.

J. Kohlas, B. Meyer, and A. Schiper (Eds.): Dependable Systems, LNCS 4028, pp. 34–54, 2006.

operations of the transaction are preformed, or none of them. *Consistency* is a requirement on the set of operations, namely that the sequence of operations brings the database from a consistent state to another consistent state. Transactions can be executed concurrently. The *isolation* property requires that the effect of transactions executed concurrently is the same as if the transactions where executed in some sequential order (in *isolation* from each other). *Durability* requires that the effect of the operations of the transaction are permanent, i.e., survive crashes. Durability is achieved by storing data on stable storage, e.g., on disk. Atomicity and durability are the two properties specifically related to fault tolerance. A single protocol is used to ensure these two properties, the so called *atomic commitment* protocol executed at the end of the transaction. If all the data accessed by a transaction is located on the same machine, the transaction is a *centralized* transaction. If the data is located on different machines, the transaction is a *distributed* transaction. Distributed transactions are more difficult to implement then centralized transactions. The main technical difficulty lies in the atomic commitment protocol. Except for this problem, the implementation of distributed transactions derives more or less easily from the implementation of centralized transactions. We discuss atomic commitment in Section 4.5.

Checkpointing is another technique for achieving fault tolerance. It consists of periodically saving the state of the computation on stable storage; in case of a crash, the computation is restarted from the most recently saved state. The technique has been developed for long running computations, e.g., simulations that last for days or weeks, and run on multiple machines. These computations are modelled as a set of processes communicating by exchanging messages. The main problem is to ensure that, after crash and recovery, the computation is restarted in a consistent state. We do not discuss checkpointing techniques here. A good survey can be found in [13].

Replication is the technique that allows the progress of the computation during failures (which is called failure *masking*). In a system composed of several components, without replication, if one single component fails the system is no more operational. Replicating a component C, and ensuring that the replicas of C fail independently, allows the system to be tolerant to the failure of one or several replicas of C. Replicating a component is very easy if the component is stateless or if its state does not change during the computation. If the state of the component changes during the computation, then maintaining the consistency among the replicas is a difficult problem. Surprisingly, it is one of the most difficult problems in distributed computing. We concentrate here on the problems related to replication.

While replication allows us to mask failures, this is not the case of transactions or checkpointing. However, the different techniques mentioned above can be combined, e.g., transactions can be run on replicated data. Implementing such a technique requires to combine transaction techniques and replication techniques. This will not be discussed here.

The rest of the paper is structured as follows. Section 2 introduces issues related to replication, and presents the two main replication techniques. Section 3 defines group communication as the middleware layer providing the tools for implementing the different replication techniques. The implementation of these tools is discussed in Section 4. Finally, Section 5 concludes this survey.

2   Replication

In this section we first introduce a model for discussing replication. Then we define what it means for replicas to be consistent. Finally we introduce the two main replication techniques.

2.1   Model for Replication

Consider a system composed of a set of components. A component can be a *process*, an *object*, or any other system structuring unit. Whatever the component is, we can model the interaction between components in terms of inputs and outputs. A component CO receives inputs and generates outputs. The inputs are received from another component CO_{in}, and the outputs are sent to some component CO_{out}. Whether CO_{in} is equal or not to CO_{out} does not make any difference for CO. In the case $CO_{in} = CO_{out}$, the component CO is called a *server*, and the component $CO_{in} = CO_{out}$ is called a *client* (see Figure 1). In this case we will denote the server component by S and the client component by C. The input sent by the client C to the server S is called a *request*, and the output sent by the server S to the client C is called a *response*. From the point of view of the client, the pair *request/response* is sometimes called an *operation*: for a client C, an operation consists of a request sent to a server and the corresponding response. We assume here that the client is blocked while waiting for the response.

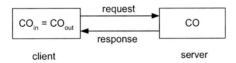

Fig. 1. Server and client

2.2   Consistency Criteria

A server S can have many clients C, C', C'', etc. For a non-replicated server S, the simplest implementation is to handle client requests sequentially, one at a time. A more efficient implementation could consist for the server to spawn a new thread for each new incoming request. However, in this case the result that the client obtains must be the same as if the operations were executed sequentially, one after the other. The same holds if the server S is replicated, with replicas S_1, ..., S_n: the result that the clients obtain must be the same as if the operations were executed sequentially by one single server. This can be defined more precisely, by the consistency criterion called *linearizability* [17] (also called *atomic consistency* [25]). A weaker consistency criterion is called *sequential consistency* [20]. We discuss only linearizability, which is the consistency criterion that is usually implemented.

Linearizability: An execution σ is linearizable if it is equivalent to a sequential execution such that *(i)* the request and the response of each operation occur both at some time t, and *(ii)* t is in the interval $[t_{req}, t_{res}]$, where t_{req} is the time when the request is issued in σ, t_{res} is the time when the response is received in σ. We explain this definition on two examples. A formal definition can be found in [17].

Consider a server S that implements a *register* with the two operations *read* and *write*:

- $S.write(v)$ denotes the request to write value v in the register managed by server S. The operation returns an empty response, denoted by *ok*.
- $S.read(\ )$ denotes the request to read the register managed by server S. The operation returns the value read.

Figure 2 shows an execution σ that is linearizable:

- Client C issues the request $write(0)$ at time t_1, and receives the empty response *ok* at time t_3.
- Client C' issues the request $write(1)$ at time t_2, and receives the empty response *ok* at time t_5.
- Client C issues the request $read(\ )$ at time t_4, and receives the response 0 at time t_7.
- Client C' issues the request $read(\ )$ at time t_6, and receives the response 1 at time t_8.

The bottom time-line in Figure 2 shows a sequential execution equivalent to σ that satisfies the two requirements *(i)* and *(ii)* above (t_a—the time at which the request and the response of $S.write(0)$ take place in σ—is in the interval $[t_1, t_3]$, t_b—the time at which the request and the response of $S.write(1)$ take place in σ—is in the interval $[t_4, t_7]$, etc.).

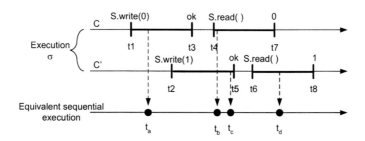

Fig. 2. A linearizable execution

Figure 3 shows an execution that is not linearizable. In an equivalent sequential execution $write(1)$ issued by C' must precede $read(\ )$ issued by C. So there is no way to construct a sequential execution in which $read(\ )$ returns 0 to C.

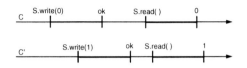

Fig. 3. A non linearizable execution

2.3   Linearizability *vs.* Isolation

Linearizability differs from the isolation property of transactions. There are two main differences. First, linearizability is defined on the *whole sequence of operations* issued by a client process in the system, while isolation is defined on a *subset of the operations* of a client process. Consider for example that process p issues operations op_1 and op_2 within transaction T_1, and later operations op_3 and op_4 within transaction T_2. Isolation does not require that the operations of T_1 are ordered before the operations of T_2 (they can be ordered after those of T_2). However, if op_i precedes op_j on process p, then linearizability requires op_i to be ordered before op_j.

The second difference is that linearizability does not ensure isolated execution of a sequence of operations. If process p issues operation $op_p^1 = S.read(\ )$ that returns v and later $op_p^2 = S.write(v+1)$, and process q issues operation $op_q^1 = S.read(\ )$ that returns v' and later $op_q^2 = S.write(v'+1)$, linearizability does not prevent the operation op_q^1 of q to be executed between the two operations op_p^1 and op_p^2 of p. There are basically two ways to prevent this from occurring. The first solution is for p and q to explicitly use locks or semaphores. The second solution is to add a new operation to the server S, e.g., *increment*, and to invoke this single operation instead of *read* followed by *write*. The second solution is better than the first one (locks and semaphores lead to problems in the presence of failures).

2.4   Replication Techniques

In the previous section, linearizability defined the desired semantics for operations issued by clients on servers. In the definition of linearizability, servers are black boxes. This means that the definition applies to non-replicated single-threaded servers, to non-replicated multi-threaded servers, to replicated single-threaded servers and to replicated multi-threaded servers. In this section we address the question of implementing a replicated server while ensuring linearizability. We discuss only the single-threaded case (the solution can easily be extended to multi-threading). The two main replication techniques are called *active replication* and *passive replication*. Other replication techniques can be seen as variants or combinations of these two basic techniques.

Active Replication: Active replication is also called *state-machine replication* [19,29]. The principle is illustrated on Figure 4, which shows a replicated server S with three replicas S_1, S_2 and S_3. The client sends its request to all the replicas, each replica processes the request and sends back the response to the client. The client waits for the first response and ignores the others. This client's behavior is correct if we assume that the servers do not behave maliciously, and the servers are deterministic:[1] in this case all the responses are identical.

In Figure 4 there is only one client. The problem becomes more difficult with multiple clients that concurrently send their requests. In this case it is sufficient that all replicas S_i receive the clients' requests in the *same order*, as shown in Figure 5. This allow the replicas to process the clients' requests in the same order. In Section 3 we introduce a group communication primitive that ensures such an ordering of client requests.

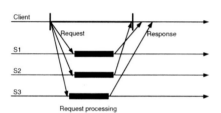

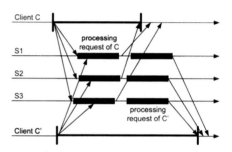

Fig. 4. Active replication

Fig. 5. Active replication: requests received in the same order

Passive Replication: The principle of passive replication is illustrated on Figure 6, which shows the same replicated server S with its three replicas S_1, S_2 and S_3. One of the replicas, here S_1, is the *primary* replica; the other replicas, S_2 and S_3 are called *backups*. The client sends its request only to the primary, and waits for the response. Only the primary processes the request. Once this is done, the primary sends an *update* message to the backups, to bring them to a state that reflects the processing of the client request. In Figure 6 the update message is also sent to the primary. The reason is that, if we include failures, it is simpler to assume that the modification of the state of the primary occurs only upon handling of the update message, and not upon processing of the request.

If several clients sent their requests at the same time, the primary processes them sequentially, one after the other. Since the primary sends an update message to the backups, the processing can be non-deterministic, contrary to active replication. Note that this superficial presentation hides most of the problems related to the implementation of passive replication. We mention them in the

---

[1] A server is deterministic if its new state and the response depend only on the request and on the state before processing the request.

next paragraph. With active replication, the implementation problems are hidden in the implementation of the group communication primitive that orders the clients' requests.

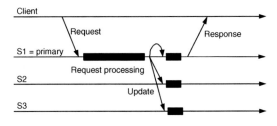

Fig. 6. Passive replication

Problems Implementing Passive Replication: When the primary crashes, a new primary must be selected. However, requiring the failure detection of the primary to be reliable (i.e., never making mistakes) is a very constraining assumption. For this reason, solutions to passive replication that do no require a reliable failure detection mechanism for the primary have been developed. The three main problems to address are the following: (a) prevention of multiple primaries being able to process requests, *(b)* prevention of multiple executions of a request, and *(c)* reception of the update message by all replicas. Problem *(a)* is related to the unreliable failure detection mechanism. Problem *(b)* arises when the current primary is falsely suspected to have crashed. Consider a client C sending its request to the primary S_1. Assume that S_1 is incorrectly suspected to have crashed, and S_2 becomes the new primary. If this happens, and C did not receive any response, it will resend its request to S_2. This may lead to execute the client request twice. Multiple execution of a request can be prevented by attaching a unique identifier to each request (this request identifier being piggybacked on the update message). Problem *(c)* arises when the primary crashes while multicasting the update message. In this case, we must prevent the undesirable situation where the update message is received by some replicas, but not by all of them. In Section 3 we present the group communication primitive that allows us to solve the problems *(a)* and *(c)*.

3   Group Communication

In the previous section we have introduced the two basic replication techniques, namely active replication and passive replication. We have also pointed out the need for communication primitives with well defined ordering properties to implement these techniques. *Group communication* is the infrastructure that provides these primitives. A group is simply a set of processes with an identifier. Messages can be multicast to the members of some group g simply by referring to the identifier of group g: the sender of the message does not need to know what processes are members of g. For example, if we consider a replicated server S with three replicas S_1, S_2 and S_3, we can refer to these replicas as the group $g_S = \{S_1, S_2, S_3\}$. As illustrated by Figure 7, group communication is a middleware layer between the transport layer and the layer that implements replication. In this section we define the two main group communication primitives for replication, namely *atomic broadcast* and *generic broadcast*. Before doing so, we introduce some concepts needed to understand the various aspects of group communication.

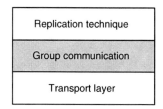

Fig. 7. Group communication

3.1   Various Group Models

Static Group *vs.* Dynamic Group: A *static* group is a group whose membership is constant over time: a static group is initialized with a given membership, and this membership never changes. This is the simplest type of group. However, static groups are often too restrictive. For example consider the replicated server S implemented by the group $g_S = \{S_1, S_2, S_3\}$. If one of the replicas S_i crashes, it might be desirable to replace S_i with a new replica, in order to maintain the same degree of replication. A group whose membership changes over time is called a *dynamic* group. Dynamic groups require to manage the addition and the removal of members to/from the group. This problem is called the *group membership* problem: it is discussed in Section 3.4.

Benign *vs.* Malicious Faults: The group (or system) model encompasses also the type of faults that are considered. The distinction is made between *benign* faults and *malicious* faults (also called *Byzantine* faults). With benign faults, a process or a channel does its job correctly, or does not do its job. A process crash, or a channel that looses a message, are benign faults. With malicious faults, a process or a channel can behave arbitrarily.

Crash-Stop *vs.* Crash-Recovery: In the context of benign faults, the distinction is made between the crash-stop and the crash-recovery process model. In the *crash-stop* model processes do not have access to stable storage. In this case, a process that crashes looses its state: upon recovery, the process is indistinguishable from a newly started process. In the *crash-recovery* model processes have access to stable storage, allowing them to periodically save their state. In this case, a process that crashes can recover its most recently saved state.

Combining These Models: Combining these three dimensions lead to different models for group communication. The simplest model is the benign static crash-stop model. Other models have been considered in the literature, but they lead to more complexity in the specification of group communication and in the algorithms. There are some subtle differences between the different models, as we explain now.

Figure 8 shows the difference between active replication with dynamic crash-stop groups (left) and active replication with static crash-recovery groups (right). In the crash-stop model, to keep the same replication degree, a crashed process (here replica S_3) must be replaced with a new process (here S_4). The initial membership of the group g_S is denoted by $v_0(g_S) = \{S_1, S_2, S_3\}$ (v stands for *view*, see Section 3.4). When S_3 crashes, the membership becomes $v_1(g_S) = \{S_1, S_2\}$. Once S_4 is added, we have the membership $v_2(g_S) = \{S_1, S_2, S_4\}$. Note that the state of p_4 must be initialized. This is done by an operation called *state transfer*: when S_4 joins the group, the state of one of its members (here S_2) is used to initialize the state of S_4. In the static crash-recovery model (Figure 8, right), the same degree of replication is kept by assuming that crashed replicas recover (here S_3). However in this context, since S_3 remains all the time a member of g_S, a message broadcast to the group while S_3 is down *must be delivered to* S_3 (here m_2). As a result, no state transfer is needed. The static crash-recovery model is preferable to the dynamic crash-stop model whenever the state of the replicas is large.

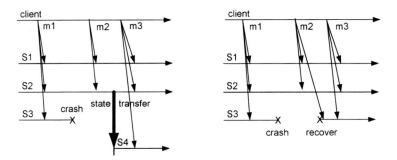

Fig. 8. Active replication with a dynamic crash-stop group (left), or a static crash-recovery group (right)

In the following we consider mainly the static crash-stop model, which is the most widely model considered in the literature, and the simplest. Dynamic groups are briefly mentioned in Section 3.4.

3.2   Atomic Broadcast for Active Replication

One of the most important group communication primitives is *atomic broadcast* [9]. Atomic broadcast is also sometimes called *total order broadcast*, or simply *abcast*. The primitive ensures that messages are delivered ordered. To give a more formal specification of the properties of abcast, we need to introduce the following notation:

- The atomic broadcast of message m to the members of some group g is denoted by $abcast(g, m)$.[2]
- The delivery of message m is denoted by $adeliver(m)$.

It is important to make the distinction between *abcast/adeliver*, and the *send/receive* primitives at the transport layer (see Figure 9). The semantics of *send/receive* is defined by the transport layer. The semantics of *abcast/adeliver* is defined by atomic broadcast. An atomic broadcast protocol uses the semantics of *send/receive* to provide the semantics of *abcast/adeliver*.

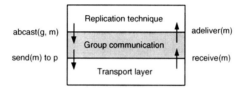

Fig. 9. *Send/receive* vs. *abcast/adeliver*

The definition of atomic broadcast in the static crash-stop model relies on the definition of a *correct* process: a process is correct if it does not crash. Otherwise it is *faulty*. Note that even though these definitions are simple, they are easily wrongly understood. Correct/faulty are predicates that characterize the *whole lifetime* of a process. This means that if some process p crashes at time $t = 10$, then p is faulty (even at time $t = 9$). With this definition, atomic broadcast in the static/crash-stop model is specified by the following four properties [16,2]:[3]

- *Validity:* If a correct process executes *abcast(g,m)*, then some correct process in g eventually adelivers m or no process in g is correct.
- *Uniform agreement:* If a process in g adelivers a message m, then all correct processes in g eventually adeliver m.
- *Uniform integrity:* For any message m, every process p adelivers m at most once, and only if p is in g and m was previously abcast to g.
- *Uniform total order:* If process p in g adelivers message m before message m', then no process in g adelivers m' before having previously adelivered m.

Validity, uniform agreement and uniform integrity define the primitive called *reliable broadcast*.[4] Atomic broadcast is defined as reliable broadcast with the uniform total order property.

---

[2] The primitive should be called atomic *multicast*. For simplicity, we keep the term *broadcast* here.

[3] More precisely, the specification corresponds to the primitive called *uniform atomic broadcast*. We will call it here simply *atomic broadcast*.

[4] More precisely, *uniform* reliable broadcast.

It is easy to see that active replication is easily implemented using atomic broadcast. If g_S is the group of replicas that provide some service S, clients C send requests using the primitive $abcast(g_S, req)$. The validity property ensures that if C does not crash, its request is received by at least one member of g_S (unless all members of g_S crash). Combining this guarantee with uniform agreement ensures that all correct processes in g_S eventually adeliver m. The uniform total order property ensures that all replicas adeliver the clients' requests in the same order.

The response from a replica in g_S to a client is sent using a unicast message, i.e., a point-to-point message. The transport layer must ensure the following *quasi-reliable channel* property [1]: if a correct process p sends message m to a correct process q, then q eventually receives m. This property is stronger than the property provided by TCP (if a TCP connection breaks, reliability is no more guaranteed).

3.3   Generic Broadcast for Passive Replication

Atomic broadcast can also be used to implement passive replication, but this is not necessarily the best solution in terms of cost. Atomic broadcast can be used as follows. Consider a replicated server S defined by the (static) group g_S, and assume that the members of g_S are ordered in a list. Initially, the member at the head of the membership list is the primary. The primary sends the update message to g_S using abcast. Whenever some member of g_S suspects the current primary to have crashed, it abcasts the message ⟨*primary change*⟩. Upon adelivery of this message every process moves the process at the head of the list to the tail. The new primary is the new process at the head of the list.

Passive replication can also be implemented using the group communication primitive called *generic broadcast* [26,2], which can be cheaper to implement than atomic broadcast. While atomic broadcast orders *all* messages, generic broadcast orders only messages that *conflict*. Conflicts are defined by a relation on the set of messages. This conflict relation is part of the specification of the primitive, and makes the primitive *generic*. The generic broadcast of message m to the group g is denoted by $gbcast(g, m)$; the delivery of message m is denoted by $gdeliver(m)$. Formally, generic broadcast is defined by the same properties that define atomic broadcast, except that the uniform total order property is replaced with the following weaker property:

- *Generic total order:* If process p in g gdelivers message m before message m', and m, m' conflict, then no process in g gdelivers m' before having previously gdelivered m.

We have seen that passive replication can be implemented with atomic broadcast for the *update* messages and the *primary-change* messages. Consider the following conflict relation between these two types of messages:

- Messages of type *primary-change* do not conflict with messages of the same type, but conflict with messages of type *update*.

– Messages of type *update* conflict with messages of the same type, and also with messages of type *primary-change*.

This ensures enough ordering to implement generic broadcast correctly. Note that most of the time one single process considers itself to be the primary, and during this period no concurrent update messages are issued. So most of the time no concurrent conflicting messages are issued.

The implementation of generic broadcast (and atomic broadcast) is discussed in Section 4.

3.4   About Group Membership

With dynamic groups, the successive membership of a group is called a *view*. Consider for example a group g, with initially three processes p, q, r. This initial membership is called the *initial view* of g, and is denoted by $v_0(g)$. Assume that later r is removed from g. The new membership is denoted by $v_1(g) = \{p, q\}$. If s is added later to the group the resulting membership is denoted by $v_2(g) = \{p, q, s\}$. So the history of a dynamic group is represented as a sequence of views, and all group members must see the sequence of views in the same order. The problem of maintaining the membership of a dynamic group is called the *group membership problem* [28].

3.5   About View Synchronous Broadcast

View synchronous broadcast or *vscast* (sometimes also called *view synchrony*), is another group communication primitive, defined in a dynamic group model [4,8]. However, the importance of vscast has been overestimated, and stems from a time where the difference between static groups and dynamic groups was not completely understood.

Consider some message m vscast by process p in view $v_i(g)$: vscast orders m with respect to view changes. In other words, vscast ensures that m is delivered by all processes in the same view v_j. The property is also called *same view delivery* [8]. A stronger property, called *sending view delivery*, requires $i = j$: the view in which the message is delivered is the view in which the message was sent [8].

The overestimated importance given to view synchronous broadcast has led to several misunderstandings. The first is that dynamic groups are needed to implement passive replication: Section 3.3 has sketched an implementation of passive replication with a static group. The second misunderstanding is that the specification of group communication with dynamic groups is inherently different from the specification of group communication with static groups. This is not the case, as shown in [27].

3.6   Group Communication *vs.* Quorum Systems

In the previous sections we have shown the use of group communication for implementing replication. *Quorum systems*, which generalize the *majority voting* technique, is another technique for replication, anterior to group communication and also more widely known. In this section we explain the advantage of group communication over quorum systems in the context of replication [12].

Definition of Quorum Systems: Consider a set $\Pi = \{p_1, \ldots, p_n\}$ of processes. The set of all subsets of Π is called the *powerset* of Π, and is denoted by 2^Π. We have for example:

$$\{p_1\}, \{p_2\}, \{p_1, p_2\}, \{p_2, p_3, p_4\}, \ldots, \{p_1, \ldots, p_n\} \in 2^\Pi.$$

A *quorum system* of Π is defined as any set $Q \subset 2^\Pi$ such that any two $Q_i \in Q$ have a non empty intersection:

$$\forall Q_1, Q_2 \in Q, \text{ we have } Q_1 \cap Q_2 \neq \emptyset.$$

Each $Q_i \in Q$ is called a *quorum*. For example, if $\Pi = \{p_1, p_2, p_3\}$, then the set $Q = \{\{p_1, p_2\}, \{p_1, p_3\}, \{p_2, p_3\}\}$ is a quorum system of Π; $\{p_1, p_2\}$, $\{p_1, p_3\}$, $\{p_2, p_3\}$ are quorums.

Quorum Systems for Implementing a Fault Tolerant Register: The use of quorums systems for fault tolerance can be illustrated on a very simple example: a server that implements a *register*. A register is an object with two operations *read* and *write*: *read* returns the value of the register, i.e., the most recent value written; *write* overwrites the value of the register.

The register can be made fault tolerant by replication on three replicas e.g., $\Pi = \{p_1, p_2, p_3\}$ with the quorum system $Q = \{\{p_1, p_2\}, \{p_1, p_3\}, \{p_2, p_3\}\}$. Each operation needs only to be executed on one quorum of Q, i.e., on $\{p_1, p_2\}$, on $\{p_1, p_3\}$, or on $\{p_2, p_3\}$. In other words, the quorum system Q tolerates the crash of one out of the three replicas. Using the quorum system Q, linearizability of the read and write operations is easy to implement [12].

Requiring Isolation: A fault tolerant register is easy to implement using quorum systems. However, clients usually want to perform more complex operations. Consider for example the operations *(a) increment* a register and *(b) decrement* a register. These two operations can be implemented as follows: (1) read the register, then (2) update the value read, and finally (3) write back the new value. However, one client C may increment the register, while at the same time another client C' decrements the register. To ensure a correct execution, the two operations must be executed in mutual exclusion. With group communication, no mutual exclusion is needed: atomic broadcast can be used to send the corresponding operation to the replicated servers.

This difference between quorum systems and group communication is illustrated in Figure 10. The left part illustrates the quorum solution, and the right part the group communication solution. In the quorum solution, the increment operation is performed by the client, after reading the register and before writing the new value. The implementation requires mutual exclusion, represented by E_{CS} (enter critical section) and L_{CS} (leave critical section). In the group communication solution, the increment operation is sent to the replicas using atomic

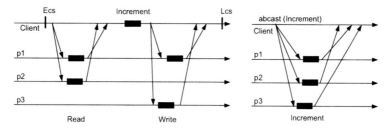

Fig. 10. Replication: quorum systems (left) *vs.* group communication (right)

broadcast; no mutual exclusion is required.[5] Implementing atomic broadcast requires weaker assumptions about the crash detection mechanism than implementing mutual exclusion [12].

4   Implementation of Group Communication

In the previous section we have seen the role of group communication for replication. We discuss now the implementation of the two group communication primitives that we have introduced, namely atomic broadcast and generic broadcast. We consider only static groups, non Byzantine processes and the crash-stop model.

4.1   Impossibility Results

Consider a static group g, and processes in g communicating by message exchange. The most general assumption is to consider that the time between the sending of a message m and the reception of m by its destination is not bounded, i.e., the transmission delay can be arbitrarily long. Similarly, if we model the execution of a process as a sequence of steps, the most general assumption is to consider that while the slowest process performs one step, the fastest process can perform an unbounded number of steps. These two assumptions define the *asynchronous system model*. The absence of bounds for the message transmission delay models an open network in which the load of the links are unknown. The absence of bounds on the relative speed of processes models processes running on CPUs with an unknown load. The asynchronous system model is the most general model, but it has a major drawback: several problems are impossible to solve in that model when one single process may crash.

One of these problems is *consensus*. The problem is defined on a set of processes, e.g., on some group g. Every process p in g starts with an initial value v_p, and all correct processes in g have to decide on some common value v that is the initial value of one of the processes. Formally, the consensus problem is defined by the following properties [7]:

---

[5] The reader may wonder why no *increment* operation can be sent with quorum systems. Sending the *increment* operation requires atomic broadcast!

- *Validity:* If a process decides v, then v is the initial value of some process.
- *Agreement:* No two correct processes decide differently.
- *Termination:* Every correct process eventually decides some value.

An explanation of *problem solvability* is needed here. Consider a distributed algorithm A_P that is supposed to solve problem P. Algorithm A_P can be launched many times. Due to the variability of the transmission delay of messages, each execution of A_P can go through a different sequence of states. However, in all of these executions, A_P must solve P. If there is one single execution in which this is not the case, then we say that algorithm A_P does not solve P. This clarification is important in the context of the consensus problem: it has been shown that consensus is not solvable by a deterministic algorithm in an asynchronous system with reliable links if one single process may crash. This result is known as the *FLP impossibility result* [14].

The FLP impossibility result is easy to extend to atomic broadcast by the following argument [10]. Assume for a contradiction that atomic broadcast can be implemented in an asynchronous system with process crashes. Then consensus can be solved as follows (in the context of some group g):

- Each process p in g executes $abcast(v_p)$, where v_p is p's initial value.
- Let v be the first message adelivered by p.
- Process p decides v.

If there is a least one correct process, then at least one message is adelivered. By the property of atomic broadcast, every correct process adelivers the same first message, and so decides on the same value. Consensus is solved, which shows the contradiction.

4.2 Models for Solving Consensus

Consensus and atomic broadcast are not solvable in an asynchronous system when processes may crash. We thus need to find a system model in which consensus is solvable (whenever consensus is solvable, atomic broadcast is also solvable, see Section 4.3). One such system is the *synchronous* system model, defined by the following two properties:

- There is a known bound on the transmission delay of messages.
- There is a known bound on the relative speed of processes.

Consensus is solvable in a synchronous system [24], but the synchronous system model has drawbacks from a practical point of view. The model requires to consider the *worst case*: the worst case for the transmission delay of messages, the worst case for the relative speed of processes. These bounds have a direct impact on the time it takes to detect the crash of a process: the higher these bounds are, the higher the time it takes to detect a process crash, i.e., the longer it takes to react to a crash. In a replicated service a long reaction to a crash leads to a long delay before clients get the replies.

The drawback of the synchronous model has led to look for system models weaker than the synchronous model, but strong enough to solve consensus (and so atomic broadcast). The first of these models is called the *partially synchronous* model [11]. The model considers bounds on the message transmission delay and on the relative speed of processes. There are two variants of the model:

1. There is a bound on the relative speed of processes and a bound on the message transmission delay, but these bounds are *not known*.
2. There is a *known* bound on the relative speed of processes and on the message transmission delay, but these bounds hold only from some unknown point on.

The two definitions are equivalent, but the first variant seems more appealing from a practical point of view.

A different approach was proposed later in [7]. It consists in *augmenting* the asynchronous model with an *oracle* that satisfies some well defined properties. In other words, the system is assumed to be asynchronous, but the processes can query an oracle about the status *crashed/not crashed* of processes. For this reason the oracle is called *failure detector oracle*, or simply *failure detector*. If the failure detector returns the reply *crashed q* to process p, we say p *suspects q*. Note that this information may be incorrect: failure detectors can make mistakes. The legal replies to a query of the failure detector are defined by two properties called *completeness* and *accuracy*. For example, the replies of the failure detector called $\Diamond S$ must satisfy the following completeness and accuracy properties [7]:

- *Strong completeness:* Eventually every process that crashes is permanently suspected to have crashed by every correct process.
- *Eventual weak accuracy:* There is a time after which some correct process is never suspected by any correct process.

Consensus is solvable in the asynchronous system augmented with the failure detector $\Diamond S$ and a majority of correct processes [7]. Moreover, it has been shown that $\Diamond S$ is the weakest failure detector that allows us to solve consensus in an asynchronous system [6]. This result shows the power of the failure detector approach and explains its popularity.

4.3   Solving Consensus

The first algorithm to solve consensus in a model weaker than the synchronous model is the consensus algorithm by Dwork, Lynch and Stockmeyer for the partially synchronous model [11]. The algorithm – called here *DLS* – requires a majority of correct processes, and is based on the *rotating coordinator* paradigm. In this paradigm, the computation is decomposed into rounds $r = 0, 1, 2, \ldots$, and in each round another process, in some predetermined order, is the coordinator. Typically, with n processes $p_0, \ldots p_{n-1}$, the coordinator of round r is process $p_{r \bmod n}$. In each round the coordinator leads the computation in order to try to decide on a value. The algorithm is based on the notions of *locked* value and *acceptable* value. The coordinator of round r tries to lock a value, say v, and if it learns that a majority of processes have locked v in round r, it can decide v. If the coordinator of round r is suspected to have crashed, then the computation proceeds to the next round $r + 1$ with a new coordinator. Note that a process can become coordinator more than once, e.g., in rounds k, $n + k$, $2n + k$, etc. The key property of the *DLS* algorithm is that the safety properties of consensus (validity and agreeement) hold even if the properties of the partially synchronous model do not hold. In other words, these properties are only needed for liveness, i.e., to ensure the termination property of consensus.

Two other consensus algorithms had a major impact and led to the development of variations of these algorithms. The first one is the *Paxos* algorithm proposed by Lamport [21,22]. The second one is the Chandra-Toueg consensus algorithm (denoted *CT* hereafter) based on the failure detector $\Diamond S$ [7]. *Paxos* and *CT*, similarly to *DLS*, require a majority of correct processes. *CT*, similarly to *DLS*, is based on the rotating coordinator paradigm. *Paxos* is also based on a coordinator, but the coordinator role is not predetermined as in the rotating coordinator paradigm, but determined during the computation (the algorithm tolerates multiple coordinators for the same round). *Paxos* and *CT* are also based on the notion of *locked* value (but there is no notion of *acceptable* value): each coordinator, one after the other, tries to lock a value v, and if it learns that a majority of processes have locked v, it can decide v. In this sense *Paxos* and *CT* are very similar. The two algorithms also share the key property of *DLS*, namely that no matter how asynchronous the system behaves, the safety properties of consensus are never violated. However, *Paxos* and *CT* differ on the following issues:

- *CT* requires reliable channels, while *Paxos* tolerates message loss (similarly to *DLS*).
- The condition for termination is rigorously defined for *CT*, namely the *eventual weak accuracy* property of $\Diamond S$. No such condition that ensure termination exists for *Paxos*.

Note that after the publication of *Paxos*, the failure detector Ω – which eventually outputs at each process the identity of the same correct process [6] – has been mentioned as ensuring the termination of *Paxos*. However, this makes sense only if we consider *Paxos* with reliable channels.

4.4   Implementing Atomic Broadcast and Generic Broadcast

A large number of atomic broadcast algorithms have been proposed in the last 20 years. These algorithms can be classified according to several criteria. One of those criteria is the mechanisms used for message ordering [9]: *fixed sequencer*, *moving sequencer*, *privilege-based*, *communication history*, *destinations agreement*. For example in a *fixed sequencer* algorithm, one process is elected as the sequencer and is responsible for ordering messages. Obviously this solution is not tolerant to the crash of the sequencer. The solution must be completed by a mechanism for electing a new sequencer in case the current sequencer crashes. This is usually done using a group membership service (see Section 3.4) to remove the current sequencer from the group. Once this is done, a new sequencer can be elected. Thus the solution implements atomic broadcast in the context of dynamic groups (see Section 3.1). The same comment applies to most of the implementations of atomic broadcast described in the literature. These implementations *require order to provide order*: the group membership service orders views, and this order is used to implement the ordering required by atomic broadcast.

Atomic broadcast can also be solved in the context of static groups. The solutions rely on consensus (which explains the fundamental role of the consensus problem in the context of fault tolerance computing). The consensus problem allows processes to agree on a value. This value can be of any type. Atomic broadcast can be implemented by solving a sequence of consensus problems, where each instance of consensus agrees on a *set of messages*. The idea is the following [7]. Consider a static group g and $abcast(g, m)$. Each process p in g has a variable k_p used to number the various instances of consensus. Whenever p has received messages that need to be ordered, p starts a new instance of consensus, uniquely identified by k_p, with the set of messages to be ordered as its initial value. By the properties of consensus, all processes agree on the same set of messages for consensus $\#k_p$, say $msg(k_p)$. Then the messages in the set $msg(k_p)$ are adelivered in some deterministic order (e.g., according to their IDs), and before the messages in the set $msg(k_p + 1)$. This solution for static groups can be extended to dynamic groups [27].

The implementation of generic broadcast is more difficult to sketch. The basic idea of the implementation is to control whether conflicting messages have been gbcast. As long as only non conflicting messages are gbcast, these messages can be gdelivered without invoking consensus, i.e., without the cost of consensus. However, as soon as conflicting messages are detected, the gdelivery of messages require to execute an instance of the consensus problem. More details can be found in [26,2].

4.5 Solving the Atomic Commitment Problem

In Section 1 we have mentioned the *atomic commitment* problem as the main problem related to the implementation of distributed transactions. The problem has similarities with the consensus problem, but also has significant differences.

In the atomic commitment problem, each process involved in the transaction votes at the end of the transaction. The vote can be *yes* or *no*. A *yes* vote indicates that the process is ready to commit the transaction; a *no* vote indicates that the process cannot commit the transaction. As in the consensus problem, all processes must decide on the same outcome: *commit* or *abort*. The conditions under which commit and abort can be decided make the difference between consensus and atomic commitment. If one single process votes *no*, the decision must be *abort*; if no failure occurs and all processes vote *yes*, then the decision must be *commit*; if there are failures, the decision can be *abort*. So "failures" can influence the decision of atomic commitment, which is not the case for consensus.

Another important difference is that, for practical reasons, the atomic commitment problem needs to be solved in the crash-recovery model (in the context of transactions, processes have access to stable storage). A third difference is related the notion of *blocking* vs. *non-blocking* solution, a difference that has not been made for consensus (the distinction between a blocking and a non-blocking solution exists only in the crash-recovery model). In the crash-recovery model, a protocol is *blocking* if a single crash during the execution of the protocol prevents the termination of the protocol until the crashed process recovers. In contrast, a non-blocking protocol can terminate despite one single process crash (or even despite more than one crash).

The most popular atomic commitment protocol is the blocking *2PC* (2 Phase Commit) protocol [3]. The first non-blocking atomic commitment protocol was proposed by Skeen [30]. At that time the consensus problem was not yet identified as the key problem in distributed fault tolerant computing. This explains that the protocol proposed in [30] does not solve atomic commitment by reduction to consensus. Today such a reduction is considered to be the best way to solve the non-blocking atomic commitment problem (see for example [15], for a solution in the crash-stop model).

5   Conclusion

More than twenty years of research have contributed to a very good understanding of many issues related to fault tolerance, replication and group communication. However, the understanding of theoretical issues is not the same in all models. For example, while static group communication in the crash-stop model has reached maturity, the same level of maturity has not yet been reached for dynamic group communication or for group communication in the crash-recovery model. More work needs also to be done to quantitatively compare different algorithms in the context of replication. Typically, while a lot of atomic broadcast algorithms have been published, little has been done to compare these algorithms from a quantitative point of view. Specifically, more work needs to be done to compare these algorithms under different fault-loads, as done for example in [31]. Addressing real-time constraints, e.g., [18], needs also to get more attention. Finally, note that recent advances in the design and implementation of group communication middeleware are presented in another chapter of this book [5].

Acknowledgments. I would like to thank Sergio Mena and Olivier Rütti for their comments on an earlier version of the paper.

References

1. M. K. Aguilera, W. Chen, and S. Toueg. Heartbeat: a timeout-free failure detector for quiescent reliable communication. In *Proceedings of the 11th International Workshop on Distributed Algorithms (WDAG'97)*, pages 126–140, Saarbrücken, Germany, September 1997.
2. M. K. Aguilera, C. Delporte-Gallet, H. Fauconnier, and S. Toueg. Thrifty generic broadcast. In *Proceedings of the 14th International Symposium on Distributed Computing (DISC'2000)*, October 2000.

3. P.A. Bernstein, V. Hadzilacos, and N. Goodman. *Concurrency Control and Recovery in Distributed Database Systems.* Addison-Wesley, 1987.

4. K. Birman and T. Joseph. Reliable Communication in the Presence of Failures. *ACM Trans. on Computer Systems*, 5(1):47–76, February 1987.

5. D. Bünzli, R. Fuzzati, S. Mena, U. Nestmann, O. Rütti, A.Schiper, and P. Wojciechowski. Advances in the Design and Implementation of Group Communication Middleware. This book, Part III, Chapter 8.

6. T. D. Chandra, V. Hadzilacos, and S. Toueg. The Weakest Failure Detector for Solving Consensus. *Journal of ACM*, 43(4):685–722, 1996.

7. T. D. Chandra and S. Toueg. Unreliable failure detectors for reliable distributed systems. *Journal of ACM*, 43(2):225–267, 1996.

8. G. V. Chockler, I. Keidar, and R. Vitenberg. Group Communication Specifications: A Comprehensive Study. *ACM Computing Surveys*, 4(33):1–43, December 2001.

9. X. Défago, A. Schiper, and P. Urban. Totally Ordered Broadcast and Multicast Algorithms: Taxonomy and Survey. *ACM Computing Surveys*, 4(36):1–50, December 2004.

10. D. Dolev, C. Dwork, and L. Stockmeyer. On the minimal synchrony needed for distributed consensus. *Journal of ACM*, 34(1):77–97, January 1987.

11. C. Dwork, N. Lynch, and L. Stockmeyer. Consensus in the presence of partial synchrony. *Journal of ACM*, 35(2):288–323, April 1988.

12. Richard Ekwall and André Schiper. Replication: Understanding the Advantage of Atomic Broadcast over Quorum Systems. *Journal of Universal Computer Science*, 11(5):703–711, May 2005.

13. E.N. Elnozahy, L. Alvisi, Y-M. Wang, and D.B. Johnson. A Survey of Rollback-Recovery Protocols in Message-Passing Systems. *ACM Computing Surveys*, 34(3):375–408, September 2002.

14. M. Fischer, N. Lynch, and M. Paterson. Impossibility of Distributed Consensus with One Faulty Process. *Journal of ACM*, 32:374–382, April 1985.

15. R. Guerraoui, M. Larrea, and A. Schiper. Reducing the cost for Non-Blocking in Atomic Commitment. In *IEEE 16th Intl. Conf. Distributed Computing Systems*, pages 692–697, May 1996.

16. V. Hadzilacos and S. Toueg. Fault-Tolerant Broadcasts and Related Problems. Technical Report 94-1425, Department of Computer Science, Cornell University, May 1994.

17. M. Herlihy and J. Wing. Linearizability: a correctness condition for concurrent objects. *ACM Trans. on Progr. Languages and Syst.*, 12(3):463–492, 1990.

18. J.-F. Hermant and G. Le Lann. Fast Asynchronous Uniform Consensus in Real-Time Distributed Systems. *IEEE Transactions on Computers*, 51(8):931–944, August 2002.

19. L. Lamport. Time, Clocks, and the Ordering of Events in a Distributed System. *Comm. ACM*, 21(7):558–565, July 1978.

20. L. Lamport. How to make a multiprocessor computer that correctly executes multiprocess programs. *IEEE Trans. on Computers*, C28(9):690–691, 1979.

21. L. Lamport. The Part-Time Parliament. TR 49, Digital SRC, September 1989.

22. L. Lamport. The Part-Time Parliament. *ACM Trans. on Computer Systems*, 16(2):133–169, May 1998.

23. J.C. Laprie, editor. *Dependability: Basic Concepts and Terminology.* Springer-Verlag, 1992.

24. N. A. Lynch. *Distributed Algorithms.* Morgan Kaufmann, 1996.

25. J. Misra. Axioms for memory access in asynchronous hardware systems. *ACM Trans. on Progr. Languages and Syst.*, 8(1):142–153, 1986.

26. F. Pedone and A. Schiper. Handling Message Semanticas with Generic Broadcast Protocols. *Distributed Computing*, 15(2):97–107, April 2002.
27. A. Schiper. Dynamic Group Communication. *Distributed Computing*, 18(5):359–374, April 2006.
28. A. Schiper and S. Toueg. From Set Membership to Group Membership: A Separation of Concerns. *IEEE Transactions on Dependable and Secure Computing (TDSC)*, 3(1):2–12, Jan.-March 2006.
29. F. B. Schneider. Implementing Fault Tolerant Services Using the State Machine Approach: A Tutorial. *Computing Surveys*, 22(4):299–319, December 1990.
30. D. Skeen. Nonblocking Commit Protocols. In *ACM SIGMOD Intl. Conf. on Management of Data*, pages 133–142, 1981.
31. Péter Urbán, Ilya Shnayderman, and André Schiper. Comparison of failure detectors and group membership: Performance study of two atomic broadcast algorithms. In *Proc. Int'l Conf. on Dependable Systems and Networks*, pages 645–654, San Francisco, CA, USA, June 2003.

Survey on Dependable IP over Fiber Networks

Maciej Kurant, Hung X. Nguyen, and Patrick Thiran

LCA-School of Communications and Computer Sciencs
EPFL, CH-1015 Lausanne, Switzerland
`maciej.kurant, hung.nguyen, patrick.thiran@epfl.ch`

Abstract. This paper gives a survey of the techniques for failure location, protection and restoration in IP over optical fiber networks.

The first part of the paper reviews failure location algorithms at the optical and the IP layers. We classify the failure location algorithms at the optical layer into two main categories: the model based approach, that builds an abstract model of the network and uses this model to diagnose failures, and the learning based approach, that views the network as a black box and diagnoses failures using a set of rules obtained either by learning or by the expertise of the human manager. At the IP layer, we focus on the location of one of the main sources of failure: lossy links. The lossy link location algorithms can also be classified into two categories: the correlation approach, that requires strong correlation between monitoring packets, and the simple tomography approach, that requires some knowledge of the distribution of lossy links.

The second part of the paper describes the main strategies that ensure survivability in IP-over-fiber networks. After a failure, traffic can be restored either at the optical layer or at the IP layer. Protection at the optical layer amounts to dedicate some lightpaths to reroute the traffic disrupted by the failure. Restoration at the IP layer eliminates the need to set up back-up optical paths, but requires to map the IP layer on the optical layer in a survivable way. We describe the most common approaches achieving this.

1   Introduction

Communication networks in general, and the Internet in particular, are overlays of multiple layers. Each layer has different functions and all the layers cooperate to deliver data from the source to the destination. The simplest layer stack is IP (Internet Protocol) over physical. The physical layer is the one where bits of data are sent. It can be wired or wireless. We consider the case where the physical layer is optical and where quick failure detection and restoration are crucial because a failure can result in the loss of tetra (10^9) bits of data per second. In today's backbone networks, to increase the capacity of the optical fibers, the optical layer uses the Wavelength Division Multiplexing (WDM) technique to send data simultaneously at different wavelengths over a single fiber. The upper layer in this simple stack is the IP layer, where packets of data are routed. Although there exist layers on top of IP (e.g., application layer), they are beyond the

J. Kohlas, B. Meyer, and A. Schiper (Eds.): Dependable Systems, LNCS 4028, pp. 55–81, 2006.

scope of this paper and we do not consider them here. In reality, there may exist some other layers in between the IP and WDM layers; the most frequent layer in backbone networks is SONET/SDH. SONET and SDH are a set of network interface standards and multiplexing schemes developed to support the adoption of optical fiber as a transmission medium. They use Time Division Multiplexing (TDM). SDH is the European standard whereas SONET is the US counterpart. This means that IP packets are transported over optical fibers that multiplex several connections either in time (TDM) at the SONET or SDH layer or in frequency (WDM) at the optical layer.

Failures occur frequently in communication networks. For instance, an average inter-failure time for the Sprint backbone network is about 12 hours [1]. Every network needs therefore to have a failure management system that can detect failures and take measures to guarantee the successful and timely delivery of data. When a failure occurs, it first needs to be detected and located. Then the traffic needs to be rerouted around the failure and the failing component has to be replaced [2]. In communication networks, failures at a lower layer will affect the performance of its upper layers, but the latter also have their own failures, unrelated to the lower layers. For example, a high optical signal-to-noise ratio (SNR) caused by a bent fiber will cause heavy losses on the IP links traversing the optical link, but heavy losses on these IP links can also be caused by overloaded network traffic, which is not visible at the optical layer. For this reason, each network layer uses its own failure management system. Moreover the failure management mechanisms at different layers need to cooperate with each other to avoid task duplication and increase efficiency.

We begin the paper with the first failure management task, which is to detect and locate a failure. Section 2 explores the various methods that are used, first to locate a faulty link at optical layer and next to locate a lossy link at the IP layer. In Section 3, we move to the second step in failure management, which is to engineer the network so that traffic is restored after the occurrence of a failure. We review the main methods used at the optical and the IP layer of an IP-over-fiber network. We conclude the paper in Section 4.

2 Failure Location in Optical and IP Networks

All existing techniques performing failure diagnosis rely on the analysis of symptoms and events that are generated during the occurrence of the failure. Simple failure location mechanisms are often based on locally monitored variables, such as the temperature of a device. The irregular values reached by these variables are logged as errors. Critical errors are sent to the network manager as alarms. Based on them, a failure is located. This is not a trivial task because some particular sets of alarms can have multiple possible explanations. Moreover, the set of alarms is sometimes noisy making the problem even more difficult. The noise is introduced by corrupted alarms, which are those alarms that unexpectedly arrive at the management system when they should not (*false alarms*) or those that do not arrive at the management system when they should (*missing alarms*).

The nature of failures and the available monitoring information are significantly different for the optical and the IP layer. Therefore, each layer needs to have its own failure location method. We address them separately in the following two subsections.

2.1 Failure Location at the Optical Layer

We are interested in detecting and locating failures of equipments at the optical layer. Some of the most common optical equipments and their operations are shown in the simple network of Fig. 1. A detailed survey of the failure location algorithms at the optical layer of an IP/SDH/WDM network can be found in [3]. In this section, we summarize the the most important algorithms discussed in [3] and add new developments that were not covered in that paper. We begin with a discussion of the available monitoring information. We then describe the types of failures that can be found at the optical layer and the alarms they generate. Finally, we compare and contrast the various methods that have been proposed in the literature to solve the failure location problem at the optical layer.

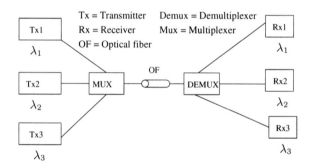

Fig. 1. A simple WDM network with three transmitters and three receivers. The three wavelengths coming out of Tx1, Tx2 and Tx3 are multiplexed at the multiplexer MUX before being transmitted on fiber OF. At the destination, these three wavelengths are demultiplexed at the demultiplexer DEMUX and then forwarded to Rx1, Rx2 and Rx3, respectively.

Available Monitoring Information. A failure at the optical layer can generate a large number of alarms within the optical layer, as well as from all of the layers above, such as SONET/SDH and IP. A failure location algorithm at the optical layer needs therefore to correlate alarms from all of these layers.

- At the optical layer, the monitoring information is delivered by the microcontrollers that control the optical equipments. Not all optical equipments are controlled. In an optical network, the most common optical equipments able to provide monitoring information and generate alarms are transmitters, receivers, switches, 3Rs (Re-generators/Re-shaper/Re-timer), protection switches, and amplifiers (a more detailed description can be found in [4]). Transmitters send alarms when either the temperature or the incoming power is beyond a prescribed range. Receivers send alarms when the input optical power is under an acceptable level. 3Rs send alarms when they cannot lock to the incoming signal. Protection switches send alarms when they change the switch position due to an unacceptable incoming optical power. Switches send alarms when the connection of a particular input and a particular output cannot be established. Amplifiers send alarms when the pump laser does not work properly or when incoming power is not sufficient. Furthermore, if adequate testing equipment is deployed, the management system can obtain information about the quality of the optical signal such as signal to noise ratio and crosstalk by measuring the Bit Error Rate (BER) [5]. Devices measuring direct optical signal can be divided into two categories. (i) Global testing equipment (GTE), such as spectrum analyzers, measures the quality of the overall optical signal in a fiber. GTEs are able to produce the measurements of frequency and time of all wavelengths in a fiber. Examples of the GTEs are the MS26665C and MS2667C of Anritsu [6]. (ii) Individual testing equipment(ITE) can measure only properties of a single wavelength and depends on the transmission technology (ATM, SONET, SDH, etc.). An example of the ITEs is the MP1552 of Anritsu [6].

– At the SDH/SONET layer, the important failure notifications handled by SDH are loss of signal (LOS), loss of frame (LOF), loss of pointer(LOP) [7], degraded signal, and excessive error [8]. The SDH/SONET interface has also a set of mechanisms that are used for sending alarms upstream and downstream of the optical path to guarantee fast failure detection and recovery [9].

All of the above monitoring information is obtained passively without introducing any additional traffic into the network. We call this approach *passive* monitoring. A complementary technique is *active* monitoring where additional end-to-end connections (called probes) are created to measure the optical signal quality, see e.g. [10]. A degradation of the probing signal indicates failures at some of the optical devices used by the connection. More details of the recent progress in monitoring the performance of optical networks can be found in [11].

Fig. 2 provides a simple illustration of the available monitoring information for failures at the optical layer in an IP/SDH/WDM optical network. The data format at the IP layer is in packets, at the SDH/SONET layer it is in frames multiplexed in several time channels, and at the WDM layer it is in connections multiplexed in several wavelengths. When there is a failure at the physical layer, alarms from several layers will be sent to their own management platforms and failure protection and restoration mechanisms will be triggered at each layer. In the example of Fig. 2, when Node 1 fails, the WDM layer could start a failure location mechanism based on the alarms generated at the physical layer (for example a *Loss of Optical Power* at the receiver of Node 2). Otherwise, the SDH/SONET layer will react by applying protection in order to restore the interrupted connection based on the SDH alarms *Loss of frame*, *Loss of Pointer*, etc. issued by the SDH equipments. If the SDH layer cannot restore the end-to-end connection, the IP routers will detect the failure and try to find an alternative IP path.

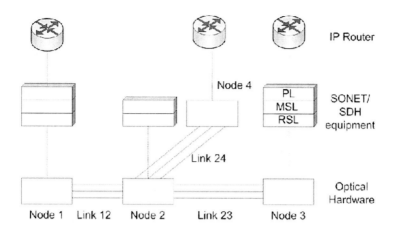

Fig. 2. Example of available monitoring information in an IP/SDH/WDM network. The notations PL, MSL, and RSL represent SDH Path, Multiplex Section and Regenerator Section layers, respectively.

Failures at the Optical Layer. We distinguish two types of failures at the optical layer: *hard* and *soft* failures.

- Hard failures are unexpected events that suddenly interrupt the optical channel. An example of a hard failure is a fiber cut. These failures can be detected at the optical layer from alarms sent by hardware devices.
- Soft failures are events that progressively degrade the quality of the signal transmission. An example of a soft failure is the variation of temperature of a laser: the output wavelength will drift as the laser heats up or cools down. In this case, the wavelength drift creates interferences with adjacent channels. The detection of soft failures often requires information from the upper layers, such as a SDH/SONET error frame rate. For example, when the wavelength is shifted, devices at the WDM layer will not detect any abnormality, but monitoring devices at the SDH and IP layer will observe increases in BER or SNR.

Failure Location Algorithms. In optical networks, a failure at an optical component not only results in faulty behavior at that component, but can also cause degradations in the signals sent from that component to other components. The other components may also forward the abnormal signals further. This manifestation is called *failure propagation*, and needs to be taken into account by the failure location mechanisms. Locating failures from the information provided by monitoring devices in systems with failure propagation such as optical networks is known to be NP-hard [12, 13, 14]. Many approaches have been proposed to solve this intractable problem. We divide them into two main categories: the *model based* methods and the *learning based* methods.

The model based methods [15, 16, 17, 18, 4] first construct an accurate and workable model for the networks on the basis of the functional and physical properties of the network components, and then make a diagnosis by comparing actual observations with forecasts from the model. The advantages of the model based methods are that they are able to cope with incomplete information and unforeseen failures, and do not require learning. Their drawback is the difficulty of developing a good model for complex networks. We study three model based methods in this paper:

- (1a) the probabilistic reasoning system developed by Katzela and Schwartz [15],
- (1b) the FSM system developed by Li and Ramaswami [17],
- (1c) the deterministic system developed by Mas and Thiran [13].

The learning based methods view the system as a black box delivering outputs when a particular failure occurs. They learn the relationship between input events and output diagnosis, which can be done in different ways: by capturing the human expert knowledge and implementing it in an efficient way (expert systems) [19, 20, 21], by recording the history of previous cases that occurred in the past (cased-based systems) [22], by artificial neural networks [23, 24] or by any other algorithm with statistical learning capabilities [25]. The main advantage of the black box methods is that they do not require detailed model of the networks. However they need long learning processes. We consider the two learning based methods:

- (2a) the expert system presented by Jakobson et al. [26],
- and (2b) the case based system proposed by Lewis [22].

There are also hybrid methods [27,28,29] that combine the two aforementioned approaches and inherit both their advantages and disadvantages.

Comparison of Failure Location Algorithms. We now compare the failure location methods introduced in the previous section (1a, 1b, 1c, 2a, and 2b) by applying them to the example network in Fig. 2. These techniques are compared with respect to the *input data* they need and their *methodology*.

Input data is the information required by the failure location algorithms from the monitoring tools (timestamps, failure probabilities). It is different for the five studied algorithms.

- Method (1a) needs (i) network topology, (ii) the failure probabilities of each node and link and (iii) the probabilities that a failure at one component will propagate to the others (failure propagation probability). For the example network in Fig. 2, the graph representing the physical layer could look like the one shown in Fig. 3, where each element is either a network node or a fiber, and has an associated failure probability p_i. Every link between two nodes has a weight p_{ij}, which is the failure propagation probability.
- Method (1b) needs the network topology and the finite state machine (FSM) for that specific network. In order to design the FSM, the network manager

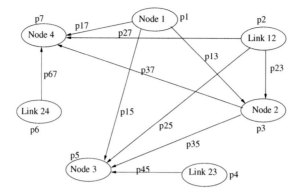

Fig. 3. The probabilistic graph model for the network in Fig. 2

has to define the failures that have to be located, and the events that determine the status of the network, which can be either alarms informing about a problem or notifications informing about the resolution of a problem. In the simple example network in Fig. 2, considering up to two simultaneous failures, the FSM looks like the set of interconnected states shown in Fig. 4.

– Method (1c) does not need the topology but instead requires the set of established end-to-end connections in the network. Each connection is then viewed as a channel containing an ordered set of network elements. Fig. 5 shows the model for the example network with three channels.

– Method (2a) needs to have the manager experiences and translates these experiences into a set of "if/then/else" rules. In our example, the rules could be:

> **If loss of light 23 then**
>> **If loss of light 24 then**
>>> **If loss of light 12 then link 12 fails**
>>> **else node 2 fails**
>> **else link 23 fails**

– Method (2b) takes as input the history of all previous solved failures: sets of alarms that are received and their diagnosis results. In our example, some solved scenarios would be:

> **Loss of light 23 is caused by failure of link 23.**
> **Loss of light 23 and loss of light 24 are caused by failure of node 2.**

Methodology is the actual algorithm used to locate the failure. The methodologies of the five studied techniques are:

– Method (1a) first designs the directed dependency graph as in Fig. 3 and then applies a divide and conquer algorithm [15], in two phases. In the first phase, called the *partitioning phase* that can be done off-line, it groups iteratively the nodes by taking the two nodes of the graph i, j, for which the failure propagation probability p_{ij} is largest, and by replacing them by a single

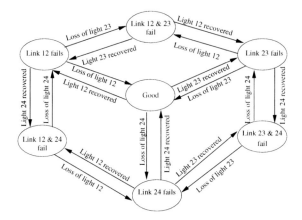

Fig. 4. The FSM model for the network in Fig. 2

new node k whose failure probability is $p_k = p_i + p_j \times p_{ji} + p_j + p_i \times p_{ij}$. The new propagation probabilities p_{kl} and p_{lk}, involving another node l and the new node k are the maximum of the previous propagation probabilities: $p_{kl} = \max\{p_{il}, p_{jl}\}$, $p_{lk} = \max\{p_{li}, p_{lj}\}$. The iterations stop when the all nodes in the dependency graph are merged into a single node that is also the root of the tree. The second phase, called the selection phase, is carried out on-line when alarms arrive at the management system. The algorithm starts from the root node of the tree obtained at the end of the partitioning phase and traverses the tree by choosing the branches that explain most alarms and that have a greater probability of containing the faulty element. It stops when it finds the smallest most likely set of elements explaining all the received alarms.

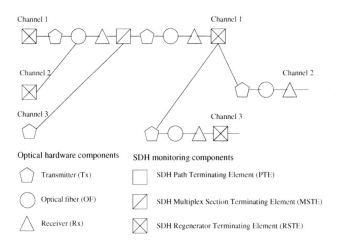

Fig. 5. The deterministic graph model for the network in Fig. 2

– Method (1b) needs to design the FSM that models the failure behavior of the network. It first defines a set of states, each state being associated to a failure scenario that may occur in the network. A last state is added to this set to represent the normal operation of the network. Given this set of states, the transition between states is defined by the events that have to be received from the network. When events (alarms or repairs) arrive, the FSM changes its state. The output of the FSM is the actual state that the system is in.

– Method (1c) consists of two stages. In the first stage, which can be done off-line, the algorithm determines which alarms will ring when a network component fails. In the second stage, which is carried out when alarms arrive, the algorithm first corrects possible alarm errors by determining the most likely set of erroneous alarms. The algorithm then solves the resulting failure location problem with the cleaned alarms by iteratively picking the network component whose failure generates the largest number of alarms, until all alarms are covered by at least one failure.

– Method (2a) first defines all the rules given by the expert knowledge of the manager. When alarms are received, the corresponding rule will provide a diagnosis. If no rule has been established for the received alarms, either no result or a default result will be given.

– In method (2b), given the alarm input, the delivered outputs are the already solved failure scenarios corresponding to the closest match in the history database. When the result is confirmed by the manager, the new case is then added to the database.

Table 1 summarizes the comparisons of different failures location methods at the optical layer.

Table 1. Comparative table of the properties of the failure location algorithms at the optical layer described in this section: *HF=* Hard failure, *SF=* soft failure, *Memory=* Memory usage, *Diagn.=* On-line diagnostic phase (alarm processing) complexity, *Prepr.=* Off-line pre-processing phase complexity, *FP=* Knowledge of failure probabilities required. *Ext.* means that the method could have this property, but at the expense of a quite important extension of the database/rules/etc.

	HF	SF	Memory	Diagn.	Prepr.	FP
1(a) Probabilistic model	Yes	No	Medium	Medium	High	Yes
1(b) FSM	Yes	No	Low	Low	High	Yes
1(c) Deterministic model	Yes	Yes	High	Low	High	No
2(a) Expert System	Yes	Ext.	Low	Low	Low	No
2(b) Case based System	Yes	Ext.	High	Medium	Low	No
2(c) Neural network	Yes	Ext.	Low	Low	High	No
2(d) Proactive system	Yes	Yes	Medium	High	Low	No

2.2   Failure Location at the IP Layer

In this section we survey failure detection and location mechanisms at the IP layer. As in the previous section, we begin with a discussion of the available monitoring information. We then describe the types of failures that occur at this layer. Finally, we will compare and contrast the various methods that have been proposed in the literature.

Available Monitoring Information at the IP Layer. At the IP layer, performance information can be obtained in different ways, depending on the accessibility to the individual routers.

- **Direct measurements at routers:** Network managers can configure routers in their network to maintain information about their own performance. For example, routers can keep count of the numbers of packets dropped due to some reasons. These information can be collected and transmitted to the network manager using mechanisms such as SNMP [30] at regular time intervals. Collecting performance information requires significant memory and computing resources from the routers. Even though sampling techniques can be used to reduce these requirements, in practice, the direct measurements can only be made at intervals of minutes (typically five minutes). Therefore, despite their potential to give accurate information for the network manager, direct measurements are the least reliable and informative way to collect performance data.
- **Passive measurements using dedicated monitors:** Network managers can also deploy passive monitors in the network at multiple points to measure the performance of packets, such as the arrival time of a packet at a specific monitor [31]. From these measurements, performance metrics such as one way delay and packet losses on the segments between monitors can be inferred. These methods have the advantages of being non-intrusive and quite accurate, see e.g. [32]. The drawback is that they require monitors to be installed at multiple locations and can be deployed only by the network owner. Even though packet monitors are cheap, their deployment and maintenance costs are substantial.
- **End-to-end measurements:** In this approach, one infers the state of the network devices through the observed performance of end-to-end monitoring packets. A special feature of the probing approach is that it allows people without privilege rights to measure the networks. This approach is important in today's IP networks where traffic traverses different administrative domains and there is no incentive for the owners of each sub-network to collect and freely distribute vital statistics of their networks. There are many different types of probes one can use, namely ICMP response packets, TCP SYN/ACK, DNS, HTTP page downloads, as well as dedicated probe protocols. These factors have led the end-to-end measurement approach to be the most the widely deployed method [33, 34]. Note here that end-to-end information can be obtained either actively by injecting probing traffic into the network, or passively by listening to existing traffic in the network.

Since most of the measurement data available for the failure diagnosis of wide area IP networks is end-to-end, we only consider these measurements in this paper.

Failures at the IP Layer. The IP layer employs a sophisticated set of routing mechanisms to carry data between end points whenever possible. However, the IP layer can only provide a best effort service and does not guarantee the timely nor even the successful delivery of the data.

Many applications, such as voice or video, require strict loss and delay requirements for acceptable quality. For example, at loss rates of 4-6% or more, video conferencing becomes irritating and non-native language speakers are unable to communicate. The occurrence of long delays of 4 seconds or more at a frequency of 4-5% or more is also irritating for interactive activities, such as telnet or X windows. Paxson [33] reports that a loss of 5% has a significant adverse effect on TCP performance, because it will greatly limit the size of the congestion window and hence the transfer rate, whereas 3% is often substantially less serious. A loss rate of 2.5% makes conversations using Voice over Internet Protocol (VoIP) slightly annoying. A more realistic burst loss pattern results in VoIP distortion going from not annoying to slightly annoying when the loss rate goes from 0 to 1% [35]. Round trip times (RTTs) should be $RTT < 400ms$ for the interactive applications. VoIP requires a $RTT < 250ms$ or it is hard for the listener to know when to speak [35].

Failure management at the IP layer is mainly concerned with the ability of the network to deliver data within some bounds on loss rates and/or delays. Of the various metrics (loss, delay, throughput) that one can use to evaluate the performance of an IP network, loss is the most critical; this is because other metrics can be inferred from it. For example, the throughput of a TCP connection can be calculated using loss and delay information [36]. In this section, we concentrate only on the detection and location of IP links that have loss rates above 1% (*lossy links*). A lossy link can be caused either by failures at the optical layer or by congestions at the IP layer. We do not distinguish these two cases in this paper. Knowing the locations of lossy links, an application can significantly improve its performance by rerouting around them [37].

Lossy Link Location Problem Definition. We focus on the techniques that can be used to infer lossy links using end-to-end measurements. The inference of internal link properties given end-to-end observations is called network tomography. Most tomography works consider tree topologies like the one depicted in Fig. 6. Each node in the tree represents a router or an end-host. Each link represents a connection between two routers/hosts. Note here that the link can be a single physical link or a chain of physical links connected by intermediate routers. Probing packets are sent from the source at the root node to the receivers at the leaf nodes along paths that pass through several internal nodes. The goal of loss tomography is to estimate individual link loss rates based on the loss rate perceived at a few end nodes.

The network is modelled as a directed graph $\mathcal{G} = (\mathcal{V}, \mathcal{E})$, where the set $\mathcal{V}$ of nodes denote the network routers/hosts and the set $\mathcal{E}$ of edges represent the communication links connecting them. The number of nodes and edges is denoted by $n_v = |\mathcal{V}|$, and $n_e = |\mathcal{E}|$, respectively. For a known topology $\mathcal{G} = (\mathcal{V}, \mathcal{E})$ and a set of end-to-end paths $\mathcal{P}$, $n_p = |\mathcal{P}|$, we compute the routing matrix D of dimension $n_p \times n_e$ as follows. The entry $D_{ij} = 1$ if the path P_i contains the link e_j and $D_{ij} = 0$ otherwise. A row of D therefore corresponds to a path, whereas a column corresponds to a link.

Let ϕ_i denote the packet transmission probability on path P_i and ϕ_{e_j} the packet transmission probability on link e_j. Clearly, the loss rate of a link e_j equals to $1 - \phi_{e_j}$. Therefore, estimating the link loss rates amounts to estimating the variables ϕ_{e_j} from the measured path transmission rates ϕ_i. Assuming independence among loss events on links, the relation between the path-wise and link-wise transmission rates reads

$$y = Dx = \left[\sum_{j=1}^{n_p} x_j D_{ij} \right]_{1 \le i \le n_e} \tag{1}$$

where $y_i = \log(\phi_i)$ and $x_j = \log(\phi_{e_j})$: y is the vector of measurements, e.g. path packet transmission rates, and x is the vector of link transmission rates.

The network loss tomography problem boils down to solving the linear system of equations (1) to find x given y and D.

Lossy Link Location Algorithms at the IP Layer. Equations (1) cannot be solved directly because most of the time the matrix D is rank deficient, that is, $\text{rank}(D) < \min(n_p, n_e)$ (the rank of D is the maximal number of columns (rows respectively) of D which are linearly independent). The non-uniqueness of link loss rates is illustrated in the example of Fig. 6 [38].

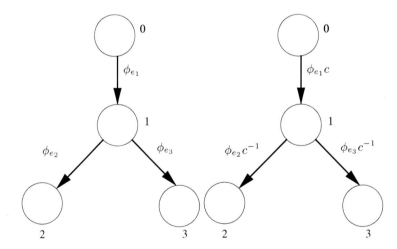

Fig. 6. In the figure, the nodes are the network routers/hosts and the directed links are the communication links connecting them. ϕ_{e_j} denotes the transmission rate of link e_j and c is a constant between $\max\{\phi_{e_2}, \phi_{e_3}\}$ and $1/\phi_{e_1}$. Both set of link transmission rates give the same end-to-end transmission rates. Link transmission rates therefore cannot be uniquely calculated from end-to-end transmission rates.

Two techniques can overcome the non-uniqueness solution problem to identify lossy links at the IP layer. The first approach, called the *correlation* approach, introduces additional constraints to (1) by creating a correlation between probing packets. The second approach, called the *simple tomography* approach, exploits the distribution of link loss rates on the Internet to solve (1).

The correlation approach can be realized by either using multicast [39] or unicast probing packets [40,41]. Multicast packets are sent to a group of subscribing receivers. At internal branching points, each multicast packet is replicated and sent along each branching path. In contrast, unicast packets are sent to only one receiver. To correlate them, the unicast packets to different receivers are sent almost at the same time such that they experience the same loss behavior on the common links shared by different receivers. Several challenges exist in bringing the multicast or unicast methods into widespread fruition. On one hand, multicast is not widely deployed. On the other hand, methods based on unicast probing incur costs to deploy appropriate data collection softwares. We study in this paper three correlation based methods:

- (1a) the multicast method developed by [39],
- (1b) the unicast packet pair method developed by [40],
- (1c) the unicast packet train method developed by [41].

The difficulties encountered in the previous methods motivate the simple tomography approach that does not require the correlations between probing packets [42, 38]. The simple tomography approach is based on the assumption that network links are generally lossless and that only a few links are responsible for dropped packets. The major advantage of this approach is that applications already monitor packets from end-to-end. Simple tomography methods do not seek to calculate the exact loss rate for each link. Instead, they use a threshold t_l, called link threshold, to determine whether a link e_k is good ($\phi_{e_k} \geq t_l$) or bad (lossy) ($\phi_{e_k} < t_l$). The threshold t_l can be set either to meet a given transmission rate target, or on the basis of data history that shows a clear value separating well and badly performing links. The problem of identifying lossy links without finding exact link loss rates amounts to finding the most probable solution for the observed end-to-end data. Knowing that bad links are not frequent, the most probable solution is the one giving the least number of lossy links. Let us consider the example in Fig. 6. Assuming that the threshold separating good and bad links is 0.99, if the end-to-end transmission rates to the sink of both nodes 2 and 3 are below 0.98 ($\approx 0.99 \times 0.99$), the most probable explanation is that link 0-1 is lossy (having transmission rate less than 0.99). Other explanations require at least two links to be lossy, and are therefore much less likely. We consider in particular two simple tomography methods:

- (2a) the simple tomography using Monte-Carlo simulation method developed in [42],
- and (2b) the simple tomography using set-cover heuristic method in Duffield [38].

Comparison of Lossy Link Location Algorithms at the IP layer. We now compare the lossy link location methods introduced in the previous section (1a, 1b, 1c, 2a, and 2b) by applying them to the example network in Fig. 6. These techniques may be compared with respect to the *network support* they require and their *methodology*.

Network support is the additional support needed by the loss link location algorithms in addition to the network topology. It is different for the five studied algorithms.

- Method (1a) requires (i) multicast support from all the routers and (ii) specific software packages installed at the multicast sender and receivers to send, collect and analyze the multicast traffic.
- Methods (1b) and (1c) need to have some specific softwares installed at the unicast sender and receivers to send, collect and analyze the unicast traffic.
- Methods (2a) and (2b) do not need any additional support from the network.

Methodology is the actual algorithm used to locate the lossy links. The methodologies of the five studied techniques are:

- Method (1a) uses multicast packets to calculate the link loss rates. In the network of Fig. 6, if a multicast packet is sent by the sender at node 0 and received by the receiver at node 2 but not the one at node 3, then it can be immediately determined that the loss occurred on link 3 (successful reception at node 2 implies that the multicast packet reached the internal node 1). By performing such measurements repeatedly, the loss rates on the two links 2 and 3 can be estimated; these estimates and measurements enable to deduce the loss rate on link 1. To illustrate the method further, let $\phi_{2|3}$ be the ratio of the number of multicast packets simultaneously received at both nodes 2 and 3, relatively to the total number received at node 3. In other words, $\phi_{2|3}$ is the empirical probability of success on link 2 conditional upon success on link 3, which provides a simple estimate of ϕ_{e_2}. Similarly, we define $\phi_{3|2}$ as the probability of success on link 3 conditional upon success on link 2, and let ϕ_1 and ϕ_2 be the transmission rates of multicast packets for node 2 and 3. We can then write

$$
\begin{pmatrix} \log \phi_2 \\ \log \phi_2 \\ \log \phi_{2|3} \\ \log \phi_{3|2} \end{pmatrix} = \begin{pmatrix} 1\,1\,0 \\ 1\,0\,1 \\ 0\,1\,0 \\ 0\,0\,1 \end{pmatrix} \begin{pmatrix} \log \phi_{e_1} \\ \log \phi_{e_2} \\ \log \phi_{e_3} \end{pmatrix}. \tag{2}
$$

A least square estimate of ϕ_{e_j} is easily computed for this over-determined system of equations. Sophisticated and effective algorithms have been derived for large scale network tomography in [39].
- Method (1b) was introduced in [40] to overcome the fact that most routers in the Internet today do not support multicast and that performance observed

by multicast packets differs significantly from that observed by unicast traffic. In method (1b), back-to-back packet pairs, each consisting of two packets sent one after the other by the sender, are sent to every pair of receivers. When two packets of a pair arrive back-to-back in a common queue, the successful transmission of one packet indicates, with high probability, the successful transmission of the other packet. If two back-to-back packets are sent to node j from the previous node $\rho(j)$ on a path, then let β_j be the conditional probability that the first packet of a pair arrives at node j from $\rho(j)$ given that the second packet sent by $\rho(j)$ has arrived successfully at node j. β_j is very close to 1. Denote the complete set of conditional success probability by $\beta = \{\beta\}_{j=1}^{n_e}$, where n_e is the number of links. In this case, the network tomography problem boils down to determining the values of ϕ_{e_j} and β_j that best explain the probing results. Maximizing the likelihood is not simple and, consequently, numerical optimization strategies are required. The most commonly used method is the expectation-maximization algorithm (EM) [40].

– Method (1c) also uses back-to-back unicast packets but in a different way. The main objective of method (1c) is to create multicast probing using unicast packets. In method (1c), the sender sends a sequence (a train) of many back-to-back packets to all receivers (instead of packet pairs to all pairs of receivers as in method (1b)). Contrary to method (1b) where the conditional probabilities β_j are treated as variables, method (1c) assumes that $\beta_j = 1$ for all j. By viewing each packet train as a multicast packet, method (1c) then uses techniques in method (1a) to infer the link loss rates.

– Method (2a) is a simple tomography method proposed by [42], which means that it does not seek to calculate the exact link loss rates, but that it determines whether a link is lossy or not. Method (2a) uses the sophisticated Monte Carlo Markov Chain Simulation (*MCMC* method) to determine the lossy link. It tries to determine the posterior distribution, $\mathbb{P}(x|y)$, of the link loss rates in logarithmic scale x given the observed path data, y. Knowing $\mathbb{P}(x|y)$, one can draw samples from this distribution where each sample is a vector containing the transmission rates for all links in the network that can explain the observed data. The method then collects the transmission rates of each link in all samples and compares them with the threshold t_l. If the majority of the sampled transmission rates of a link are bad ($< t_l$), then the link is declared as bad. Otherwise it is declared as good. In general, it is hard to compute $\mathbb{P}(x|y)$ directly because of the complex integrations, especially when x is a vector, as in the present case. It is also difficult to obtain samples of the distribution $\mathbb{P}(x|y)$. Hence method (2a) uses an indirect approach to collect them by constructing a Markov chain whose stationary distribution is exactly equal to $\mathbb{P}(x|y)$. When such a Markov chain is run for a sufficiently large number of steps, it converges to its stationary distribution. The method then gathers samples from this stationary distribution and views them as samples from the posterior distribution $\mathbb{P}(x|y)$. This way, it does not have to determine the distribution $\mathbb{P}(x|y)$ and then draw the

Table 2. Comparative table of the properties of the methods described in this section for lossy link location at the IP layer: the column *Loss Rates* indicates whether the method can infer the exact loss rates, and the column *Meas. Errors* indicates whether the method can handle measurements errors, e.g., errors in estimating the end-to-end loss rates.

	Monitoring Costs	Processing Time	Loss Rates	Meas. Errors
1(a) Multicast tomography	High	Low	Yes	Yes
1(b) Unicast packet pair	Medium	High	Yes	Yes
1(c) Unicast packet train	Medium	Low	Yes	Yes
2(a) MCMC	Low	High	No	Yes
2(b) SCFC	Low	Low	No	No

samples from it. For the detailed construction of the Markov chain, we refer to [42].

– Method (2b) is a simple tomography method proposed by Duffield [38] (Duffield called this approach the *SCFC* algorithm). It first determines a threshold $t_p = t_l^{n_{link}}$, with n_{link} is the number of links in the path, for all paths. It then determines all end-to-end paths that have bad transmission rates, that is, whose transmission rate is below t_p. By observing that a path is bad if and only if one of its links is bad and that bad links are rare, it tries to find the smallest number of links whose badness can explain the badness of all bad end-to-end paths. The SCFC method adopts a greedy heuristic that iteratively chooses at each step the link that can explain the largest number of bad paths and infers that the link is lossy.

Table 2 gives a summary of the comparisons of different lossy link location methods at the IP layer.

3   Failure Protection and Restoration in IP/WDM Networks

Failures must not only be identified and located. The network must be designed so that the traffic is protected against them, which implies rerouting rapidly the traffic when a failure occurs, until it is repaired.

So far, we distinguished between a first generation IP/SONET/WDM network and a second generation IP/WDM network. In the context of failure protection, however, speaking at a functional level, there are no big differences between IP/SONET/WDM networks protecting traffic at the SONET layer, and IP/WDM networks protecting traffic at the optical layer, since the optical layer should take over all protection and restoration functionalities of the SONET layer. Therefore in this section we do not make a distinction between both architectures and we use the SONET/SDH and optical layer indifferently. This brings us to the analysis of two layers: the *physical layer* (optical) and the *logical layer* (IP).

The physical layer topology is a set of optical switches (nodes) and fibers (links) interconnecting them. Each logical link is mapped on the physical topology as a *lightpath*. A lightpath may span multiple fiber links. A set of all light-paths defines a *mapping* of the logical graph on the physical graph. Given the physical and logical topologies, the problem of finding a mapping and assigning wavelengths to all logical links is called the Routing and Wavelength Assignment (RWA) problem. In its general form, the RWA problem does not take failure resilience into account - its objective is to minimize the network resources. A survey on RWA algorithms can be found in [43]. The difficulty of the RWA problem depends partially on the type of physical nodes used in the network. Perhaps the simplest kind of physical node is an optical crossconnect (OXC). It switches the optical signal from an input port to an output port without wavelength conversion. In this case a lightpath must occupy the same wavelength on all fiber links it traverses, which is called a *wavelength continuity constraint*. Physical nodes can be equipped with *wavelength converters* to alleviate this constraint: some can offer a full conversion capability (that is, any wavelength can be converted to any other wavelength), others only offer limited conversion capability (that is, a wavelength can only be converted to the neighboring wavelengths on the spectrum). When the full wavelength conversion is available at every node, the RWA problem is in fact reduced to the routing problem only.

Generally, there are two approaches for providing survivability of IP-over-WDM networks: protection and restoration [44]. *Protection* is the mechanism in which the traffic is switched to available resources when a failure occurs. It needs to be very fast, the commonly accepted standard for physical layer is 50 ms. Protection routes must therefore be pre-computed, and wavelengths must be reserved in advance at the time of connection setup. For speed requirements, protection may require fairly simple topologies (rings rather than complex meshes) and may be performed in a distributed way, without relying on a central management entity to coordinate actions. *Restoration* is the mechanism in which new routes are established on the fly, after a failure has occurred. This is much slower than protection and requires enough free resources available at the moment of the failure.

The failure protection and restoration tasks can be carried out at different layers. Often, the logical layer uses restoration (IP restoration) and the physical layer uses protection (optical protection). We illustrate these approaches in the toy example in Fig. 7, where three IP connections are mapped on a six-node physical topology. Assume that each fiber can carry two wavelengths λ_1 and λ_2, each of the capacity of one unit of traffic. Fig. 7a shows an example of protection at the physical layer. This is achieved by setting up three primary lightpaths (set in bold), all on wavelength λ_1, which are used to carry the traffic in absence of failures. For each primary lightpath we also prepare a backup lightpath (dashed) on wavelength λ_2. If the fiber (5,6) fails then all the traffic on the primary lightpath (1,6,5,4) on λ_1, is routed over the backup lightpath (1,3,4) on λ_2. Note that due to very small reaction times, these mechanisms are transparent to the logical layer.

The Internet Protocol (IP) is also capable of restoring the traffic around a failed facility. It is illustrated in Fig. 7b. Here each logical (IP) link has only one corresponding lightpath. Routers periodically exchange keep-alive or hello messages to check the health of neighboring links and nodes. A failure of the fiber (5,6) does not trigger any action at the physical layer. Instead, after the loss of a few successive hello messages between the routers 1 and 4, the logical link (1,4) is deduced to have failed. Now, the traffic between the nodes 1 and 4 is rerouted in the logical topology via node 3. In order to enable this, two requirements must be met; first, a single physical failure cannot cut the connectivity at the logical layer, and second, the links at the logical layer must be overprovisioned, in order to be able to absorb the additional traffic rerouted after a failure. Let us assume that in the example in Fig. 7b all logical links initially carry (before a failure) the same amount t of traffic. In order to enable the IP restoration, t can be, at most, half of one traffic unit (i.e., half of the optical channel capacity). Note, however, that overprovisioning has a positive side effect of keeping the links under-utilized during regular operations and therefore of maintaining all delays short in the network.

Despite the requirements it imposes, the IP restoration approach turns out to be more resource efficient than optical protection. This is partially due to the

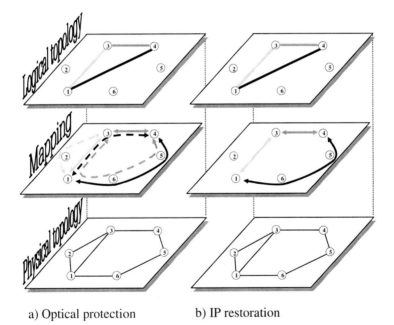

a) Optical protection   b) IP restoration

Fig. 7. An illustration of the basic concept of optical protection (left) and IP restoration (right). The logical topology consisting of three IP links is mapped on the physical topology with six nodes and seven optical fibers. Each fiber can carry two wavelengths λ_1 and λ_2, each of the capacity of one unit of traffic. The lightpaths are represented by the arrows in the mapping. For example, the logical link (1,4) uses the lightpath (1,6,5,4). In the WDM protection scheme, the primary lightpaths use λ_1 and are set in solid, whereas the backup lightpaths use λ_2 and are dashed.

different granularity of the approaches: at a packet level in IP restoration vs. at a wavelength level in optical protection. Assume, for instance, that initially every logical link is loaded with at most half a unit of traffic. Under this assumption, both failure protection schemes in Fig. 7 can deal with any single fiber failure. Note that the primary lightpaths in the optical protection scheme are exactly the same as the lightpaths set up in IP restoration, hence the resources used by them are the same. The optical protection approach, however, commits additional resources by setting up the backup lightpaths, which makes it more resource-consuming. This effect is even stronger in denser and bigger topologies.

A major difficulty in optical networks that support various upper layers is that each layer performs its own protection and mechanisms independently from the others. This can lead to undesirable races between layers to protect traffic. For example, if the optical layer is protection enabled and if it did not recover from the failure very rapidly, the logical layer might happen to detect the failure. It will start rerouting the IP traffic around the failed link(s) or router(s). The lack of coordination between layers can therefore create a quite intricate situation. The problem of inter-layer coordination is addressed for example in [45, 46, 47]. Having protection at only one layer might simplify the problem, but one still needs then to choose the layer at which it should be done. It is not obvious which layer is more suitable for failure protection/restoration; each has pros and cons [48, 44]. First of all, some failures, such as a failed line card in a router, cannot be detected at the lower layer, but only at the IP layer (i.e., by IP restoration). Another advantage of IP restoration, as we have seen above, is its resource efficiency. Unfortunately, it is also inherently slow - failure detection at the logical layer takes tens of seconds at least, and time scales at which restoration occurs are typically at least three orders of magnitude larger than the protection processes at the physical layer. However, many real network operators deploy IP restoration only, and find it an effective and cost-efficient solution (see e.g., [49]). Some multi-layer protection/restoration schemes can adequately combine the advantages of each layer and still avoid most of their disadvantages [46], but do not eliminate the complexity of coordinating the different restoration schemes at the various layers (some solutions are proposed in [46]). One way to bypass some of this complexity race is to allocate the restoration task to a different layer for different traffic classes[1], which also brings benefits in resource usage [50].

We discuss now in more details the techniques used to protect and restore traffic, first at the physical layer, and next at the logical layer.

3.1   Protection and Restoration at the Physical Layer Only

All protection techniques involve some redundant capacity with the network to reroute traffic in case of a failure. There are essentially two basic protection mechanisms used in point-to-point links: 1+1 protection, and 1:1 protection(and its generalization to 1:n protection).

---

[1] A traffic class might be defined for instance by its origin/destination, bandwidth or maximal delay and jitter.

In 1+1 protection, traffic is transmitted simultaneously on two separate fibers on disjoint routes. The receiver selects the signal at the destination that has the largest incoming power. If that fiber is cut, it will automatically switch to the other fiber. This is the fastest and simplest protection, because no signalling is needed. It is however very inefficient in terms of resources, as every unit of traffic requires twice as much capacity. As a result, it is used in some ring networks (Unidirectional path-switched rings, see [51]), but not in large, meshed WDM networks.

In 1:1 and, more generally speaking, 1:n protection, traffic is transmitted only on one fiber (called working or primary fiber). If this fiber is cut, the sender and receiver both switch to the other fiber (called protection or back-up fiber). This is not as fast nor as simple as 1+1 protection, because the destination must detect the failure first and then signal it to the source, which will then switch over to the protection fiber. The advantage of 1:1 protection is that the capacity on the back-up fiber can be spared for unprotected traffic, which will be preempted in case of a failure, or can be shared between n multiple, physically disjoint working paths, in which case one speaks of 1:n protection rather than 1:1 protection (the latter applies only to a back-up path which is not shared among multiple primary paths). Sharing a back-up path among n disjoint working paths can spare a large amount of bandwidth, but at the cost of an increased amount of signalling. On the contrary, having a dedicated path requires the reservation of many more resources, but requires less signalling. The gain in spatial reuse of 1:1 protection schemes over 1+1 is already important for rings [51], but gets even much larger in meshed WDM networks.

Protection around the failed facility can be done at different points in the network: either around the two end-points of the the failed link, by line protection; or between the source and destination of each connection traversing the failed link, by path protection. Protection at the line layer is simpler, but path protection requires less bandwidth and can better handle node failures.

Routing and assigning wavelength in an optical network to guarantee its survivability by either 1+1 or 1:1 protection can be formulated as an Integer Linear Programming (ILP) problem. Ramamurthy and Mukherjee [52] use the ILP formulation to compare quantitatively the two schemes, together with the variants of link and path protection. The 1:1 path protection leads to significant savings in capacity utilization over the 1:1 link and 1+1 protection schemes. Since for large topologies the ILP formulation approach becomes computationally difficult, a number of heuristics have been proposed [53].

Protection is the most common mechanism deployed at the optical layer, because WDM or SONET/SDH connections are usually long-lived, and rarely set up on demand. Some authors advocate the possibility of restoration at the optical layer, which would spare more bandwidth than protection, but can also introduce significant delays to restore the traffic [54]. The complexity of restoring traffic at the optical layer (compared to protection at same layer, or restoration at the IP layer) makes it unlikely that operators rely primarily on restoration at the optical layer in the near future.

3.2 Restoration at the Logical Layer by Survivable Mapping

Recall from the beginning of Section 3, that in order to make the IP restoration work, the logical topology must remain connected after a failure. This requirement can be met by an appropriate mapping of the logical topology on the physical topology.[2] More specifically, if the logical topology remains connected after any single physical link failure, then the underlying mapping is called a *survivable mapping*.

Although the survivable mapping problem can be viewed as a specific version of the Routing and Wavelength Assignment (RWA) problem, it is often defined relaxing some basic assumptions of RWA, such as the wavelength continuity or even the capacity constraints. This results in a survivable mapping problem that is independent of RWA and can be addressed separately.

The problem of finding survivable mapping is NP-complete [55] and has drawn recently a lot of attention. It was first identified by Crochat et.al. [56], and named "design protection". Some authors focused on simplified versions of the survivable mapping problem, assuming a cycle (ring) topology at the physical layer [57,58] or the logical layer [55,59]. The others addressed the general case, with arbitrary topologies at both layers. In general, the existing approaches can be divided into three groups: (i) exact algorithms based on Integer Linear Programming (ILP), (ii) pure heuristics and (iii) heuristics with provable properties. Below we describe each of them in more details, and compare in Table 3.

ILP. The ILP solutions can be found for example in [55,44,60]. In [55] it was observed that a mapping is survivable if and only if no physical link is shared by all logical links belonging to a cut-set of the logical graph.[3] This observation is used in [55] to formulate an ILP model for the survivable mapping problem: for each logical link and for each cut-set of the logical graph, a constraint is added to the ILP. This leads to exact solutions, but also to excessive run-times [61] for networks of a non-trivially small size (few tens of nodes). To overcome this difficulty two relaxations to ILP are proposed in [55], by including only cut-sets of small sizes. This considerably accelerates the algorithm, but can easily lead to suboptimal solutions. Facing the same time-complexity problem of ILP, the authors of [44] and [60] decided to try a heuristic approach.

Heuristics. Despite many differences, the heuristics used to solve the survivable mapping problem share the same general methodology. They start with some initial mapping (e.g., shortest path) and try to improve it at subsequent iterations. Probably the most often used heuristic is *Tabu Search*. It is a version of a steepest descent search algorithm that stores a list (called a Tabu List) of recent moves to avoid them. This allows Tabu Search escape the local minima.

---

[2] We assume that the logical and the physical topologies are given and cannot be changed.

[3] A *cut-set* of a network is defined by a cut of the network: a cut is a partition of the set of nodes V into two sets S and $V - S$, and the cut-set defined by this cut is the set of edges which have one endpoint in S and one in $V - S$.

Table 3. Comparison of efficiency and functionalities of four approaches to search for a survivable mapping. The question mark "?" means that the option might be possible to realize, but, to the best of our knowledge, nobody did it to date.

Functionality	ILP	Tabu Search	FastSurv	SMART
Scalability	Low	Average	High	Very high
Capacity and other constraints	Yes	Yes	Yes	No
Verification of a solution existence	Yes	No	No	Yes
Node/span/multiple failures	?	?	Yes	Yes
Tracing and repairing the vulnerable areas	No	No	No	Yes

For more details refer to [62]. Tabu Search was used with success to solve the survivability problem in many settings, e.g., without capacity constraints [56], with capacity constraints [63, 64] or additionally meeting maximum delay requirements [60]. Another general heuristic applied to solve the survivable mapping problem is Simulated Annealing in [48]. There is also a number of heuristics developed specifically to solve this problem, e.g., in [44] and [65]. The FastSurv algorithm introduced recently in [65], exploits the observation already mentioned in the ILP paragraph, which takes use of cut-sets in the logical topology. However, unlike in [55], the FastSurv algorithm systematically and indirectly learns about the importance of particular cut-sets and focuses only on the most relevant ones. This approach results in much better efficiency and scalability than those of other heuristics.

Heuristics with Provable Properties. The SMART algorithm proposed in [66, 67] does not fall in either group above. It is based on a breakdown of the problem into a set of independent smaller problems, which are easy to solve. Each of them is solved separately, and then the solutions are combined to obtain a survivable mapping of the entire topology. This makes SMART the fastest and most scalable heuristic to date. Moreover, the formal analysis in [67] revealed that SMART can also serve as a scalable method of verification of the existence of a survivable mapping and a tool tracing and repairing the vulnerable areas of the network. These two features are completely novel in the field.[4] It should be noted, however, that one of the main assumptions of the analysis in [67] is relaxing the capacity constrains. In the presence of some additional real-life constraints such as limited fiber capacity or maximum delay, the SMART approach loses its efficiency and properties. Therefore SMART is more used to getting some topological insight into the problem than to finding an engineering solution, which makes this approach in a sense complementary to others.

3.3   Other Types of Failures

So far we have only considered single physical link failures. They may result from a fiber cut, a fault of a single interface card in the optical switch, or a fault of an

---

[4] The ILP can also verify the existence of a survivable mapping, but as we argued before, it is not scalable.

optical amplifier. They are the most common type of failures in optical networks, but not the only one. If we allow for the physical location of the fibers, we extend single link failures to single *span failures*. A *span* is a bundle of fibers partially placed together for cost reasons (e.g., along railway and electricity lines). A single cut can break all of these fibers at once, in which case we speak of a span failure. We can also encounter *node failures*; they are the consequence of a failure of equipment at nodes, such as switches. In our context a node failure is equivalent to a failure of all physical links neighboring to the node. Finally, we consider *double–link failures*, i.e., independent failures of any two physical links. Usually such a situation takes place when the second failure occurs before the first one is repaired. This is not very common, but possible. For example, in the Sprint network, the time between two successive optical failures ranges from 5.5 sec to 7.5 days with a mean of 12 hours [1]. Most of them are repaired automatically within several minutes, but those requiring human intervention (e.g., after a fiber cut) may last hours or days. It is quite probable that during that period another physical failure occurs.

These failure scenarios were addressed mainly by physical layer protection: the span failures in [68,69], the node failures in [70], and the double-link failures in [71, 72, 73]. The IP restoration mechanisms considered these failures in [66] (all types of failures) and [67] (link and node failures).

4   Conclusion

We have addressed the failure management problem in IP/WDM optical networks. This issue can be decomposed with respect to two criteria. First, we distinguish the failure location from the failure restoration. The former aims at identifying the failing component based on the feedback from the network, whereas the latter consists in rerouting the traffic affected by the failure. These two tasks have different objectives and require different approaches. The second line of division is defined by the existence of at least two layers in the network: the IP layer and the optical layer. Each layer applies its own specific mechanisms to transport traffic, which significantly affects the way a failure is handled.

Following this view, we have discussed and made a detailed comparison of numerous failure management techniques, separately for failure location and restoration, and distinguishing between the IP and the optical layer. In contrast to previous surveys that have focused only on some particular aspects, our approach results in a global overview of failure management possibilities in IP/WDM networks.

References

1. Markopoulou, A., Iannaccone, G., Bhattacharyya, S., Chuah, C.N., Diot, C.: Characterization of Failures in an IP Backbone. In: Proceedings of the IEEE INFO-COM'04. (2004)
2. Abek, F., Hegerin, H., Neumair, B.: Integrated Management of Networked Systems. Morgan Kaufmann Publishers (1998)

3. Mas, C., Thiran, P.: An efficient algorithm for locating soft and hard failures in WDM network. JSAC special issue on Protocols and Architectures for next generation optical WDM networks **18** (2000) 1900–1911
4. Mas, C., Nguyen, H.X., Thiran, P.: Failure location in WDM networks. In: Optical WDM Networks: Past Lessons and Path Ahead. Kluwer Academic Publishers (2004)
5. ITU-T COM 15 121: Signal Quality Monitoring in Optical networks. (1999)
6. Anritsu: Catalog of measuring instrument (1993)
7. ITU-T Rec. G.872. Architecture of Optical Transport Networks (1998)
8. ITU-T Rec. G.806. Characteristics of Transport Equipment - Description Methodology and Generic Functionality (2000)
9. Wautersa, N., Ocahoglu, G., Struyve, K., Falcao, P.: Survivability in a new paneuropean carrier's network based on WDM and SDH technology: Current implementations and future requirements. IEEE Communication Magazine **37(8)** (1999) 63–69
10. Tao, W., Somani, A.K.: Attack monitoring and monitor placement in all-optical networks. In: Proceedings of IEEE GBN 2001. (2001)
11. Kilper, D., Bach, R., Blumenthal, D.J., Einstein, D., Landolsi, T., Ostar, L., Preiss, M., Willner, A.E.: Optical performance monitoring. Journal of Lightwave Technology **22** (Jan 2004) 294–304
12. N.S.V.Rao: Computational complexity issues in operative dianosis of graph based systems. IEEE Transactions on Computers **42** (1993) 447–457
13. Nguyen, H.X., Thiran, P.: Failure location in all optical networks: the assymetry between false and missing alarms. In: Proceedings of ITC 19. (2005)
14. Ducatelle, F., Gambardella, L.M., Kurant, M., Nguyen, H.X., Thiran, P.: Algorithms for Failure Protection in Large IP-over-Fiber and Wireless Ad Hoc Networks. In Dependable Systems: Software, Computing, Networks, eds. J. Kohlas, B. Meyer, A. Schiper, Lecture Notes in Computer Science 4028, Springer, 2006 (this volume)
15. Katzela, I., Schwartz, M.: Scheme for fault identification in communication networks. IEEE/ACM Transaction on Networking **3** (1995)
16. Wang, C., Schwart, M.: Identification of faulty links in dynamics-routed networks. IEEE Journal on selected Areas in Communications (1993) 1449–1460
17. Li, C.S., Ramaswami, R.: Fault Detection and Isolation in transparent All-Optical Networks. In: IBM Research Report. Volume RC-20028. (1995)
18. Bouloutas, A., Hart, G., Schwartz, M.: Fault identification using a fsm model with unreliable partially observed data sequences. IEEE Transactions on Communications **41** (1993) 1074–1083
19. Gu, K., et al.: Realization of an expert system for an online fault diagnosis and restoration in a bulk power system. In: Proc. 4th International Symposium expert Systems Application Power Systems. (1993)
20. Brugnoni, S., et al.: An expert system for rel time fault diagnosis of the italian communications network. In: Proceedings of Integrated network management. Volume 3. (1993) 617–628
21. Jakobson, G., Weissman, M.E., Brenner, L., Lafond, C., Matheus, C.: Grace: Building next generation event correlation services. In: IEEE/IFIP: Network Operations and Management Symposium NOMS, 2000. (2000)
22. Lewis, L.: A case-based reasoning approach to the resolution of faults in communications networks. In Integrated network management III (1993) 671–682

23. Maki, Y., Loparo, K.A.: Neural network approach to fault detetin and diagnosis in industrial processes. IEEE Transactions on Control Systems Technology **5(6)** (2001) 529–541

24. Rodriguez, C., Rementeria, S., Martin, J., Lafuente, A., Perez, J.: A modular neural network approach to fault diagnosis. IEEE Transactions on Neural Networks (March 1996)

25. Ho, L., Cavuto, D., Papavassilou, S., Zawadzki, A.: Adaptive and automated detection of service anomalies in transaction-oriented wans. IEEE Journal on Selected Areas Communications **18(5)** (May 2000) 744–757

26. Jakobson, G., Weissman, M.E.: Alarm correlation. IEEE Network (1993) 52–59

27. Hood, C., Ji, C.: Proactive network-fault detection. IEEE Transactions on reliability **46(3)** (Sep 2000)

28. Lin, A.: A hybrid approach to fault diagnosis in network and system management. HP Technical Report (1998)

29. Gardner, R., Harle, D.: Alarm correlation and nerwork fault resolution using kohonen self-organising map. In: In proceedings of Globecom 97. (1997) 1398–1402

30. Stallings, W.: SNMP, SNMPv2, SNMPv3 and RMON 1 and 2. Addision-Wesley Longman Inc (1999)

31. Zhang, Y., Breslau, L., Paxson, V., Shenker, S.: On the characteristics and origins of internet flow rates. In: Proceedings of the ACM SIGCOMM Conference. (2002)

32. Choi, B.Y., Moon, S., Zhang, Z.L., Papagiannaki, K., Diot, C.: Analysis of point-to-point packet delay in an operatinal network. In: Proceedings of the INFOCOM. (2004)

33. Paxson, V.: Measurement and Analysis of End-to-End Internet Dynamics. PhD thesis, Univ. of Cal., Berkeley (1997)

34. Almes, G., Kalidini, S., Zekauskas, M.: A one-way delay metric for IPPM. IETF, IP Performance metrics, request for comments:2680 (1999)

35. ITU-T Rec. G.113. [G.113 Appendix I (05/02)] Provisional planning values for the equipment impairment factor Ie and packet-loss robustness factor Bpl (2002)

36. Mathis, M., Semke, J., Mahdavi, J., Ott, T.: The macroscopic behaviour of the TCP congestion avoidance algorithm. Computer Communication Review **27** (1997)

37. Tao, V., Xu, K., Estepa, A., Fei, T., Gao, L., Guerin, R., Kurose, J., Towsley, D., Zhang, Z.L.: Improving voip quality through path switching. In: Proceedings of IEEE Infocom. (March 2005)

38. Duffield, N.: Simple network perormance tomography. In: Proceedings of the IMC'03, Miami Beach, Florida (2003)

39. Caceres, R., Duffield, N.G., Horowitz, J., Towsley, D.: Multicast-based inference of network-internal loss characteristics. IEEE Transactions on Information Theory **45** (1999) 2462–2480

40. Coates, M., Nowak, R.: Network loss inference using unicast end-to-end measurement. In: Proceedings of the ITC Seminar on IP Traffic, Measurements and Modelling, Monterey (2000)

41. Duffield, N., Presti, F.L., Paxson, V., Towsley, D.: Inferring link loss using striped unicast probes. In: Proceedings of the IEEE Infocom 2001, Alaska (2001)

42. Padmanabhan, V.N., Qiu, L., Wang, H.J.: Server-based inference of internet performance. In: Proceedings of the IEEE INFOCOM'03, San Francisco, CA (2003)

43. Zang, H., Jue, J.P., Mukherjee, B.: A review of routing and wavelength assignment approaches for wavelength-routed optical wdm networks. SPIE Optical Networks Magazine **(1)** 47–60

44. Sahasrabuddhe, L., Ramamurthy, S., Mukherjee, B.: Fault management in IP-Over-WDM Networks: WDM Protection vs. IP Restoration. IEEE Journal on Selected Areas in Communications **20** (2002) 21–33
45. Demeester, P., et al.: Resilience in multilayer networks. IEEE Communications Magazine (August 1999) 70–75
46. Colle, D., et al.: Data-centric optical networks and their survivability. IEEE Journal on Selected Areas in Communications **20** (2002) 6–20
47. Zhang, H., Durresi, A.: Differentiated Multi-Layer Survivability in IP/WDM Networks. Proceeding of Network Operations and Management Symposium (2002)
48. Fumagalli, A., Valcarenghi, L.: IP Restoration vs. WDM Protection: Is There an Optimal Choice? IEEE Network (2000)
49. Iannaccone, G., Chuah, C.N., Bhattacharyya, S., Diot, C.: Feasibility of IP restoration in a tier-1 backbone. (Sprint ATL Research Report Nr. RR03-ATL-030666)
50. Nucci, A., Taft, N., Barakat, C., Thiran, P.: Controlled use of excess backbone bandwidth for providing new services in IP-over-WDM networks. IEEE Journal on Selected Areas in Communications **JSAC-22** (2004) 1692–1707
51. Gerstel, O., Ramaswami, R.: Optical Layer Survivability-An Implementation Perspective. IEEE Journal on Selected Areas in Communications **18** (2000) 18851923
52. Ramamurthy, S., Mukherjee, B.: Survivable WDM mesh networks, Part I - Protection. Proc. of IEEE INFOCOM'99 (1999)
53. Mohan, G., Somani, A.K.: Routing dependable connections with specified failure restoration guarantess in WDM networks. Proc. of IEEE INFOCOM'02 (2002)
54. Ramamurthy, S., Mukherjee, B.: Survivable WDM mesh networks, Part II - Restoration. Proc. of IEEE ICC'99 (1999)
55. Modiano, E., Narula-Tam, A.: Survivable lightpath routing: a new approach to the design of WDM-based networks. IEEE Journal on Selected Areas in Communications **20** (2002) 800–809
56. Armitage, J., Crochat, O., Boudec, J.Y.L.: Design of a Survivable WDM Photonic Network. Proceedings of IEEE INFOCOM 97 (1997)
57. Lee, H., Choi, H., Subramaniam, S., Choi, H.A.: Survival Embedding of Logical Topology in WDM Ring Networks. Information Sciences : An International Journal, Special Issue on Photonics, Networking and Computing (2002)
58. Lee, H., Choi, H., Choi, H.A.: Restoration in IP over WDM optical networks. In Proceedings of the 30th ICPP Workshop on Optical Networks (2001)
59. Sen, A., Hao, B., Shen, B., Lin, G.: Survivable routing in WDM networks logical ring in arbitrary physical topology. Proceedings of the IEEE International Communication Conference ICC02 (2002)
60. Giroire, F., Nucci, A., Taft, N., Diot, C.: Increasing the Robustness of IP Backbones in the Absence of Optical Level Protection. Proc. of IEEE INFOCOM 2003 (2003)
61. Leonardi, E., Mellia, M., Marsan, M.A.: Algorithms for the Logical Topology Design in WDM All-Optical Networks. Optical Networks Magazine (2000)
62. Glover, F., Taillard, E., Werra, D.: A user's guide for tabu search. Annals of Operations Research (1993) 3–28
63. Crochat, O., Boudec, J.Y.L.: Design Protection for WDM Optical Networks. IEEE Journal of Selected Areas in Communication **16** (1998) 1158–1165
64. Nucci, A., Sansò, B., Crainic, T., Leonardi, E., Marsan, M.A.: Design of Fault-Tolerant Logical Topologies in Wavelength-Routed Optical IP Networks. Proc. of IEEE Globecom 2001 (2001)
65. Ducatelle, F., Gambardella, L.: Survivable routing in ip-over-wdm networks: An efficient and scalable local search algorithm. Optical Switching and Networking (2005) To appear.

66. Kurant, M., Thiran, P.: Survivable Mapping Algorithm by Ring Trimming (SMART) for large IP-over-WDM networks. Proc. of BroadNets 2004 (2004)

67. Kurant, M., Thiran, P.: On survivable routing of mesh topologies in IP-over-WDM networks. Proc. of IEEE INFOCOM'05 (2005)

68. Li, G., Doverspike, B., Kalmanek, C.: Fiber Span Failure Protection in Mesh Optical Networks. Optical Networks Magazine **3** (2002) 21–31

69. Zang, H., Ou, C., Mukherjee, B.: Path-protection routing and wavelength-assignment (rwa) in wdm mesh networks under duct-layer constraints. IEEE/ACM Transactions on Networking **11** (2003) 248–258

70. Kim, S., Lumetta, S.: Addressing node failures in all-optical networks. Journal of Optical Networking **1** (2002) 154–163

71. Choi, H., Subramaniam, S., Choi, H.A.: On Double-Link Failure Recovery in WDM Optical Networks. Proc. of IEEE INFOCOM'02 (2002)

72. He, W., Sridharan, M., Somani, A.K.: Capacity Optimization for Surviving Double-Link Failures in Mesh-Restorable Optical Networks. Proc. of OptiComm'02 (2002)

73. Clouqueur, M., Grover, W.D.: Mesh-restorable Networks with Complete Dual-failure Restorability and with Selectively Enhanced Dual-failure Restorability Properties,. Proc. of OptiComm'02 (2002)

SCOOP – Concurrency Made Easy

Volkan Arslan, Patrick Eugster, Piotr Nienaltowski, and Sebastien Vaucouleur

Chair of Software Engineering
Swiss Federal Institute of Technology Zurich
CH-8092 Zurich, Switzerland
scoop@se.inf.ethz.ch
http://se.inf.ethz.ch/research/scoop.html

Abstract. The metaphor of objects as entities encompassing both logic and state, simplifying the design and development of particularly large-scale applications, is well established in the industry. However, large applications are rarely monolithic components that carry out a single sequential task; most applications are composed of many components running in parallel. Yet, the vast majority of such applications are built in a rather ad-hoc manner, typically by making use of threading libraries and explicit synchronization through low-level mechanisms such as semaphores, locks, or monitors layered on top of objects.

The Simple Concurrent Object-Oriented Programming (SCOOP) model strives for a higher-level abstraction for concurrency, naturally woven into "traditional" object-oriented constructs. Thanks to the full support for contracts and other object-oriented mechanisms and techniques — inheritance, polymorphism, dynamic binding, genericity, and agents — SCOOP offers the programmer a simple yet powerful framework for efficient development of concurrent systems.

This paper presents a survey of SCOOP, including (1) the foundations of the SCOOP paradigm, its computation and synchronization models (focusing on *simplicity*), and our more recent developments. These are (2) an extended type system for eliminating synchronization defects (improving *safety*), (3) support for transactional semantics for subcomputations (enforcing *atomicity*), and (4) an event library for programming real-time concurrent tasks (allowing for *predictability*).

1 Introduction

The object-oriented paradigm promotes ease of design, development, and maintenance of applications by reflecting in a *natural* manner the real-world scenarios which these applications are portraying. Its support for intuitive reasoning has made object-orientation a widely adopted choice for devising large-scale industrial applications. The object paradigm however suffers from a weakness that may soon become a show-stopper: *concurrency*. Though nature presents itself as concurrent in many ways, the integration of objects with concurrency has namely not taken place in a natural way. Problems arise from aliasing, or substitution, which are cornerstones of the object paradigm. Yet, virtually all

J. Kohlas, B. Meyer, and A. Schiper (Eds.): Dependable Systems, LNCS 4028, pp. 82–102, 2006.
© Springer-Verlag Berlin Heidelberg 2006

industrial-scale applications developed currently span several concurrent tasks that proceed autonomously from time to time, and require controlled interaction at chosen points.

Established practices for concurrent programming include the explicit use of threading libraries and rather low-level synchronization mechanisms such as locks, semaphores, or monitors, for protecting objects from conflicting accesses and modifications, hampering the consistency of these objects. Threading models and precise semantics of basic concurrency control mechanisms however may diverge on different platforms, slightly only at first glance, but actually with sensible effects, making concurrent programming still a closed book reserved to experts. The software field badly needs a concurrent programming technique enjoying the same simplicity and inspiring the same confidence as the accepted constructs of sequential programming.

As its name suggests, the Simple Concurrent Object-Oriented Programming (SCOOP) [1] model is an attempt to provide this simple basis. SCOOP follows the ambition of supporting programmers in writing correct and efficient software, by taking object-oriented programming as given, in a form based on the concepts of Design by Contract [2]. SCOOP extends these concepts in a minimal way (essentially one language keyword and a few library mechanisms) to cover concurrency and distribution. To address requirements of concurrent processing (e.g., mutual exclusion, wait conditions) SCOOP gives new semantics to well-known constructs (e.g., argument passing, preconditions) where the standard sequential semantics could not be applied anyway.

Being high-level, the SCOOP model is applicable to many different physical setups, including multiprocessing, multithreading, or distributed computing. By taking advantage of the *inherent* concurrency in object-oriented programming, programmers are shielded from low-level concepts such as explicit thread creation, manipulation, and synchronization. In short, the SCOOP model associates one or more objects with a *conceptual processor*, which is the only one to execute on these objects, and can be mapped to an operating system process, thread, etc. The keyword **separate** is used to denote entities that reference objects which, from the point of view of the client object, may be under the control of a different processor. The appearance of such variables inherently triggers synchronization in certain situations, according to well-defined *consistency rules*.

The contributions of this paper consists in providing a concise overview of the SCOOP model and its recent refinements, divided into four aspects:

- *Simplicity.* We present the basic SCOOP paradigm, by laying out its architecture, its basic model of computation, as well as its synchronization scheme. The latter perspective on SCOOP is elucidated by explaining the consistency rules defining the semantics of "traditional" object-oriented constructs such as feature calls, argument passing, or preconditions, and by summarizing scheduling policies.
- *Safety.* By having a single processor execute a single operation at a time on a given object, the SCOOP model avoids data races. Nonetheless, there are situations in which the basic SCOOP model may exhibit synchronization

defects. We propose an ownership-like *type system* to address these issues, and derive from it the consistency rules for SCOOP. The proposed type system makes it possible to eliminate potential synchronization faults at compile-time; it also integrates with SCOOP other advanced mechanisms of Eiffel, such as *agents* and *attached types*.

- *Atomicity.* The SCOOP model is augmented with transactional semantics, in order to support *atomic* features, features whose use takes either full effect or none, even in the face of hardware failures. This effort has also been initiated in view of exploiting the many recent efforts on transactional support at the operating system level. We provide the programmer the choice between *cooperating concurrency* (traditional SCOOP semantics) and *conflicting concurrency* (transactional semantics) and the possibility of combining these. Our approach also marries two error recovery modes for transaction aborts, namely *backward recovery* (rollback) and *forward recovery* (*compensation* [3] for cases where the effects of partial computations can not simply be undone).

- *Predictability.* We present a real-time event library (RTEL) which is built on top of an existing event library [4] designed initially without real-time concerns in mind. Introducing both concurrency and timing constraints enables the successful application of event-driven programming techniques to embedded real-time applications. The known advantages of modular development and reasoning of object-oriented languages, as well as the separation of concerns enforced by the event-driven style of programming [5] are retained. To achieve predictability in real-time applications, the RTEL is designed to support in particular the modeling of *periodic*, *sporadic*, as well as *aperiodic* tasks of real-time applications, thus ensuring their timing constraints such as *worst-case execution time* (WCET), *deadline*, and *periodicity*.

The design of the basic SCOOP model, as well as any of the amendments represented by the last three contributions outlined above has followed the same directives, which consist namely in guiding the programmer with language constructs which (1) anchor safety statically, yet (2) are minimally intrusive, and (3) preserve flexibility. By abiding to these principles, SCOOP makes concurrent object-oriented programming simple and can easily be integrated with other languages.[1] The three additions are presented by providing motivating scenarios, examples, and reporting on their implementation status.

Roadmap. Section 2 overviews the basic SCOOP model. Section 3 presents improvements to the type system fostering safety. Section 4 describes **atomic** features – features supporting transactional semantics. Section 5 reports on our real-time event library (RTEL), an event library for modeling and devising real-time tasks within SCOOP. Section 6 presents conclusions and future work.

---

[1] Note that contracts have been recently added to several mainstream programming languages, e.g., Java (JML [6]), C# (Spec# [7]).

2 Simplicity: The SCOOP Model

2.1 Computation

In object-oriented computation, the basic mechanism is a feature call such as $x.f\,(a)$, with the following semantics (Figure 1): the client object calls feature f on the supplier object attached to x, with argument a. In a sequential setting, such calls are synchronous, blocking the client until the supplier has terminated the execution of the feature.

To support concurrency, SCOOP allows the use of more than one *conceptual* processor to handle execution of features. More precisely, every object in SCOOP is associated with a single processor, which represents a thread of control. The processor associated with an object is the only one to execute feature calls on that object. We say that a processor *handles*, and *owns* the object; a processor in the general case owns several objects, and this set of objects owned by a processor constitute the *domain* of that processor.

If the client and supplier objects in a feature call have different handlers, the call becomes asynchronous: in Figure 1, the computation on Object 1 can move ahead without waiting for the call on Object 2 to terminate. Processors are the principal new concept for adding concurrency to the framework of sequential object-oriented computation. A processor does not have to be associated with a physical processor; it may be implemented by a process of the operating system, or a thread in a multithreading environment. In the .NET Framework, processors can be mapped to application domains [8].

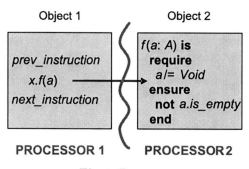

Fig. 1. Processors

Viewed by the software, a processor is an abstract concept; the same concurrent application may be executed on very different architectures without any change to its source text.

2.2 Separateness

Since the effect of a call depends on whether the client and the supplier objects are handled by the same processor or by different ones, the software text must distinguish unambiguously between these two cases. For declarations of variables or functions, normally appearing as x: *SOME_CLASS*, a new form is now possible, x: **separate** $SOME\_CLASS$. The keyword **separate** indicates that x is *potentially* handled by a different processor, so that calls on x will be asynchronous. With such a declaration, any creation instruction **create** $x.make$ ( ) will use a new processor to handle calls on x. The declaration does not specify *which* processor to use for handling the object. What matters is that this processor is different from the processor handling the current object.

If a target of a call is a separate expression, i.e., a separate entity or an expression involving at least one separate entity, such a call is referred to as *separate call*. In Figure 1, x is a separate entity for Object 1, Object 2 referred to by x is a separate object, and $x.f$ (a) is a separate call.

2.3   Synchronization

SCOOP addresses the synchronization and communication needs of concurrent programming, including mutual exclusion, locking and waiting, through argument passing and Design by Contract.

Argument Passing. A basic rule of SCOOP is that a separate call — $x.f$ (a) where x is separate — is only permitted if x itself is an argument of the enclosing routine, and that calling a routine with such a separate argument will cause waiting until the corresponding separate object is exclusively available to the caller. So if the client calls r (a), or $y.r$ (a), where r is defined as

r (x: **separate** $SOME\_TYPE$) **is** ...

the call will wait until no other client is using a in this way. This rule provides the basic synchronization mechanism for SCOOP. It avoids a pitfall of concurrent programming, which consists in assuming that in two successive calls on a separate object, such as

> $that\_stack$. $push$ ($some\_value$)
> ...
> x := $that\_stack$. top

nothing may have happened to the object in between – so that in the example above the object assigned to x is the object referred to by *some_value* previously stored at the top of the stack. In a concurrent setting, other clients may interfere with the object *that_stack* between the two calls. As mentioned, both calls above require *that_stack* to be an argument of the enclosing routine(s) in SCOOP. If these are different routines, no confusion is likely; if they are the same routine, the rule guarantees that the routine will hold the object for the entire duration of every call, to the exclusion of any other clients.

Preconditions. In Eiffel, a routine such as *put* in Figure 2 may have a precondition and a postcondition. A precondition clause involving a call with a separate target, such as *buffer* . *is_full* , is called a *separate precondition*. The other clause appearing here, *value* /= **Void**, is not separate. In sequential programs, preconditions are correctness requirements that the client object must fulfill before calling the routine on the supplier object. If one or more preconditions are not met, the client has broken the contract; for example, it has tried to store a value into a full buffer. Since the execution is sequential, the state of the buffer cannot change (no other client can try to consume an element from the buffer in the meantime). In a concurrent context this does not apply any more; the buffer may be full when the client object is trying to store a value into it, but nothing prevents another client object from consuming an element from the buffer later on. A non-satisfied separate precondition does not necessarily break the contract; it just forces the client object to *wait* until the precondition is satisfied. This inapplicability in a concurrent context of the usual sequential interpretation of preconditions leads to the SCOOP use of separate preconditions, namely as *wait conditions* rather than correctness conditions. We have shown the basic synchronization rule: in the case of a separate argument, any call will wait until the object is available. To obtain the full synchronization mechanism, we add the rule that if the routine has a precondition clause using such a separate argument as target, for example **not** *buffer. is_full* the call will wait until both of the following conditions are satisfied:

a. The object is available.
b. The separate precondition is satisfied.

The wait semantics only apply to separate preconditions. Others, such as *value* /= **Void**, retain their usual meaning as correctness conditions.

2.4   Scheduling

In the following paragraphs we illustrate the concepts of SCOOP and scheduling through the well-known producer-consumer scenario. Some objects are producing values and storing them into the shared buffer *buf* (see Figure 2); others are consuming elements from that buffer (see Figure 3). For both producers and consumers, the respective *buf* object is a separate object, declared as such in the source code. To perform any call to *buf*, a client (producer or consumer) must obtain an exclusive lock on *buf*. The SCOOP rule then implies embedding all the calls to *buf* in routines *store* and *consume_one*. Direct calls to *buf. put*, *buf. item*, and *buf. remove* would be invalid.

To call *consume_one* from routine *consume_n*, a consumer will pass *buf* as argument. In the SCOOP access control policy, when one or more arguments of a routine are separate objects, the client must obtain exclusive locks on all these objects before executing the routine. Here the consumer object must obtain an exclusive lock on *buf* before executing *consume_one*. If another object is currently holding the lock, the client must wait until the lock has been released, then try to acquire it. The default policy is FIFO. More precisely, locking takes place as follows:

I. A client attempts to acquire the locks on all the relevant objects.
II. The separate precondition clauses are evaluated. If they do not all hold, the object releases the lock and goes back to 1.

III. The routine is executed.

IV. The locks are released.

Releasing all locks in case not all separate preconditions are satisfied allows other clients to access corresponding supplier objects and change their state, so that the wait conditions required by another client may eventually be met.

The above locking policy facilitates building correct concurrent programs and reasoning about them:

- No interference between client objects is possible since at most one client may hold a lock on a supplier object at any time. This helps find which object is responsible for possible breaches in the contract, such as breaking the supplier's invariant.
- The precondition rules ensure that correct calls do not violate the integrity of the supplier object.

```
class PRODUCER
feature
   store (buffer: separate BUFFER [G]; value: G) is
          -- Store value into buffer.
      require
         buffer_not_full : not buffer.is_full
         value_provided:   value /= Void
      do
         buffer.put (value)
         ensure
         buffer_not_empty: not buffer.is_empty
      end
   random_gen: RANDOM_GENERATOR
   buf: separate BUFFER [INTEGER]
   produce_n (n: INTEGER) is
          -- Produce n integer values and store them into a buffer.
      local
         value: INTEGER
         i: INTEGER
      do
         from i := 1
         until i > n
         loop
            value := random_gen.next
            store (buf, value)
            -- buf.put (value) is forbidden here
            i := i + 1
         end
      end
end
```

Fig. 2. Producers

```
class CONSUMER
feature
   consume_one (buffer: separate BUFFER [G]) is
        -- Consume one element from buffer.
     require
        buffer_specified :  buffer /= Void
        buffer_not_empty: not buffer.is_empty
     do
        value := buffer.item
        buffer.remove
         ensure
        buffer_not_full : not buffer.is_full
     end
   buf: separate BUFFER [INTEGER]
   consume_n (n: INTEGER) is
        -- Consume n elements from a buffer.
     local
        i: INTEGER
     do
        from i := 1
        until i > n
        loop
           consume_one (buf)
           -- buf.item and buf.remove are forbidden here
           i  := i + 1
        end
     end
end
```

Fig. 3. Consumers

2.5   A Note on Asynchrony

Thanks to the asynchronous semantics of separate calls, a client executing separate calls is not blocked and can proceed with the rest of its computation. Later on, however, it may need to resynchronize with the supplier. Rather than introducing a specific language mechanism for this purpose, SCOOP relies on a variant of *wait-by-necessity* [9] which consists in causing the client to wait on the result of calls to queries (in particular functions), since it needs the result to proceed, whereas commands (procedures) do not require waiting. This mechanism is automatic and does not require any effort from the programmer.

2.6   Implementation and Tools

SCOOP is not supported by any existing Eiffel compiler. Therefore, we developed the *scoop2scoopli* preprocessor that allows programmers to write SCOOP programs, have them type-checked according to the refined typing rules (see 3) and translated into standard Eiffel code with embedded library calls (library calls map SCOOP constructs to the underlying concurrency platform). We decided to provide a binding for several concurrency platforms. So far, we delivered a thread-based library implementation – SCOOPLI – that supports POSIX threads and .NET Multithreading. The preprocessor and the library are available for download at *http://se.inf.ethz.ch/research/scoop.html*.

We are developing a library for distributed computing. It is currently based on web services but we are planning to support other communication infrastructures as well. We are also thinking of a multi-threaded implementation on a widespread real-time operating system.

3   Safety: Extended Type System for SCOOP

SCOOP programs are free of data races *by construction* – since all operations on a given object are executed by its handling processor and all processors are sequential, at most one operation might be executed on the object at any time (operations cannot be preempted). Nevertheless, other synchronization defects – *atomicity violations* and *deadlocks*– might still occur. In this paper, we focus on atomicity violations.

3.1   Separateness Consistency Rules

Atomicity violations are caused by an incorrect interleaving of feature calls issued by different client objects. The synchronization policy of SCOOP (see section 2.3) should prevent them. Unfortunately, the locking mechanism alone, although very restrictive, does not solve the problem. That is why the original SCOOP model introduced four additional *separateness consistency rules* [2]. The rules impose further restrictions on operations (assignment, argument passing) that involve separate entities. For example, it is required that the target of an assignment be declared as separate if the source of the assignment is separate.

Although the rules are easily understandable by a programmer, they are too informal to be used by a compiler. Also, they do not support the *agent mechanism* (see below) and they are too restrictive – in particular the rule for *expanded types* (value types) eliminates many useful programs. We also demonstrated that they are not sound – it is possible to write programs that satisfy them and still exhibit atomicity violations.

3.2   Type System

To provide a sound basis for safe concurrency, it is necessary to refine and formalize the rules. It is impossible to check the rules statically using the standard Eiffel type system because separateness is a property of objects, not classes; the conformance of separate and non-separate entities cannot be expressed statically in terms of subclassing. Therefore, we propose a type system (inspired by the ownership type system for JavaCard [10]) that augments Eiffel's types with *processor tags*. Correctly typed programs are guaranteed to be free of atomicity violations. A type checker can check the type conformance of SCOOP programs at compile time.

Let $TypeId$ denote the set of declared type identifiers of a given Eiffel program. We define the set of tagged types for a given class as

$$TaggedType \doteq ProcessorId \times TypeId$$

where $ProcessorId$ is the set of processor tags declared in the class. Processor tags denote processors — in a similar sense as entities denote references to objects. Each class implicitly declares two processor tags: • (*current processor*) and ⊤ (*some processor*). The subtype relation $\preceq$ on tagged types is the smallest reflexive, transitive relation satisfying the following axioms, where α is a tag, $S, T \in TypeId$, and $\preceq_{Eiffel}$ denotes the conformance relation on $TypeId$:

$$(\alpha, T) \preceq (\alpha, S) \iff T \preceq_{Eiffel} S \tag{1}$$

$$(\alpha, T) \preceq (\top, T) \tag{2}$$

The extended type system allows us to reason precisely about the locality of objects that are represented by separate and non-separate entities. Typing rules are defined in such a way that all potential atomicity violations are eliminated (the interleaving of *pure queries* is not regarded as an atomicity violation since a pure query does not modify the state of the object it is applied to). The typing rules are straightforward – in fact, the proper definition of the notion of *type conformance* takes care of most problems. Here is an example rule (for assignment):

$$[Assign] \quad \frac{\Gamma \vdash l :: (\alpha, T), \quad \Gamma \vdash e :: (\beta, S), \quad \Gamma \vdash (\beta, S) \preceq (\alpha, T)}{\Gamma \vdash l := e}$$

This rule is very similar to the standard Eiffel rule for assignment — both of them state that an assignment is correctly typed if and only if the type of its target conforms to the type of its source. The only difference is that $[Assign]$ relies on the extended the notion of conformance as expressed by axioms 1 and 2.

To demonstrate the improvements brought by the enhanced type system (both in terms of safety and flexibility), we use the code examples in Figures 4 and 5. Figure 4 shows the class code written in the original SCOOP model; Figure 5 shows the same code rewritten using the enhanced syntax that allows for explicit declaration of object locality. Processor tags (here *p1*) are declared as entities of a special type *PROCESSOR*. They may only appear in type annotations, e.g. *a_list* : **separate** $<p1>$ *LIST* $[X]$ (this means " *a_list* is handled by the processor corresponding to *p1*"; more formally, *a_list* :: $(p1, LIST[X])$).

If the original SCOOP code, feature call *element.some_operation* in routine r of class C will be invalid because it is a separate call and its target does not appear as a formal argument of routine r, as required by the separate call rule. Nevertheless, feature call *a_list .item.some_operation* that has the same semantics as

element.some_operation is treated as correct although it introduces a potential
atomicity violation. The evaluation of *a_list .item* yields a separate object and
the subsequent application of *some_operation* to that object should be rejected
by the compiler because there is no guarantee that the processor handling the
target of that call is reserved by the client object. Nevertheless, there is no consistency rule that takes care of such cases. As a result, potentially unsafe code is
accepted by the compiler. With the new typing rules, the compiler will reject the
call *a_list .item.some_operation* because *a_list.item* :: $(\top, X)$ and the compiler
cannot decide whether the corresponding processor ($\top$) is locked within the scope
of the routine (see Figure 5). Therefore, the atomicity violation will be avoided.
As we can see, the new type system eliminates the sources of unsoundness in the
original SCOOP model.

On the other hand, feature *s* does not conform to the original consistency
rules. As a result, it is rejected by the compiler although it is perfectly safe,

```
class C
feature
    r ( a_list : separate LIST [X]) is
        local
            element: separate X
        do
            element := a_list .item
            element.some_operation        -- Rejected
            a_list .item.some_operation   -- This call should be rejected too!
        end

    s ( a_list : separate LIST [X]) is
        local
            element: separate X
        do
            element := a_list .item
            a_list .extend (element) -- This call should be accepted!
        end
    ...
end

class LIST [G]
feature
    item: G
        -- Item at current position

    extend (an_element: G)
        -- Add 'an_element' to end.
    ...
end
```

Fig. 4. Original SCOOP code with synchronization faults

i.e. it does not introduce any potential atomicity violations. This is because the reasoning about the locality of separate objects is very restricted in the original model – we can only say that an object is handled by the *current processor* or by *some processor*. So, when assigning the result of *a_list* . *item* to *element*, we lose the information about the exact locality of *element*. Although we know that *element* is handled by the same processor as *a_list* (the result of *item* is non-separate w.r.t. *a_list*), the type checker cannot use that information when checking the subsequent call to *a_list* . *extend*. Feature *extend* expects an argument that is non-separate w.r.t. *a_list* , but the type checker only sees *element* as being handled by *some processor* and therefore non-conforming to the required type (see Figure 4). Thanks to the possibility of specifying the locality of objects through the use of processor tags, the code of routine *s* can be

---

class *C*

feature −− Processor tags
    p1: *PROCESSOR*

feature
    r (*a_list* : **separate** *LIST* [*X*]) **is**
        local
            element: **separate** *X*
        do
            element := *a_list* . *item*
            element.some_operation   −− Rejected
              a_list . *item.some_operation* −− Rejected
        end

    s (*a_list* : **separate** *<p1>* *LIST* [*X*]) **is**
        local
            element: **separate** *<p1>* *X*
        do
            element := *a_list* . *item*
            a_list . *extend* (*element*) −− Accepted
        end
   ...
end

class *LIST* [*G*] **feature**
    item: *G*
        −− Item at current position

    extend (*an_element*: *G*)
        −− Add 'an_element' to end.
    ...
end

Fig. 5. New type rules reveal synchronization faults

enriched (see Figure 5) so that the type-checker accepts it. We explicitly say that *element* is handled by the same processor as *a_list* (in this case *p1*). The assignment *element* := *a_list* . *item* type-checks correctly because *element* :: $(p1, X)$ and *a_list.item* :: $(p1, X)$ – note that the type of an expression is evaluated taking into account the locality of its target and the locality of the result type. Similarly, the call to *a_list* . *extend* (*element*) is correctly typed – the expected type of the actual argument is $(p1, X)$ and *element* has exactly that type. Here, the new type system allows for an increased flexibility. The SCOOP model becomes much more expressive.

The augmented type system for SCOOP allows for modular checking of safety properties. The type checker only needs to know the interface of the classes that the currently checked class uses (as supplier or parent); it is not necessary to consider the full program code. In order to achieve that modularity in the presence of polymorphism, we had to refine the rules for feature redefinition. We introduced a *contravariant* rule for formal arguments, i.e. their processor tags may only be preserved or generalized to $\top$. Conversely, the rule for query results is *covariant*, i.e. the processor tag may only be preserved or specialized. Note that such specialization is only possible if the original tag is $\top$.

3.3   Agents

Agents are used in Eiffel to "wrap" routine calls [11]. One can think of agents as a more sophisticated form of .NET delegates. Typing agent expressions is tricky even in a sequential context, so we expected that the integration of the mechanism with SCOOP would be difficult. Recall that the semantics of argument passing in SCOOP is such that the processor handling a separate object passed as an actual argument to a routine call will be locked (see section 2.3). Nevertheless, when an agent is passed as actual argument to a feature call, we should lock the handler of its *target* rather than the agent itself. Also, the types of the actual arguments passed to an agent call must be evaluated w.r.t. the the agent's target; this is complicated by the fact that the arguments are wrapped in a *tuple*.

We decided to treat agents as any other objects but give appropriate rules for agent creation, so that the type of an agent expression reflects the locality of its target. More precisely, the processor tag of the agent's type is identical to the processor tag of the target's type. A special typing rule is given for agent calls – the tuple of arguments is "stripped down" and each of its elements is considered separately.

The proposed solution supports polymorphism. Unfortunately, it cannot be applied to agents with an open target because the locality of the potential target is not known at the time of agent construction. This is not an issue if the agent under consideration is declared as non-separate. We are currently investigating the possibility of using detachable types for typing open-target agent expressions. Another, somewhat less satisfactory solution would be to impose a run-time check at call time for separate agents with an open target.

4   Atomicity: Transactional Semantics

Numerous fundamental impossibility results in the field of distributed systems [12] make many of the simple approaches taken in the concurrent case simply not viable in a typical asynchronous distributed setting. Hence, the distributed version of the SCOOP model requires special care. We propose a transactional extension to the initial SCOOP model in order to help programmers in the construction of reliable distributed software.

4.1   Introduction to the Transactional Model

We propose programming language support for the specification of atomicity properties of particular features (routines or attributes). With such support, the application programmer is assisted by the compiler in constructing reliable distributed software. This extension to the initial SCOOP model aims at supporting *atomic features* - features whose use takes either full effect or none. The rollback capabilities introduced allows for an optimistic concurrency model and hence to a potential increase in the level of concurrency. Some computations cannot be rolled-backed. In order to circumvent this problem we propose to add support for *compensation*. We define the concept of compensation and explain how we provide explicit support for compensation at the language level.

Our approach builds on the extensive work which has already been done in the field of transactional systems [13] (the concept of nested transactions has been thoroughly explored since the seminal work of Moss [14]). Butler et al. [3] proposed a formalization of a compensation language in CSP which influenced the compensation scheme that we describe in this section.

4.2   Syntactic Extensions

We propose the addition of a keyword **atomic** to the programming language. Routines can be declared to be atomic by replacing respectively the usual **do** ... **end** block delimiters by **atomic** ... **end**. Attribute accesses are inherently atomic. That is, any read and write of an attribute is atomic. Calling an atomic feature implicitly results in creating a corresponding transaction (a commit is attempted at the end of the feature). Figure 6 illustrates the syntax.

Semantics. Naturally atomic features, like non-atomic ones, can have pre- and postconditions. Just like in the original SCOOP model, preconditions on separate objects have wait condition semantics in the case of atomic features. An atomic feature fails and returns with an exception if its processing encounters an error other than a conflict with the computations performed by any concurrently executing atomic feature (i.e., any competing transaction). The composition of atomic features will be discussed in Section 4.3.

Inheritance and Atomicity. Inheritance is a fundamental concept for code reuse. *Redefinition* of a feature should only provide equal or stronger guarantees to a client. The guarantees provided by atomic features are clearly stronger than those provided by non-atomic features. In others terms, atomicity is a

---

class *BANK_ACCOUNT*
feature

    deposit(*sum*: *INTEGER*)
      require
      sum >= 0
    atomic
        balance = *balance* + *sum*
    ensure
        balance = **old** *balance* + *sum*
    end

      ...
end −− class BANK_ACCOUNT

class *ATM*
  −− An ATM client with an atomic transfer feature
feature

    transfer(*source*: **separate** *BANK_ACCOUNT*;
             destination: **separate** *BANK_ACCOUNT*;
             sum: *INTEGER*)
  require
    sum >= 0
    source. *may_withdraw*(*sum*)
  atomic
    source. *debit*(*sum*)
    destination. *credit*(*sum*)
  ensure
      source.*balance* = **old** *source.balance* − *sum*
      destination.*balance* = **old** *source.balance* + *sum*
  end
end −− class ATM

Fig. 6. Bank account and ATM with atomicity

special case of non-atomicity. This leads to the rule that features can be redefined from non-atomic to atomic but not vice-versa. This rule will be enforced at compilation.

4.3   Composition of Atomic Features

Nesting. Atomicity can be straightforwardly ensured if it is transitive. That is, if all features called within atomic features are atomic themselves, one can ensure that the (partial) effects of an atomic feature can be "undone". A nested call to an atomic feature can then trigger the start of a nested transaction, i.e., a *sub-transaction* [14].

---

class *CLIENT*
feature

    client_id : *INTEGER*

    plan_holidays(*agency*: **separate** *TRAVEL_AGENCY*;
                        atm: **separate** *ATM*;
                                client_account : **separate** *BANK_ACCOUNT*)
    local
        ticket_id : **separate** *INTEGER_REF*
    atomic
        −− compensated call
        agency. order_ticket (*client_id*) ÷ *agency.cancel_ticket*(*client_id*)
        −− atomic call
        atm. transfer(*client_account* , *agency. account,amount*)
        ...
    end

   ...
end −− class CLIENT

Fig. 7. Compensation example

Compensation. Constraining atomic features to calling only other atomic features would however be overly restrictive, as it would eliminate the possibility of including many routines whose effects can by their very nature simply not be undone. For such situations, in which rollbacks are unfeasible, we adopt the approach of "rolling forward" computation to *compensate* [3] as best as possible for the operations that can not be undone. Calls within an atomic feature can be issued to an atomic feature, or to any other feature if the client defines a corresponding compensation clause. That is, the compiler will reject any atomic features that contains calls to non-atomic features for which no compensation clause is mentioned.

Syntactically, a compensation clause is demarked by separating it from associated feature through a character '÷'. Consider the example in Figure 7. A client orders a ticket from a travel agency (a non-atomic operation where the obvious parameters such as departure date, destination etc. are omitted for simplicity). The code declares a command call to the same travel agency to cancel a possibly issued ticket in case of a transaction abort. Let's assume that the command call to *order_ticket* completed successfully. Its corresponding compensation operation will be listed in the sequence of compensation routines to be called in case of a rollback. If the ATM fails for some reason before the final commit, the processor executing the call to the routine *plan_holidays* will execute the compensation routines in the reverse of the order in which they were defined. In this case, this simply results in calling the travel agency to cancel the ticket order.

Limitations of Compensation. Depending on the application and on the specific operations performed, a compensation can not always recover completely the initial state (the state at the beginning of the transaction). It is thus important to note that compensation is not a perfect solution, but is more a trade-off that allows to partially tackle the problem of non-recoverable actions. It should also be emphasized that the goal of compensation is *not* to replace the usual exception mechanisms (see [15]).

5   Predictability: A Real-Time Event Library

The ability to model periodic, sporadic and aperiodic tasks in a way ensuring their timing constraints such as worst-case execution time (WCET), deadline and periodicity is a major concern in embedded real-time programming. Through the use of our real-time event library (RTEL) based on SCOOP the predictability of such embedded real-time programs can be achieved, while retaining the advantages of modular development and reasoning of object-oriented languages and the benefit of event-driven programming.

5.1   Overview

The basic goal of RTEL is to support the modelling of periodic, sporadic and aperiodic tasks. RTEL is built on top of an existing event library ([4]) designed initially without concurrency and real-time concerns in mind. In order to model e.g. a periodic task using RTEL the following steps must be carried out:

- The *publisher* creates an event type
- The *subscriber* subscribes an object (which is called *subscribed object*) to an event type
- The *publisher* publishes an event

Following our previous ([4]) and recent work ([16]) we use a small sample application to show the basic capabilities of the concurrent event library for embedded and real-time programming. The details of the RTEL have been omitted due to space limitations, but they can be found in [16]. In our simple application we want to observe the temperature, humidity, and pressure of containers in a chemical plant. The measurements are supposed to originate from external physical sensors. Whenever the value(s) of one or more measured physical attributes change(s), the concerned parts of our system (e.g. an actuator and/or display units) are notified, so that they can update the values or take appropriate actions.

Now assume that in our example we would like to control a certain actuator, e.g., a valve which adjusts the heater according to temperature changes. Since the temperature can change at any time, it is modeled using a periodic task (i.e. a real-time task which is activated regularly at fixed rates/periods [17]). In order to model a periodic task, the timing constraints periodicity T, the deadline d and the WCET c (cost) must be specified. The deadline d is the point in time by

---

class *SENSOR*

feature – *Access*

    temperature: *INTEGER*
        – – Container temperature

    set_temperature (*t*: *INTEGER*)
        – – Set temperature to t.

feature – *Events*

    temperature_event: **separate** *EVENT_TYPE* [*TUPLE* [*INTEGER*]]
        – – Event associated with attribute temperature

end – **class** *SENSOR*

Fig. 8. SENSOR

which a real-time job must be completed, where a job is defined as an instance of a task [17]). The WCET is the maximum amount of time needed to finish a task. Assume that the periodicity is $T = 10$ ms, $c = 5$ ms, and $d = T = 10$ ms. This means that every 10 ms the task is released anew, assuming that the total time needed for reading the temperature value from the physical temperature sensor and for the actuator to perform the necessary actions is $c = 5$ ms.

5.2 Creating an Event Type

Class *SENSOR* (Figure 8) is an abstraction of a sensor that measures among others the temperature.

Furthermore, an event type *temperature_event* corresponding to the change of attribute temperature (through the feature *set_temperature*) is defined in class *SENSOR* as follows:

temperature_event: **separate** *EVENT_TYPE* [*TUPLE* [*INTEGER*]]

The temperature event is defined using the class *EVENT_TYPE*, declared as *EVENT_TYPE* [*EVENT_DATA* → *TUPLE*]. It is a generic class with constrained generic parameter *EVENT_DATA* representing a tuple of arbitrary types. In the case of *temperature_event*, the value of this generic parameter is *TUPLE* [*INTEGER*] since the actual event data (i.e., temperature value) is of type *INTEGER* [4]. Note that other attributes such as humidity and pressure have been omitted due to space limitations.

The keyword **separate** reflects the concurrent nature of the temperature event. In this context, the object to which the attribute *temperature_event* is attached will be handled by a different processor than the processor of the object declaring *temperature_event*. As a consequence, all feature calls on the *temperature_event* attribute will be executed asynchronously.

After having declared *temperature_event* in class *SENSOR*, we should make sure that the corresponding event is published whenever the temperature changes. Feature *set_temperature* of class *SENSOR* performs the following call for this purpose:

call_temperature (*temperature_event*, [*temperature*])

An instance of class *SENSOR* is a **publisher** of the temperature event *temperature_event*.

5.3   Subscribing to an Event Type

Our example includes two further classes, which will subscribe to the event published by *SENSOR*. First, we introduce class *ACTUATOR* with the feature *adjust_valve* (*t: INTEGER*). An instance of *ACTUATOR* is a **subscribed object**: it reacts to the published events by executing the corresponding routine, e.g. *adjust_valve*.

Second, we introduce class *CONTROLLER*, which is in charge of subscribing the feature *adjust_valve* of class *ACTUATOR* listed above to the corresponding event type *temperature_event*. An instance of class *CONTROLLER* is a **subscriber**. In order to subscribe feature *adjust_valve* of actuator (of type *ACTUATOR*) to event type *temperature_event*, the subscriber (instance of *CONTROLLER*) makes the following call:

sensor.temperature_event. subscribe_periodic
(..., **agent** *actuator.adjust_valve* (?), ...)

As a result, feature *adjust_valve* of actuator will be called each time *temperature_event* is published. The actual argument of feature *subscribe_periodic* (actually *subscribe_periodic* has five formal arguments) in class *EVENT_TYPE* is a so-called agent which can be roughly viewed as a function pointer. The question mark reflects an open argument that will be filled with concrete event data (a value of type *INTEGER* here) when feature *adjust_valve* is actually executed [11]. To be more precise, the first formal argument of *subscribe_periodic* requires actually another agent expression; the complete feature call to *subscribe_periodic* is thus:

if *sensor.temperature_event. subscribe_periodic*
(**agent** *physical_sensor.read_and_set_temperature*,
 agent *actuator.adjust_valve* (?), 10, 10, 5) **then**
     −− here periodic subscription was successful .
end

Note that class *PHYSICAL_SENSOR* is responsible for accessing the low-level device, i.e., the physical sensor for reading the temperature, humidity, and pressure. Class *SENSOR* (representing a software sensor) on the other hand is more abstract and hence application-specific, e.g. it adds event types such as *temperature_event*, *humidity_event*, and *pressure_event*.

5.4 Publishing an Event

By executing *set_temperature* (of class *SENSOR*) through *physical_sensor*, the temperature event *temperature_event* (in class *SENSOR*) will be published. The event type guarantees (by relying on an appropriate scheduler) that the agent *physical_sensor.read_temperature* is released every $T = 10$ ms. In order to do this, the feature *subscribe_periodic* of class *EVENT_TYPE* returns a boolean value to indicate that class *EVENT_TYPE* can indeed fulfill the subscription with the specified timing constraints $T = 10$ ms, $d = 10$ ms, and $c = 5$ ms. If this is infeasible, the return value will be false, and the subscription will not take place.

6 Conclusions and Future Work

We have presented the SCOOP model for concurrent object-oriented programming. SCOOP offers a comprehensive approach for building high-quality concurrent and distributed systems. The simplicity and expressive power of the model is achieved by taking object-oriented programming in a simple and pure form, based on the concepts of *Design by Contract* that have proved highly successful in improving the quality of sequential programs, and extending them in a minimal way to cover concurrency and distribution. The mechanism largely derives from examining the consequences of the notion of contract in a non-sequential setting. The model is applicable to many different physical setups, from multiprocessing to multithreading, network programming, Web services, highly parallel processors for scientific computation, and distributed computation.

We have proposed three refinements of SCOOP whose purpose is to improve the crucial aspects of the model: *safety, predictability, support for atomicity*. We achieve safe concurrency through the use of an augmented type system that refines and formalizes the separateness consistency rules to statically eliminate synchronization defects. We also provide a support for transactional semantics of features. Finally, we present an event library for programming real-time concurrent tasks within the SCOOP framework.

We are currently working on several mechanism that have not been discussed in this paper. In particular, we want to reduce the amount of necessary locking by allowing the interleaving of *pure query* calls made by different clients, and use *detachable types* to better express the need for locking. We are planning to provide a uniform treatment of *exceptions* in sequential and concurrent contexts. We are also investigating the feasibility of providing specific support for aperiodic real-time tasks.

Acknowledgements

We are very grateful to the Hasler Foundation who provided the financial support for the SCOOP project. We would also like to thank the Swiss National Science Foundation and Microsoft Research for their support.

References

1. Meyer, B.: Systematic Concurrent Object-Oriented Programming. Communications of the ACM **36** (1993) 56–80
2. Meyer, B.: Object-Oriented Software Construction. Second edn. Prentice Hall (1997)
3. Butler, M., Hoare, C., Ferreira, C.: A Trace Semantics for Long-Running Transactions. In: 25 Years Communicating Sequential Processes. (2004) 133–150
4. Arslan, V., Nienaltowski, P., Arnout, K.: Event Library: An Object-Oriented Library for Event-Driven Design. In: Joint Modular Languages Conference on Modular Programming Languages (JMLC 2003). (2003) 174–183
5. Eugster, P., Felber, P., Guerraoui, R., Kermarrec, A.M.: The Many Faces of Publish/Subscribe. ACM Computing Surveys **35** (2003) 114–131
6. Burdy, L., Cheon, Y., Cok, D., Ernst, M., Kiniry, J., Leavens, G., Leino, K.R.M., Poll, E.: An Overview of JML Tools and Applications. Eighth International Workshop on Formal Methods for Industrial Critical Systems (FMICS '03) (2003)
7. Mike Barnett and K. Rustan M. Leino, and Wolfram Schulte: The Spec# Programming System: An Overview. In: CASSIS 2004. Springer (2004)
8. Nienaltowski, P., Arslan, V., Meyer, B.: Concurrent object-oriented programming on .NET. IEE Proceedings - Software **150** (2003) 308–314
9. Caromel, D.: Towards a Method of Object-Oriented Concurrent Programming. Communications of the ACM **36** (1993) 90–102
10. Dietl, W., Müller, P., Poetzsch-Heffter, A.: A type system for checking applet isolation in Java Card. In Barthe, G., Burdy, L., Huisman, M., Lanet, J.L., Muntean, T., eds.: Construction and Analysis of Safe, Secure and Interoperable Smart devices (CASSIS). Volume 3362 of Lecture Notes in Computer Science., Springer-Verlag (2004) 129–150
11. ECMA: Eiffel Analysis, Design and Programming Language. ECMA Standard 367 (2005)
12. Fich, F.E., Ruppert, E.: Hundreds of Impossibility Results for Distributed Computing. Distributed Computing **16** (2003) 121–163
13. Weikum, G., Vossen, G.: Transactional Information Systems: Theory, Algorithms, and the Practice of Concurrency Control and Recovery. Morgan Kaufmann Publishers, San Francisco, CA (2002)
14. Moss, J.E.B.: Nested Transactions: an Approach to Reliable Distributed Computing. Technical Report 260, Massachusetts Institute of Technology, Laboratory for Computer Science (1981)
15. Vaucouleur, S., Eugster, P.: Atomic Features. In: Proceedings of the Workshop on Synchronization in Concurrent Object-Oriented Languages (SCOOL), OOPSLA. (2005)
16. Arslan, V., Eugster, P.: Modeling Embedded Real-time Applications with Objects and Events (to appear). In: Proceedings of the 3rd Workshop on Object-Oriented Modelling of Embedded Real-Time Systems (OMER-3). (2005)
17. Brega, R.: A Combination of System Software Techniques Aimed at Raising the Runtime-Safety of Complex Mechatronic Applications. PhD thesis, ETH Zurich, Switzerland (2002)

Scalable Programming Abstractions
for XML Services

Burak Emir, Sebastian Maneth*, and Martin Odersky

School of Computer and Communication Sciences
EPFL, CH-1015 Lausanne, Switzerland
burak.emir@epf.ch, sebastian.maneth@nicta.com.au,
martin.odersky@epfl.ch

Abstract. Traditional programming paradigms and styles do not lend
themselves easily to XML services. This has led to engineered systems
that are characterized by a mix of special purpose and general purpose
languages. Such systems are brittle, hard to understand and do not scale
well - hence they are not dependable. We describe some facets of the
Scala programming language targeted at XML services that unify the
disparate worlds through a judicious combination of existing and new
programming language constructs. More concretely, we describe use cases
of case classes, regular pattern matching and comprehensions. Programs
that use these abstractions can deliver XML services in a scalable and
manageable way. We discuss the essential design decisions we took, the
experience we gained during development, and identify directions of further research.

1 Introduction

Service-orientation is an emerging paradigm that promises a deep impact on programming. Similar to the rise of object-oriented systems when graphical user interfaces became the norm, service-oriented systems are motivated by two strong
trends: the move from single-machine, homogeneous execution environments to
distributed and heterogeneous ones, and the move from fine-grained and propri-
etary transmission formats to coarse-grained, standardized and semistructured
ones.

The reasons behind this paradigm shift lie in new challenges posed by programming applications and services for the internet. For the last 20 years, the
most common programming model has been object-oriented: System components
are objects, and computation is done by method calls. Methods themselves take
object references as parameters. This is a beautifully simple abstraction, which
describes computation adequately as long as we are dealing with a single computer. At first, it seems that the concept of remote method calls lets one extend
this programming model to distributed systems. However, this approach does
not scale up well to wide-scale networks where messages can be delayed and
components may fail.

---

* Present address: National ICT Australia, Kensington NSW 1466, Australia.

J. Kohlas, B. Meyer, and A. Schiper (Eds.): Dependable Systems, LNCS 4028, pp. 103–126, 2006.
© Springer-Verlag Berlin Heidelberg 2006

Web services address the message delay problem by increasing granularity, using method calls with larger, structured arguments, typically represented as XML data. They address the failure problem by using transparent replication and avoiding server state. Conceptually, they are *tree transformers* that consume incoming message documents and produce outgoing ones.

Should this paradigm shift have an effect on programming languages? There are at least two arguments that suggest this: First, today's object-oriented languages are not very good at analyzing and transforming structured data, such as XML trees. Since such trees usually contain only fields but no methods, they have to be decomposed and constructed from the "outside", that is from code that is external to the tree definition itself. In an object-oriented language, the ways of doing so are limited. In the most common solution (characterized by W3C's Document Object Model [16]), all tree nodes are values of a common type. This makes it easy to write generic traversal functions, but forces applications to operate on a very low conceptual level, which often loses important semantic distinctions present in the XML data. More semantic precision is obtained if different internal types model different kinds of nodes. But then tree decompositions require the use of run-time type tests and type casts to adapt the treatment to the kind of node encountered. Such type tests and type casts are generally not considered good object-oriented style. They are rarely efficient, and not easy to use.

By contrast, tree transformation is the natural domain of functional languages. Their algebraic data types, pattern matching and higher-order functions make these languages ideal for the task. It's no wonder, then, that specialized languages for transforming XML data such as W3C's XSLT [16] are functional.

The second reason for the popularity of functional languages in web-service programming is the fact that handling mutable state is problematic in this setting. Components with mutable state are harder to replicate or to restore after a failure. Data with mutable state is harder to cache than immutable data. Functional language constructs make it relatively easy to build components without mutable state.

Many web services are constructed by combining different languages. For instance, a service might use XSLT to handle document transformation, XQuery for database access, and Java for the "business logic". The downside of this approach is that the necessary amount of cross-language glue can make applications cumbersome to write, verify, and maintain. A particular problem is that cross-language interfaces are usually not statically typed. Hence, the benefits of a static type system are missing where they are needed most – at the join points of components written using different paradigms.

Conceivably, the glue problem could be addressed by a "multi-paradigm" language that would express object-oriented, concurrent, as well as functional aspects of an application. But one needs to be careful not to simply replace cross-language glue by awkward interfaces between different paradigms within the language itself. Ideally, one would hope for a fusion which unifies concepts found in different paradigms instead of an agglutination, which merely includes them side by side. This fusion is what we try to achieve with the Scala programming language [13].

Scala is both object-oriented and functional. It is a pure object-oriented language in the sense that every value is an object. Types and behavior of objects are described by classes. Classes can be composed using mixin composition. Scala is designed to work seamlessly with two mainstream object-oriented languages – Java and C#.

Scala is also a functional language in the sense that every function is a value. Nesting of function definitions and higher-order functions are naturally supported. Scala also supports a general notion of pattern matching which can model the algebraic types used in many functional languages. Furthermore, this notion of pattern matching naturally extends to the processing of XML data.

In this paper, we focus on the elements that make Scala suitable for programming web services and applications. These are in particular its support for pattern matching, with its specialization to XML data, as well as its support for higher-order functions, with for-comprehensions as a convenient front-end syntax for querying. Other innovations of Scala, which have to do with component abstraction and composition, are described elsewhere [14].

Related Work

There has been extensive research in general purpose languages that tackle data integration and concurrency in innovative ways, yet retain some form of static type safety.

The designers of the research language Mawl [2] have introduced a notion of forms and a notion of session with the goal to produce valid HTML services. Their form language is a custom extension of HTML, and the language ensures that only valid HTML is sent to the client.

Sessions were taken up by the authors of Bigwig [5] and its successors JWig [6]. While the former is aimed at HTML, the latter provides more general XML transformations, while keeping the statically checked validity guarantees. Widespread use of JWig seems however inhibited because of its reliance on a particular validation language.

Bierman et al. propose Cω [4] an object-oriented language in which an overloaded dot operator can be used for XPath like querying. Distribution is approached by chords, which in turn are based on the join calculus. This language furthermore integrates Benton et al.'s concurrency abstractions for C# [3].

XJ [11] is an extension to Java that aims at binding types from XML schemata and providing XPath primitives in an imperative context. XPath expressions are used for bulk updates, and a combination of static analysis techniques and runtime checks is used to guarantee type safety.

Xtatic [10] is an extension to C# that introduces regular expression types and sophisticated runtime representation of XML values. Programmers can take advantage of the underlying .NET concurrency model.

Our work in data binding is similar to the approach Wallace and Runciman take for Haskell XML integration [17]. The authors create specialized type definitions from a given DTD.

The W3C has standardized the XSLT and XQuery languages [16] for transformation and querying of XML. The former was intended as a language for simple transformations but quickly grew beyond its initial goal. The latter is designed as the XML equivalent of the database-hosted structured query language (SQL). Both languages are functional in the sense that they do not permit imperative update of XML trees.

The rest of this paper is structured as follows. Section 2 gives an introduction to case classes and pattern matching; these features, known from the functional programming domain, are useful for handling algebraic datatypes and structured data in particular. Section 3 is the core section of this paper; it describes the XML library of Scala. Starting with the XML data model in Scala, it describes parsing and validation, regular sequence pattern matching, and querying XML using for comprehensions. Section 4 shows two examples of simple XML services, and their implementation in Scala. When dealing with more advanced service architectures one will have to deal with concurrent requests and events. Scala's programming abstractions for concurrency are shortly described in Section 5. Section 6 concludes.

2   Case Classes and Pattern Matching

In this section we start by recalling the conventional, object-oriented way of decomposing data. Then we introduce case classes and describe the semantics of pattern matching. Finally, regular sequence patterns are discussed; as will be seen in the next section, these are particularly useful for decomposing XML data.

2.1   Object-Oriented Decomposition

When dealing with structured data, a common object-oriented design pattern is to create a set of classes, some of which act as structural containers for others (cf. the Composite pattern [9]). For inspecting structured data, a programmer can solely rely on virtual method calls of methods provided by such classes.

As an example, consider a simple evaluator for propositional logic, consisting of propositional variables and connectives. We can decompose the evaluator according to the term structure as follows:

```scala
trait Term {
  def eval(env: Array[Boolean]): Boolean;
}
class True() extends Term {
  def eval(env: Array[Boolean]) = true;
}
class Var(i: Int) extends Term {
  def eval(env: Array[Boolean]) = env(i);
}
class Not(term: Term) extends Term {
  def eval(env: Array[Boolean]) = !term.eval(env);
}
```

```
class And(left: Term, right: Term) extends Term {
  def eval(env: Array[Boolean]) = left.eval(env) && right.eval(env);
}
```

The given program models propositional formulas with an abstract class (called *trait*) `Term` which defines a deferred `eval` method that takes an environment as a parameter. Concrete subclasses of `Term` model the various term variants. Note that the compiler has enough information to infer the result type, it is thus omitted for brevity.

This object-oriented decomposition scheme generally requires the anticipation of all operations traversing a given structure. Moreover, non-local inspections cannot be implemented by one method alone, several dispatches are necessary. Often internal methods have to be exposed to some degree. Adding new methods is tedious and error-prone, because it requires all classes to be either changed or subclassed. A related problem is that implementations of operations are distributed over all participating classes making it difficult to understand and change them.

The Visitor pattern [9] can be used to separate operations from structure, however, it still breaks encapsulation, it does not deal with non-local inspections either and requires significant amounts of boilerplate code.

2.2   Pattern Matching over Class Hierarchies

Functional languages like ML and Haskell have embraced *algebraic datatypes* for the purpose of separating structure from operations. Operations on such datatypes are simply functions which use *pattern matching* as the basic decomposition principle. Such an approach makes it possible to implement a single `eval` function without exposing artificial auxiliary functions.

Scala provides a natural way for tackling the above programming task in a functional way by supplying the programmer with a mechanism for creating structured data representations similar to algebraic datatypes and a decomposition mechanism based on pattern matching.

Instead of adding algebraic types to the core language, Scala enhances the class abstraction mechanism to simplify the construction of structured data. Classes tagged with the **case** modifier automatically define a constructor with the same arguments as the primary constructor. Singleton objects (or objects, for short) are classes that have only one instance, hence serve as constants:

```
abstract class Term ;
case object True extends Term ;
case class Var(i: Int) extends Term ;
case class Not(term: Term) extends Term ;
case class And(left: Term, right: Term) extends Term ;
```

Given these definitions, it is now possible to create the propositional formula $x_1 \wedge \neg(\neg x_2 \wedge x_3)$ without using the **new** primitive, simply by calling the constructors associated with case classes: `And(Var(1), Not(And(Not(Var(2)), Var(3))))`. The fields of each case class can be accessed with the usual dot notation, e.g. as in x.left. Furthermore, Scala's pattern matching expressions provide a concise means of decomposition that uses these constructors as patterns:

```
def eval(term: Term, env: Array[Boolean]): Boolean = term match {
  case True             => true;
  case Var(i)           => env(i);
  case Not(t)           => !eval(t, env);
  case And(left, right) => eval(left, env) && eval(right, env); }
```

Note that apart from the pleasing localization of the intended behavior in one method, there is now a way to change the representation of environments to bitfields without needing to touch the source code of the Term classes. Moreover, it becomes easy to perform non-local inspections through the use of nested patterns as happens in the following function.

```
def simpl(term: Term): Term = term match {
  case True | Var(_)    => term
  case Not(Not(x))      => simpl(x)
  case Not(x)           => Not(simpl(x1))
  case And(left, right) => And(simpl(left), simpl(right)) }
```

The matching expression x match { case pat_1 => e_1 case pat_2 => e_2 ...} matches value x against the patterns pat_1, pat_2, etc. in the given order. The value x is called the *scrutinee*. A pattern pat_i is a term built up from variables, case class constructors, and some predefined match primitives (like the wildcard _ and the choice operator |). To match the scrutinee against pat_1, pat_2, etc. means to find the first pattern pat_i that can be made equal to x by binding its variables to terms appropriately. If such a pattern is found then e_i is executed, after replacing in e_i each variable of pat_i by its binding. If no such pattern is found, then a run time error is generated. The wildcard pattern _ matches any value. Choice patterns $p_1|p_2$ may not contain variables and match the union of values that are matched by their subpatterns. A constructor pattern $Constr(p_1, ..., p_n)$ matches any value that is an instance of the corresponding case class, and whose arguments match the arguments patterns. Hence, patterns can be terms of arbitrary depth (cf. the pattern Not(Not(x)) in the function simpl.

Such a functional decomposition scheme has the advantage that new functions can be added easily to the system. On the other hand, integrating a new case class might require changes in all pattern matching expressions. For extensibility, the Scala compiler does not check *exhaustiveness* of patterns, meaning to ensure that any scrutinee must match at least one of the patterns. For the moment it neither checks *redundancy*, i.e. when a pattern can never match due to a more general earlier pattern. We plan to add redundancy checks in the future.

Patterns in Scala are linear in the sense that a variable may appear only once within a pattern. However, it is possible to add to a pattern p a "guard", i.e., an if expression that involves the variables of *pat*. For instance, the pattern case And(x, y) if x == y matches only terms of the form And(t, t). Hence, using such equality guards it is possible to express arbitrary constraints between variables.

The **case** modifier can appear anywhere on a class hierarchy. It is possible to extend a case class, and case classes can extend non-case classes, which enables more involved designs than the flat one presented above. The only restriction that applies is that a case class may not directly or indirectly be derived from another case class.

2.3   Regular Sequence Pattern Matching

The case class declarations introduced above determine the exact number of contained objects, similar to a function declaration determining the exact number of arguments. But often programmers need to deal with a number of sequence elements that is not known in advance. This can be done using *sequence parameters*.

The last parameter of a formal parameter list can be turned into a sequence parameter by marking its type T with a star ($*$), which is a shorthand for the type $Seq[T]$. This works for case class declarations as well as for function declarations. The example from above can thus be extended with a conjunction over an arbitrary number of terms as follows:

case class BigAnd(terms: Term*) **extends** Term ;

The field `terms` is of the type `Seq[Term]`. The `Seq` trait offers functionality to obtain the length of the sequence, to access its elements, and to iterate over them. Such a sequence parameter offers syntactic convenience by permitting an arbitrary number of arguments in function and constructor calls. A conjunction over an arbitrary number of terms like $\neg x_1 \wedge x_2 \wedge x_3$ can now be expressed as BigAnd(Not(Var(1)),Var(2),Var(3)).

The following code transforms BigAnds into a series of Ands.

```
def toAnd(b:BigAnd): Term = {
  val it = b.terms.elements;
  var t  = True;
  while(it.hasNext) { t = And(it.next, t); }
  return t; }
```

In practice, the data to be passed to the constructor may often already be in some sequence representation. In this case, a *sequence escape* is used to guide the compiler. The code **val** xs = List(Not(Var(1)),Var(2),Var(3)); BigAnd(xs:_*) constructs the same conjunction as above, using the sequence escape xs:_*. If the annotation were missing, the compiler would signal a type error since xs of type Seq[Term] cannot be used as a Term.

Let us now discuss how sequences can be decomposed, using pattern matching. A *regular sequence pattern* is a regular expression that possibly is annotated with variable bindings [8]. A variable binding is written x@p where p is a regular pattern that may not contain other variable bindings. For regular expression constructs we use the following standard notations;

- concatenation: p,p concatenates sequence patterns
- the star operator: $p*$ denotes zero or more occurrences of p

- the plus operator: *p+* denotes one or more occurrences of *p*
- the option operator: *p?* denotes *p* or the empty sequences.

A choice pattern is a sequence pattern if one of its branches is a sequence pattern. Variables binding a sequence pattern that matches elements of some type `T` are of type `Seq[T]`.

Regular patterns can be applied to sequences of any type, not just case classes. Here is an example of a text-processing task using regular patterns:

```
def findRest(z: Seq[Char]): Seq[Char] = z match {
  case Seq(_*, 'G', 'o', 'o'*, 'g', 'l', 'e', rest@(_*)) => rest }
```

This pattern is used to search for the sequence of letters `"Gogle"` or `"Google"`, or .... If the input `z` matches, then the function returns what remains after the occurrence, otherwise it generates a runtime error. Possible ambiguities (e.g., for several occurrences of 'Goo*gle-words' in z) are resolved using the (left) shortest match policy which chooses the shortest match for each possibility (such as _*), coming from the left. In the example this coincides with matching the *first* occurrence of `"Goo*gle"` in `z`.

As (conventional) pattern matching is well suited for decomposing ranked trees (i.e., trees in which each node has a fixed number of children), regular sequence pattern matching is the counterpart for decomposing *unranked* trees. As we will see in the following section, regular sequence pattern matching is particularly useful in the context of XML, because XML documents are naturally modeled as unranked trees.

3   XML Facilities in Scala

XML [16] has emerged as the *lingua franca* of the web. Henceforth, all major programming languages are providing, in varying degrees, support to handle XML data. XML documents describe tree-structured data. Functional programming languages, starting with Lisp, have always been particularly well-suited in dealing with trees and tree-structured data. It therefore comes as no surprise that Scala with its functional features is well-suited for XML processing.

The next two subsections describe basic features of XML processing in Scala: our data model of XML, how to express XML documents in Scala code, how to parse XML documents, and how to validate a document against a given schema while parsing. Then, in Section 3.3 we describe how regular sequence pattern matching can be applied to XML data. After a short discussion on namespaces and attributes, section 3.5 describes how to express XML queries with for comprehensions. Finally, we show how to realize queries on XML data, using Scala's elegant concept of for comprehensions.

3.1   Data Model

We give an introduction to Scala's XML data model by contrasting it with the W3C's Document Object Model (DOM), which is characteristic for a number

```
<?xml version="1.0"?>
<purchaseOrder orderDate="1999-10-20">
  <shipTo country="US">
    <name>Alice Smith</name>  <street>123 Maple Street</street>
    <city>Mill Valley</city> <state>CA</state> <zip>90952</zip>
  </shipTo>
  <billTo country="US">
      <name>Robert Smith</name>      <street>8 Oak Avenue</street>
      <city>Old Town</city>      <state>PA</state> <zip>95819</zip>
  </billTo>
  <comment>Hurry, my lawn is going wild!</comment>
  <items>
  <item partNum="872-AA">
      <productName>Lawnmower</productName>     <quantity>1</quantity>
      <USPrice>148.95</USPrice> <comment>Confirm this is electric</comment>
  </item>
  <item partNum="926-AA">
      <productName>Baby Monitor</productName>   <quantity>1</quantity>
      <USPrice>39.98</USPrice>          <shipDate>1999-05-21</shipDate>
  </item>
  </items>
</purchaseOrder>
```

Listing 1.1. Extract from XML document

of related object-oriented XML data models. The DOM has been implemented
in several programming languages, including Java. We will also compare code
written using Java and DOM with code written using Scala.

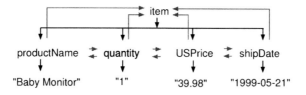

Fig. 1. DOM of a purchase order item

Consider the XML fragment in Listing 1.1. It shows a purchase order consisting of two items. The tree structure inherent in such a purchase order is
essentially an unranked, ordered tree. Within DOM, such tree structures are
doubly-linked: there are pointers to each child of a node and back, and pointers
from each node to its next and previous sibling. Figure 1 depicts the DOM tree
structure of a purchase order.

From a programmer's perspective the availability of many tree pointers
(parent-child, child-parent, next-sibling, previous-sibling) might offer high flexibility. However, code that uses parent and previous-sibling pointers is hard to

```
import org.w3c.dom.Document;
import org.w3c.dom.Element;
...
//Retrieve the Document object
DocumentBuilder fact =DocumentBuilderFactory.newInstance()newDocumentBuilder();
Document po = fact.parse(new File("po.xml"));
Element root = po.getDocumentElement();

//Retrieve all partNums and compute the grand total for the purchase order
double total = 0;
NodeList children = root.getChildNodes();
for (int i = 0; i < children.getLength(); i++) {
   Node node = children.item(i);
   //Find the items child element
   if ("items".equals(node.getLocalName())) {
      NodeList itemList = node.getChildNodes();
      for (int j = 0; j < itemList.getLength(); j++) {
         Node item = itemList.item(j);

         //Get the partNum attribute value
         NamedNodeMap attrs = item.getAttributes();
         System.out.println("partNum:" + attrs.getNamedItem("partNum"));

         //Find the USPrice child element
         NodeList itemChildren = item.getChildNodes();
         for (int k = 0; k < itemChildren.getLength(); k++) {
            Node child = itemChildren.item(k);
            if ("USPrice".equals(child.getLocalName()) {
               total += Double.valueOf(child.getNodeValue()).doubleValue();
} } } } }
System.out.println("Grand_total_=_" + total);
```

Listing 1.2. Processing with Java and DOM

read and possibly introduces circularities thus leading to nontermination. Moreover, it increases the footprint of DOM: (1) DOM representations are very *memory costly* (usually at least 4-5 times the space of the original XML document on disk) and (2) program code using DOM is *overly verbose*.

In contrast, Scala has a much thinner model of XML: an XML document is seen as an immutable, ordered (singly-linked) unranked tree. This model agrees with the functional view of a tree in which no pointers to parent or previous-sibling nodes are provided. Programmers can obtain those nodes by storing them in temporary variables upon a traversal. Two major advantages of this representation are (1) memory efficiency (usually around 1-2 times the space of the original XML document on disk) and (2) clean, concise program code.

Before describing the library classes, we demonstrate the latter point consider as example simple programming task over the purchase order data. We want to

```
import scala.xml.XML;
val doc = XML.loadFile("po.xml");
var total = 0;
for(val z <- doc \\ "item";
    val y <- z \ "USPrice") {
  Console.println("partnum:_" + z \ "@partNum");
  total = total + Double.valueOf(y.text)
}
Console.println("Grand_total_" + total);
```

Listing 1.3. Processing with Scala

- collect the partNum attributes and
- compute the sum of the prices in the USPrice elements.

Using DOM within Java, this task is realized by the code shown in Listing 1.2. Each node is mapped to an object, whose children are accessed by obtaining a NodeList using the getChildNodes() method, and then accessing each child using a call like item(i). The label of a node is accessed via the getLocalName().

A corresponding Scala code is shown in Listing 1.3. It uses a for comprehension to search for all pairs (z,y) such that z is an item-node and y is a USPrice-child of z. For comprehensions are explained in detail in Section 3.5.

The Node class embodies Scala's tree model of XML. It describes the components of an XML node, namely the namespace prefix, the label, a pointer to the namespace bindings in scope, the attributes and the children. This library class provides also methods for XML serialization, namespace/attribute lookup, XPath selection etc.

```
abstract class Node extends NodeSeq {
    def prefix:     String;
    def label:      String;
    def scope:      NamespaceBinding;
    def attributes: MetaData;
    def child:      Seq[Node];   ... }
```

NodeSeq is a wrapper class that acts as a proxy for an arbitrary sequence of nodes – this can be a list, an array, or any other custom representation (a single Node acts as a singleton sequence). It adds methods \ and \\ than can be used like corresponding XPath operators / and //.

```
abstract class NodeSeq extends Seq[Node] {   ...
    def \(that: String): NodeSeq  = {...}
    def \\(that: String): NodeSeq = {...} }
```

Note that the operators \\ and \ are *not* build-in operators of the Scala language, but, are just ordinary methods, since operator characters can be used as method names. Scala resolves an expression of the form a id b into the more familiar a.id(b). A fixed precedence scheme guides the parser and determines in which direction operations associate.

Concrete subclasses of Node exist for elements, text nodes, comments, processing instructions, and entity references. The informed reader might wonder about namespace and root nodes – the root node is represented by a class Document, and namespace nodes are instances of NamespaceBinding which is described further down.

Elements are by default represented using the scala.xml.Elem class, which is – not surprisingly – a case class. The accessor methods for the constructor arguments provide exactly the methods required by the superclass scala.xml.Node.

```
case class Elem(prefix: String, label: String, attributes: MetaData,
           scope: NamespaceBinding, child: Node*) extends Node { ... }
```

3.2   Literals, Parsing, and Validation

XML syntax can be used directly in a Scala program, e.g., in value definitions.

```
val labPhoneBook =
  <phonebook>
    <descr>Phone numbers of<b>XML</b> hackers.</descr>
    <entry>
      <name>Burak</name>
      <phone where="work">    +41 21 693 68 67 </phone>
      <phone where="mobile"> +41 78 601 54 36 </phone>
    </entry>
  </phonebook>;
```

The value labPhoneBook is an XML tree; for instance, one of its nodes has the label phone, a child sequence consisting of a single text node labeled by +41 2.., and a map from the attribute key where to the value "work". Within XML syntax it is possible to escape to Scala using the brackets { and } (similar to the convention used in XQuery). For example, a date node with a child text node consisting of the current date can be defined by <date>{ df.format(new java.util.Date()) }</date>.

Parsing XML data is done by means of the load method of the object scala.xml.XML. Scala's XML parser is of course entirely written in Scala, and is also used to parse the XML literals described above. The XML standard actually describes two variants of XML parsers – the validating and the non-validating ones. The parser library parser provides support for validation, which can be enabled as shown in the following lines.

```
val fil = new java.io.File("data.xml");
val prs = new scala.xml.parsing.ConstructingParser(fil, true)
    with ValidatingMarkupHandler ;   // true = preserve whitespace
prs.nextch;                          // initialize parser
val d = prs.document();              // returns Document instance
val elem = d.docElem;
val dtd  = d.dtd;
```

The above code is a case of so-called mixin composition: a mixin class ValidatingMarkupHandler overrides certain members of the existing class

`ConstructingParser`, changing their behavior from non-validating to validating. In general, mixin composition is a flexible means to pull together pieces of code that have been factored out into components [14].

The user also has the possibility to connect an event handler to the parser, which gets called back whenever a subelement has been successfully parsed. This allows to traverse the document without necessarily constructing it in memory. It can be useful, for instance, in order to run an optimized query directly during parse time of the document and without actually constructing the document, or, if based on the element name different representations (of different types) are to be constructed.

3.3   Regular Matching on XML Nodes

XML nodes can be decomposed using pattern matching. Scala allows to use XML syntax here too, albeit only to match elements. The following example shows how to add an entry to a phonebook element.

```
import scala.xml.{ Node, XML } ;
def add(pbook: Node, newEntry: Node): Node =
  pbook match {
    case <phonebook>{ cs @ _* }</phonebook> =>
      <phonebook>{ cs }{ newEntry }</phonebook>
  }
val newPhoneBook =
  add(XML.load("savedPhoneBook"),
      <entry>
        <name>Sebastian</name>
        <phone where="work">+41 21 693 68 67</phone>
      </entry>);
```

The add function performs a match on the phonebook element, binding its child sequence to the variable cs (the regular sequence pattern _* matches an arbitrary sequence). Then it constructs a new phonebook element with child sequence cs followed by the node newEntry. Note that the pattern cs @ _* appears inside code braces, it would otherwise be interpreted as literal text.

The compiler turns the above shorthand into constructor calls of the class scala.xml.Elem. New temporary variables are introduced to deal with namespace definitions and redefinitions and prefixed and unprefixed attributes. If we ignore those for a moment, the resulting code is equivalent to the following (which could equally well be written by a user that despises angle brackets)

```
import scala.xml._ ;
def add(pbook: Node, newEntry: Node): Node =
  pbook match {
    case Elem(_,"phonebook",_,_,cs @ _*) =>
      Elem(null, "phonebook", Null, $scope,
           (new scala.xml.NodeBuffer() &+ ch &+ newEntry):_*)
  }
val newPhoneBook = add(XML.load("savedPhoneBook"),
```

```
Elem(null, "entry", Null, $scope, Null,
   Elem(null, "name", Null, $scope, Text("Sebastian"))
   Elem(null, "phone", new UnprefixedAttribute("where","work", Null), $scope,
            Text("+41_21_693_68_67"))));
```

More involved patterns are possible. The following pattern traverses the children of a node and finds out whether a book with the title <scala/xml> comes before a book with the title XSLT Reference, and if so, returns the book elements between those two.

```
books match {
  case <books>{ _*, <book><title>&lt;scala/xml&gt;</title>{ _ * }</book>,
        mid @ _*, <book><title>XSLT Reference</title>{ _ * }</book>,
              _* }</books> => mid
    case _                 => Nil
}
```

3.4   Namespaces and Attributes

Attributes and namespaces are implemented as immutable, linked lists. Attributes with namespace prefixes are distinguished from ones without. For the reader not versed in the namespace issues regarding XML, it might suffice to know that the Namespaces in XML Recommendation [16] specification, which has been introduced long after the XML specification, provides a means to 'package' related names by associating them with a uniform resource identifier (URI). The association avoids name collisions and happens indirectly by (1) binding URIs to prefixes and (2) prefixing names using the syntax ns:localname.

For convenience, a *default namespace* may be declared that applies to unprefixed names. Finally, it is also possible to undeclare prefix bindings. As an example, consider the following element:

```
<seat class="Y" ht:class="blink" xmlns:ht="urn:hypertext">33B</seat>
```

This element defines two distinct class attributes, the second being in the namespace determined by the ht prefix. This prefix is bound by a namespace declaration xmlns:html="urn:hypertext", which happens to be in the same element. Here is the equivalent Scala code, with an explanation below:

```
Elem(null, "seat",
  new UnprefixedAttribute("class","Y",
      new PrefixedAttribute("ht","class","blink", Null)),
  new NamespaceBinding("ht","urn:hypertext", TopScope),
  Text("33B"))
```

The default namespace is identified by the null reference. Namespaces are encoded in a linked list of namespaces bindings (and "un-bindings"). The nodes of the list are shared among nodes of the same subtree. In this way, we fully support namespaces in Scala's literal syntax and library. The programmer can extend an existing scope scp with the above binding is achieved by writing

new NamespaceBinding("html","urn:hypertext", p), with object TopScope acting as the top-level (empty) scope.

3.5   XML Queries through For Comprehension

For comprehensions are a functional feature used e.g. in Haskell to concisely express computations on lists. In general, a for comprehension consists of generators (a sequence expression whose elements will subsequently be assigned to a variable) and filters (boolean expressions that eliminate some of the elements). The following code shows how to concisely compute a list pairs of numbers i, j between 0 and 100 where $i = 3n$ and $j < i$.

```
for (val i <- List.range(0, 100); i % 3 == 0; val j <- List.range(0, i); )
  yield Pair(i, j);
```

For comprehensions are related to queries on XML data in a way that complements pattern matching. Where the latter yields at most one result for a pattern, queries are usually used to compute *all* matches of a query. Scala's flexible comprehension mechanism can be used to this end, allowing for a concise and elegant style that closely resembles XQuery. In the following example, we select all **entry** elements from **labAddressbook** and from **labPhoneBook** into the variables **a** and **p**, respectively. Whenever the name contents of two such entries coincide, a **result** element is generated which has as children the address and phone number, taken from the appropriate entry.

```
for (val a <- labAddressBook \\ "entry";
     val p <- labPhoneBook \\ "entry";
     a \ "name" == p \ "name") yield
  <result>{ a.child }{ p \ "phone" }</result>
```

Note the variable order inside the for comprehension: labAddressBook is traversed in document order (=depth-first left-to-right) and for each entry found, labPhoneBook is traversed in document order. Hence, the order of entries in the result will be the order of entries in labAddressBook; If a and p are exchanged inside the **for**, then the order of results will be as in labPhoneBook.

3.6   Data Binding

Types of XML documents are usually specified by so called schemas. The act of checking conformance to a schema is called validation. Popular schema formalisms are DTD (Document Type Definition), XML Schema [16], and RELAX NG [12]. At this moment a simple support for DTDs is available through the schema2src tool. It converts a DTD to a set of class definitions which can only be instantiated with XML data that is valid with respect to the DTD.

The idea here is to map the generic tree representation to case classes. We can create one case class per element tag, and place code that validates in the constructor. The validating code uses Scala's regular expression library. The validation functions can also be called separately, and the tool is written in an

```
<!ELEMENT phonebook (descr, entry*)>
<!ELEMENT descr     (#PCDATA | b)*>
<!ELEMENT b         (#PCDATA)>
<!ELEMENT entry     (name, phone+)>
<!ELEMENT name      (#PCDATA)>
<!ELEMENT phone     (#PCDATA)>
<!ATTLIST phone where (home|mobile|work) "home">
```

Listing 1.4. A typical DTD

extensible way to accommodate user-defined modules for custom schema languages.

XML documents that are represented generically can be validated and optionally translated into the specialized representation, by using the so-called binder object.

```
val pb = dtd.binder.validate(<phonebook> ... </phonebook>);
pb match {
  case phonebook(_, _*,
          entry(md,
            name(Text("Sebastian")),
            p@phone(_,_*)), _*)) => p }
```

Existing XML documents can then be validated against the DTD using a special load method which tries to instantiate the corresponding classes. Scala's regular expression library is used to convert content models to finite automata.

4   Services

In this section, we will give some examples that show how Scala can be used to create web services. For reasons of space, we will only give basics of servlet programming and refer the interested reader to the real life applications that were written in Scala and are in active use.

4.1   Common Gateway Interface

Web services were born out of ad hoc interfaces to webservers that became standardized in one way or another. The earliest of them, the Common Gateway Interface (CGI), may be considered as the first defining protocol of web services. CGI programs can be written in almost any language, but the cost of real life CGI programs is influenced by two crucial issues:

First, new variants of CGI use long-running processes that communicate with the web server and handle requests concurrently. Scala's suitability for concurrency will be analyzed in detail in the next section. Second, writing server side programs is made hard due to inversion of control and state [15]. We are currently working on an implementation for an infrastructure for web services that

```scala
class MyServlet extends HttpServlet {
  def getTime = java.util.Calendar.getInstance().getTime();

  def doGet(req:HttpServletRequest, res:HttpServletResponse) = {
    val page = <html>
                 <head> <title>Hello, Servlet World!</title> </head>
                 <body>
                   <h1>Hello, Servlet World!</h1>
                   <p> The time is <b>{ getTime.toString() }</b> </p>
                 </body>
               </html>;
    res.getWriter().write( page.toString() );
} }
```

Listing 1.5. A friendly Scala servlet

solves the control issue using continuations. This task is greatly simplified by having first-class functions in the language.

4.2 Servlets

On the Java platform, using the CGI is usually discarded in favor of *servlets*. These are small portions of object-oriented code centered around a *servlet container* or *servlet engine* which maps URL requests of the HTTP protocol to method calls.

Programmers can choose among many servlet containers to run their Java servlets It is easy to write servlets in Scala making use of the tight integration between the two languages. A sample servlet is given in Listing 1.5.

Built on top of the servlet technology, we have implemented a range of web services that are in active use. These are the Scala bugtracking system, and an online auction software. Both are three-tier systems that generate XHTML for presentation purposes. We found developing real life applications quite useful to guide the design of the XML library and testing the implementation of the literal syntax.

4.3 Remote Invocations

The concept of a web services does not (and might never) benefit from an agreed upon definition. Nevertheless, specifications like XMLRPC and the Simple Object Access Protocol (SOAP) have emerged as language-independent remote method invocation protocols that enjoy some popularity in this context. Space limitations hinder us from giving a full example; given the above explanations it is clear that Scala provides everything needed to handle SOAP fragments like the following one of a Google service. For the networking tasks, the relevant Java network library are at the programmer's disposal.

```
<SOAP-ENV:Envelope xmlns:SOAP-ENV="http://schemas.xmlsoap.org/soap/envelope/"
                   xmlns:xsi="http://www.w3.org/1999/XMLSchema-instance"
                   xmlns:xsd="http://www.w3.org/1999/XMLSchema">
  <SOAP-ENV:Body>
    <ns1:doSpellingSuggestion xmlns:ns1="urn:GoogleSearch"
        SOAP-ENV:encodingStyle="http://schemas.xmlsoap.org/soap/encoding/">
      <key xsi:type="xsd:string">00000000000000000000000000000000</key>
      <phrase xsi:type="xsd:string">Boogle</phrase>
    </ns1:doSpellingSuggestion>
  </SOAP-ENV:Body>
</SOAP-ENV:Envelope>
```

We can summarize that by these properties of Scala's XML syntax and data model, applications benefit from improved integration over present solutions built from Java plus XML libraries.

5 Concurrency

Finally, we shall point out that concurrency is an application area for which Scala is particularly well suited. Consider the task of implementing an electronic auction service. We focus here on an Erlang-style actor process model [1] to implement the participants of the auction. An alternative approach to concurrent programming in Scala using pi-calculus is described elsewhere [7].

Actors are objects to which messages are sent. Every process has a "mailbox" of its incoming messages which is represented as a queue. It can work sequentially through the messages in its mailbox, or search for messages matching some pattern.

For every traded item there is an auctioneer process that publishes information about the traded item, that accepts offers from clients, and that communicates with the seller and winning bidder to close the transaction. We present an overview of a simple implementation here.

In Listing 1.6, we define the messages that are exchanged during an auction. There are two traits: `AuctionMessage` for messages from clients to the auction service, and `AuctionReply` for replies from the service to the clients. Both classes are extended with a number of cases.

Listing 1.7 presents a Scala implementation of a class `Auction` for auction processes that coordinate the bidding on one item. Objects of this class are created by indicating (1) a seller process which needs to be notified when the auction is over, (2) a minimal bid, and (3) the date when the auction is to be closed.

The process behavior is defined by its `run` method. That method repeatedly selects (using `receiveWithin`) a message and reacts to it, until the auction is closed, which is signaled by a `TIMEOUT` message. Before finally stopping, it stays active for another period determined by the `timeToShutdown` constant and replies to further offers that the auction is closed.

```
trait AuctionMessage;
case class Offer(bid: int, client: Actor)   extends AuctionMessage;
case class Inquire(client: Actor)            extends AuctionMessage;

trait AuctionReply;
case class  Status(asked: int, expire: Date) extends AuctionReply;
case object BestOffer                         extends AuctionReply;
case class  BeatenOffer(maxBid: int)          extends AuctionReply;
case class  AuctionConcluded(seller: Actor, client: Actor)
                                              extends AuctionReply;
case object AuctionFailed                     extends AuctionReply;
case object AuctionOver                        extends AuctionReply;
```

Listing 1.6. Implementation of an Auction Service

```
class Auction(seller: Actor, minBid: int, closing: Date) extends Actor {
  val timeToShutdown = 36000000; // msec
  val bidIncrement = 10;
  override def run() = {
    var maxBid = minBid - bidIncrement;
    var maxBidder: Actor = _;
    var running = true;
    while (running) {
      receiveWithin ((closing.getTime() - new Date().getTime())) {
        case Offer(bid, client) =>
          if (bid >= maxBid + bidIncrement) {
            if (maxBid >= minBid) maxBidder send BeatenOffer(bid);
            maxBid = bid; maxBidder = client; client send BestOffer;
          } else {
            client send BeatenOffer(maxBid);
          }
        case Inquire(client) =>
          client send Status(maxBid, closing);
        case TIMEOUT =>
          if (maxBid >= minBid) {
            val reply = AuctionConcluded(seller, maxBidder);
            maxBidder send reply; seller send reply;
          } else {
            seller send AuctionFailed;
          }
          receiveWithin(timeToShutdown) {
            case Offer(_, client) => client send AuctionOver
            case TIMEOUT => running = false;
} } } }    }
```

Listing 1.7. Implementation of an Auction Service

Here are some further explanations of the constructs used in this program:

- The `receiveWithin` method of class `Actor` takes as parameters a time span
  given in milliseconds and a function that processes messages in the mailbox. The function can be expressed directly as a matching expression. The
  `receiveWithin` method selects the first message in the mailbox which matches
  one of these patterns and applies the corresponding action to it.
- The last case of `receiveWithin` is guarded by a `TIMEOUT` pattern. If no other
  messages are received in the meantime, this pattern is triggered after the time
  span which is passed as argument to the enclosing `receiveWithin` method.
  `TIMEOUT` is a particular instance of class `Message`, which is triggered by the
  `Actor` implementation itself.
- Reply messages are sent using syntax of the form `destination send`
  `SomeMessage`, which expands to `destination.send(SomeMessage)` as described
  before.

All the constructs discussed above are offered as methods in the library class
`Actor`. That class is itself implemented in Scala, based on the underlying thread
model of the host language (e.g. Java, or .NET). The implementation of all
features of class `Actor` used here is given in Section 5.2.

5.1   Mailboxes

Mailboxes are high-level, flexible constructs for process synchronization and communication. They allow sending and receiving of messages. A *message* in this
context is an arbitrary object. There is a special message `TIMEOUT` which is used
to signal a time-out.

```
case object TIMEOUT;
```

Mailboxes implement the following signature.

```
class MailBox {
  def send(msg: Any): unit;
  def receive[a](f: PartialFunction[Any, a]): a;
  def receiveWithin[a](msec: long)(f: PartialFunction[Any, a]): a;
}
```

The state of a mailbox consists of a multi-set of messages. Messages are added
to the mailbox using the `send` method. Messages are removed using the `receive`
method, which is passed a message processor `f` as argument. This is a partial
function from messages to some result type, which can be implemented as a
pattern matching expression. The `receive` method blocks until there is a message
in the mailbox for which its message processor is defined. The matching message
is then removed from the mailbox and the blocked thread is restarted by applying
the message processor to the message.

Here's how the mailbox class can be implemented:

```
class MailBox {
  private abstract class Receiver extends Signal {
    def isDefined(msg: Any): boolean;
    var msg = null;
  }
```

We define an internal class for receivers with a test method `isDefined`, which indicates whether the receiver is defined for a given message. The receiver inherits from class `Signal` a `notify` method which is used to wake up a receiver thread. When the receiver thread is woken up, the message it needs to be applied to is stored in the `msg` variable of `Receiver`.

```
  private val sent = new LinkedList[Any];
  private var lastSent = sent;
  private val receivers = new LinkedList[Receiver];
  private var lastReceiver = receivers;
```

The mailbox class maintains two linked lists, one for sent but unconsumed messages, the other for waiting receivers.

```
  def send(msg: Any): unit = synchronized {
    var r = receivers, r1 = r.next;
    while (r1 != null && !r1.elem.isDefined(msg)) { r = r1; r1 = r1.next }
    if (r1 != null) {
      r.next = r1.next; r1.elem.msg = msg; r1.elem.notify;
    } else {
      lastSent = insert(lastSent, msg);
  } }
```

The **send** method first checks whether a waiting receiver is applicable to the sent message. If yes, the receiver is notified. Otherwise, the message is appended to the linked list of sent messages.

```
  def receive[a](f: PartialFunction[Any, a]): a = {
    val msg: Any = synchronized {
      var s = sent, s1 = s.next;
      while (s1 != null && !f.isDefinedAt(s1.elem)) { s = s1; s1 = s1.next }
      if (s1 != null) {
        s.next = s1.next; s1.elem
      } else {
        val r = insert(lastReceiver, new Receiver {
          def isDefined(msg: Any) = f.isDefinedAt(msg);
        });
        lastReceiver = r;
        r.elem.wait();
        r.elem.msg
    } }
    f(msg)
  }
```

The `receive` method first checks whether the message processor function `f` can be applied to a message that has been sent but not consumed yet. If yes, the thread continues immediately by applying `f` to the message. Otherwise, a new receiver is created and linked into the `receivers` list, and the thread waits for a notification on this receiver. Once the thread is woken up again, it continues by applying `f` to the message that was stored in the receiver. The insert method on linked lists is defined as follows.

```
def insert(l: LinkedList[a], x: a): LinkedList[a] = {
  l.next = new LinkedList[a];
  l.next.elem = x;
  l.next.next = l.next;
  l }
```

The mailbox class also offers a method `receiveWithin` which blocks for only a specified maximal amount of time. If no message is received within the specified time interval (given in milliseconds), the message processor argument f will be unblocked with the special `TIMEOUT` message. The implementation of `receiveWithin` is quite similar to `receive`:

```
def receiveWithin[a](msec: long)(f: PartialFunction[Any, a]): a = {
  val msg: Any = synchronized {
    var s = sent, s1 = s.next;
    while (s1 != null && !f.isDefinedAt(s1.elem)) {
      s = s1; s1 = s1.next ;
    }
    if (s1 != null) {
      s.next = s1.next; s1.elem
    } else {
      val r = insert(lastReceiver, new Receiver {
          def isDefined(msg: Any) = f.isDefinedAt(msg);
      });
      lastReceiver = r;
      r.elem.wait(msec);
      if (r.elem.msg == null) r.elem.msg = TIMEOUT;
      r.elem.msg
    }
  }
  f(msg)
}
} // end MailBox
```

The only differences are the timed call to `wait`, and the statement following it.

5.2   Actors

The auction service was based on high-level actor processes, that work by inspecting messages in their mailbox using pattern matching. An actor is simply a thread whose communication primitives are those of a mailbox. Actors are hence defined as a mixin composition extension of Java's standard `Thread` class with the `MailBox` class.

```
abstract class Actor extends Thread with MailBox;
```

6 Conclusion

We have discussed Scala's facilities for dealing with semistructured data and concurrency. We have shown that the combination of functional and object-oriented programming constructs lets one design expressive high-level libraries that are also easy to use. Two examples of this approach were Scala's libraries for XPath-style XML navigation and Erlang-style actors.

Of course, moving a construct from a language to a library is not a silver bullet by itself. However, the library-based approach has two benefits. First, the core language can be kept simpler and more general. Second, libraries are much easier to upgrade and extend than core language constructs.

In future work, we plan to further pursue the library based approach. Our next targets are a framework for database integration and a web service infrastructure based on continuations. Scala is available under a free software license under http://scala.epfl.ch.

Acknowledgments. The Scala design and implementation has been a collective effort of many people. Besides the authors, Philippe Altherr, Vincent Cremet, Julian Dragos, Gilles Dubochet, Stéphane Micheloud, Nikolay Mihaylov, Michel Schinz, Erik Stenman and Matthias Zenger have made important contributions. The work was partially supported by grants from the Swiss National Fund under project NFS 21-61825, the European Framework 6 project PalCom, the Swiss National Competence Center for Research MICS, Microsoft Research, and the Hasler Foundation.

References

1. J. Armstrong, R. Virding, C. Wikström, and M. Williams. *Concurrent Programming in Erlang*. Prentice-Hall, second edition, 1996.
2. D. Atkins, T. Ball, G. Bruns, and K. Cox. Mawl: a domain-specific language for form-based services. *IEEE Trans. Software Eng.*, 25(3):334–346, 1999.
3. N. Benton, L. Cardelli, and C. Fournet. Modern concurrency abstractions for C#. In *Proc. of the 16th European Conference on Object-oriented programming.*, LNCS 2374, 2002.
4. G. Bierman, E. Meijer, and W. Schulte. The essence of data access in $C\omega$. In *Proc. of the 19th European Conference on Object-Oriented Programming*, LNCS 3586, 2005.
5. C. Brabrand, A. Møller, and M. I. Schwartzbach. The <bigwig> project. *ACM Transactions on Internet Technology*, 2(2):79–114, 2002.
6. A. S. Christensen, A. Møller, and M. I. Schwartzbach. Extending Java for high-level web service construction. *ACM Transactions on Programming Languages and Systems*, 25(6):814–875, 2003.
7. V. Cremet and M. Odersky. PiLib: A hosted language for pi-calculus style concurrency. In *Dagstuhl proc.: Domain-Specific Program Generation*, 2003.
8. B. Emir. Extending pattern matching with regular tree expressions for XML processing in Scala. Master's thesis, Rheinisch-Westfählische Technische Hochschule Aachen, 2003.

9. E. Gamma, R. Helm, R. Johnson, and J. Vlissides. *Design Patterns.* Addison-Wesley, 1995.
10. V. Gapeyev, M. Y. Levin, B. C. Pierce, and A. Schmitt. The Xtatic experience. In *Workshop on Programming Language Technologies for XML (PLAN-X)*, Jan. 2005. University of Pennsylvania Technical Report MS-CIS-04-24, Oct 2004.
11. M. Harren, M. Raghavachari, O. Shmueli, M. G. Burke, R. Bordawekar, I. Pechtchanski, and V. Sarkar. Xj: facilitating XML processing in Java. In *Proc. of the 14th International Conference on World Wide Web*, 2005.
12. Oasis. RELAX NG. See http://www.oasis-open.org/.
13. M. Odersky, P. Altherr, V. Cremet, B. Emir, S. Maneth, S. Micheloud, N. Mihaylov, M. Schinz, E. Stenman, and M. Zenger. An overview of the scala programming language. Technical Report IC/2004/64, Ecole Polytéchnique Fédérale de Lausanne, 2004.
14. M. Odersky and M. Zenger. Scalable component abstraction. In *Proc. of the 20th Annual Conference on Object-Oriented Programming, Systems, Languages and Applications*, 2005.
15. C. Quiennec. The influence of browsers on evaluators or, continations to program web servers. In *Proc. of the 5th ACM SIGPLAN International Conference on Functional Programming*, 2000.
16. World wide web committee. http://www.w3.org/
17. M. Wallace and C. Runciman. Haskell and XML: Generic combinators or type-based translation? In *Proc. of the 4th International Conference on Functional Programming*, 1999.

Definition and Correct Refinement of Operation Specifications

Thomas Baar, Slaviša Marković,
Frédéric Fondement, and Alfred Strohmeier

École Polytechnique Fédérale de Lausanne (EPFL)
School of Computer and Communication Sciences
CH-1015 Lausanne, Switzerland
{thomas.baar, slavisa.markovic, frederic.fondement,
alfred.strohmeier}@epfl.ch

Abstract. Modern incremental and iterative software engineering processes advocate to build software systems by first creating a highly simplified and abstract model of the system which is then moved by applying a series of model improvements toward implementation. Models of software systems at any level of abstraction should contain, besides structural information, a precise description of the expected system behavior. This paper formalizes relations between models of the same system at different levels of abstraction, classifies approaches for describing behavior of system operations, and investigates how these system operation descriptions can be kept synchronized with frequent changes of the system's structure.

Keywords: Design by Contract, Refactorings, Refinements, System Operations, Graph Transformations, UML, OCL, QVT.

1 Introduction

In the Analysis phase of the software development lifecycle, the expected behavior of the system under development has to be described as clearly as possible. Many methodologies, e.g. Rational Unified Process [1], Catalysis [2], and Fusion [3], propose to start with a high-level class model that represents only coarsely the actual state space of the system. The system's behavior is modeled by operations attached to classes and precisely described by a contract consisting of a pre- and postcondition [4,5] (see also the survey [6] in this volume). In practice, contracts are often given only informally. Formal contracts – written in a formal specification language – have some obvious advantages such as being a non-ambiguous criterion for the correctness of the implemented system. After the Analysis phase has been finished, the developed class model serves as a starting point for further design activities. In the Design phase, the state space of the system is typically explored thoroughly in order to define the best possible way *how* the system can provide the behavior that has been specified in the Analysis phase. This includes to iteratively refine the

J. Kohlas, B. Meyer, and A. Schiper (Eds.): Dependable Systems, LNCS 4028, pp. 127–144, 2006.
© Springer-Verlag Berlin Heidelberg 2006

current class model until it can be implemented directly in a chosen programming language.

Although the sketched development process can help to master the complexity of software development and to implement provably correct systems, it has not been widely adopted in industry yet. Many practitioners shy away from the effort to annotate class diagrams with formal contracts and to apply formal refinements when working on the system's design. We see two main reasons for the resistance to develop software by stepwise refinement. Firstly, the semantics of a contract language does not always meet the needs of developers. It is much more common to annotate a contract in an informal language such as English than in a formal language. Secondly, there is no common understanding on what refinement should mean and what it is good for in practice. Both problems are amplified by the lack of tool support. The contract language for UML, the Object Constraint Language (OCL), is not supported yet by any of the major UML tool vendors. A useful support for a contract language has to include also support for rewriting contracts when refining a (more) abstract class diagram to a (more) concrete one.

Despite their rare usage in practice, formal contract languages offer many advantages that fit well with recent trends in software engineering. Component-based development [7] is based on the idea of assembling applications from pre-fabricated modules (components). The functionality of a component is described best by a formal contract. Ideally, a component would carry also a formal proof to have implemented this contract correctly. Another motivation for using formal contract languages is model-driven development [8], which puts the modeling artifacts and not the implementation code to the forefront. The Model Driven Architecture (MDA) initiative of the OMG [9] aims at a framework for defining systems using a wide range of structural and behavioral views. The ultimate goal of MDA is to raise the level of abstraction at which systems are developed.

This paper discusses the purpose and semantics of contract languages and refinement steps. In Sect. 2, we divide existing formal contract languages into two groups called restrictive and constructive languages. After giving in Sect. 3 some formal definitions on the syntax and semantics of contracts, it is shown in Sect. 4 by example how a class diagram can be refined. Furthermore, the impact of a refinement on the syntactical correctness of operation contracts is shown. We make a proposal how refinement can be defined not as a syntactic transformation but based on the semantics of the involved class diagram. Based on this notion of refinement, we introduce correctness criteria for rewritten contracts in the refined diagram. For refactorings, which can be seen as a specific form of refinement, we discuss how operation contracts can be rewritten fully automatically without changing their semantics. In Sect. 5, constructive specification languages are discussed in more detail. Sometimes, constructive languages only allow to describe deterministic contracts. This shortcoming, however, can be remedied by integrating some elements of restrictive languages into constructive languages. Section 6 concludes the paper.

2   Restrictive vs. Constructive Languages

Formal languages for defining a contract, i.e. a pair of pre- and postcondition, can be divided into two groups. The distinction is based on the technique of formulating the postcondition of a contract. *Restrictive languages* focus in the postcondition on *Which properties must be satisfied in the post-state?* The postcondition is formalized as a predicate (a Boolean expression), which is evaluated to true in all valid post-states. Otherwise stated, the postcondition *restricts* the set of possible post-states. Well-known examples for restrictive languages are Eiffel [10], OCL [11], JML [12], and Z [13]. *Constructive languages*, instead, focus in the postcondition on *Which state transition is realized by the operation?* The contract prescribes how for a given pre-state the post-state is *constructed*. Well-known examples for constructive languages are Abstract State Machines (ASMs)[14], B [15], and UML's Action Language [16].

If an operation would be specified both with a restrictive and a constructive contract, then the properties of the post-state, which are given in the restrictive contract, could be entailed from a constructive contract. Some special purpose logics such as Hoare-Logic [17], Dynamic Logic [18] or even tools such as KeY [19] could be used to formally show this entailment relationship. The fact that restrictive contracts are comparably weak is also illustrated by the presence of the well-known *frame problem* [20,21]. Constructive languages, on the other hand, have the tendency to allow only deterministic specifications, which prevent any variations among the implementations of the specified operation.

We illustrate here briefly the main problems faced by restrictive and constructive specifications on a trivial example. A more detailed discussion on how the frame problem can be handled in restrictive languages is found in [22].

Let class A have two integer attributes a1, a2 and one operation op(). The intended behavior of op() is to double the value of attribute a1. A contract in the restrictive language OCL typically looks as follows:

context A::op()
    post: self.a1 = self.a1@pre + self.a1@pre

Since this contract has no precondition the predicate true is implicitly assumed. The postcondition is given in form of a restriction on the post-state: a post-state is valid as long as the value of attribute a1 on object self (which is the object on which op() is invoked) is doubled compared to the value of a1 in the pre-state (represented by a1@pre). Although it was intended, the OCL contract does not imply that the change of attribute a1 is the only effect of operation op(). According to this contract, also implementations of op() are correct that change the value of a2, or create new objects, or delete existing objects. A version of the OCL contract that really captures completely the intended behavior would be possible but its postcondition would be longwinded and had to mention explicitly all properties of the underlying class diagram that are not affected by op() (e.g. self.a2=self.a2@pre and A.allInstances()=A.allInstances()@pre).

The intended behavior could be given more easily and directly if a constructive language is used for formulating the contract. Operation op() could be specified in B by

    op() $\triangleq$ a1 := a1*2

Here, the precondition is omitted as well (implicitly true) and the postcondition is given in form of a pseudo-program which is 'executable' on a given pre-state. In difference to the restrictive contract, the semantics of the pseudo-program assumes an additional 'and nothing else changed' policy. Thus, implementations of op() that change, for instance, the value of attribute a2 would be not correct according to this contract written in B.

As discussed more detailed in Sect. 5, constructive languages suffer from a problem that is opposite to the frame problem. Whereas restrictive contracts can hardly express which parts of the system state remain unchanged, constructive contracts can hardly expressed that some parts of the system can arbitrarily change.

3   A Formal Contract Language

This section formalizes a contract language, giving its syntax and semantics. We have chosen the language of UML class diagrams (see [23,24] for a general introduction) and the Object Constraint Language (OCL) [25,11] as a formal, restrictive language to specify contracts for operations. Our formalization will be the basis to define precisely our notion of refinement and correctness presented in Sect. 4.

The first two definitions formally capture the notion of class and object diagrams in a mathematical way. The well-known graphical notation of these diagrams are intentionally ignored here, but can be added straightforwardly as Fig. 1 illustrates.

Definition 1 (Class Diagram). *A class diagram cd is a tuple (*CLASS, ATT, ASSO, OPER, *owner, atttype, associates, mult, opsig, $\preceq$) where*

- CLASS, ATT, ASSO, OPER *are disjunctive finite sets containing symbols for classes, attributes, associations, and operations*
- *owner, atttype are total functions on* ATT *yielding the owning class and the type of attributes*
- *associates is a total function on* ASSO *yielding the list of classes connected by associations*
- *mult is a total function on* ASSO *yielding the list of multiplicities (sets of non-negative natural numbers) annotated on association ends*
- *opsig is a total function on* OPER *yielding the list of parameter types; we assume the owning class of the operation to be always the first element of the list*
- $\preceq$ *is a partial order on* CLASS *reflecting its generalization hierarchy*

The information given in a class diagram can easily be converted into a signature Σ of a sorted, first-order predicate logic. Every class name C becomes a sort symbol C, every attribute at becomes a function symbol $at : owner(at) \rightarrow atttype(at)$, the generalization hierarchy $\preceq$ is embedded in the sort hierarchy $\preceq$. Furthermore, we assume signature Σ to contain also entries for all declarations made in the standard OCL library. Thus, the set of sort symbols in Σ contains

OCL's standard types `Integer`, `Real`, `String`, `Set`(T). There are function symbols in Σ for all pre-defined OCL operations such as `includes`: `Collection`(T) $\times\ T \rightarrow$ `Boolean` and the sort hierarchy $\preceq$ has entries for pre-defined types, e.g. `Integer` $\preceq$ `Real`, etc.

The first-order predicate logic for Σ is semantically interpreted by usual first-order structures. For the pre-defined symbols of the OCL library, a fixed interpretation is assumed. For example, the standard sort `Integer` is always interpreted as the set of natural numbers, the symbol `includes` is always interpreted as the set-theoretical *is-element-of* relationship, etc.

In our context, it is useful and common to call interpretations also *states*. That is the reason why the interpretations $\mathcal{I}$ of signature Σ are also denoted as *State$_\Sigma$*. Two interpretations for Σ can differ only in the interpretation of the symbols that stem from the class diagram. This part of interpretations can be depicted by *object diagrams*. Consequently, object diagrams and states are isomorphic structures. Object diagrams are denoted as a mathematical tuple in the same style as class diagrams. Figure 1 shows a simple example of a class and an object diagram both in the usual graphical notation and as mathematical tuples.

Definition 2 (Object Diagram). *Let cd=(*CLASS, ATT, ASSO, OPER, *owner, atttype, associates, mult, opsig, $\preceq$) be a given class diagram. An object diagram od for cd is a tuple (*OBJ, SLOT, LINK*) where*

- OBJ *is a total function on* CLASS. OBJ*(C) yields the finite set of all existing objects (we also say all instances) of class C.*
  We also write OBJ$_C$ *instead of* OBJ*(C).*
- SLOT *is a total function on* ATT. SLOT*(at) yields a total function from* OBJ*(owner(at)) to* OBJ*(atttype(at)).*
  We also write SLOT$_{at}$ *instead of* SLOT*(at).*
- LINK *is a total function on* ASSO. LINK*(as) yields a set of object lists where the i-th object in each list must be an instance of the i-th element of accociates(as).*
  We also write LINK$_{as}$ *instead of* LINK*(as).*

  If as is a binary association (i.e. associates(as) is a list of length two), we use opp$_{as}$(o) as an abbreviation for $\{o' \mid (o,o') \in Link_{as} \vee (o',o) \in Link_{as}\}$. Otherwise stated, opp$_{as}$(o) denotes the set of opposite ends of links in which object o is participating. If opp$_{as}$(o) is a singleton set, we use opp$_{as}$(o) also to refer to the contained element, i.e. opp$_{as}$(o) might also stand as an abbreviation for $\mu o' \mid (o,o') \in Link_{as} \vee (o',o) \in Link_{as}$.
- *The cardinality of* LINK$_{as}$ *must satisfy the restrictions expressed by the multiplicities attached to as. More formally: Let as be an n-ary association and i=1,...,n. The function prj(i, list) extracts the i-th element from list. Then, for all i, for all tuple $\in Link_{as}$ the following holds:*
  $$\#\{tuple' \mid \textstyle\bigwedge_{j=1..i-1,1+1,..,n} prj(j,tuple') = prj(j,tuple)\} \in prj(i,mult(as))$$
- *If C1 $\preceq$ C2 then Obj$_{C1} \subseteq$ Obj$_{C2}$.*

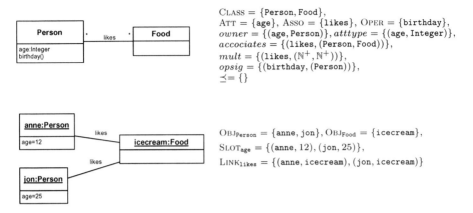

Fig. 1. Class and object diagram in both graphical and textual notation

A *contract* for an operation $op()$ is a pair $(pre, post)$ where pre, $post$ are predicate formulas over Σ. Both formulas can contain variables that are declared as formal parameters of $op()$ (note, that the pre-defined OCL variable *self* is handled in our formalism also as a formal parameter of $op()$). The precondition pre is evaluated on a given pre-state $s1$ and a given binding $argval$ of the formal parameters. The evaluation is defined formally by structural induction on all OCL expressions (see OCL's language definition [11] for details). We write $(s1, argval) \models_\Sigma pre$ iff pre is evaluated in $s1$ under the binding $argval$ to *true*. The postcondition $post$ is similarly evaluated in a pre-state $s1$, an argument binding $argval$, and a post-state $s2$. We write $(s1, argval, s2) \models_\Sigma post$ iff $post$ is evaluated to *true*.

Definition 3 (Semantics of Contract). *Let cd be a given class diagram, Σ the induced signature, $op()$ an operation in cd, and $(pre, post)$ a contract for $op()$.*

A label transition system (LTS) for $op()$ is a pair $(State_\Sigma, \rho)$ where $State_\Sigma$ denotes all possible states for Σ and ρ is a subset of $State_\Sigma \times Argval \times State_\Sigma$. Here, Argval denotes all bindings of the formal parameters of $op()$ to concrete values.

We say that $lts1 = (State_\Sigma, \rho_1)$ is larger then $lts2 = (State_\Sigma, \rho_2)$, denoted by $lts2 \sqsubseteq lts1$, iff $\rho_2 \subseteq \rho_1$.

The semantics of contract $(pre, post)$ is the largest LTS $sem_{op} = (State_\Sigma, \rho)$ such that $(s1, argval, s2) \in \rho$ implies that either $(s1, argval) \not\models_\Sigma pre$ or $(s1, argval, s2) \models_\Sigma post$.

Informally stated, the semantics of a contract is a LTS where the relation ρ contains exactly the state transitions which are possible according to the contract.

Definition 4 (Implementation, Partial/Total Correctness). *Let cd be a given class diagram, Σ the induced signature, $op()$ an operation in cd, and $(pre, post)$ a contract for $op()$.*

An implementation *of operation op() is a deterministic LTS* $(State_\Sigma, \rho)$ *on all possible states and argument bindings. A LTS* $(State_\Sigma, \rho)$ *is called* deterministic *on state s1 and argument binding argval iff* $(s1, argval, s2) \in \rho$ *and* $(s1, argval, s2') \in \rho$ *implies* $s2 = s2'$.

An implementation $(State_\Sigma, \rho)$ *of operation op() is called* partially correct *if* $(State, \rho) \sqsubseteq sem_{op}$.

An implementation $(State_\Sigma, \rho)$ *of operation op() is called* totally correct *if it is partially correct and* ρ *is total on all pre-states allowed by precondition pre. More formally: If* $(s1, argval) \models_\Sigma pre$ *then there exists s2 such that* $(s1, argval, s2) \in \rho$.

Definition 5 (Non-deterministic Contract). *Let* $(pre, post)$ *be a contract for operation op(). We call this contract* deterministic *if* sem_{op} *is deterministic on all allowed states s1 and argument bindings argval that satisfy the precondition:* $(s1, argval) \models_\Sigma pre$. *Otherwise, the contract is called* non-deterministic.

Note that deterministic contracts allow only one implementation on the allowed pre-states.

4   Correct Refinement of OCL Contracts

This section proposes a refinement notion that is purely based on the semantics of the involved class diagrams and does not impose any syntactical restrictions on them. Our approach is motivated by a simple case study on developing software to control a Drink Vending Machine (DVM). For some types of refinement, called *refactorings*, we derive in Sect. 4.4 some automatic rewriting rules for the contracts attached to the abstract class model.

4.1   Example: Drink Vending Machine (DVM)

A Drink Vending Machine (DVM) must be able to interact with both customers and service persons. The main functionality offered to customers is selling a drink. When a customer wants to buy a drink, s/he first has to select among the different drink kinds the machine offers, then to insert sufficient money, and finally to take the delivered drink from the drawer. A service person should be able to replenish the DVM with new drinks, to empty the money box of the DVM, to fix problems with the drawer, etc. For a realistic model of the DVM (see [26] for details), all possible exceptional cases have to be taken into account, e.g. that all drinks of a certain kind are sold out when a customer wants to buy it or that the capacity of the moneybox has been exceeded.

In this paper, we concentrate only on the formal specification of system operation `sellDrink()`. The operation `sellDrink()` is responsible for delivering drinks and for maintaining the number of available drinks in the DVM. Informally, this operation (1) checks, if the money inserted by the customer, called credit, is sufficient for buying the desired drink, (2) checks, if the desired drink is available, and (3) decrements the counter of how many drinks of the selected type are available in the system.

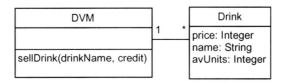

context DVM **inv**:
    self.drink−>forAll(d1,d2| d1.name=d2.name **implies** d1=d2)

Fig. 2. System description on abstract layer

An initial model for the DVM could look like the class diagram given in Fig. 2. The operation `sellDrink()` declared on class `DVM` has two parameters. The parameter `drinkName` (of type `String`, what has been suppressed in the diagram) denotes the kind of drink the customer has selected, for instance tomato juice, orange juice, cola, beer, etc. The parameter `credit` (of type `Integer`) represents the amount of money inserted by the customer. The class `Drink` represents all possible kinds of drinks offered by the DVM. The attributes `name` and `price` are self-explaining, the attribute `avUnits` represents the number of units that are still available within the DVM for sale. The invariant attached to the class diagram ensures the uniqueness of drink names.

The intended behavior of `sellDrink` is deterministic. Whenever the selected kind of drink is available and the inserted money is sufficient to buy the drink, the value of attribute `avUnits` on the corresponding `Drink` object should be decremented by 1 and nothing else should happen. Be aware that at the beginning of a software development project, most operations are specified by deterministic contracts. This is due to the fact that the system model is quite abstract and hides most of the details that cause the complexity of the real system.

For the initial system model given in Fig. 2, a restrictive contract for operation `sellDrink()` would typically look like the following OCL specification:

context DVM::sellDrink(drinkName:**String**, credit:**Integer**)
pre:
    self.drink−>select(d|d.name=drinkName **and**
                         d.price<=credit **and**
                         d.avUnits>0)−>size() = 1
post:
    self.drink−>select(d|d.name=drinkName)
                    −>forAll(d1| d1.avUnits=d1.avUnits@pre−1)

The precondition formalizes the steps (1) and (2), which have been informally given above, and the postcondition decrements the attribute `avUnits` on the selected `Drink` object by one. This contract written in OCL, however, does not capture the intended behavior since it is not deterministic and would allow within the execution of `sellDrink()`, for example, to change the name of the drink, what is surely not intended. In other words, the semantics of the contract language does not fit the needs of developers working on analysis documents. Some restrictive languages have made provision to handle the frame problem by

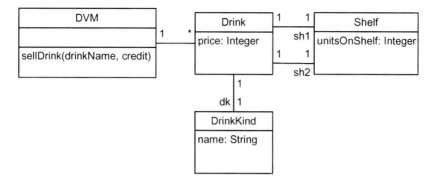

context DVM inv :
    self.drink.dk–>forAll(d1,d2| d1.name=d2.name implies d1=d2)

Fig. 3. System description on concrete layer

adding to the two standard clauses of a contract, pre- and postcondition, a third clause that is often called 'modifies'. The language OCL does not have such a third clause, yet. Nevertheless, we will use, despite all its weaknesses, the above shown contract for sellDrink() as the starting point for the next refinement of the system model.

4.2   Refinement of Class Diagrams

The initial system model shown in Fig. 2 has some obvious drawbacks, also known as *design smells*. The class Drink has three attributes, which all serve different purposes. The name of a drink is something very static whereas the price for one unit might be subject of very frequent changes. Furthermore, the number of units currently available is rather an attribute of the DVM than one of class Drink. Thus, all three attributes should be owned by different classes.

Let us assume that in addition to addressing these smells an improved model should take into account a new detail on DVMs, namely that for each kind of drinks a DVM has exactly two shelves. A new class diagram reflecting these changes is shown in Fig. 3. In the remainder of the paper, we name this diagram *cdiag* whereas the diagram in Fig. 2 is named *adiag* (for concrete and abstract diagram).

The improvements of the new diagram *cdiag* are basically two changes. Firstly, the attributes name and price were decoupled by (1) introducing a new class DrinkKind, (2) connecting it with class Drink using an association with multiplicities 1-1, and (3) moving attribute name from Drink to DrinkKind. Secondly, the new class Shelf became the owner of attribute avUnits (after renaming it to unitsOnShelf). Moreover, the new detail of the state space that each kind of drinks is stored on exactly two shelves is reflected by the two new associations sh1 and sh2.

This informal definition how *adiag* has been refined to *cdiag* is not enough if one wants to argue formally on the correctness of such a step, e.g. in respect of the expected behavior of both original and refined system. Thus, we present now what refinement should mean in our context and how one can define the refinement relationship between two given (potentially completely different) diagrams in a formal way. Unlike the types of refinement foreseen in the UML (see [24]), our refinement definition does not map syntactical constructs from the concrete diagram to the abstract diagram. Instead, the main idea is to give a mapping from states of the concrete system to states of the abstract system. This technique goes back to a proposal made by Hoare in [27]. Please note that, unlike the refinement calculus presented in [28] for Eiffel, we do not aim here to bridge the gap from a UML model of a system to its implementation written in an implementation language such as Java.

Definition 6 (State Mapping). *Let cd^a, cd^c be two class diagrams, which are called* abstract *and* concrete *class diagram, respectively. A refinement is a relationship between them and is defined by a mapping function* map *for states and a mapping function* argmap *for argument vectors of operations.*

A state mapping is a total function $map : State_{\Sigma_{cd^c}} \rightarrow State_{\Sigma_{cd^a}}$. *We will consider only such refinements for which a surjective mapping function* map *can be defined.*

The function argmap *is defined as a family of functions*
$argmap_{op} : \mathcal{I}(opsig^c(op)) \rightarrow \mathcal{I}(opsig^a(op))$ *where* $op \in \text{OPER}$.

It is often possible to define for the same class diagrams cd^a, cd^c more than one mapping function. For example, let cd^a be the class diagram consisting of only one class B and two attributes b1, b2 of type Integer, and cd^c be the class diagram consisting of class B and two attributes b3, b4 of type Integer. Then, two possibilities of how *map* could be defined are:

1. $\text{OBJ}_B^a := \text{OBJ}_B^c$,
   $\text{SLOT}_{b1}^a(o) := \text{SLOT}_{b3}^c(o)$, $\text{SLOT}_{b2}^a(o) := \text{SLOT}_{b4}^c(o)$ where $o \in \text{OBJ}_B^c = \text{OBJ}_B^a$
   $\text{LINK}^a := \text{LINK}^c = \emptyset$
2. $\text{OBJ}_B^a := \text{OBJ}_B^c$,
   $\text{SLOT}_{b1}^a(o) := \text{SLOT}_{b4}^c(o)$, $\text{SLOT}_{b2}^a(o) := \text{SLOT}_{b3}^c(o)$ where $o \in \text{OBJ}_B^c = \text{OBJ}_B^a$
   $\text{LINK}^a := \text{LINK}^c = \emptyset$

In its first version, *map* assigns the value for attribute b3, b4 to the values for the abstract attributes b1, b2. In the second version, it is vice versa, b3 is mapped to b2 and b4 is mapped to b1. For the sake of brevity, we often omit in the definition of *map* the assignment for those components in the abstract object diagram that remain the same as in the concrete object diagram. For example, the first refinement could also be given as $\text{SLOT}_{b1}^a(o) := \text{SLOT}_{b3}^c(o)$, $\text{SLOT}_{b2}^a(o) := \text{SLOT}_{b4}^c(o)$ since OBJ_B^a, LINK^a are the same as OBJ_B^c, LINK^c. An even shorter definition would be possible: $\text{SLOT}_{b1}^a := \text{SLOT}_{b3}^c$, $\text{SLOT}_{b2}^a := \text{SLOT}_{b4}^c$.

The second mapping function *argmap* maps the input parameters for the operation of the concrete layer to input parameters for the operation of the abstract layer. Suppose, class B had an operation inc(Integer) in both cd^a and cd^c. The mapping function $argmap_{op}$ could be defined as follows:

$$argmap_{op}((o, i)) = (o, i + 3)$$

The variable o represents the object on which op is invoked. An invocation with parameter i at the concrete layer is mapped to an invocation on the same object o with parameter $i + 3$ at the abstract layer. As for map, we will omit the definition for $argmap$ if it maps argument vectors of the concrete layer to identical vectors on the abstract layer.

The intended mapping for the DVM example is:

$$\text{SLOT}^a_{name}(opp_{dk}(o)) = \text{SLOT}^c_{name}(o)$$
$$\text{SLOT}^a_{avUnits}(opp_{sh1}(o)) = \text{SLOT}^c_{unitsOnShelf}(o) + \text{SLOT}^c_{unitsOnShelf}(opp_{sh2}(opp_{sh1}(o)))$$

4.3   Refinement of Contracts

It is obvious that the formal contract for sellDrink() in *adiag* cannot be simply copied to *cdiag*. The copied contract would be neither syntactically nor semantically correct. Contracts have to be adapted to the new class diagram, a new version for sellDrink() could look like the following:

context DVM::sellDrink(drinkName:**String**, credit:**Integer**)
pre:
    self.drink—>select(d|d.dk.name=drinkName **and**
                d.price<=credit **and**
                (d.sh1.unitsOnShelf>0 **or**
                d.sh2.unitsOnShelf>0))—>size() = 1

post:
    self.drink—>select(d|d.dk.name=drinkName)
    —>forAll(d1|
        d1.sh1.unitsOnShelf+d1.sh2.unitsOnShelf=
        d1.sh1.unitsOnShelf@pre+d1.sh2.unitsOnShelf@pre−1)

For the precondition, the attribute access d.name in the original contract was changed to d.dk.name in order to reflect moving of attribute **name** from Drink to DrinkKind. Furthermore, it must be tested now if at least one shelf has units available. More interesting changes have been made in the postcondition. The original postcondition, which strived to describe a deterministic state change, now became intentionally non-deterministic. Instead of decreasing attribute avUnits, an implementation of sellDrink() could change attribute unitsOnShelf either for the first or the second shelf (sh1, sh2). This is achieved by the *under-specified* postcondition saying that the sum of unitsOnShelf for both shelves is decreased by one.

Note that the new contract leaves the decision open *which one* of the shelves decreases its number of units. In other words, an implementation of sellDrink() that first makes the first shelf empty before selling drinks from the second shelf should be possible as well as an implementation that sells units from the second shelf before the ones from the first shelf or an implementation that alternates between both shelves. Of course, an implementation has to realize a concrete, fixed algorithm but the decision which algorithm to take is deferred here to a later phase of the software development project.

In the following, we want to answer the question whether the new version of the OCL contract is correct in respect to the contract given for `sellDrink` in *adiag*. A very basic criterion for correctness of the refined system is that every state transition which the concrete system is allowed to make has its 'counterpart' in the abstract system. Otherwise stated, whenever one can observe a behavior on the concrete system, 'the corresponding behavior' on the abstract system is allowed as well. The, somehow, imprecise terms 'counterpart' and 'corresponding behavior' are made clear in the following formal definition as a projection of behavior from the concrete layer to the abstract layer under the state mapping, which is defined when the underlying class diagram is refined.

Definition 7 (Correct Contract Refinement). *Let class diagrams cd^a, cd^c and refinement functions map, argmap be given. Furthermore, let $op()$ be an operation declared in both diagrams, and $(pre^a, post^a)$, $(pre^c, post^c)$ be its contracts. The semantics of the contracts are the LTSs $sem_{op}^a = (State_{\Sigma_{cd^a}}, \rho^a)$, $sem_{op}^c = (State_{\Sigma_{cd^c}}, \rho^c)$.*

The contract $(pre^c, post^c)$ for $op()$ is called to be a correct refinement *of the abstract contract $(pre^a, post^a)$ if the following holds:*

For all argument bindings argval for $op()$ at the concrete layer, for all $s1, s2 \in State_{\Sigma_{cd^c}}$: if $(s1, argval, s2) \in \rho^c$ then $(map(s1), argmap_{op}(argval), map(s2)) \in \rho^a$

After giving a formal correctness criterion for the refinement of contracts, it is, of course, interesting to discuss whether or not the refined contract for `sellDrink()` shown above is correct according to this criterion. We do not answer this question immediately but will describe in the next subsection a technique to ensure the correctness of simple refinements. The same technique is powerful enough also to argue on the correctness of more complicated refinements.

4.4 Refactorings as Simple Refinements

The refinement from *adiag* to *cdiag* was defined so far as a monolithic step. One could also think to achieve the same by a concatenation of much smaller refinements: 1) create class `DrinkKind` and connect it to `Drink` with 1-1 association 2) move attribute `name` from `Drink` to `DrinkKind` 3) create class `Shelf` and connect it to `Drink` with 1-1 association 4) move attribute `avUnits` from `Drink` to `Shelf` 5) rename attribute `avUnits` as `unitsOnShelf` 6) add a second 1-1 association between `Drink` and `Shelf`.

From these six steps, the first five steps do not change (up to isomorphism) the state space of the system but just restructure the model. Such steps, called *refactorings*, are small improvements that lead to better design since they directly address poor structures of the model (smells). A smell can be the duplication of attributes or operations, a heavy class having too many responsibilities, too many dependencies between classes, etc. Typical changes done by refactorings include moving attributes and operations up and down in the inheritance hierarchy of the classes, moving attributes and operations to newly created classes, giving attributes, operations, classes a new name, etc. The main characteristic of these changes is that they do not make the system description closer to the implementation level but keep it at the same level of abstraction.

In recent years, much research has been devoted to refactoring (see [29] for an overview). Most of these works, however, have concentrated on the refactoring of implementation code. Fowler gives in [30] a catalog of refactorings for Java programs. A typical refactoring rule describes in a first step changes on the Java declarations, e.g. moving a field to a new class to make the original class less heavy, and in a second step, how the remaining Java program must be updated in order to become consistent with the changed declaration, e.g. every access to the original field must be forwarded to the new class.

In [31], we have formalized a catalog of basic refactorings for UML class diagrams together with the necessary changes on attached OCL constraints. The above given correctness criterion offers now the possibility to argue on the semantical correctness of the refactorings. To do this, we have to assume that every refactoring is associated with a unique mapping function. This mapping function is not part of refactoring catalogs yet, but is in most cases obvious.

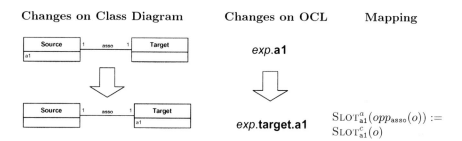

Fig. 4. Refactoring MoveAttribute

As an example we formalize in Fig. 4 the refactoring *MoveAttribute*, which moves in a first step the attribute from the source class to a target class if both classes are connected by an 1-1 association. Actually, there are even more side conditions that must hold, e.g. that the target class has not already an attribute with the same name as the moved attribute. These side conditions are dropped here for the sake of brevity, the interested reader is referred to the formalized version of this rule given in [31]. In a second step, all OCL constraints attached to the class model must be updated by substituting each attribute access of form $exp.\mathtt{a1}$ with the new expression $exp.\mathtt{target.a1}$. The expression $exp.\mathtt{target}$ is a navigation from source to target class. Note that updating the attached OCL constraints can be done automatically.

We finish this section with a theorem on the correctness of the defined refactoring.

Theorem 1 (Correctness of MoveAttribute). *The refactoring Move-Attribute refines contracts correctly.*

Proof. Let cd^a, cd^c be the original and refactored diagram, $op()$ an operation, and $(pre^a, post^a)$, $(pre^c, post^c)$ the original and the refactored contract for $op()$. The two contracts induce the two LTSs $sem^a_{op} = (State^a_\Sigma, \rho^a)$ and $sem^c_{op} = (State^c_\Sigma, \rho^c)$. According to the correctness criterion we have to show that for every tuple $(s1, argval, s2) \in \rho^c$, there is a tuple $(map(s1), argmap(argval), map(s2)) \in \rho^a$.

The condition $(s1, argval, s2) \in \rho^c$ means $(s1, argval) \models_{\Sigma_{cd^c}} pre^c$ and $(s1, argval, s2) \models_{\Sigma_{cd^c}} post^c$. The constraints pre^c, $post^c$ are by construction only different from pre^a, $post^a$ at subexpressions of form $exp.\texttt{target.a1}$. According to the semantics of OCL, this expression is evaluated in s to the same value as $exp.\texttt{a1}$ in $map(s)$. Thus, we have $(s1, argval) \models_{\Sigma_{cd^c}} pre^c$ if and only if $(map(s1), map(argval)) \models_{\Sigma_{cd^a}} pre^a$ and, furthermore, $(s1, argval, s2) \models_{\Sigma_{cd^c}} post^c$ if and only if $(map(s1), argmap(argval), map(s2)) \models_{\Sigma_{cd^a}} post^a$.   □

5   Constructive Specifications

In the preceding section, we have discussed the problems related with refinement of class diagrams and how contracts have to be updated accordingly. We have seen, that a refinement sometimes requires to rewrite a deterministic contract by a non-deterministic one.

For the DVM example we tried to capture the intended behavior of operation `sellDrink()` with a restrictive constraint in OCL. Due to the immanent frame problem of restrictive languages, it is practically impossible to formalize deterministic contracts, which, however, are often needed in the first phases of a software development project.

In this section, we discuss how more appropriate contracts for `sellDrink()` can be given using a constructive specification language. The specification language of our choice is QVT [32], a special form of graph transformations.

5.1   Graph Transformations

Graph transformations (see [33] for an overview) were originally developed to manage the manipulation of graphs. Since system states are easily representable as graphs, they can also be used as a tool to describe state changes, i.e. the intended behavior of operations.

A graph is manipulated by applying a graph transformation rule on it. Every graph transformation rule consists of a Left Hand Side (LHS) pattern and a Right Hand Side (RHS) pattern. Both patterns consist of labeled nodes and links, which might occur in both patterns. The rule is applied by, firstly, searching subgraphs in the given graph that match with LHS and, secondly, by rewriting the matching subgraphs with new subgraphs derived from RHS. If a node/link in the given graph matches with a node/link that occurs, according to its label, only in LHS then this node/link is removed from the given graph. If a node/link occurs only in RHS then a corresponding element is created. Nodes can also have slots for attribute values. These values are updated according to the allowed values of variables occurring in the rule. Finally, a rule has a name (reflecting the operation it specifies) and parameters (reflecting the signature of the operation).

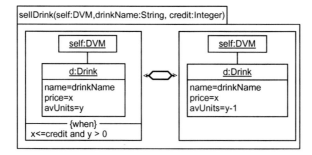

Fig. 5. Constructive contract for `sellDrink()` on abstract layer

As an example, we consider the specification of `sellDrink()` as shown in Fig. 5. This rule has to be read – as an operation contract – as follows: Whenever in a pre-state an object d of class `Drink` is linked with the object `self` on which `sellDrink()` was invoked and the value of its attribute `name` matches with parameter `drinkName` and the value for attribute `price` is less than or equal to parameter `credit` and the value of attribute `avUnits` is greater than 0, then the post-state is derived from the pre-state by decreasing the value of attribute `avUnits` by 1.

Note that the post-state is *constructed* from the pre-state. This is despite the fact that the specification is, unlike in B or ASM, not given in form of a pseudo-program but by a pair of matching patterns. The given contract is truly deterministic since it completely prescribes the update from the pre- to the post-state. The semantics of the graph transformation rules stipulates that all parts of the pre-state that do not match with LHS remain unchanged.

5.2   Graph Transformations for Non-deterministic Specifications

One common problem of constructive languages is the tendency to allow only the formulation of deterministic contracts (due to the construction of a unique post-state). Actually, many graph transformation systems, e.g. AGG [34], allow only to describe deterministic rules because they insist on having an executable specification. The formalism of our choice, QVT, is an exception and allows to use variables that only occur in RHS. Consequently, these variables are not bound after the first step of the rule application (the matching of a subgraph with LHS). The value for the variables can freely be chosen in the second rule application step, when the matching subgraph is rewritten with a new graph derived from RHS. The variable values, however, can be restricted by an OCL constraint given in the when-clause of the rule.

The non-deterministic contract for sellDrink on the concrete layer is shown in Fig. 6. There are two new variables y1' and y2' in RHS whose values can be chosen non-deterministically as long as the restrictions imposed by the OCL constraint in the when-clause are obeyed.

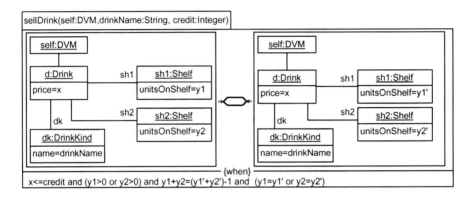

Fig. 6. Constructive, non-deterministic contract for sellDrink on concrete layer

The integration of a when-clause into transformation rules can be seen as an attempt to mix constructive with restrictive specification style. This idea is actually not new, also the constructive language B provides with ANY-WHERE and the language ASM with its non-deterministic choices analogous constructs. These non-deterministic constructs in turn have again inspired the language designers of restrictive languages to include them. For instance offers OCL a construct any() that should mimic the ANY-WHERE construct of B. The integration of any() in OCL has caused, however, a lot of contradictions in the language semantics as analyzed in [35]. This is another striking example for a mis-conception, if the fundamental differences between restrictive and constructive specifications languages are not sufficiently understood.

6   Conclusions

In this paper, we have formalized relations between models of the same software system situated at different levels of abstraction. We assume the system to be described by UML class diagrams with OCL constraints attached, but our results can easily be applied also to other specification formalisms.

Moreover, we have given a classification of formal contract definition languages in respect to the underlying specification technique they offer. For graph transformations, which can be seen as a constructive specification language, we propose an approach to express non-determinism by enriching them with restrictive specification elements.

Another contribution of this paper is the investigation how changes made on structural part of a model can influence contracts for operations. In order to cope with this problem, we have defined criteria for the correctness of contract refinements. We were able to prove for a simple kind of standard refinement, a well-known refactoring rule, that its application preserves the semantical correctness of contracts.

Acknowledgements

This work was supported by HASLER-Foundation, project DICS-1850 and by Swiss National Science Foundation, grant 200020-101596.

References

1. Phillippe Kruchten. *The Rational Unified Process*. Object Technology Series. Addison-Wesley, 1999.
2. Desmond D'Souza and Alan Wills. *Objects, Components and Frameworks With UML: The Catalysis Approach*. Object Technology Series. Addison-Wesley, 1998.
3. Derek Coleman, Patrick Arnold, Stephanie Bodoff, Chris Dollin, Helena Gilchrist, Fiona Hayes, and Paul Jeremaes. *Object-Oriented Development: The Fusion Method*. Prentice Hall, 1994.
4. Bertrand Meyer. Applying "design by contract". *IEEE Computer*, 25(10):40–51, October 1992.
5. Bertrand Meyer. *Object-Oriented Software Construction*. Prentice-Hall, Englewood Cliffs, second edition, 1997.
6. Bertrand Meyer. Dependable software. In Jürg Kohlas, Bertrand Meyer, and André Schiper, editors, *Dependable Systems: Software, Computing, Networks*, volume 4028 of *LNCS*. Springer, 2006. (this volume).
7. Clemens Szyperski. *Component Software – Beyond Object-Oriented Programming*. Addison-Wesley, 1997.
8. Stuart Kent. Model driven engineering. In Michael J. Butler, Luigia Petre, and Kaisa Sere, editors, *Proceedings of Third International Conference on Integrated Formal Methods (IFM 2002)*, volume 2335 of *LNCS*, pages 286–298. Springer, 2002.
9. Stephen J. Mellor, Kendall Scott, Axel Uhl, and Dirk Weise. *MDA Distilled*. Addison-Wesley, 2004.
10. Bertrand Meyer. *Eiffel – The Language*. Prentice-Hall, Englewood Cliffs, 1992.
11. OMG. UML 2.0 OCL Specification – OMG Final Adopted Specification. OMG Document ptc/03-10-14, Oct 2003.
12. Gary T. Leavens, Albert L. Baker, and Clyde Ruby. Preliminary design of JML: A behavioral interface specification language for java. Technical Report TR 98-06-rev28, Department of Computer Science, Iowa State University, 2005. Last revision July 2005, available from www.jmlspecs.org.
13. J. M. Spivey. *The Z Notation: A Reference Manual*. Prentice-Hall, 1992.
14. Egon Börger and Robert Stärk. *Abstract State Machiness*. Springer, 2003.
15. Jean-Raymond Abrial. *The B Book: Assigning Programs to Meanings*. Cambridge University Press, August 1996.
16. OMG. UML 1.5 Specification. OMG Document formal/03-03-01, March 2003.

17. K. R. Apt. Ten years of Hoare logic: A survey – part I. *ACM Transactions on Programming Languages and Systems*, 1981.
18. David Harel, Dexter Kozen, and Jerzy Tiuryn. *Dynamic Logic*. Foundations of Computing. MIT Press, October 2000.
19. Wolfgang Ahrendt, Thomas Baar, Bernhard Beckert, Richard Bubel, Martin Giese, Reiner Hähnle, Wolfram Menzel, Wojciech Mostowski, Andreas Roth, Steffen Schlager, and Peter H. Schmitt. The KeY tool. *Software and System Modeling*, 4(1):32–54, 2005.
20. J. McCarthy and P. J. Hayes. Some philosophical problems from the standpoint of artificial intelligence. *Machine Intelligence*, pages 463–502, 1969.
21. A. Borgida, J. Mylopolous, and R. Reiter. ...And Nothing Else Changes: The Frame Problem in Procedure Specifications. In *Proceedings of ICSE-15*, pages 303–314. IEEE Computer Society Press, 1993.
22. Thomas Baar. OCL and graph transformations – a symbiotic alliance to alleviate the frame problem. In Jean-Michel Bruel, editor, *Satellite Events at the MoDELS 2005 Conference: MoDELS 2005 International Workshops OCLWS, MoDeVA, MARTES, AOM, MTiP, WiSME, MODAUI, NfC, MDD, WUsCAM, Montego Bay, Jamaica, October 2-7, 2005, Revised Selected Papers*, volume 3844 of *LNCS*, pages 20–31. Springer, 2006.
23. Grady Booch, James Rumbaugh, and Ivar Jacobson. *The Unified Modeling Language User Guide*. Object Technology Series. Addison-Wesley, second edition, 2005.
24. James Rumbaugh, Ivar Jacobson, and Grady Booch. *The Unified Modeling Language Reference Manual*. Object Technology Series. Addison-Wesley, second edition, 2005.
25. Jos Warmer and Anneke Kleppe. *The Object Constraint Language: Precise Modeling with UML*. Addison-Wesley, 1998.
26. Alfred Strohmeier, Thomas Baar, and Shane Sendall. Applying Fondue to specify a drink vending machine. *Electronic Notes in Theoretical Computer Science, Proceedings of OCL 2.0 Workshop at UML'03*, 102:155–173, 2004.
27. C. A. R. Hoare. Proof of correctness of data representation. In Friedrich L. Bauer and Klaus Samelson, editors, *Language Hierarchies and Interfaces*, volume 46 of *LNCS*, pages 183–193. Springer, 1975.
28. Richard F. Paige and Jonathan S. Ostroff. ERC – an object-oriented refinement calculus for Eiffel. *Formal Aspects of Computing*, 16:51–79, April 2004.
29. Tom Mens and Tom Tourwé. A survey of software refactoring. *IEEE Trans. Software Eng.*, 30(2):126–139, 2004.
30. Martin Fowler. *Refactoring: Improving the Design of Existing Programs*. Addison-Wesley, 1999.
31. Slaviša Marković and Thomas Baar. Refactoring OCL annotated UML class diagrams. In Lionel Briand and Clay Williams, editors, *Proc. ACM/IEEE 8th International Conference on Model Driven Engineering Languages and Systems (MoDELS)*, volume 3713 of *LNCS*, pages 280–294. Springer, 2005.
32. OMG. Revised submission for MOF 2.0, Query/Views/Transformations, version 1.8. OMG Document ad/04-10-11, Dec 2004.
33. Grzegorz Rozenberg, editor. *Handbook of Graph Grammars and Computing by Graph Transformations, Volume 1: Foundations*. World Scientific, 1997.
34. AGG team. AGG homepage. http://tfs.cs.tu-berlin.de/agg, 2005.
35. Thomas Baar. Non-deterministic constructs in OCL – what does any() mean. In Andreas Prinz, Rick Reed, and Jeanne Reed, editors, *Proc. 12th SDL Forum, Grimstad, Norway, June 2005*, volume 3530 of *LNCS*, pages 32–46. Springer, 2005.

Formal Test Generation from UML Models[*]

Didier Buchs, Luis Pedro, and Levi Lúcio

Software Modeling and Verification laboratory
University of Geneva, Switzerland
didier.buchs, luis.pedro, levi.lucio@cui.unige.ch
http://smv.unige.ch

Abstract. In this paper we will explain our approach for generating test cases for a UML system model. Despite the fact that UML authors claim that UML semantics are precise enough to define non-ambiguous models, we find that the overlap of the different views makes it difficult to explore and make deductions on the state space of the modeled system in order to generate test cases. Our approach is thus based on a subset of UML (inspired from the Fondue approach) for which we have defined clear transformation semantics. We provide these semantics by delineating transformation rules using the MDA (Model Driven Architecture) architecture. We transform UML models into CO-OPN (Concurrent Object Oriented Petri Nets) ones, CO-OPN being a formal specification language defined in our Laboratory.

We have also defined a language for expressing test intentions for CO-OPN models. This language allows selecting interesting executions (tests) cases) of a model by providing constraints over all possible traces of that model. By exploring the model's semantics with the tools we have built for our CO-OPN language we are able to generate test cases based on those test intentions. We are also able to partially eliminate redundancy in the produced test cases by finding equivalence classes in the model operation's inputs.

1 Introduction

As the complexity and size of a system increases, modeling techniques that address abstraction and decomposition play a very important role. At the same time different view points of the system are envisaged in order to fully describe it by means of a model. This raises the problem of relating and keeping consistent the different models that represent, sometimes orthogonally, several perspectives of the system. At the same time, the need to isolate errors in the implementation motivates our work that aims to automatically generating test sets from a well defined model. Figure 1 shows the general picture of our approach that will be explained in detail during this article.

---

[*] This project was partially funded by the DICS project of the Hasler foundation, with number 1850.

J. Kohlas, B. Meyer, and A. Schiper (Eds.): Dependable Systems, LNCS 4028, pp. 145–171, 2006.

Our development approach encompasses three steps: *Analysis – Prototyping – Implementation*. For the analysis phase we use the UML Fondue[1] development method that allows specifying a system using different view points by means of different diagrams - at the same time with Fondue we can produce a complete description of the system by providing a logical relation between each individual diagram.

The product of the implementation phase is a system that will be used to execute the tests produced by the test case generation framework. In our Model-based testing approach, there is an implementation relation between the model (developed during the *Analysis* phase) and the System Under Test (SUT) based on the idea that the observational behavior of both model and implementation are compatible.

Taking into account that the objective of our current work is to automatically generate a set of tests that will afterwards be applied to the SUT, we need to transform the system specification into the language that we use for the purpose of test case generation - CO-OPN [2] (Concurrent Object Oriented Petri Nets).

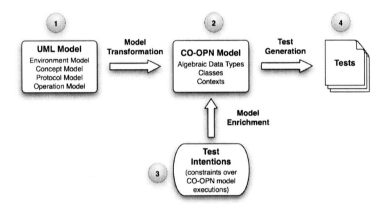

Fig. 1. The process of test generation from UML

In order to produce test sets from the system's model, we developed a language (*TestSel*) that allows expressing test intentions for the system specification. This language provides the syntax and semantics that permits narrowing the initial (usually infinite) number of tests present in a system specification.

2   From UML to CO-OPN

Our approach aims at easily generating tests from a well known and widely used modeling language. One of the key points to achieve this is being able to transform UML Fondue models into models of a specification language that provides an unambiguous representation of the system. In this section we will focus on the activities that allow achieving point *2* from point *1* in Fig. 1, i.e. UML model creation and transformation into CO-OPN. Before we continue detailing how this process is accomplished, we will briefly introduce: Fondue [1] (UML Dialect) - the source language; and CO-OPN [3] the target language.

UML Fndue provides two main artifacts: *Concept* and *Behavior* Models. The first one is represented as *UML class diagrams* and defines the static structure of the system. The *Behavior Model* defines the input and output communication of the system, and is divided in three models: *Environment*, *Protocol* and *Operation* - represented respectively by *UML collaboration diagrams*, *UML state charts* and *OCL operations*.

CO-OPN is a formal specification language built to allow the expression of models of complex concurrent systems. Its semantics is formally defined in [4], making it a precise tool not only for modeling, but, thanks to its operational semantics, also for prototyping and test generation. It groups a set of object-based concepts such as the notion of class (and object), concurrency, sub-typing and inheritance that we use to define the system specification coherently regarding notions used by other standard modeling approaches. An additional coordination layer provides the designer with an abstract way of representing interaction between modeling entities and an abstract mapping to distributed computations.

The CO-OPN object oriented modeling language is based on Algebraic Data Types (ADT) and Petri Nets. It's syntax and semantics allow using heterogeneous Object Oriented (OO) concepts for system specification. The specifications are collections of *ADT*s, *classes* and *context* - the CO-OPN modules. Detailed information about CO-OPN language can be found in [2].

2.1 The Model by Example

This section will explain, by means of an example, how we use UML Fondue in order to model our system. We start presenting the case study by stating the problem description and we continue defining the model using the Fondue methodology. The example is not intended to be a complete and exhaustive one, but rather an illustration of the full process for our approach.

The proposed system consists of a mobile phone with a SIM card that can be authenticated with a PIN number. The phone has three different functioning states: phoneOff - when the phone is not operating; phoneStandBy - when the mobile phone is waiting for the user to insert a PIN number; phoneOn - corresponding to the state where the phone is ready to perform calls.

The behavior of the system is such that the user is asked for a PIN number in order to be able to turn the phone to the phoneOn state that allows performing calls. The inserted PIN (stored in the SIM card) is checked and there can be at most three consecutive wrong attempts. If this number is reached the card's state changes from unlockedPin to lockedPin.

Environment Model: This model precises the incoming and outgoing messages of the system. In Fig. 2 it is possible to observe the incoming messages:

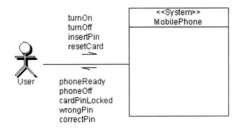

Fig. 2. Fondue Environment Model for the Mobile Phone System

turnOn, turnOff, insertPin and resetCard. The last one is used for demonstration purposes in case the SIM card becomes locked after the maximum number of unsuccessful insertPin operations is reached. The system is able to send the user the following messages with self-descripting meanings: phoneReady; phoneOff; cardPinLocked; wrongPin; and correctPin.

Concept Model: The static structure of the system is accomplished by the realization of the *Concept Model*. This structure is defined as an UML class diagram and it is presented in Fig. 3 for our example system.

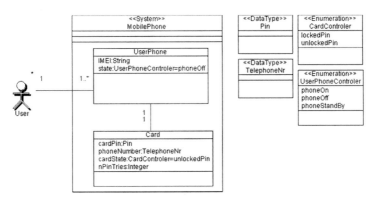

Fig. 3. Fondue Concept Model for the Mobile Phone System

We consider the system composed by two classes related as presented in the figure. The diagram shows a system in which one user can have one or more mobile phones (represented by the association User ⟶ UserPhone). The UserPhone is identified by its IMEI[1] and by its state (state attribute in UserPhone class) and provides an association of cardinality 1..1 with class Card. The SIM card

---

[1] International Mobile Equipment Identity Number (IMEI) is an unique electronic serial number of the Global System for Mobile Communication (GSM) mobile phone handsets.

(class Card in the figure) is identified by phoneNumber, cardPin, cardState and nPinTries representing respectively: the phone number associated to the card; its valid Pin; the card's state; the number of previous Pin insertions with a wrong value. Both state and cardState attributes are defined by the CardControler and UserPhoneControler enumerators. These enumerators provide the allowed states of the two transition systems that will be further specified by the two *Protocol Diagrams*.

Protocol Model: With Fondue's *Protocol Model* it is possible to specify the dynamic behavior of the system over logical time. This model is expressed by means of UML state charts which capture the way the system responds to requests depending on its current state.

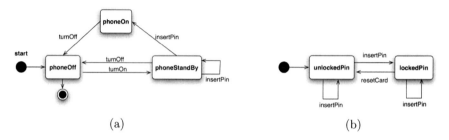

(a)   (b)

Fig. 4. Fondue Protocol Models - (a): UserPhoneControler state machine; (b): CardControler state machine

As can be seen in Fig. 4, some of the actions (in the same system state) can lead to more than one system state - this presents a typical example of unwanted non-determinism in the system's specification. The non-determinism can be suppressed in the *Operation Schemas* by means of OCL constraints expressed using pre and post-conditions.

Operation Schemas: Describe the services offered by the system. For simplicity, in this section we are going to present only one of the Operation Schemas: the operation insertPin(pin:Pin) that is presented in Fig. 5.

This operation describes the behavior that the system should have when the message insertPin is sent. Albeit the sequence of allowed transitions has already been defined in the *Protocol Model*, this definition identifies possible points of non-determinism in system's state **phoneReady** and provides the necessary logic in order to solve them.

2.2   Transformation Process

In order to perform the transformation from Fondue to CO-OPN we need to clearly define the methodology both in terms of technology used and in what concerns the formal definitions: Regarding the former one, our approach proposes that we use the MDA [5] technology as base framework. This implies using the

```
Operation: MobilePhone:insertPin(pin:Pin)
Description: This operation describes how the system behaves during the Pin insertion
process.
Messages: User::{phoneReady; wrongPin; correctPin; cardPinLocked}
New: c: Card;
Alias: u:UserPhone IS sender.UserPhone
Pre: u.state::phoneStandBy and
     not u.state::phoneOn
Post: if c.cardState::lockedPin then
          sender^cardPinLocked
      elseif c.cardPin <> pin
          c.nPinTries = c.nPinTries@pre + 1 and
          sender^wrongPin
          if c.nPinTries = 3 then
             c.CardStatus::lockedPin and
             c.nPinTries = 0
          end
      else
          c.nPinTries = 0 and
          u.state::phoneOn and
          c.cardState::unLockedPin and
          sender^correctPin and
          sender^phoneReady
      end
```

Fig. 5. Fondue Operation Schema for operation insertPin(pin:Pin) for the Mobile Phone System

metamodel of both languages and defining the transformation based on them; The *metamodel* of a language is a description of all the concepts that can be used in that language - it is also known as its *abstract syntax*. A *metamodel* is composed of *metaclasses* and their *relationships* - in conjunction they compose the complete *metamodel* of the language. Thus, every element in an ordinary language is an instance of the respective *metaclass*. *Metamodels* are models and this implies that we can manipulate them - they simply reside in another level of abstraction; The second aspect implies a clear and formal definition of transformation rules and mapping. This definition must be formally expressed and mapped into a transformation language (see for example [6] or [7]). The transformation language is the artifact that will allow executing the transformation and will act as the bridge between the technology used and the transformation definition. Transformations are composed of a series of rules which are applied to the source Fondue model. Each rule attempts to find some pattern in the source model and, if successful, generate some corresponding pattern in a target CO-OPN model. One can see the transformation rule as consisting of two parts of a graph: a left-hand side (LHS); and a right-hand side (RHS).

These two aspects together can precisely define and execute a transformation from a *Language A* to a *Language B* - In particular we are interested in the transformation from UML Fondue to CO-OPN that we are going to detail in the remaining parts of this section.

The sequence of the transformation is presented in Fig. 6 using a Petri Net. The places with a token represent the set of different types of Fondue Diagrams. When firing transitions $T1$ to $T4$ in the figure, the transformation will evolve transforming, step by step, each one of the Fondue diagrams. Each transition represents the process of transforming one diagram and the place after it contains the result of that process together with the result of the previous transformation.

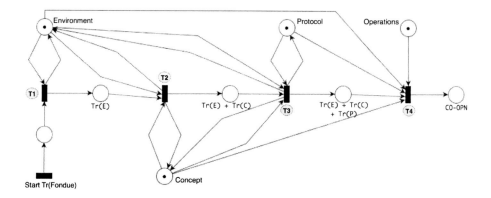

Fig. 6. UML Fondue to CO-OPN transformation sequence

Albeit each transition is meant to represent the transformation of a specific type of Fondue diagram, with the exception of $T1$ all the others need information from other diagram(s) besides the one that the transition concerns. More specifically:

- Transition $T2$ (transformation of the *Concept Model*) includes two distinct tasks: transformation of the *Concept Model* itself: and a second iteration in the *Environment Model* transformation to complement the transformation of the input messages with their parameters. The *Environment Model* provides the input messages to the system but no information is specified in what concerns the possible parameters for each message.
- Transition $T3$ (*Protocol Model's* transformation) needs the availabilty of the *Environment Model* information so that it can check if the specified system transitions correspond to messages previously defined in the *Environment Model*. At the same time, information regarding the *Concept Model* is also required in order to inspect if the names of the *Protocol Models* have any class/enumerator with the same name in the *Concept Model* and if the states defined in the *Protocol Diagram* correspond to the ones provided by the *Concept Model*.
- Transition $T4$ (*Operation Schema* transformation process) requires information from all the other Fondue models: from the *Environment Model* in order to understand if the name of the Operation is already defined; from the *Concept Model* to analyze if the invoked methods (and the classes that correspond to the type of the object) have been defined; from the *Protocol Model* to control if the states defined in the pre and post-conditions have been defined.

2.3   Transformation Description

The transformation process from Fondue to CO-OPN consists in the composition of the transformation of each one of the Fondue models. A transformation from Fondue to CO-OPN is a function:

$$\forall F \in Fondue, \exists C \in COOPN : T_r(F) = C \tag{1}$$

At the same time, the transformation $T_r(F)$ is a composition of the transformation of each one of the Fondue models:

$$\forall F =< e, c, p, o >\in Fondue, e \in E, c \in C, p \in P, o \in O :$$
$$T_r(F) = T_r^{env}(e) + T_r^{con}(c) + T_r^{prot}(p) + T_r^{op}(o) \quad (2)$$

with, E the set of *Fondue Environment* diagrams, C the set of *Fondue Concept* diagrams, P the set of *Fondue Protocol* diagrams and O the set of *Fondue Operation Schemas*. The '+' operator is the disjoint union.

Having generically defined the transformation from Fondue to CO-OPN, in the following lines we will particularize how the transformation from each type of Fondue diagram is done.

Environment Diagram: This transformation constitutes the first iteration in order to achieve the complete transformation from Fondue to CO-OPN. The *Environment Diagram* is composed of one System, messages going to the system and messages sent by the system to the outside - as presented in Fig. 2. Being S, M_i, M_o the System, the set of input messages and the set output messages respectively we can formalize the transformation of a Fondue Environment diagram as:

$$\forall s \in S, m_i \in M_i, m_o \in M_o :$$
$$T_r^{env}(E) = T_r^{env}(s) + T_r^{env}(m_i) + T_r^{env}(m_o) \quad (3)$$

Taking into account that one system is transformed in a CO-OPN Context, the input messages into methods of the Context and the output messages into gates of the CO-OPN Context, and being Γ the set of CO-OPN Contexts, M the set of CO-OPN Methods and G the set of CO-OPN gates:

$$\forall s \in S, m_i \in M_i, m_o \in M_o :$$
$$T_r^{env}(E) = Id(co) + Id(m) + Id(g) \quad (4)$$

where Id is the isomorphic transformation between Fondue and CO-OPN.

Concept Model: The transformation of the *Concept Model* is basically the transformation of a reduced UML class model.

Generically, the transformation of the *Concept Model* is performed as follows:

- the class name in the *Concept Model* is transformed into the name of a class in CO-OPN;
- the attributes are transformed in Places[2] in the CO-OPN class;
- the class associations are CO-OPN classes with source and target values;
- **get** and **set** methods must be created in order to access and modify each one of the class attributes;

---

[2] A Place in a CO-OPN class is like a place in a Petri Net with the difference that, in CO-OPN, a Place is of a certain type provided by the associated ADT.

− both the user defined and primitive data types are transformed in CO-OPN
ADTs.

Taking this into account, for class Card in the *Concept Model* from Fig. 3, the
result of the transformation of a CO-OPN class will be as presented in Fig. 7.

```
Class Card;
Interface
 Type
     card;
...
Body
 Use
     Naturals;
     CardControler;
     TelephoneNr;
     Pin;
 Places
     cardPin _ : pin;
     nPinTries _ : natural;
     cardState _ : cardControler;
     phoneNumber _ : telephoneNr;
 Initial
     cardState unlockedPin;
 ...
 ...
End Card;
```

Fig. 7. Class Card transformed from Fondue to CO-OPN

Protocol Model: This transformation is similar to transformations from UML
state charts to Petri Nets (like in [8]). Fig. 8 present the equivalent Petri Net in
the CO-OPN MobilePhoneController class to the *Protocol Model* in 4(b).

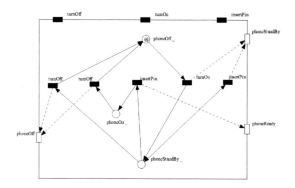

Fig. 8. Protocol Model UserPhoneController transformed from Fondue to CO-OPN

Operation Schemas: The transformation in what concerns the *Operation
Schemas* can be defined as:

$$\forall op \in M_i, msg \in M_o, pre \in PRE, post \in POST, \exists o \in O :$$
$$T_r(o) = < T_r(op), T_r(msg), T_r(pre)..T_r(post) > \tag{5}$$

taking into account that: O is the set of Fondue Operation Schemas; PRE set of pre-conditions; $POST$ the set of post-conditions;

The pre and post-conditions are based on control operators ($if...then...else...$), affectation based on OCL expressions.

For transformation, all expressions of type

$$\{if \quad lexpr \quad then \quad expr \quad else \quad expr | logicalvar \quad := \quad oclexpr | expr, expr\} \quad (6)$$

will be transformed into only positive conditional axioms. For example, for an OCL expression like the one that follows:

```
if cond1 then
  if cond2 then do1 else do2
else
  do3
```

The transformation will result into three positive conditional axioms:

```
if cond1 and cond2 then do1; if cond1 and not(cond2) then do2; if
not(cond1) then do3;
```

or, more specifically in CO-OPN syntax:

```
(cond1) = true & (cond2) = true => op With do1 (cond1) = true &
(cond2) = false => op With  do2 (cond1) = false => op With do3
```

In general, the transformation will produce several components in CO-OPN of format: $TrOCL(lexpr) = < logical\ expr, synchronisation >$.

We should note that, for logical expressions that are simple boolean conditions without access to elements in Class model, we will have $synchronization = \varnothing$. Moreover, the ".." operator is used to gather the result of each sub expressions. It means conjunction of logical expressions and sequence of synchronizations. The result will be one CO-OPN axiom for each flatenned axiom.

Consider the following piece of the *Operation Schema* in Fig. 5:

```
elseif c.cardPin <> pin
  c.nPinTries = c.nPinTries@pre + 1 and
  sender^wrongPin
  if c.nPinTries = 3 then
    c.CardStatus::lockedPin and
    c.nPinTries = 0
end
```

The CO-OPN resulting axioms for class Card will be of form:

```
(c.getcardPin p = pin)=false
  =>insertPin pin With wrongPin // c.getnPinTries n .. c.setnPinTries n+1

(c.getcardPin p = pin)=false and (c.getnPinTries 3 = true)
  =>insertPin pin With c.setcardStatus lockedPin // c.setnPinTries 0
```

where the operator // represents the execution in parallel of the different expressions.

2.4   Transformation Execution

The transformation execution is the "map" from the transformation formalization into one (or several) transformation languages. Since not all of the transformation languages provide the same functionalities we decided to adopt several of them. Thus, we will use them in order to "enrich" each other and to be able to provide an execution to our transformation. In Fig. 9 it is possible to see the general process of the transformation execution. The grey parts of the Fig. represent what was previously mentioned: more than one approach of transformation can be adopted. In this case we present an architecture using a transformation language that is based on a transformation model (e.g. the Model Transformation Language [7] (MTL)) and another based on directly specifying transformation rules (e.g. Mod-Transf - a XML and ruled based transformation language [9]).

In general, the mechanism of executing the transformation follows the standard process defined by the Object Management Group (OMG). This means defining and using the Meta Model of each one of the languages as an instance of the Meta Object Facility[10] (MOF). The transformation rules (or transformation model that is also an instance of MOF) can be written profiting from the fact that the source (Fondue in our approach) and the target (CO-OPN) languages' abstract syntaxes are defined using the exact same methodology. As for the technology used, standards for (meta)model exploration and creation have been defined meaning that we can use them in order to coherently execute the transformation.

The basic idea of this particular transformation is to give part of the source language semantics using the transformation rules applied to the abstract syntax, being the other part provided directly and automatically by the fact that the transformation leads to a CO-OPN model (like described in [11]). This leads to a model in the CO-OPN formal specification language allowing state space exploration and thus automatic test generation as explained in the next sections.

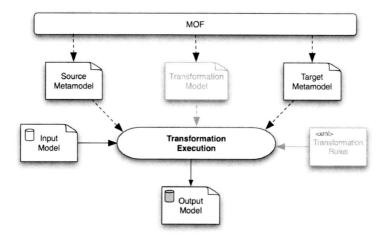

Fig. 9. General transformation execution

2.5   Tools

The software utilities we have under development in our laboratory that support the work described previously include: model transformation tools that handle MOF models exploration; generic model browsing; Java interfaces generation in order to generically explore a model of a given type; model transformation features. The tool is capable to cope with plugins (basically the definition of the transformation rules and their algorithms) that will use existing generated Java interfaces to achieve the transformation. These interfaces are a direct Java mapping for accessing the metamodels (and their instances) of both target and source languages.

3   Introduction to Model Based Testing (Using CO-OPN Specifications)

Our approach to test case generation stems from the pioneer works of Bernot, Gaudel and Marre [12] on model-based testing using formal specifications. This work has been extended by Barbey and Péraire in their Phd. Thesis which address the problematic of testing Object Oriented systems and finding practical tools for doing so.

In a nutshell, the approach can be described as follows: given a non-ambiguous model of the SUT (System Under Test), the test engineer will provide hypotheses about the functioning of the SUT. The purpose of these hypotheses is to generalize the SUT's behavior so that equivalent behaviors can be mapped into classes of system inputs – the test cases. By generalizing the behavior of the SUT we reduce the amount of system inputs necessary to perform exhaustive testing, which is in the general case infinite as Bernot, Gaudel and Marre describe in [12]. In fact, if we look at an SUT as being a black box with a number of available operations, the number of test cases necessary to fully test that system will include all possible sequences of calls to the SUT's operations. Moreover, if the operations the SUT makes available include parameters, all the possible values of those parameters will have to be explored. The generalization hypotheses are then provided either about sequences of calls to operations of the SUT, or about the values that are the parameters of those operations. Ideally, our approach will reduce a test set of infinite size to one of finite size that can be applied the SUT in practicable time.

Clearly, the approach is biased by the quality of the hypotheses the test engineer will provide about the functioning of the SUT: while hypotheses which are too weak will lead to test sets which are too large to be practical, hypotheses which are not correct generalizations of the SUT's behavior will lead to test sets which are not representative of the full behavior of the SUT.

3.1   The Model and the SUT (System Under Test)

Since in model-based testing the idea is to compare the SUT with its model, let us now discuss the model. Firstly, it is necessary that there exists a one-to-one morphism between the signatures of the operations of the SUT and the ones of the model – otherwise is makes no sense to try to compare them. By being non-ambiguous, the model allows exploring a state space which is in principle more abstract but equivalent to the one of the SUT. The test cases that are inferred from the hypotheses about the SUT behavior can be "run" through the model in order to provide them with semantics (i.e., are the test cases valid or invalid behaviors according to the model).

Another purpose of the SUT's model is to provide a means for automatically determining classes of input parameters to SUT's operations that will produce an equivalent behavior in those operations (see chapter 4 of the well-known book [13] from Glenford J. Meyers for an introduction to the subject). Given that our modeling language CO-OPN includes syntactic constructs to define the behavior of operations over the SUT, we perform an analysis of these constructs in order to find those equivalence classes.

3.2   Oracle and Test Driver

Other important issues related to testing are the *test driver* and the *oracle* as Péraire, Barbey and Buchs describe in [14,15]. The purpose of the test driver is to provide a means of applying the generated tests to the SUT. The test driver will also be in charge of recovering the observable results of executing the test cases. These results will be passed to the oracle which will decide of the success of the test, i.e., of the conformance of the results observed in the SUT to the ones predicted by the model. We will not go further into these topics in this paper, although some experiments we have realized which have produced interesting results are reported in [16].

3.3   Formalization of the Approach

We can then summarize the objective of model-based testing as follows: being P a program belonging to the class of all possibles SUTs, SP a CO-OPN specification, $\vDash$ a satisfaction relation between SUTs and CO-OPN specifications and $\vDash_o$ an oracle satisfaction relation between SUTs and test sets:

$$P \vDash SP \Leftrightarrow P \vDash_o T_{SP} \tag{7}$$

We would like to find T_{SP} which is a set of tests having the same semantics as SP. Ideally, comparing the SUT to the model would be equivalent to comparing the SUT to the test set T_{SP}. The latter comparison is done by the oracle which examines the result of running the test cases through the test driver. However, our approach includes hypotheses about the SUT, which means we extend equation 7 to the following (where $T_{SP,H}$ stands for a test set having the same semantics as SP but reduced by hypotheses H[3] which generalize behaviors of P):

$$(P \text{ satisfies } H) \Rightarrow (P \vDash SP \Leftrightarrow P \vDash_o T_{SP,H}) \tag{8}$$

---

[3] In fact, since the oracle cannot always decide P satisfies a test case, it may become necessary to include in H additional hypotheses that extend the oracle's capability of observation.

The equivalence on right hand side of equation 8 holds only when SUT P satisfies hypotheses H. Since it is not trivial to prove that an SUT satisfies hypotheses about its behavior, the quality of the obtained test set will necessarily depend on the quality of the hypotheses – which reflect the knowledge the test engineer has about the functioning of the SUT.

In the following sections of this paper we will focus on how tests are actually generated from a CO-OPN specification which results from the transformation of the initial UML model of the SUT. Figure 1 puts in evidence this test generation process, which consists on enriching the CO-OPN model with test intentions (or hypotheses about the SUT's behavior) and deriving the resulting tests using a set of tools we have developed for that purpose.

4   Testing CO-OPN Specifications: Brief Discussion on Methodology

As previously described, the CO-OPN specification language is an Object-Oriented formalism. When designing an approach to test CO-OPN specifications we want to take into consideration the fact that we want to test specifications as a whole, but also its parts. A first important remark to be done about our test methodology is that since it follows the model-based philosophy, we will always perform back-box testing. However, we can perform black-box testing focusing on a part of the specification. In Fig. 10 we exemplify testing at different levels of detail of the same specification. Three cases can be differentiated:

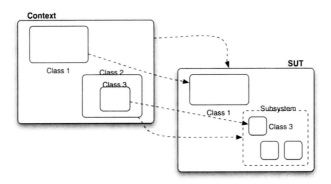

Fig. 10. Testing a CO-OPN specification at different level of detail

- *Testing a context*: A context is a particular feature of the CO-OPN language given it only acts as a coordinator for the objects it holds. Since a CO-OPN context does not have its own state, only one instance of a given context exists in a specification and there are no variables of type context. Typically contexts are used as the outermost layer of a specification, defining methods and gates which correspond to inputs and outputs of the system. In terms of test artifacts, the outermost context corresponds to the interface of the SUT;

- *Testing a class*: In figure 10 it is possible to differentiate two scenarios while testing a class:
  - *A class in the model corresponds to a class in the SUT*: In this case we are in the scenario of unit testing a class. We can consider the class to be an SUT on its own and generate tests for it. We can envisage using a commercially well known unit test driver such as JUnit [17] for Java in order to practically apply the tests. However, if a class has references to objects (as they usually do), these references need to be initialized so the class can be tested correctly. If the references are initialized when the object is built, there is no problem. However, if the references are passed by reference to the class constructor, it may become necessary that the test is also able to pre-generate those references;
  - *A class in the model corresponds to a subsystem in the SUT*: It may happen that there is no direct mapping between a CO-OPN class and an implementation class. A CO-OPN class may correspond to a subsystem of several classes in the implementation. In this case the implementation subsystem has to be encapsulated by the interface defined in the specification. The test driver will then have to perform the connections between the calls to the interface and their mapping on the subsystem.

5   The Test Selection Language *TestSel*

The test intentions appearing in figure 1 are expressed in our test selection language *TestSel*. Barbey, Péraire and Buchs present in [15,14] specifically devised templates of hypotheses (can be considered as building bricks for more complex hypotheses) and a methodology for applying them. They claim in their work the methodology they present leads to a good quality of hypotheses, thus to test sets that uncover errors in a wide range of possible SUTs. *TestSel* extends their work by introducing language constructs to compose templates of hypotheses. With these constructs we are able to build refined hypotheses about the SUT's behavior. In order to present *TestSel* we will start by the language we have chosen to represent our test cases which is called HML (Hennessy-Milner Logic).

5.1   Test Representation Media - The HML Formalism

HML is a simple temporal logic built to express properties of processes. Its capability to express process properties as graphs of events over time makes it an interesting language for expressing test cases. In particular, HML_{SP} stands for the language of HML formulas over a given CO-OPN specification SP. By this we mean that HML_{SP} corresponds to HML formulas over CO-OPN events, where a CO-OPN event corresponds to a pair $\langle Input, Output \rangle$ – *Input* and *Output* being synchronizations over the CO-OPN specification's methods and gates respectively. In the following definition of the abstract syntax of HML_{SP}, T represents the always true constant (verified by any process in any state) and $Event_{SP}$ is the set containing all the Input/Output synchronization pairs over SP.

Definition 1. *Syntax of HML_{SP}*

- $T \in HML_{SP}$
- $f \in HML_{SP} \Rightarrow (\neg f) \in HML_{SP}$
- $f, g \in HML_{SP} \Rightarrow (f \wedge g) \in HML_{SP}$
- $f \in HML_{SP} \Rightarrow (\langle e \rangle f) \in HML_{SP}$ *where* $e \in Event_{SP}$

We express CO-OPN's semantics using transition systems, so before providing the semantics of HML_{SP} let us start by defining the notion of transition system: the transition system denoted by a CO-OPN specification SP is a quadruple $\langle Q, Event_{SP}, \rightarrow, i \rangle \in \Gamma$ (Γ being the class of all transition systems) where Q is the set of all states in SP, $\rightarrow \subseteq Q \times Event_{SP} \times Q$ and i is a non empty initial state. We also define equivalence in the CO-OPN world as the *bisimulation* equivalence $\Leftrightarrow$ (see Biberstein's Phd thesis [4] on CO-OPN's semantics) between the transition systems denoting the semantics of CO-OPN models. Taking again equation 7, we can better define the satisfaction relation $\vDash$ between an SUT P and a CO-OPN specification SP using the bisimulation relation. Being $G(P)$ and $G(SP)$ transition systems representing the semantics of P and of SP we can write:

$$P \vDash SP \Leftrightarrow G(P) \Leftrightarrow G(SP)^4 \qquad (9)$$

The semantics of HML_{SP} is defined in terms of the satisfaction relation $\vDash_{HML_{SP}}$ between the transition system denoted by specification SP and HML_{SP} formulas. Formally, given a transition system $G = \langle Q, Event(SP), \rightarrow, i \rangle$ denoting SP and a state $q \in Q$, the satisfaction relation $\vDash_{HML_{SP}} \subseteq \Gamma \times Q \times HML_{SP}$ is defined as:

Definition 2. *Semantics of HML_{SP}*

- $G, q \vDash_{HML_{SP}} T$
  (specification SP always satisfies formula T at state q)
- $G, q \vDash_{HML_{SP}} (\neg f) \Leftrightarrow G, q \nvDash_{HML_{SP}} f$
  ($\neg f$ is satisfied by specification SP at state q if SP in that same state q does not satisfy f)
- $G, q \vDash_{HML_{SP}} (f \wedge g) \Leftrightarrow G, q \vDash_{HML_{SP}} f$ *and* $G, q \vDash_{HML_{SP}} g$
  ($f \wedge g$ is satisfied by specification SP at state q if f is satisfied by SP at state q and g is satisfied by SP at state q)
- $G, q \vDash_{HML_{SP}} (e\langle f \rangle) \Leftrightarrow \exists e \in Event_{SP}$ *such that* $q \xrightarrow{e} q' \in \rightarrow$ *and* $G, q \vDash_{HML_{SP}} f$
  ($e\langle f \rangle$ is satisfied by SP at state q if there is an event $e \in Event_{SP}$ leading from state q to q' and f is satisfied by SP at from state q').

If we consider G to be the transition system representing the semantics of a CO-OPN specification SP and $q \in Q$ the initial state of model SP, the test set obtained from a set of HML_{SP} formulas is such that:

---

[4] We will not discuss how to obtain a transition system from a CO-OPN specification SP, given that the purpose of this paper is not to explain the semantics of a CO-OPN specification – we rather aim at expressing the relation between the test language and the specification language.

Definition 3. *Test Set for a given set of formulae $F \subseteq HML_{SP}$:*

$$Test_{SP,G}(F) = \{\langle f, Result \rangle \in F \times \{true, false\} \mid$$
$$(G, q \vDash_{HML_{SP}} f \ and \ Result = true) \ or$$
$$(G, q \nvDash_{HML_{SP}} f \ and \ Result = false)\} \quad (10)$$

In this way we classify HML_{SP} formulas as valid or invalid behaviors of the model of the SUT described by SP.

5.2   Full Agreement Between HML and CO-OPN Semantics

We are now in measure to define more precisely the satisfaction relation $\vDash_o$ used in equation 8. Being $G(P)$ the transition system representing the semantics of SUT P (which we want to observe through the execution of test cases), $G(SP)$ the transition system representing the semantics of the CO-OPN specification SP and $F \subseteq HML_{SP}$, the $\vDash_o$ relation is given by:

Definition 4. *Oracle satisfaction $\vDash_o$*

$$P \vDash_o Test_{SP,G(SP)}(F) \Leftrightarrow Test_{SP,G(P)}(F) = Test_{SP,G(SP)}(F) \quad (11)$$

Equation 4 illustrates the fact of applying a test set to an SUT. It states that a CO-OPN specification SP and an SUT P should satisfy any set of HML_{SP} formulas is the same manner. In other words, SP and P should have the same behavior.

We will not go deeply into this subject, but it is possible to use HML as a testing language because there exists a full agreement between CO-OPN equivalence and HML equivalence. CO-OPN equivalence is given by the bisimulation relation and Hennessy has shown in [18] that two transition systems can be distinguished by HML if and only if they are not bisimulation equivalent.

According to equation 7 we are checking if SUT P has the same semantics as specification SP. We do this by first calculating a test set T_{SP} with the same semantics as SP (definition 3) and then checking if P also satisfies T_{SP} through black-box observation of its behavior when the tests are ran. This said, the full agreement between CO-OPN equivalence and HML equivalence is fundamental for our approach. It is this result that allows us to say that comparing an SUT P to a CO-OPN specification SP through the usage a test set T_{SP} is equivalent to comparing directly the transition systems denoted by P and SP using bisimulation. In other words, this means that we don't lose discriminating power between $\vDash$ and $\vDash_o$.

5.3   Advantages and Disadvantages of HML as a Test Formalism

Another interesting aspect of using HML as a test representation media is the fact that we can make use of *not* ($\neg$) and *and* ($\wedge$) operators. The *not* operator allows us to state that an SUT does not produce a given behavior, while the *and* operator allows us to discriminate branching non-determinism. While the semantics of these operators is straightforward as previously explained in this paper, it may be not trivial to apply them in practice while testing a real SUT. Let us exemplify by imagining the application of a negative HML formula (a negative test case) to an SUT. In this case, the *oracle* would have to decide about the satisfaction of the negative formula which is not a trivial task. In fact if the SUT blocks during the execution of a negative test case, the oracle may not always be able to distinguish between the blockage required by the specification and a blockage provoked by a fault present in the SUT. By a blockage in a CO-OPN specification we understand the fact that an operation is not available from a given state. In that sense the we need the oracle to able to distinguish between that kind of blockages and the blockages that are due to errors in the code of the SUT.

On the other hand, if we would like to apply to an SUT a test case represented by a conjunctive HML formula (including *and* operators) other problems would arise: the semantics of the *and* operator are so that for a transition system to verify a formula $(f \wedge g)$ both f and g have to be satisfied starting from the same state. Practically, to apply a formula $(f \wedge g)$ to an SUT a test driver would have to be able to either first test f and then g, or the reverse. In order to be able to do this, a "backtracking" capability of the SUT would be necessary in order to go back to the state where the formula splits. Although we do not provide solutions for an oracle and a test driver capable of testing negative or conjunctive formulas, we point these two problems as issues to take into consideration while using HML as a test case formalism.

5.4   Example – A Set of Selection Hypotheses for the Mobile Phone Example

Before presenting formally the structure of $TestSel$ we will provide an example of a set of test selection hypotheses for the mobile phone example provided in section 2.1. The example in Fig. 11 is given in the concrete syntax of $TestSel$ that we have implemented in our IDE for the CO-OPN language. This IDE is called CoopnBuilder and includes editors for context, class and ADT modules of CO-OPN specifications. $TestSel$ is implemented as an extra module for CO-OPN specifications. Instances of these types of modules are called *constraint* modules – is the sense that they constrain the whole set of possible executions of the SUT.

Fig. 11 depicts a single *constraint* module called *NatelCons*. CoopnBuilder allows multiple constraints modules per CO-OPN specification. Informally, the structure of a constraint module includes the following sections:

- *Interface*: defines the name of the constraints that are defined by a module. Each constraint name corresponds to a set of HML formulas and the union of all these sets is the final test set defined by the module. In the future we would like to compose constraints coming from several modules;
- *Body*: declares the properties necessary to the construction of the constraints declared in the interface. It includes five sections:

```
ConstraintSet NatelCons;
    Interface
        Constraints
            pinTest;
            block;
            reachOn;

    Body
        Constraints
            nWrongPins

        Use
            Boolean
            Pin

        Axioms
1           subUniformity(p) => HML(<turnOn with null>,<insertPin(p) with g> T) in pinTest;

2           [] in nWrongPins;

3           f in nWrongPins => f . HML(<insertPin(newPin(1 1 1 1)) with g> T) in nWrongPins;

4           f in nWrongPins & nbEvents(f) < 4 => HML(<turnOn with null>) . f .
            HML(<insertPin(newPin(1 2 3 4)) with g> T) in insertPins;

        Variables
            p : Pin
            f : HML
            g : gate

        External
End NatelCons;
```

Fig. 11. Test selection hypotheses for the Mobile Phone example

- *Contraints*: declares the constraints defined locally to help in the construction of the exported constraints. They are not exported from the module;
- *Use*: declares specification modules (namely class and ADT modules) that are used to build the constraints;
- *Axioms*: declares axioms and rules that establish elementary behaviors of the SUT. The conjunction of these behaviors in the *constraint* module corresponds to the reduction hypotheses as it was stated in section 3;
- *Variables*: establishes the type of the variables used in the definitions of the *Axioms* section;
- *External:* declares functions used in HML formulas (test cases) during testing time (as opposed to test generation time). The purpose of these functions is to calculate values over non-deterministic outputs of the SUT. For further explanations on this subject we direct the interested reader to [19].

The *Axioms* section is clearly the most relevant one. In this paper we will not provide a textual description of the semantics of the language of constraint module's axioms since it can be found in [19]. However, some comments about the axioms that can be found in Fig. 11 follow. Please keep in mind that an axiom is of the form `condition => assignment` where the *assignement* (of a set of HML formulas to the set represented by the constraint name) only happens if the *condition* holds.

- **axiom 1**

  ```
  subUniformity(p) => HML(<turnOn with null>,<insertPin(p) with g> T) in pinTest;
  ```

  This axiom generates test cases that start by turning on the phone and then insert a pin value. The *subuniformity* operator selects for variable p values according to the behavior of the operation *insertPin*, which either validates or invalidates the introduced pin number. This axioms will then produce two tests: turn on the phone and insert a correct pin; turn on the phone and insert an incorrect pin. The language makes available two more operators *exhaust* and *uniformity* that are similar to *subuniformity* but that select all values or only one value in the domain from the variable in parameter, respectively.

- **axioms 2 and 3**

  ```
                        [] in nWrongPins;
  f in nWrongPins => f . HML(<insertPin(newPin(1 1 1 1)) with g> T) in nWrongPins;
  ```

  This couple of axioms is used to produce the same set of tests. Axiom 3 is recursive since it builds an HML formula that inserts a wrong pin and then concatenates it (".." is the concatenation symbol for HML formulas) with formulas of the same type. Axiom 2 represents the base HML formula T, which is the stop condition for the recursion in axiom 3 (given that axiom 3 is defined in terms of itself). The tests produced by these axioms are sequences of any size of wrong pins insertions (assuming *(newPin 1 2 3 4)* is the correct pin).

- **axiom 4**

  ```
  f in nWrongPins & nbEvents(f) < 4 => HML(<turnOn with null>) . f .
       HML(<insertPin(newPin(1 2 3 4)) with g> T) in insertPins;
  ```

  This axiom uses a *nbEvents* operator that limits the number of events in HML formula f. In this case the idea is to use the previously defined constraint name *nWrongPins* to build sequences of at most four wrong pins. These sequences are then concatenated at the beginning with an operation to turn on the phone and at the end with a correct pin insertion (notice however that the output of the event is variable). The idea in this case is to test if the system only blocks at the introduction of more than three wrong pins and behaves correctly in the remaining cases. Examples of other operators over HML formulas are: *depth* – number of events of the deepest branch of an HML formula; *nbOccurences* – number of occurrences of a method name in an HML formula; *positive* – HML formulas without *not* ($\neg$) operators; *sequence* – HML formulas without *and* ($\wedge$) operators.

5.5   The Structure of *TestSel*

As its name indicates, *TestSel* is a test selection language rather than a test reduction language. Despite the fact that we have defined in 3 the process of finding tests as the progressive reduction of exhaustive test set, this process cannot be reproduced in the real world for a simple reason: it is not possible to generate the exhaustive (infinite) test set in finite time and then reduce it. In order to overcome this operational difficulty while still employing the presented theoretical framework, we have thus decided to implement practically the test finding process as one of selection – using logic programming principles. The basic approach is explained by Barbey in [15], where he starts by defining the language $HML_{SP,X}$ – our HML_{SP} language extended with variables. The test selection is then practically achieved by instantiation of the variables present in $HML_{SP,X}$ formulas. Given a CO-OPN specification SP, the set X_{HML} of variables over HML formulas and the set X_{Event} of variables over SP's events, the syntax of $HML_{SP,X}$ is defined as follows:

Definition 5. *Syntax of* $HML_{SP,X}$

- $T \in HML_{SP}$
- $x \in X_{HML} \Rightarrow x \in HML_{SP,X}$
- $f \in HML_{SP,X} \Rightarrow (\neg f) \in HML_{SP,X}$
- $f, g \in HML_{SP,X} \Rightarrow (f \wedge g) \in HML_{SP,X}$
- $f \in HML_{SP} \Rightarrow (\langle e \rangle f) \in HML_{SP}$ *where* $e \in Event_{SP,X}$)

The set $Event_{SP,X}$ *includes CO-OPN pairs* $\langle Input, Output \rangle$, *Input and Output being synchronizations including variables. Two CO-OPN events can be synchronized simultaneously, in sequence or in parallel. A CO-OPN event is a method or a gate name, followed by a set of parameters.* $Event_{SP,X}$ *includes variables on methods or gates names of the specifications (which we will call* X_{MG}) *as well as variables over event parameters – these can be sets of values described in ADT modules (which we will call* X_S) *of the specification or references to objects of classes defined in the specification (which we will call* X_C).

We can then consider the exhaustive test set to be represented by $\langle f, r \rangle$ where $f \in HML_{SP,X}$. In fact, given that f has free variables it cannot be applied directly to the SUT. Hypotheses about the behavior of the SUT will serve the purpose of instantiating those free variables – leading to ground HML formulas that can be used as a test cases for an SUT. The process of test selection can then be seen as the process of transforming an $HML_{SP,X}$ formula into an HML_{SP} one, by means of hypotheses about the SUT that can be translated in constraints on the formula's variables.

The Abstract Syntax of *TestSel*. Before providing an example of using *TestSel* we will present its abstract syntax. The purpose of this section is to layout the basis for being able to precisely define the semantics of *TestSel*. While reading this section, please keep in mind section 5.4 of this paper where the syntax and the semantics of *TestSel* was informally introduced. *TestSel* has three syntactic layers, namely:

- *CO-OPN event*: includes the possible Input/Output synchronizations pairs of a CO-OPN specification. The set of these pairs for a specification SP is given in definition 5 by the set $Event_{SP,X_S}$;

- *HML*: set of $HML_{SP,X}$ formulas over a CO-OPN specification SP;
- *Constraints*: constraints over variables of $HML_{SP,X}$ formulas. Our language allows constraints over variables that represent: execution paths – sequences of events with HML operators $\wedge$ and $\neg$); values that are parameters of operations – CO-OPN class instances or CO-OPN sorts (sets of values) defined in ADT modules.

The abstract syntax of the first two layers in the above list has already been provided in definition 5. In what concerns the third layer we will provide the abstract syntax of a constraint module over a specification SP. The language will be defined in a top-down fashion:

Definition 6. *Constraint module*
A constraint module over a CO-OPN specification SP is a quintuplet
$\langle SP, K, ax, X, F_{SP} \rangle \in \Psi_{SP}$, where:

- *SP is a CO-OPN specification;*
- *K is the set of constraint names defined by the constraints module;*
- *X is a set of typed variables $X_{HML} \cup X_{MG} \cup X_C \cup X_S$;*
- *F_{SP} is a set of function signatures defined in ADT modules of specification SP;*
- *$ax \subseteq AX_{K,X,SP}$ is a set of axioms defined over $HML_{SP,X}$ formulas, predefined operators, constraint names in K and variables in X;*

Intuitively speaking, a constraint module for a specification SP will define a set of constraint names – each name representing a different generalization of a behavior of the SUT. The constraints are defined by axioms that belong to the $AX_{K,X,SP}$ language. Still, before proceeding with the definition of this language we will present the syntax of terms over $HML_{SP,X}$ formulas as this will be necessary for subsequent definitions:

Definition 7. *The terms $T_{HML_{SP,X}}$ over $HML_{SP,X}$*

- $t \in HML_{SP,X} \Rightarrow t \in T_{HML_{SP,X}}$
- $t1, t2 \in HML_{SP,X} \Rightarrow t1 \,.\, t2 \in T_{HML_{SP,X}}$

The intuition behind this definition 7 is to provide us with the necessary syntax for the concatenation of $HML_{SP,X}$ formulas. We thus define the language of constraint axioms over a CO-OPN specification SP as follows:

Definition 8. *Given K, X and SP as defined previously, a constraint axiom is a triplet belonging to the relation $AX_{K,X,SP}$ such that:*

$$AX_{K,X,SP} = Cond_{K,X,SP} \times T_{HML_{SP,X}} \times K$$

where:

- *$Cond_{K,X,SP}$ is a conjunction of atomic conditions;*
- *$T_{HML_{SP,X}}$ is term built from $HML_{SP,X}$ formulas;*
- *K is a constraint name.*

This syntax for constraint axioms allows us to see constraints as sets of HML formulas – an instantiated $HML_{SP,X}$ formula *Formula* is produced by a constraint *ConsName* only if we can find a substitution to the variables of *formula* that satisfies the condition *Condition*. We are now missing the definition of $Cond_{K,X,SP}$:

Definition 9. *Conditions $Cond_{K,X,SP}$ of a behavioral axiom*
    Given K, X and SP as defined previously, the set $Cond_{K,X,SP}$ is a conjunction of atomic conditions such that:

$$\forall n \in \mathbb{N}, ac_i \in AC_{K,X,SP}, i \in \{0..n\}, ac_1 \wedge ac_2 \wedge \ldots ac_n \in Cond_{K,X,SP}$$

Finally we will define the set $AC_{K,X,SP}$ of atomic conditions. An atomic condition is a constraint over variables of X.

Definition 10. *Atomic conditions $AC_{K,X,SP}$*
    $\forall k \in K, t \in T_{HML_{SP,X}}, tn, tn' \in T_{NAT}, tb, tb' \in T_{BOOL}, x \in X_S,$

$t\,in\,k,\ uniform(x),\ exhaust(x),\ tn\,cmpOp_\mathbb{N}\,tn',\ tb\,cmpOp_\mathbb{B}\,tb' \in AC_{K,X,SP}$

where $cmpOp_\mathbb{N} \in \{=, <>, <, >, <=, >=\}$ and $cmpOp_\mathbb{B} \in \{=, <>\}$.

T_{NAT} represents the set of terms over arithmetic expressions. Given $t \in T_{HML_{SP,X}}$, T_{NAT} is defined as:

$$n,\ depth(t),\ nbEvents(t),\ nbOccurrences(m,t),\ tn\,op_\mathbb{N}\,tn' \in T_{NAT}$$

where $n \in \mathbb{N}$, m is a method name defined in SP, $tn, tn' \in T_{NAT}$ and $op_\mathbb{N} \in \{+, -, *, /\}$.

T_{BOOL} represents the set of terms over boolean expressions. Given $t \in T_{HML_{SP,X}}$, T_{BOOL} is defined as:

$$\{true, false\},\ onlyConstructor(t),\ onlyMutator(t),\ onlyObserver(t),\ sequence(t),$$
$$positive(t),\ trace(t) \in T_{BOOL}$$

Semantics of $TestSel$. After having described the abstract syntax of $TestSel$, we are now in measure of providing its semantics:

Definition 11. *Semantics of TestSel*
    Given a CO-OPN specification SP, the semantics of a constraint module $CONS = \langle SP, K, ax, X, F_{SP} \rangle \in \Psi_{SP}$ is the set of all HML_{SP}^{CONS} formulas such that:

$$HML_{SP}^{CONS} = \bigcup_{axiom \in ax} \{f \in HML_{SP} \mid f \vdash axiom\}$$

The informal meaning of definition 11 is the following: for each axiom of the constraints module all the HML_{SP} formulas (without variables) that satisfy it are collected in a set. The set of test cases produced by a constraint module is the union of all sets of test cases produced by each individual axiom. We will not further develop the $\vdash$ relation in this paper. In order to verify if $f \vdash axiom$ we have to find a substitution of the variables of $axiom$ so that we can find f. In particular, the substitution of variables that are quantified with the $subuniformity$ operator is complex given that it becomes necessary to analyze the behavior of the operations in the CO-OPN specification.

In order to finish this section of the paper we will state the validity of the test sets obtained by the $constraint$ modules of our $TestSel$ language:

Theorem 1. *Given a CO-OPN specification SP and a constraint module $CONS$, the test set $Test_{SP,G(SP)}(HML_{SP}^{CONS})$ obtained from $CONS$ is a valid test set, meaning it does not reject correct programs.*

Proof.
$$Test_{SP,G(SP)}(HML_{SP}^{CONS}) \subseteq Test_{SP,G(SP)}(HML_{SP})$$
is trivial by construction. □

In theorem 1 we show that test sets that are selected by $TestSel$ for a CO-OPN specification SP are part of the exhaustive test set. Thus the selection process does not introduce invalid test cases in the final test set. Validity of the tests is necessary but not sufficient for measuring the quality of a test set. In fact, we would have to prove that the union of all the behaviors described by all the constraint modules about a specification corresponds to a correct generalization of the behavior of the specification. This can be reduced to the problem of measuring the coverage of the obtained test set.

5.6   Tools for Test Production

As we have already mentioned in this paper, an IDE for the CO-OPN language called CoopnBuilder already exists. We have used this infrastructure in order to implement our language $TestSel$, as can be seen from the example in 5.4. From this front end we are able to produce $Prolog$ code that generates the test sets. The reason why we have used Prolog for this task has to do with the fact that the resolution mechanism of this language allows relatively straightforward mapping between its semantics and the semantics of $TestSel$. In fact, $Prolog$ is a theorem prover that tries to verify if a logical clause can be induced from the available rules. If the logical clause to be proved includes variables, Prolog will find all the substitutions for those variables that make the clause true. This is similar to the semantics of $TestSel$ – we want to find substitutions for the axioms of a constraint module that make the constraints over the variables of those axioms true. In this process we find fully instantiated HML formulas which are sequences of inputs for the SUT.

On the other hand, only (syntactically) finding is sequences of inputs is not enough. We also need to provide them with semantics in order to turn them into test cases, as shown in definition 3. To do that we have two options at our disposal: a prototyping tool that turns CO-OPN specifications into Java programs [20]; a translator that converts CO-OPN specifications into Prolog programs [21]. Both options are currently implemented and allow verifying if an HML formula is a valid behavior of a CO-OPN specification. We are inclined to pursue the latter option given that the integration with the Prolog code produced from the constraint modules becomes more natural. Other reasons for this choice have to do with the fact that Prolog is a language where the concepts of code and data are mixed. This allows a natural reflection which is extremely useful for analyzing and decomposing the behavior of the operations defined in the specification.

In figure 12 we present some of the tests which are (semi) automatically generated by our tool. In fact, the four lines in the Fig. represent four solutions to the constraint name *insertPins* declared in the constraint module of figure 11 for the Mobile Phone example. Our tool is not yet able to verify if the tests generated are valid or invalid behaviors of the specification, so we have chosen them by hand. In fact, given that in the axiom for the *insertPins* constraint (and previously, in the axiom for the *nWrongPins* constraint) the variable g is a gate that remains to be instantiated, many other solutions are possible. However, they will all represent invalid behaviors of the specification.

6   Related Work

A large number of papers on model-based test case generation exists in the literature. However, not many deal with models expressed in semi-formal languages such as UML.

At the university of Franche-Comté an approach to test case generation similar to ours is being developed. Legeard and Peureux explain in [22] their method which consists in: translating a UML specification into a program in an adapted logic programming language similar to Prolog; explore symbolically the state space of the model searching for values for parameters of operations that are interesting to test.

```
X = next(coopnEvent(method(turnOn)), next(coopnEvent(method(insertPin(newPin
1 2 3 4)), gate(coopnSyncSim(correctPin,phoneReady)))), t)) ;

X = next(coopnEvent(method(turnOn)), next(coopnEvent(method(insertPin(newPin
1 1 1 1)), gate(pinResult(false))), next(coopnEvent(method(insertPin(newPin 1
2 3 4)), gate(coopnSyncSim(correctPin,phoneReady)))), t))) ;

X = next(coopnEvent(method(turnOn)), next(coopnEvent(method(insertPin(newPin
1 1 1 1)), gate(wrongPin)), next(coopnEvent(method(insertPin(newPin 1 1 1
1)), gate(wrongPin)), next(coopnEvent(method(newPin 1 2 3 4)), gate
(coopnSyncSim(correctPin, phoneReady)))), t)))) ;

X = next(coopnEvent(method(turnOn)), next(coopnEvent(method(insertPin(newPin
1 1 1 1)), gate(wrongPin)), next(coopnEvent(method(insertPin(newPin 1 1 1
1)), gate(wrongPin)), next(coopnEvent(method(insertPin(newPin 1 1 1 1)), gate
(coopnSyncSim(wrongPin,cardPinLocked))), next(coopnEvent(method(insertPin
(newPin 1 2 3 4)), gate(cardPinLocked))), t))))) ;
```

Fig. 12. Tests generated for the Mobile Phone example

Jan Philipps et al explain in [23] their approach which starts from a model described in AUTOFOCUS^{TM}, a tool based on UML-RT (for Real-Time systems). The framework also makes use of a logic programming language to explore symbolically the state space.

7   Conclusion

In this paper we have presented our work on automatic test case generation for UML (Fondue) models. We have decided to tackle the problem in two phases, the first one being the translation of UML into a the formal specification language CO-OPN. CO-OPN has clearly defined semantics which allow us to explore the model soundly in order to produce test cases. The translation process that we formally define is based on the decomposition of the Fondue sub-models (environment, concept, protocol and operations) and their individual mapping into CO-OPN modules (ADT, classes and contexts). We also take into consideration the fact that the Fondue modules overlap or complement each other at certain points and include these implicit semantics in the translation. The process is introduced also by means of an example of a specification of a mobile phone.

The second phase of the problem concerns the automatics test generation. Here also we present a formal process, insisting on the definition of a language that will enable this process. We define the language at several layers of complexity, which allow to take our theory of testing into consideration while adapting it to the test selection needs of an engineer. We also provide a semi formal semantics for this language and illustrate it generating a test set for the mobile phone specification.

Tools are currently being implemented for the process we describe. We are already able to partially automate the processes we describe.

References

1. Alfred Strohmeier. Fondue: An Object-Oriented Development Method based on the UML Notation. In *X Jornada Técnica de Ada-Spain, Documentación, ETSI de Telecommunicación, Universidad Politécnica de Madrid*, Madrid, Spain, November 2001.
2. Didier Buchs and Nicolas Guelfi. A formal specification framework for object-oriented distributed systems. *IEEE Transactions on Software Engineering*, 26(7):635–652, july 2000.
3. Olivier Biberstein, Didier Buchs, and Nicolas Guelfi. CO-OPN/2: A concurrent object-oriented formalism. In *Proc. Second IFIP Conf. on Formal Methods for Open Object-Based Distributed Systems (FMOODS), Canterbury, UK, July 21-23 1997*, pages 57–72. Chapman and Hall, Lo, 1997.
4. Olivier Biberstein. *CO-OPN/2: An Object-Oriented Formalism for the Specification of Concurrent Systems*. PhD thesis, University of Geneva, 1997.
5. Object Management Group. Mda guide version 1.0.1. Technical report, OMG, June 2003.

6. Octavian Patrascoiu. YATL:Yet Another Transformation Language. In *Proceedings of the 1st European MDA Workshop, MDA-IA*, pages 83–90. University of Twente, the Nederlands, January 2004.
7. Triskell team. MTL Documentation. URL: http://modelware.inria.fr/rubrique4. html.
8. Zhaoxia Hu and Sol M. Shatz. Mapping uml diagrams to a petri net notation for system simulation. In Frank Maurer and Günther Ruhe, editors, *SEKE*, pages 213–219, 2004.
9. Triskell team. Mod-Transf - xml and ruled based transformation language. URL: http://modelware.inria.fr/rubrique15.html.
10. Object Management Group. Meta-Object Facility specification, April 2002. url: http://www.omg.org/technology/documents/formal/mof.htm.
11. Luis Pedro, Levi Lucio, and Didier Buchs. Prototyping Domain Specific Languages with COOPN. In *Rapid Integration of Software Engineering techniques*, volume LNCS 3943. Springer-Verlag, 2006.
12. M.-C. Gaudel G. Bernot and B. Marre. Software testing based on formal specifications: a theory and a tool. *IEEE Software Engineering Journal*, 6(6):387–405, 1991.
13. Glenford J. Myers. *The Art of Software Testing*. John Wiley & Sons, Inc., New York, NY, USA, 1979.
14. Cécile Péraire, Stéphane Barbey, and Didier Buchs. Test selection for object-oriented software based on formal specifications. In *PROCOMET '98: Proceedings of the IFIP TC2/WG2.2,2.3 International Conference on Programming Concepts and Methods*, pages 385–403, London, UK, UK, 1998. Chapman & Hall, Ltd.
15. Stéphane Barbey, Didier Buchs, and Cécile Péraire. A theory of specification-based testing for object-oriented software. In *EDCC*, pages 303–320, 1996.
16. Levi Lucio, Luis Pedro, and Didier Buchs. A Methodology and a Framework for Model-Based Testing. In N. Guelfi, editor, *Rapid Integration of Software Engineering techniques*, volume LNCS 3475, pages 57–70. LNCS, 2005.
17. Erich Gamma and Kent Beck. Junit.org. URL: http://www.junit.org/.
18. Matthew Hennessy and Colin Stirling. The power of the future perfect in program logics. *Inf. Control*, 67(1-3):23–52, 1986.
19. Levi Lucio, Luis Pedro, and Didier Buchs. A test selection language for co-opn specifications. In *IEEE International Workshop on Rapid System Prototyping*, pages 195–201, 2005.
20. Ali Al-Shabibi, Didier Buchs, Mathieu Buffo, Stanislav Chachkov, Ang Chen, and David Hurzeler. Prototyping object oriented specifications. In *Proceedings of the 24th International Conference on Applications and Theory of Petri Nets (ICATPN 2003), Eindhoven, The Netherlands — Lecture Notes in Computer Science / Wil M. P. van der Aalst and Eike Best (Eds.)*, volume 2679, pages 473–482. Springer-Verlag, June 2003.
21. M. Buffo and D. Buchs. Symbolic simulation of coordinated algebraic petri nets using logic programming. University of Geneva – Internal Note.
22. Bruno Legeard and Fabien Peureux. Generation of functional test sequences from b formal specifications-presentation and industrial case study. In *ASE*, pages 377–381, 2001.
23. Jan Philipps, Alexander Pretschner, Oscar Slotosch, Ernst Aiglstorfer, Stefan Kriebel, and Kai Scholl. Model-based test case generation for smart cards. *Electr. Notes Theor. Comput. Sci.*, 80, 2003.

Advances in the Design and Implementation of Group Communication Middleware

Daniel Bünzli, Rachele Fuzzati, Sergio Mena, Uwe Nestmann[*]
Olivier Rütti, André Schiper, and Paweł T. Wojciechowski[**]

Ecole Polytechnique Fédérale de Lausanne (EPFL)
1015 Lausanne, Switzerland
<firstname>.<lastname>@epfl.ch

Abstract. Group communication is a programming abstraction that allows a distributed group of processes to provide a reliable service in spite of the possibility of failures within the group. The goal of the project was to improve the state of the art of group communication in several directions: protocol frameworks, group communication stacks, specification, verification and robustness. The paper discusses the results obtained.

1 Introduction

Group communication is a programming abstraction that allows a distributed group of processes to provide a reliable service in spite of possible failures within the group. Group communication encompasses broadcast protocols (e.g., reliable broadcast, atomic broadcast), membership protocols, and agreement protocols.Group communication is a middleware technology, lying between an application layer and a transport layer. Developing and maintaining a group communication middleware is a non-trivial, error-prone and complex task. In this context, the goal of the project was to improve the state of the art in several directions: flexibility, reusability, formalization, verification and validation. Due to space constraints, a detailed presentation of all the contributions was not possible. The paper gives an overview of the results obtained, structured as shown in Figure 1. Details can be found in the referenced papers.

Protocol frameworks: Flexibility and reusability of a middleware layer—and of any piece of software—can be achieved by decomposing the middleware into protocols that can be assembled. The glue that allows to assemble the protocols is called a protocol *framework*. The features of a protocol framework are essential to the protocol composer: they can make life more or less easy. Typically, adequate features can reduce the errors at assembly time, i.e., when the protocols are glued together to build a group communication middleware. Protocol frameworks are addressed in Section 2, where we start by presenting the features of traditional protocol frameworks, before presenting the novel aspects that have been designed and implemented within the project.

---

[*] Now at Berlin University of Technology, 10587 Berlin, Germany.
[**] Now at Poznań University of Technology, 60-965 Poznań, Poland.

J. Kohlas, B. Meyer, and A. Schiper (Eds.): Dependable Systems, LNCS 4028, pp. 172–194, 2006.

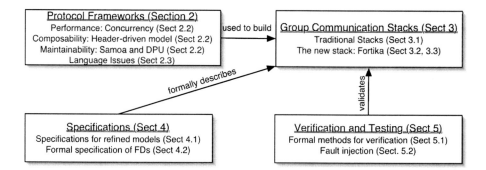

Fig. 1. Structure of the paper

Group communication stacks: A good protocol framework is essential to achieve flexibility and reusability, but is by itself not sufficient. It is also required to identify the "right" components (or protocols). In the context of group communication this is a difficult task, because of the difficulty of the problems to solve. Components derive from algorithms that solve these problems. In Section 3 we explain that the traditional architecture of a group communication middleware has considered *group membership* as one of its most basic components. We discuss the deficiencies of this choice and propose a different architecture. We believe that the new architecture has a much better chance to be flexible, i.e., to adapt to a changing environment. As a consequence, the components are much more likely to be reusable.

Specifications: In group communication, formalization plays an important role at two levels: *(i)* at the level of the specification of the problems to be solved, and *(ii)* at the level of solving these problems. At the specification level, we need a precise characterization of the desired properties of group communication primitives or services. At the solution level, we need to characterize the assumptions that allow us to solve the problems. These issues have been addressed in the past. However, it is only for static groups and in the so-called crash-stop model (in which processes do not recover after a crash) that specifications of group communication are widely accepted and agreed upon. Specifications for dynamic group communication have been proposed, but they differ significantly from static specifications, which is not satisfactory. In Section 4 we show that it is possible to specify dynamic group communication in such a way that, if the group happens to be static, then we obtain the well-known static specifications. We also address specifications of group communication in the crash-recovery model (in which processes have access to stable storage to save their state). Specifications for the crash-recovery model have been proposed in the past, but they fail to capture the fundamental difference between the crash-stop and the crash-recovery model. In Section 4 we discuss how this issue can be addressed. Section 4 also addresses an important formalization issue related to solving group communication problems. The concept of *unreliable failure detectors* has been introduced some time ago. The section proposes a fresh look at failure detectors by representing them via transition systems (as known from operational semantics), with the goal of bringing the definitions closer to our formal reasoning techniques.

Verification and testing: Section 5 is devoted to verification and testing. Consensus is one of the most fundamental problems in group communication. Many of the algorithms for solving consensus have been described in pseudo code, and their proofs use concepts that are sometimes not rigorously defined. Here, we propose a formal approach to the proof of a rigorously defined consensus algorithm. Finally, Section 5 describes an experiment conducted on our new *Fortika* group communication middleware that was build within the project. Fault injection has been used to study how *Fortika* reacts to memory and network corruption— faults that *Fortika* was not designed to handle. The experiments allowed us to identify a few weaknesses and to correct them. The result is a very robust group communication middleware.

2   Protocol Frameworks

We first present the most significant existing frameworks. Then, we discuss some novel ideas that advance the state of the art of protocol composition, covering programming models, concurrency support and dynamic protocol update. Finally, we study languages to ensure the safe usage of concurrency support.

2.1   Existing Frameworks

Protocol frameworks are programming tools to build complex middleware out of simpler off-the-shelf building blocks, called *protocols*. This modular approach yields advantages such as customization, code reuse, extensibility, and ease of maintenance. Altogether, this eases the implementation of group communication middlewares (and, in turn, the implementation of fault tolerant applications).

Most of the existing frameworks are based on an event-driven programming model. In such a model, a protocol is structured as a set of events, handlers, bindings, and a state that can be private or shared with other protocols. Events carry data and are triggered by protocols. The handlers contain the code of the protocol and can modify the state and trigger events. A binding is a mapping between an event type and one or several event handlers. When a handler triggers an event, all handlers bound to its type are executed thereby possibly triggering new events. Composing protocols consists in binding events of a protocol to handlers of other protocols [14].

Cactus. Cactus [2] is an evolution of the x-kernel [4] protocol framework. Composition with x-kernel was strictly layered, i.e., a protocol could only communicate with the protocols immediately above or below. Cactus introduces a finer-grain level of composition where several *microprotocols* can be assembled to form an x-kernel protocol. Each microprotocol can communicate with any other microprotocol in the same protocol using events.

Cactus supports concurrent execution of its microprotocols. Concurrency inside composite protocols requires synchronization policies in order to preserve the properties provided by the composite protocols. The C version of Cactus offers basic guarantees in the presence of concurrency, such as atomic execution of handlers. In the Java version of Cactus, however, it wholly depends on the programmer, who must implement the required synchronization policy using standard language facilities (such as locks, semaphores, monitors, etc...). This approach, besides being tricky and error-prone, harms modularity, since a composer has to adapt the code of the microprotocols composed in order to come up with an adequate concurrency management.

Appia. Appia [1] is a re-engineering of the Ensemble group communication toolkit [3]. In Ensemble, programmers can compose protocols in layered stacks where there can only be one protocol per level in the composition. In contrast, Appia allows more flexible composition, where there may be several protocols per level.

Appia features a validation check for composition. Every protocol declares which event types it accepts, requires and provides. At composition time, Appia verifies that all required events are provided by some protocol, rejecting all compositions that do not pass this check. However, the fact that the direction of events is not taken into account makes this verification superficial.

Unlike Cactus, Appia does not allow concurrent execution of protocols. All events are dispatched by a single-threaded scheduler. This frees the protocol programmer from the burden of dealing with concurrency, deadlocks, etc. However, this absence of concurrency prevents Appia from making the most of high-performant systems (e.g., multi-processor platforms).

2.2   Novel Aspects

Our project brought up new programming abstractions that either improve over, or provide an alternative to existing protocol frameworks. First we describe a new *header-driven* programming model to program protocols in frameworks. This model solves well-known composition problems of the event-driven model and thereby enables the use of powerful composition languages (e.g. ML module systems) to structure protocols and stacks. Then, we describe a runtime system to support concurrency inside a protocol stack without the need to make the protocols themselves aware of concurrency. Finally, we describe SAMOA—a novel protocol framework that implements the runtime system, and provides other interesting features such as dynamic protocol update.

A Header-Driven Programming Model. All recent frameworks use a general-purpose event-driven programming model to manage interactions between protocols. However in complex compositions, where protocols offer their service to more than one protocol, the one-to-many interaction scheme of events introduces composition problems by mixing up the targets to which data should be delivered. In other words, protocols may receive events with data that is not targeted at them. This problem compromises the use of powerful composition languages on top of an event-driven model, because *ad hoc* mechanisms need to be introduced to "route" events to the right protocols. Moreover, the event model doesn't properly handle *peer interactions*, where a protocol interacts with its peer running on another node by using the service of a lower-level protocol. The way events handle this ubiquitous pattern is critical in three ways: (1) it is complex, because invariants known at design time need to be enforced by the composer; (2) it is obscure, because the indirections introduced by the events hide, in the code, the logical structure of peer interactions; (3) it is unsafe, because misbindings can lead to runtime type errors or erratic behaviour. To solve these problems we propose in [6] a novel and simple alternative that shifts the driving force behind interactions from events to the headers (data) they carry.

In the event-driven model, protocols typically encapsulate communication data for their peers in the messages and headers that are carried by events. A message is a list of headers and a header is a typed container for data. Protocols often use a single event handler to manage the reception of messages. Nevertheless, some protocols need to get different kinds of data via this single handler. In order to do so they introduce a *tag name* in the header to indicate the kind of information being transmitted. Since a header usually remains internal to a protocol and its peers, it is not restrictive to impose that each header shall be *named* and that each name shall be *declared by at most one protocol* in a composition. A protocol composition satisfying these constraints has the following interesting property. If we look at the names of a message's sequence of headers, we can approximately see the sequence of protocols—the route—that will handle the message when it is processed by the composition of protocols. In other words the message's sequence of headers drives its processing in the composition. The event model prevents us from exploiting this property. Thus instead of having events at the core of our interaction scheme we should have *headers*. This is the essence of our proposal.

The essential ingredients of a *header-driven model* are headers and messages. As before, a message is a list of headers. But headers are *named* containers carrying statically typed data. To construct a header, its name must be defined. A header handler defines a header name and associates a computation to the deconstruction of every message that starts with this name. Message dispatch is the interaction scheme, it deconstructs messages. When a message is dispatched, the unique header handler corresponding to the head of the message is invoked with the head's data and the tail of the message as arguments. Compared to the event model we can say that (1) header handlers replace event handlers, (2) message dispatch replaces event triggering, and (3) the event binding mechanism is dropped.

The resulting *header-driven* model has several advantages. It solves the composition problems of the event model, it simplifies inter-protocol dependencies and hence the task of composing protocols, and it concisely handles peer interactions and explicitly reveals their logical structure (no binding indirections). Moreover, the *header-driven* model provides better static typing, which avoids runtime type errors and erratic behaviours that can occur in the event model. Our approach was validated by a proof-of-concept implementation [11].

Automatic Concurrency Control for Protocol Stacks. Implementing atomic processing of concurrent messages in a protocol stack is notoriously hard and error-prone. *Atomic transactions* can greatly help programming. Every fresh message is processed by a new transaction with the guarantee of *isolation*—a property known from standard ACID (Atomicity, Concurrency, Isolation and Durability) transactions[1]. The usual implementation of atomic transactions depends however on *rollback-recovery*—if some operations of concurrent transactions conflict with respect to isolation, then the transactions are started again. Rolling back some of the *input/output (I/O)* effects is problematic, e.g. resending messages that have been output to the network may confuse the distributed protocol. To evade this problem, we have designed *rollback-free* concurrency control algorithms for protocol frameworks [28]. The algorithms implement runtime *versioning and scheduling* of transaction operations.

The basic idea of versioning is the following. Tickets (or *versions*) are assigned to isolation-only transactions (called *tasks*) that allow them to acquire *verlocks*, i.e., versioning locks protecting isolation-critical operations. On task creation, a task obtains incremented version values for all verlocks that it wants. The task can acquire a verlock only when the verlock's counter has reached the version count. The counters are monotonically increasing counters, one per verlock. The counter is increased when the verlock has been released by a given task for *the last time*.

In [28], we described three variants of versioning algorithms (*Basic, Bound*, and *Route*), which differ in the precision of detecting when verlocks are actually requested for the last time. To detect this moment, upon a task creation, the algorithms require some data about the task to be passed as the argument. Different variants of the algorithms can be characterized as follows:

- *Basic*: it gives an almost serial execution, however only verlock names must be known *a priori* (they can be inferred statically, as described in Section 2.3);
- *Bound*: it requires a least-upper-bound (supremum) on verlock access to be known *a priori*; in general, this variant allows for more parallelism than *Basic*, but it performs like *Basic* if supremum cannot be reached;
- *Route*: it allows for even more parallelism than *Bound*, however it demands *a priori* a complete tree of potential accesses to verlocks within scope of a task, where a branch in the tree corresponds to a thread of execution.

The SAMOA Protocol Framework and Dynamic Update. We have developed *SAMOA*, a novel protocol framework that improves over the existing protocol frameworks in two respects. Firstly, *type-safe* dynamic protocol (re)binding guarantees that no runtime errors can happen due to protocol interactions. Secondly, isolation-only, rollback-free transactions (or *tasks*) make it

---

[1] This property is similar to *atomicity* in the programming language community.

easier for programmers to encode concurrent protocols that may have irrevocable I/O effects; the implementation of tasks uses concurrency control algorithms described above. An experimental implementation of SAMOA as a package in Java is available [20]. Some of the key features of SAMOA are the possibility to load protocols *on-the-fly* and to dynamically bind and unbind protocols. Based on these features, we have implemented efficient mechanisms for *dynamic protocol update*. The problem of dynamic protocol update has been addressed in [27]. Essentially, we must guarantee global service availability and correctness while a distributed update operation takes place. To validate these ideas, we have implemented the *Adaptive Group Communication* (AGC) middleware in which protocols can be replaced dynamically. The AGC middleware uses the Fortika group communication protocols that supports both the crash-stop and crash-recovery models (see Sections 3 and 4.1).

2.3 Language Issues

The use of isolated tasks in our implementation of SAMOA in Java is not *safe*, i.e., the programmer must carefully determine and declare certain data about tasks for the concurrency control algorithms to work correctly. Below we describe the design of a safe programming language that removes this drawback.

Another problem with the existing protocol frameworks that support concurrency (such as SAMOA and Cactus) is that it is not possible to reuse protocols that contain any synchronization constructs, such as spawning a new task, without inspecting the code of these protocols (since these constructs may need to be removed in the new stack). To remove this drawback, we have proposed to *separate* the synchronization code and the protocol code. In the end of this subsection, we discuss the design of two languages for this separation. These languages could become an integral part of any future protocol frameworks.

Language Design For Isolated Tasks with I/O Effects. To spawn a new task, the SAMOA programmer uses a construct `isolated` R e, where e is a concurrent, isolated task. In the simplest case (Basic versioning algorithm), argument R is just a list of service names that *may* be requested by the task e. Unfortunately, a wrong argument R compromises safety (and therefore also correctness!). How could one make this construct *safe* for programmers? The idea is to design a *type system* that can verify at compile time whether the argument R is correct. A type system—implemented as part of the compilation tool—can prove that *any* program execution preserves given properties expressed as types (informally: *"well typed programs can't go wrong"*).

In [26,25], we designed a *typed language* for expressing rollback-free transactions (tasks) in modular protocols. It has a construct `isolated` R e to spawn a new task e, where task expression e is executed by a new thread. Any return result of this evaluation is ignored—the only visible outcome of task execution are any *data and I/O effects*. Any threads spawn by e are part of the *same* task. The concurrent execution of tasks satisfies the *isolation property*. The argument R in `isolated` R e is a list of verlock names. A new verlock x can be created with `newlock` x : m `in` e, where m is an *effect type* of a single verlock. We normally create a fresh verlock for each communication channel (I/O effects), and each data structure (memory change effects). Verlocks can be shared by concurrent tasks.

We can use verlocks in the expression `sync` e' e. The expression has a semantics that is roughly similar to `synchronized` in Java, i.e., expression e' is evaluated first and yields verlock x (of type m), which is then acquired when possible. Expression e is then evaluated to some v. Finally, the verlock is released and v returned by the whole expression. There is, however, an important difference. What is a locking strategy? Or, when exactly the verlock x is acquired when executing the expression `sync` x e? Verlock x of type m is *acquired* when two conditions are satisfied: (1) the effect m caused by e does not conflict (with respect to *isolation*) with the effects of other concurrent tasks, and (2) lock x is free (i.e., the standard locking principle applies). The second condition is required just to avoid races *inside* a task; it can be dropped if tasks are single-threaded.

In [26,25], we have defined the iso-calculus, a typed call-by-value lambda calculus that is extended with threads, verlocks and tasks. It gives formal semantics to the constructs described above. The iso-calculus has a type system that *guarantees* that well-typed programs satisfy isolation. Programs that do not guarantee isolation are rejected. Formally, the following *type soundness* theorem holds: if expression e is typeable, then all terminating executions that evaluate ("compute") e to value v satisfy isolation. The type system essentially guarantees two properties: (1) all operations that need to be isolated are protected by verlocks (*"no race conditions can happen"*), and (2) all verlocks required by a task are known before the task commences (*"safe versioning"*). It builds on Flanagan and Abadi's [10] type system for *safe locking* with singleton kinds. The formal proof of the type soundness theorem for the iso-calculus appeared in [25].

Declarative Synchronization for Protocol Reuse. One of the promises of modular protocol design is the reuse of protocol components in different protocol stacks. However, in practice, protocol reuse is problematic. Concurrent components within a stack implement a synchronization policy. Reusing selected components in a different stack often requires to modify component code, so that it implements a policy of the new stack. Unfortunately, this is a counterexample to protocol modularity.

The above problem does not exist if we separate the synchronization and protocol code. Two approaches to such *separation of concerns* have been developed within our project: (1) *static* [24], in which synchronization policy (that may include isolation) is declared between components using *concurrency combinators*, and (2) *dynamic* [23], in which synchronization policy is declared between *semantic rôles* using abstract types. In [24], we defined a property, called *composition safety*, that informally means that any runtime execution of a protocol can satisfy the synchronization policy declared using the language of concurreny combinators. The main result of this work was to show that the property can be verified statically, thus eliminating runtime errors due to wrong composition.

3   Group Communication Stacks

Flexibility and modularity of a group communication middleware requires a protocol framework with the right features. However, this is not enough. Flexibility
and modularity requires also to identify the right components (or protocols).
In this section we first point out common features of the most representative
group communication stacks implemented in the past. Then we describe the
new architecture of our new *Fortika* group communication stack, and explain its
advantages. A more detailed discussion can be found in [16].

3.1   Traditional Group Communication Stacks

In any group communication stack, *atomic broadcast* is one of the most fundamental communication primitives provided.[1] However, there is not one single
way to implement atomic broadcast. The architecture of traditional group communication stacks is shown on Figure 2(a). Their main characteristics are the
following:

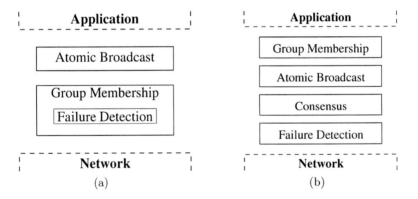

Fig. 2. (a) Traditional group communication stack, and (b) new group communication
stack

Group membership and failure detection are strongly coupled: Failure detection
is a low level mechanism that provides information (possibly incorrect) about the
status *crashed/alive* of processes in a group (see Section 3.2). This information
can be *inconsistent*, in the sense that two processes p, q might have a different
perception of the processes in the group. On the contrary, the group membership
service provides a *consistent* view of the successive membership of the group (see
Section 4.1). In traditional architectures these two components are strongly coupled: failure detection is a sub-component of the group membership component,
which acts as a failure detection for the rest of the system.

---

[1] *Atomic broadcast* delivers messages to all processes of a group in the same global
order.

Atomic broadcast algorithms rely on group membership: The traditional protocol stacks use atomic broadcast algorithms that require the help of the group membership to avoid blocking in the case of the failure of some critical process. Basically these algorithms operate in two modes, a failure-free mode and a failure mode. A notification of removal of a process from the group (e.g., due to a failure suspicion) leads the protocol to switch to the failure mode.

The consensus abstraction is barely used: The traditional protocol stacks have not recognized the important role of consensus (see [21]) for solving agreement problems, e.g., group membership, atomic broadcast. These stacks have group membership (and not consensus) as their most basic component.

3.2   *Fortika*: The New Group Communication Stack

The architecture of Fortika, our new group communication stack, is shown on Figure 2(b). Fortika's protocols can be composed using several protocol frameworks: Samoa, Cactus or Appia. The main differences in Fortika's architecture compared with the traditional one are the following:

Group membership and failure detection are decoupled: The strong coupling between failure detection and group membership in the traditional stacks was motivated by the atomic broadcast algorithms (see Section 3.1). Decoupling group membership from failure detection has the following advantage: failure suspicions do not necessarily lead to the costly process exclusion operation.

Group membership relies on atomic broadcast and not the opposite: Atomic broadcast can be solved by a sequence of instances of consensus (see [21]). Such a solution does not rely on a group membership service, and works without blocking if no more than half of the processes in the group crash.

Since the group membership component does not need to be *below* the atomic broadcast component, it can be placed *above*. This means that group membership can be implemented using atomic broadcast, which is quite natural, since the group membership service must deliver totally ordered views.

A consensus component is part of the stack: Since consensus plays a basic role in a group communication stack, it should appear as one of the bottom most component. Note that the consensus component requires the service of an (unreliable) failure detection component.

3.3   Assessment of the New Architecture

The two main advantages of the new architecture are the following.

Less complex stack: With traditional stacks, ordering is solved in two places: (1) within the group membership component for views, and (2) within the atomic broadcast component for messages. This is clearly not optimal, and introduces unnecessary complexity. The redundancy disappears in the new architecture.

Higher responsiveness: The performance of group communication must not only be measured in failure-free executions, but also in the case of failures. In the case of failures an important factor is the time needed to detect the failure (i.e., the crash of a process). The critical factor is thus the time-out of failure detectors. However, reducing the time-outs increases the probability of false suspicions. Decoupling failure suspicions from process exclusion has a big advantage: (1) a small value can be chosen for failure suspicion and (2) a large value for process exclusion. The factor that influences the performance of atomic broadcast is the short time-out value, and a wrong failure suspicion costs here very little. On the contrary, the exclusion of falsely suspected process has a high overhead, which can be avoided by choosing a large time-out value for exclusions.

4   Specifications

We discuss now more formal aspects related to group communication. We first address results related to the specification of group communication primitives. Here, we report on two contributions that each advance the state of the art, one by providing original specifications in the sparsely investigated territory of the crash-recovery model, and the other by revisiting and revising on specifications in the better investigated field of dynamic group communication. Finally, we propose an improved specification style for specifications, taking the example of unreliable failure detectors, to bring the respective mathematical definitions closer to our formal reasoning techniques.

4.1   Advances on Specifications in Refined Computing Models

Various models have been considered for group communication, namely *static/dynamic* groups, groups with *benign/malicious* faults, groups with *crash-stop/crash-recovery* processes [21]. These models not only influence the implementation of group communication, but also their specification. The model mostly considered in the literature is the static/crash-stop model with benign faults. Simple and widely adopted specifications for this model have been given in [12]. However, the static/crash-stop model does not cover the needs of a lot of applications. We discuss here group communication in the static crash-recovery model and in the dynamic crash-stop model.

Group Communication in the Crash-Recovery Model. In the crash-stop model processes do not have access to stable storage. In such a model a process that crashes loses all its state: upon recovery it cannot be distinguished from a newly starting process. The crash-stop model is attractive from an efficiency point of view: no stable storage means no costly logging operation, i.e., more efficient algorithms. However, the crash-stop model has also limitations. Algorithms developed in this model do not tolerate the crash of *all* processes. Moreover, access to stable storage is natural for many applications. This gives a strong motivation to consider group communication in the crash-recovery model. We consider here atomic broadcast.

Atomic broadcast in the crash-recovery model has been considered in [19]. However, as we explain in [15], the specification fails to capture the fundamental difference between the crash-stop and the crash-recovery model. In the crash-stop model there is no need to distinguish (1) the state of the application from (2) the state of the group communication infrastructure (if processes do not recover after a crash, the distinction is irrelevant). Indeed, in this case the two states are always trivially synchronized. This is no more the case when processes do recover. In this case the distinction—for each process—between *application state* and *group communication state*, requires to synchronize the checkpointing of these two parts of a process state. For this purpose we introduce a *commit* primitive. Thus atomic broadcast is defined in terms of the traditional *abcast* primitive (used by the application to broadcast a message), the traditional *adeliver* primitive (by which the group communication infrastructure provides a message to the application) and the new *commit* primitive. When executed by the application, *commit* tells the following to the group communication infrastructure: the application state, up to the most recent event, is saved on stable state. Implicitly, this leads the commit primitive to play two roles: (i) *veto* (e.g., no right to adeliver a message that was already adelivered before the commit), and (ii) *obligation* (e.g., for another process to adeliver a message).

Rather than giving here a formal specification of atomic broadcast in terms of *abcast*, *adeliver* and *commit*, we give the intuition of the specification on two examples.

(i) Veto role of commit. Consider the following two sequences of events on process p:
- *Scenario 1: adeliver$_p$(m); crash$_p$; recovery$_p$; adeliver$_p$(m);*
- *Scenario 2: adeliver$_p$(m); **commit$_p$**; crash$_p$; recovery$_p$; adeliver$_p$(m);*

Scenario 1 is ok, but not Scenario 2. In Scenario 2, *commit* marks the point at which p's execution will resume after a crash. So m cannot be adelivered a second time after recovery. The absence of commit in the first scenario allows m to be adelivered again after p's recovery: the crash leads p to "forget" the adelivery of m.

(ii) Obligation role of commit. Consider the following two sequences of events on process p:
- *Scenario 1: adeliver$_p$(m); crash$_p$; recover$_p$;*
- *Scenario 2: adeliver$_p$(m); **commit$_p$**; crash$_p$; recover$_p$;*

In Scenario 1, since p crashed after having adelivered m (i.e., the adelivery of m is "forgotten"), no other process is obliged to adeliver m. In Scenario 2, the execution of commit by p after the adelivery of m (i.e., upon recovery p "remembers" having adelivered m), forces other processes q to adeliver m. Note that the obligation is only on so-called *good* processes, i.e., processes that never crash or processes that crash only a finite number of times and always recover after a crash [5].

These two examples show that the execution of commit by process p makes all preceding events on p become "permanent". Without commit, events are volatile. The specification of atomic broadcast in the crash-recovery model is based on this distinction. The details can be found in [15]. A prototype has been implemented in our *Fortika* group communication middleware (see Section 3).

Dynamic Group Communication. While the specification of group communication in the crash-recovery model has been addressed only by few authors, the specification of dynamic group communication has received a lot of attention [9]. Nevertheless these specifications are not really satisfactory. The main problem is that the specifications for dynamic groups are not close to the specifications for static groups. Specifically, if we consider the specifications for dynamic groups in the special case of a static group, we do not obtain the widely adopted static specifications [12].

In the existing group communication specifications for dynamic groups, the key component is the *group membership service*, which is responsible for adding and removing processes to/from a group. Consider some group g. The successive membership of g is modelled using the notion of *view*: the requirement on the group membership is that it delivers the successive views of g to its members in the *same order*. For example if $v_0(g) = \{p, q, r\}$ is the initial view of g, and then the successive views are $v_1(g) = \{p, q\}$ and $v_2(g) = \{p, q, s\}$, then all processes see the membership changes in the same order. In the existing group communication specifications for dynamic groups, the specification of the group communication service is used to specify the basic communication primitive, called *view synchronous broadcast* or simply *vscast*. Vscast basically requires that messages that are vscast are ordered with respect to view changes [9]. Finally, atomic broadcast is defined as vscast with an additional order property.

This might look similar to the specification of atomic broadcast with static groups, where atomic broadcast is defined as *reliable broadcast* (or *rbcast*) with an additional order property [21]. Unfortunately, when comparing the specifications of (i) rbcast with static groups and (ii) vscast with dynamic groups, it is hard to see their similarities. However, it is possible to specify dynamic group communication such that the dynamic specifications reduce to the standard static specifications when the group membership does not change.

With static groups, the specification distinguishes *correct* processes (that do not crash) and *faulty* processes (that crash). The obligations (to deliver messages) are only on correct processes. With dynamic groups, the situation is slightly different. Consider a group g. The obligations (to deliver messages) must only be on *correct processes that are members of g*. If some process crashes or leaves g, its obligation with respect to g disappear. Symmetrically, if a process joins g, it starts to have obligations with respect to g. This can be expressed by the notion of *g-correct* process, derived from the notion of *v-correct* process [22]. Informally, process p is *v-correct* in some view v if p installs view v and does not crash while its view is v; process p is *g-correct* if it is correct in the first view of g it belongs to, and in all successive views of g.

With the notion of *v-correct* and *g-correct* process we can define dynamic reliable broadcast almost as (static) reliable broadcast. Reliable broadcast is defined by validity, uniform agreement and uniform integrity (for a definition of these properties, see [21]). Dynamic reliable broadcast can be defined by (i) the same uniform integrity property, (ii) slightly modified validity and uniform agreement properties (correct must be replaced with *g-correct* or *v-correct*), and (iii) a new *uniform same view delivery* property [22]:

- *Uniform same view delivery:* if two processes p and q deliver message m in view v^p (for p) and v^q (for q), then $v^p = v^q$.

This specification of dynamic reliable broadcast is a generalization of static reliable broadcast: if the group is static, dynamic reliable broadcast reduces to static reliable broadcast.

Dynamic atomic broadcast can then be defined as dynamic reliable broadcast with an additional total order property, which only slightly differs from the static total order property. Details can be found in [22], which also shows that the group membership specification can be trivially obtained from the dynamic atomic broadcast specification.

4.2   Proof-Oriented Specification Style for Failure Detectors

The concept of *unreliable failure detectors* was introduced by Chandra and Toueg [8] as a means to add weak forms of synchrony into asynchronous systems, mostly of the crash-stop model mentioned in the previous Section 4.1. Various kinds of such failure detectors, as we also use in the group communication architecture of Figure 2, have been identified as each being the weakest to solve some specific distributed programming problem [7]. Here, we provide—for the purpose of specification—a fresh look at the concept of failure detectors from the point of view of programming languages, using the formal tool of operational semantics, with the goal of bringing it closer to our formal reasoning techniques (see Section 5.1).

According to Chandra and Toueg [8], at any given time $t \in \mathbb{T}$, the failure detector (FD) of some process outputs a list of (names of) processes that it currently suspects to have crashed. As mentioned in Section 3, FDs are unreliable: they may make mistakes, they may disagree among themselves, and they may even change their mind indefinitely often.

In Table 1, we propose a uniform specification scheme—based on a two-layered transition system—to describe the operational semantics of process networks in the context of failure detectors. One layer describes—by separate sets of rules—both the transitions $N \rightarrow N'$ of process networks (here, left unspecified to keep the setting parametric, but should be derived from the description of the algorithm) and the transitions $\Gamma \rightarrow \Gamma'$ of the network's environment (keeping track of crashes and providing failure detection, as indicated by rule (ENV)). A process i in a network carries out essentially two kinds of transitions $N \rightarrow N'$, distinguished by whether it requires the suspicion of some process j by process i, or not. Formally, we use labels suspect$_j$@i and τ@i to indicate these two kinds. Another layer, with the rules (TAU) and (SUSPECT), deals exclusively with the compatibility of network and environment transitions, conveniently focusing on the environment conditions for the two kinds of transitions of process networks.

Table 1. Uniform "Abstract" Operational Semantics Scheme

$$(\text{ENV}) \; \frac{\text{`` failure detection events happens in the environment ''}}{\Gamma \to \Gamma'}$$

$$(\text{TAU}) \; \frac{\Gamma \to \Gamma' \qquad N \xrightarrow{\tau@i} N' \qquad \text{`` } i \text{ not crashed in } \Gamma \text{ ''}}{\Gamma \vdash N \to \Gamma' \vdash N'}$$

$$(\text{SUSPECT}) \; \frac{\Gamma \to \Gamma' \qquad N \xrightarrow{\text{suspect}_j@i} N' \\ \text{`` } i \text{ not crashed in } \Gamma \text{ ''} \qquad \boxed{\text{`` } j \text{ may be suspected by } i \text{ in } \Gamma \text{ ''}}}{\Gamma \vdash N \to \Gamma' \vdash N'}$$

For example, the boxed condition exploits the failure detector information that in our scheme is to be provided via the environment component Γ.

Runs are sequences of system transitions, as derivable by operational semantics rules. A process is *correct in a given run*, if it does not crash in this run.

Chandra and Toueg specified FDs by means of *failure patterns* $F : \mathbb{T} \to 2^{\mathbb{P}}$ and *failure detector histories* $H : \mathbb{T} \times \mathbb{P} \to 2^{\mathbb{P}}$. We refer to the respective runs as $\mathbb{T}$-runs, since time $\mathbb{T}$ lies at the core of the statically fixed components F and H. This (F, H)-based model is easily reformulated in our two-layered scheme [17].

Probably the main novelty of Chandra and Toueg's paper [8] was the definition and study of a number of FDs that only differ in their degree of reliability, as expressed by a combination of safety and liveness properties. These are formulated in terms of permitted and enforced suspicions according to the respective failures reported in F and the failure detection recorded in H:

completeness addresses *crashed processes that must be suspected*
by (the FDs of) "complete" processes.
accuracy addresses *correct processes that must not be suspected*
by (the FDs of) "accurate" processes.

These properties are implicitly quantified for *all possible runs*. The words "complete" and "accurate" processes indicate some flexibility in the definition of the set of processes that the property shall be imposed on. Many instantiations of completeness and accuracy have been proposed.

Inspired by the FD called Ω [7], we observed that the common principle behind the (F, H)-based notions of accuracy is that of "justified trust". The key role is played by correct processes—those that, according to F, were *immortal* in the given run—that are *trusted forever* (according to H) in the given run, either eventually or already from the very beginning. In a *dynamic* operational semantics scenario, as opposed to the static view of (F, H), we rather model the moment when such a process becomes forever trusted. Dynamically, however, we must also ensure this process not to crash afterwards—it must become immortal at this very moment. We call such a process *trusted-immortal*.

Table 2. Operational Semantics Scheme with Reliable Information

$$(\mathbb{D}\text{-ENV}) \quad \frac{(\mathsf{TI} \cup \mathit{TI}) \cap C = \emptyset \qquad (\mathsf{C} \cup C) \cap \mathit{TI} = \emptyset \qquad |\mathsf{C} \cup C| \leq \mathrm{maxfail}(n)}{(\mathsf{TI},\mathsf{C}) \quad \longrightarrow \quad (\mathsf{TI} \uplus \mathit{TI}, \mathsf{C} \uplus C)}$$

$$(\mathbb{D}\text{-TAU}) \quad \frac{(\mathsf{TI},\mathsf{C}) = \Gamma \rightarrow \Gamma' \qquad N \xrightarrow{\tau @ i} N' \qquad i \notin \mathsf{C}}{\Gamma \vdash N \rightarrow \Gamma' \vdash N'}$$

$$(\mathcal{X}\text{-SUSPECT}) \quad \frac{(\mathsf{TI},\mathsf{C}) = \Gamma \rightarrow \Gamma' \qquad N \xrightarrow{\mathrm{suspect}_j @ i} N' \qquad i \notin \mathsf{C} \qquad \boxed{\mathrm{condition}_{\mathcal{X}}(\Gamma, j)}}{\Gamma \vdash N \rightarrow \Gamma' \vdash N'}$$

Note, here, that our treatment of trusted immortals is to be seen in the very same way as Chandra and Toueg's treatment of (F, H): the ultimate goal is to provide some mathematical device to specify (not: implement) in retrospective view "what may have happened" in an acceptable run according to FD-sensitive information. They fix this information statically, while we allow it to develop dynamically and, by that, we can simplify the style of specification.

With this idea, we proposed a new model [17] capable to represent *all* of the FDs of [8] solely based on information that is not fixed before a run starts, but is dynamically appearing along its way. It turns out that two kinds of information suffice: (1) which processes have crashed, and (2) which processes have become *trusted-immortal*. Both kinds of information may occur at any moment in time, but they remain irrevocable in any continuation of the current run.

In Table 2, environments $\Gamma = (\mathsf{TI},\mathsf{C})$ record sets TI of trusted-immortal processes and sets C of crashed processes. Rule ($\mathbb{D}$-ENV) precisely models their non-deterministic appearance in full generality: in a single step, an environment may be increased by further trusted-immortal processes ($\in \mathit{TI}$) or crashed processes ($\in C$). Rule ($\mathbb{D}$-TAU) permits actions $\tau @ i$ if $i \notin \mathsf{C}$. Rule ($\mathcal{X}$-SUSPECT) requires in addition that the suspected process j is permitted to be suspected by Γ, depends on the FD accuracy that we intend to model.

Our $\mathbb{D}$-representations of FDs are proved extensionally equivalent with the $\mathbb{T}$-representations proposed in [8] via mutual "inclusion" of their sets of runs. Essentially, this works by looking for a *mutual simulation* of $\mathbb{T}$-runs and $\mathbb{D}$-runs sharing the same network run (by projecting onto the N-component). In general, proofs using the new instead of the old representation are considerably simpler.

5   Verification and Testing

Verification and testing are complementary, but equally important aspects. Up to now, in our new architecture, we have focused on two aspects: the formal verification of the consensus component, based on an operational semantics, and the experimental validation of the Fortika group communication stack, through the technique of fault injection. While the formal verification seeks to prove that a consensus component does precisely what it should, the experimental validation seeks to "stress-test" the robustness of a component by confronting with environment conditions that go beyond what it should be able to cope with.

5.1   Formal Verification of the Consensus Component

As pointed out in Section 3.2, consensus is a fundamental component that plays a basic role in the new architecture. The properties it provides to the above components are:

1. *Validity*: If a process decides a value v, then v was proposed by some process.
2. *Agreement*: No two correct processes decide differently.
3. *Termination*: Every correct process (eventually) decides some value.

Any correct implementation of the consensus component must guarantee the respect of these three properties. Since consensus is one of the basic building blocks of the new group communication stack (see Figure 2(b)), the correctness of its implementation is fundamental for the stability of the whole new architecture.

Many algorithms are available to implement the consensus component. This variety is due to the existence of different models (of communication, of failure, etc) and the necessity of taking advantage of the properties provided by underlying components. A common trait of many of these algorithms is that they are described in pseudo code—i.e., with neither formal syntax nor formal semantics—and the proofs of their correctness are given informally, with brief argumentations expressed in natural language. Thus, the pseudo code sometimes leaves space to interpretation and the correctness proofs sometimes require the readers to actually prove themselves substantial parts or subresults for which only informal arguments were given. To convincingly argue for the stability and correctness of the whole architecture, we consider it vital to rely on a consensus implementation that has been proved correct formally.

Given the model in which our architecture was placed (reliable communication, crash failure) and given the presence of failure detectors, the algorithm that we chose to implement the consensus component was the one proposed by Chandra and Toueg in [8]. This algorithm makes use of reliable broadcast and failure detector abstractions. It also assumes a majority of correct processes.

Before explaining the algorithm, it is worth here to briefly clarify the meaning of the terms Quasi-reliable Point-to-Point and Reliable Broadcast abstractions that we will use in our description. Both Quasi-reliable Point-to-Point and Reliable Broadcast are components that lie in what we call Network layer (Figure 2). As their name suggest, they are (quasi) reliable in that they guarantee the reception and non-corruption of messages sent by correct processes. Quasi-reliable Point-to-Point takes care of messages exchanged between two processes, while Reliable Broadcast distributes messages to all the correct processes in a group. Since the implementation of these two components does not influence the consensus algorithm, in our study we represent them as abstractions providing specific features and properties. Now everything is in place to describe the Chandra-Toueg consensus algorithm.

The Chandra-Toueg algorithm (Figure 3) proceeds in *rounds* and is based on the *rotating coordinator* paradigm: for each round number, a single process

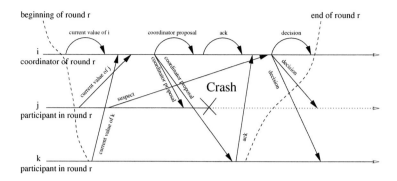

Fig. 3. A round in the Chandra-Toueg consensus algorithm

is predetermined to play a coordinator role, while all other processes in this round play the role of participants. Each of the n processes holds a local round counter and, at any time, knows who the coordinator of its current round is. For every round, each participant sends its current value to the coordinator of this round. The coordinator chooses one of the proposals it has received and sends it to all participants. These, in turn, are supposed to acknowledge the receipt. If the coordinator receives a majority of positive acknowledgments, it reliably broadcasts the value to all participants: this is going to be the decision. If a participant is not able to receive the coordinator proposal while waiting for it, and if the underlying failure detector component allows, then this participant may instead suspect the coordinator to have crashed. In this case, the participant sends a negative acknowledgement and moves to the next round, sending the very same value of the previous round to the new coordinator.

Correctness of the algorithm means that its resulting runs—more precisely: all runs satisfying the requirements on the underlying communication and coordination services—satisfy the three Consensus properties. In [8], Chandra and Toueg also provide sketches of proofs (written in natural language) of Validity, Agreement and Termination.

Such proofs make heavy reference to the concept of round. However, there is nothing like the global round number of a reachable global state in a system run. A round is only a local concept, and no relation between runs and asynchronous rounds is ever properly clarified. We consider this as problematic.

Moreover, there are two main reasons that make us argue against the approach of using only pseudo code. The first one is that the algorithm is not sufficiently complete. In fact, it describes only local behavior of processes and does not include any representation of the network. Also, the involved data structures are underspecified. In particular, there is almost no description of how and where the messages are buffered when waiting to be sent and once they have been received. The second reason is that, due to the absence of a precise formal semantics in the pseudo code, the algorithm description does not offer an unambiguous derivation of runs from the code. This is crucial because the specification of correctness properties is exclusively based on the notion of system runs. More precisely, it is based on runs of the full distributed system, including the point-to-point and broadcast messages that are buffered within the network, as well as the behavior of the failure detector mechanism.

For these reasons, the proofs would profit much from the introduction of global knowledge on:

- system states and their past, which could provide us with precise information about which processes have been in which round in the past and what they precisely did when they were there;
- broadcast messages, which could provide us with precise information about what values are the chosen ones and about the processes that already know such values and the ones that still ignore them;
- point-to-point messages, which could provide us with precise information about what messages are ready to be sent but would still be lost in the case of a crash of the sender, what messages are about to be received and cannot be lost any longer should their original sender crash, what messages have already been received thus probably influencing the following behavior of their receiver.

Thus, in our work [18], we provide a mathematical structure that describes the global idealized run-time system comprising all processes and the network. Moreover, in order to simplify the proofs, our structure also plays the role of a system history, never forgetting any information during the computation.

Formally, the consensus algorithm is specified in terms of inference rules that define computation steps as transitions between configurations of the form:

$$\frac{some\ condition}{\varGamma \vdash \langle \mathbf{B}, \mathbf{Q}, \mathbf{S} \rangle \ \rightarrow \varGamma' \vdash \langle \mathbf{B}', \mathbf{Q}', \mathbf{S}' \rangle}$$

$\varGamma$ is the environment component, presented in Section 4.2, that records sets TI of trusted-immortal processes and sets C of crashed processes. $\mathbf{B}$ contains the (histories of) messages sent during the execution of the algorithm through the Reliable $\mathcal{B}$roadcast service. $\mathbf{Q}$ contains the (histories of) messages sent during the execution of the algorithm through the $\mathcal{Q}$uasi-reliable Point-to-Point service. $\mathbf{S}$ models the *state* of the n processes. We can access the current state of each single process using its identifier, i.e. $\mathbf{S}(i)$ is the current state of process i.

The condition for the execution of the rule is usually a condition on the state of a particular process and on the messages that such process has received up to that point. For example, "process i should be in a waiting state and the message containing the coordinator proposal should not figure among the messages received by i". The condition can also be extended with requirements on the environment component. For example, "the coordinator of round r should not be in the TI set". The execution of the rule modifies the contents of (some of) the structures. For example, the state of process i changes and a new message is sent, or broadcast.

As mentioned also in Section 4.2, runs are considered as sequences of system transitions derivable by operational semantics rules. In this way we can generate all, and only, the runs that would be possible if we were executing the algorithm in reality. We can study such runs examining what happens step by step and verifying claims on the overall execution. The proofs of the properties of consensus are therefore made by showing that all the sequences of system transitions derivable by the given operational semantics rules, that represent all the possible runs generated by the algorithm, satisfy Validity, Agreement and Termination.

Summing up, in order to counter the observed incompleteness of the algorithm description in pseudo-code format, we have developed appropriate description techniques that incorporate the lacking information; also, in order to counter the observed ambiguity due to the lack of precise semantics of the pseudo-code with respect to the underlying system model, we have built the algorithm upon a formal description. We have then defined runs as sequential executions of the semantics rules and have kept track of the changes induced by the application of such rules in the $\mathbf{B}$, $\mathbf{Q}$ and $\mathbf{S}$ structures. With this apparatus, we have eventually all the formal means for reasoning on rounds, as well as on time and on messages sent/in-transit/received, thus the proofs of correctness of the algorithm are now much more detailed, rigorous and credible.

5.2   Testing the Robustness of Fortika

Fault injection is a well-known technique to assess a system's resilience to error conditions. In a joint work with the University of Illinois [13], we set up an error-injection testbed in order to study how Fortika (see Section 3.2) reacts to data corruption. We carried out several error injection campaigns, which performed thousands of error injections, consisting in flipping a random bit in main memory or in a network message. It is important to point out that Fortika has been designed with a benign-fault model in mind, that is, only crash faults were considered (see Section 4.1). The memory and network corruption errors addressed in these experiments go far beyond the model's assumptions. Thus, our goals were not to find out whether Fortika is resilient to these faults, but rather to analize (and later minimize) any unacceptable behavior of the system.

Memory Injections. We performed a preliminary injection campaign for each memory segment: code (errors directly injected into the executed code), stack (local variables altered), and heap (allocated variables dynamically corrupted).

The most important result from these experiments was the high frequency of *partial process crashes*. In many experiments (26% for stack injections) the system completely hung. Further analysis showed that multithreading was behind such system-wide hangs: quite often, an error injection threw a Java runtime exception; the Java Virtual Machine stopped the offending thread, but let the others continue execution. We call this *partial crash*: some threads were working but some were not (e.g., the injected process could be sending heartbeats but omitting other messages). We enhanced the design of Fortika to cope with memory corruption and avoid partial crashes (as well as other problems, see details in [13]). Table 3 summarizes the results of memory injections for the improved Fortika design. This table shows the low rate of executions with unacceptable behavior (between 0% and 6%) with respect to total manifested errors, which are defined as errors that visibly affect the system behavior (though not necessarily causing an incorrect execution).

Table 3. Memory injection results after improving Fortika

Memory Segment	Injected Errors	Manifested Errors	Unacceptable* Behavior
Heap	15177	1221	0
Text			
libjava.so	1000	616	36 (5.8%)
libjvm.so	910	269	7 (2.6%)
libnet.so	755	215	2 (1%)
Stack	5509	1825	109 (6.0%)

Table 4. Network injection results after improving Fortika

Total injected errors	1062
Manifested errors*	625
Message not detected	
a) No propagation	76 (12%)
b) Propagation	6 (1%)

* Percentages with respect to manifested errors are shown in parentheses.

Network Injections. In the network injection campaigns, an incoming message is altered (after checksum verification), thus resulting in an invalid input to the process. The goal is to analyze how far can an incorrect message get into the receiving process, and how badly it can affect the system. Most Fortika messages contain marshalled Java objects, thus, the desirable behavior is that Java unmarshalling routines detect and block incorrect messages.

A preliminary injection campaign evidenced a fairly high rate of incorrectly unmarshalled messages: up to 25% for certain messages types. In these experiments, the unmarshalling routines were unable to detect the corrupted message and allocated incorrect objects in memory. Further analysis showed that compatibility between different versions of the same Java class, a core feature of standard Java serialization, seriously harms robustness against corrupted messages. In the same way as with memory injections, we revised the design of Fortika in order to better react to incorrectly unmarshalled messages. The injection results for the new design are shown in Table 4, where we can see that only 13% of corrupted messages are not detected during unmarshalling, and sneak into the receiving process. Even in those cases, we see that the error seldom propagates to other processes (1% of all manifested errors).

6   Conclusion

We started from the goal to improve the state of the art of group communication by having groups with complementary scientific backgrounds—possibly characterized as distributed computing, programming languages and concurrency theory—join their forces. By now, we have already managed to achieve a number of interesting individual results that witness the potential for successful collaboration. Although much more work remains to be done, we consider our project as a promising first concrete step towards formally defined and verified implementations of flexibly reusable group communication middleware.

References

1. *The Appia project.* http://appia.di.fc.ul.pt/
2. The Cactus project. http://www.cs.arizona/Cactus/
3. The Ensemble project. http://www.cs.cornell/Info/Projects/Ensemble/
4. *The X-kernel project.* http://www.cs.arizona.edu/xkernel/
5. Marcos Kawazoe Aguilera, Wei Chen, and Sam Toueg. Failure detection and consensus in the crash-recovery model. *Distributed Computing*, 13(2):99–125, 2000.
6. Daniel C. Bünzli, Sergio Mena, and Uwe Nestmann. Protocol composition frameworks, a header-driven model. In *Proceedings of the IEEE International Symposium on Network Computing and Applications*, Cambridge, MA, USA, 2005.
7. Tushar Deepak Chandra, Vassos Hadzilacos, and Sam Toueg. The weakest failure detector for solving consensus. *Journal of ACM*, 43(4):685–722, 1996.
8. Tushar Deepak Chandra and Sam Toueg. Unreliable failure detectors for reliable distributed systems. *Journal of ACM*, 43(2):225–267, 1996.
9. G. V. Chockler, I. Keidar, and R. Vitenberg. Group Communication Specifications: A Comprehensive Study. *ACM Computing Surveys*, 4(33):1–43, December 2001.
10. Cormac Flanagan and Martin Abadi. Types for safe locking. In *Proc. ESOP '99*, LNCS 1576, March 1999.
11. Christophe Gensoul. Implementing Nuntius in the Objective Caml System. Master's thesis, EPFL, 2004.
12. V. Hadzilacos and S. Toueg. Fault-Tolerant Broadcasts and Related Problems. Technical Report 94-1425, Department of Computer Science, Cornell University, May 1994.
13. Sergio Mena, Claudio Basile, Zbigniew Kalbarczyk, André Schiper, and Ravi Iyer. Assessing the crash-failure assumption of group communication protocols. In *Proceedings of 16th IEEE Int'l Symp. on Software Reliability Engineering (ISSRE)*, November 2005.
14. Sergio Mena, Xavier Cuvellier, Christophe Grégoire, and André Schiper. Appia vs. Cactus: Comparing protocol composition frameworks. In *22nd Symposium on Reliable Distributed Systems. Florence, Italy*, October 2003.
15. Sergio Mena and André Schiper. A new look at atomic broadcast in the asynchronous crash-receovery model. In *Proceedings of the 24th Symposium on Reliable Distributed Systems (SRDS 2005)*, Orlando, Florida, October 2005.
16. Sergio Mena, André Schiper, and Paweł T. Wojciechowski. A Step Towards a New Generation of Group Communication Systems. In Markus Endler and Douglas Schmidt, editors, *Proceedings of Middleware 2003: The 4th ACM/IFIP/USENIX International Middleware Conference (Rio de Janeiro, Brazil)*, volume 2672 of *LNCS*, pages 414–432. Springer, June 2003.
17. Uwe Nestmann and Rachele Fuzzati. Unreliable failure detectors via operational semantics. In Vijay A. Saraswat, editor, *Proceedings of ASIAN 2003*, volume 2896 of *LNCS*, pages 54–71. Springer, December 2003.
18. Uwe Nestmann, Rachele Fuzzati, and Massimo Merro. Modeling consensus in a process calculus. In Roberto Amadio and Denis Lugiez, editors, *Proceedings of CONCUR 2003*, volume 2761 of *LNCS*, pages 399–414. Springer, August 2003.
19. L. Rodrigues and M. Raynal. Atomic Broadcast in Asynchronous Crash-Recovery Distributed Systems and Its Use in Quorum-Based Replication. *IEEE Transactions on Knowledge and Data Engineering*, 15(5):1205–1217, September 2003.
20. *The SAMOA Protocol Framework.* http://lsrwww.epfl.ch/samoa.
21. A. Schiper. Dependable Systems. This book, Part I, Chapter 2.

22. A. Schiper. Dynamic Group Communication. *ACM Distributed Computing*, 18(5):359–374, April 2006.
23. Vlad Tanasescu and Paweł T. Wojciechowski. Role-based declarative synchronization for reconfigurable systems. In Manuel Hermenegildo and Daniel Cabeza, editors, *Proceedings of PADL 2005: The 7th International Symposium on Practical Aspects of Declarative Languages (Long Beach, CA, USA)*, volume 3350 of *LNCS*, pages 52–66. Springer, January 2005.
24. Paweł T. Wojciechowski. Concurrency combinators for declarative synchronization. In Wei-Ngan Chin, editor, *Proceedings of APLAS 2004: The 2nd Asian Symposium on Programming Languages and Systems (Taipei, Taiwan)*, volume 3302 of *LNCS*, pages 163–178. Springer, November 2004.
25. Paweł T. Wojciechowski. Isolation-only transactions by typing and versioning. Technical Report IC-2004-104, School of Computer and Communication Sciences, Ecole Polytechnique Fédérale de Lausanne (EPFL), December 2004. 47pp.
26. Paweł T. Wojciechowski. Isolation-only transactions by typing and versioning. In *Proceedings of PPDP '05: The 7th ACM-SIGPLAN International Symposium on Principles and Practice of Declarative Programming (Lisboa, Portugal)*, July 2005.
27. Paweł T. Wojciechowski and Olivier Rütti. On correctness of dynamic protocol update. In *Proceedings of FMOODS '05: The 7th IFIP Conference on Formal Methods for Open Object-Based Distributed Systems (Athens, Greece)*, volume 3535 of *LNCS*, pages 275–289. Springer, June 2005.
28. Paweł T. Wojciechowski, Olivier Rütti, and André Schiper. SAMOA: Framework for Synchronisation Augmented Microprotocol Approach. In *Proceedings of IPDPS 2004: The 18th IEEE International Parallel and Distributed Processing Symposium (Santa Fe, USA)*, April 2004.

Fault-Tolerant Parallel Applications with Dynamic Parallel Schedules: A Programmer's Perspective

Sebastian Gerlach, Basile Schaeli, and Roger D. Hersch

Ecole Polytechnique Fédérale de Lausanne (EPFL),
School of Computer and Communication Sciences,
Station 14, 1015 Ecublens, Switzerland
dps@epfl.ch

Abstract. Dynamic Parallel Schedules (DPS) is a flow graph based framework for developing parallel applications on clusters of workstations. The DPS flow graph execution model enables automatic pipelined parallel execution of applications. DPS supports graceful degradation of parallel applications in case of node failures. The fault-tolerance mechanism relies on a set of backup threads stored in the volatile storage of alternate nodes that are kept up to date by both duplicating transmitted data objects and performing periodical checkpointing. The current state of a failed node can be reconstructed on its backup threads by re-executing the application since the last checkpoint. A valid execution order is automatically deduced from the flow graph. The addition of fault-tolerance to a DPS application requires only minor changes to the application's source code. The present contribution focuses on the development of fault-tolerant parallel applications with DPS from a programmer's perspective.

1 Introduction and Related Work

Clusters of commodity workstations are rapidly growing in size and complexity as computation power requirements increase. The large number of computing nodes incorporated within a cluster dramatically increases the likelihood of node failures during program executions. Therefore, ongoing research focuses on graceful degradation and the continuation of program execution despite individual node failures.

In the context of message-passing systems, two major classes of recovery schemes have been proposed: checkpoint-based and message log-based recovery [8].

Checkpoint based approaches store the current state of computation to stable storage. Coordinated checkpointing on all participating nodes [16] may be achieved by stopping in an ordered manner all computations and communications, and performing a two-phase commit in order to create a consistent distributed checkpoint. Checkpointing can also be performed independently on

J. Kohlas, B. Meyer, and A. Schiper (Eds.): Dependable Systems, LNCS 4028, pp. 195–210, 2006.
© Springer-Verlag Berlin Heidelberg 2006

all participating nodes (uncoordinated checkpointing). This removes the performance bottlenecks induced by the global synchronization required for coordinated checkpoints and allows checkpointing at convenient times, for example when the data size associated with a checkpoint is very small. Several checkpoints need to be stored on each node, and a consistent state from which to restart has to be found when a failure occurs [4]. In unfavorable situations, the recovery can lead to the domino effect, where no consistent checkpoint other than the initial state can be found. In order to eliminate the domino effect, additional constraints on checkpointing sequences need to be introduced, for example based on the applications' communication patterns [17].

Message logging approaches store in addition to checkpoints all the messages flowing through the system. The logged messages allow bringing a node to any given state by re-executing its application code with the corresponding sequence of logged input messages. Three types of message logging are usually considered: pessimistic, optimistic and causal. Pessimistic logging logs every received message to stable storage before processing it. This ensures that the log is always up to date, but incurs a performance penalty due to the blocking logging operation. The penalty can be reduced by using specific storage hardware, or by using sender-based message logging [13][5]. Optimistic logging begins processing messages without waiting for a successful write to stable storage [15]. The overhead of pessimistic logging is removed, but several messages might be lost in case of failures. When the system is restarted it must roll back to a previous consistent state on all nodes. Finally, causal logging also provides low overhead and limits the backtracking that has to be performed during recovery. It does however require the construction of an antecedence graph for messages, and requires a rather complex recovery scheme [9].

These mechanisms make no assumptions about the internal structure of the applications other than the use of message passing for communications between processes. They are thus very well suited for applications written with general-purpose message passing libraries such as MPI [7]. When parallel applications are described using high-level approaches, additional information about the structure of the application is available. For example, task graphs [6] or Calypso [2] make use of such information for recovering and resuming computation after a failure. In order to keep the fault-tolerance mechanism efficient, the application developer often needs to provide specific hints or to use certain constructs within the application. These modifications are required for example in order to allow an application to be restarted from a stored checkpoint.

Fault-tolerance schemes also vary in the assumptions they make about the number and nature of failures that can be recovered. Placing additional limitations on the recoverable cases may enable significant optimizations when compared to the general case. For example, if the system has never more than one failure at a time, stable storage can be replaced with transfers to neighboring nodes [14]. Such a scheme has the advantage of allowing the application to recover without having to fetch data from the stable storage of the failed node.

Dynamic Parallel Schedules (DPS) is a high-level framework for developing parallel applications [10]. The DPS framework supports fault-tolerance using a combined message logging and checkpointing approach [11]. The fault-tolerance mechanism uses the parallel application's structure exposed in the application's high-level description in order to hide most of the complexity of fault-tolerance from the application developer. However, the support for fault-tolerance is not fully transparent; the developer needs to take some specific requirements into account. In the present paper, we describe the implications of developing fault-tolerant applications from a developer's perspective.

2   The Dynamic Parallel Schedules Framework

DPS applications are defined as directed acyclic graphs of operations. The fundamental types of operations are leaf, split, merge and stream operations. The inputs and outputs of the operations are strongly typed data objects. Figure 1 illustrates the flow graph of a simple parallel application, describing the asynchronous flow of data between operations.

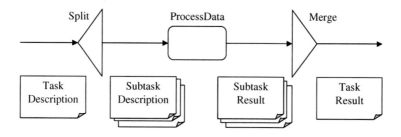

Fig. 1. Flow graph describing data distribution (split), parallel processing, and collection of results (merge)

The split operations are used to divide the incoming data objects into smaller objects representing subtasks. These subtasks are subsequently sent to the next operations specified by the flow graph (e.g. *ProcessData*). The leaf operations process the incoming data objects, and produce one output data object for each input data object. The merge operations are used to collect the results into a single large output object. Once all the results corresponding to the data objects originally sent by a split operation have been collected, the larger resulting data object is sent out. Successive data objects arriving at the entry of a split operation yield successive new instances of the split-merge operation pair.

The stream operations combine a merge operation with a subsequent split operation. Instead of waiting for the merge operation to receive all its data objects before allowing the subsequent split operation to send new data objects, the stream operation can stream out new data objects based on groups of incoming data objects. Stream operations allow programmers to finely tune their processing pipeline and therefore to ensure a maximal utilization of the underlying hardware.

All operations, including split and merge operations are extensible constructs where the developer provides his own code to control how processing requests or data are distributed, and how processed sub-results are merged into one result. The data objects circulating in the flow graph may contain any combination of simple types or complex types such as arrays or lists. The following source code shows a typical implementation for a split operation within DPS, where a task is split into smaller parts.

```
class Split : public dps::SplitOperation
  <SplitInDataObject, SplitOutDataObject> // Data object types
{
  IDENTIFY(Split)
public:
  // This method is called when the input data object is received
  void execute(SplitInDataObject *in)
  {
    // Split task into NB_PARTS small parts
    for(Int32 splitIndex=0;splitIndex<NB_PARTS;splitIndex++)
    {
      SplitOutDataObject *sot=new SplitOutDataObject();

      // Fill the output data object with meaningful data

      postDataObject(sot);
    }
  }
};
```

Other operations are implemented by deriving them from other base classes depending on their functionality, such as *dps::LeafOperation* or *dps:: MergeOperation.*

Operations within a flow graph are carried out within threads grouped in thread collections. Figure 2 illustrates the distribution of flow graph elements into thread collections for a simple compute farm application. Two thread collections are created. The first, *MasterThread*, handles the global split and merge operations, and contains only a single thread. The second, *WorkerThreads*, handles the parallel computation, and contains one thread for each compute node.

A DPS thread is a logical construct representing an execution environment for a set of operations. In data parallel applications, data is stored within threads that are distributed across the available compute nodes. Threads are implemented as standard C++ objects. Figure 3 shows an example of a grid-based data structure distributed on 3 threads. Each thread stores additional data in order to enable neighborhood dependent computations. DPS threads are mapped to operating system threads, although not necessarily in a one-to-one relationship. For instance several DPS threads residing on a single processor node may share a single operating system thread.

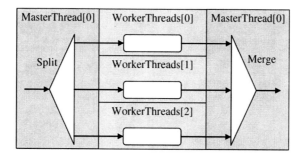

Fig. 2. A flow graph and its associated thread collections

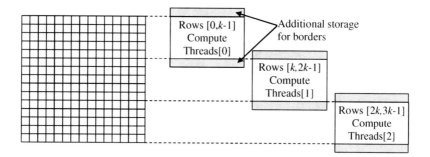

Fig. 3. Distribution of a grid-based data structure on 3 threads, each thread also storing copies of its neighboring grid lines (borders)

The selection of the thread within a thread collection on which an operation is to be executed is accomplished by evaluating at runtime a user defined routing function attached to the corresponding directed edge of the flow graph. Communication patterns such as the neighborhood exchanges illustrated in Figure 4 required for updating a distributed data structure (Figure 3) can easily be specified by using relative thread indices. The first part of the flow graph ensures that all nodes have sufficient neighborhood information available, and the second part performs the computation on all nodes. The intermediate synchronization ensures that the global state remains consistent.

By transferring data objects as soon as they are computed, and maintaining queues of arriving data objects, execution of DPS applications is fully pipelined and asynchronous. Data object queues are associated with the thread that contains the operations that will consume them. This macro data flow behavior enables automatic overlapping of communications and computations. In order to limit the size of the data object queues stored in threads, DPS provides a flow control mechanism that can be used to limit the number of data objects in circulation between a split operation and the corresponding merge operation. The flow control mechanism suspends the split operation until the processed data objects have been received by the corresponding merge operation.

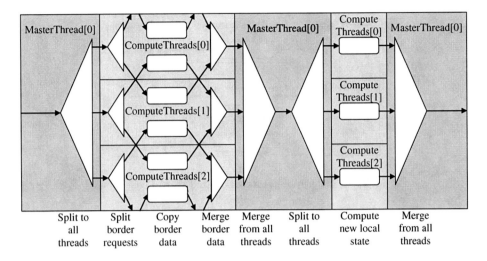

| Split to all threads | Split border requests | Copy border data | Merge border data | Merge from all threads | Split to all threads | Compute new local state | Merge from all threads |

Fig. 4. A flow graph for one iteration of an iterative neighborhood-dependant parallel computation

The flow graph together with its collections of threads and its routing functions forms a parallel schedule. A parallel schedule describes a fine to medium-grained parallel application. Its operations represent the small subtasks that are executed in a pipeline-parallel manner according to the flow graph. The DPS communication layer, hidden from the application programmer, relies on TCP sockets, and uses an optimized data serialization scheme that minimizes memory copies.

3   Fault-Tolerance in DPS

DPS provides a fault-tolerance mechanism that allows applications to continue execution despite node failures. The fault-tolerance mechanism is implemented by providing a scheme for the recovery of flow graph program execution segments located on a failed node. The scheme is composed of two distinct recovery mechanisms. The first general purpose mechanism enables the reconstruction of the state of a thread upon node failure. The second specialized mechanism is an optimization for threads that do not store any local state information.

DPS detects node failures by monitoring communications. A node is considered to be failed when it is not able to communicate with another node. The TCP/IP network layer used by DPS reports failures when communications fail or disconnections occur.

3.1   General Purpose Recovery Mechanism

The general purpose mechanism relies on a set of backup threads that are mapped onto an alternate set of nodes as illustrated in Figure 5. When a data object is sent to an operation on a given thread, a copy is also sent to the backup thread. Upon occurrence of a failure, the current state of the threads that were on the failed node is reconstructed on the backup threads by re-executing operations. The valid execution sequence of operations is automatically deduced from the flow graph of the corresponding DPS application by applying a simple data object numbering scheme.

Operations are assumed to be deterministic, i.e. for a given initial thread state and a set of incoming data objects, they will always produce the same output. This assumption is necessary to ensure that the reconstruction on a backup thread will yield a state identical to the state that was present on the failed thread.

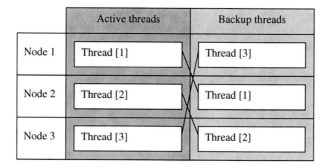

Fig. 5. Mapping of a thread collection with backup threads

In order to shorten the reconstruction time of a failed node, one may replicate the state of the active threads onto the corresponding backup threads (periodic checkpointing). When the backup thread is subsequently used for reconstructing the thread state after a failure of the active thread, reconstruction is initiated from the replicated state rather than from the initial state. Each DPS thread has three components that must be conserved for successful reconstruction: the current local thread state, the queue of data objects that wait for processing, and the state of suspended operations within that thread. Since replicating the current state also removes part of the pending data object queue on the backup thread, it reduces the memory requirements on the backup nodes. This checkpointing operation can be carried out asynchronously and independently on all individual threads. Independent checkpointing of individual threads enables the compute nodes to remain potentially busy during the checkpointing process by executing operations attached to other threads mapped to the same node. The effective overhead induced by stopping a thread in order to checkpoint can therefore be kept very low.

Since both active and backup threads are stored in the volatile storage of the processing nodes, only a single copy of the thread is left after a failure. In order to ensure that the application can survive successive failures, it is necessary to rapidly create a new backup thread for the remaining copy. The new backup thread is created by checkpointing the surviving thread copy immediately after activation, in order to minimize the time during which the application is fragile. This general-purpose fault-tolerance mechanism allows the computation to continue as long as for each thread within every thread collection either the active thread or its backup thread remains valid.

3.2   Recovery for Threads Without Local State Data

For threads that do not store any local state data (*stateless* threads), the recovery mechanism can be simplified. If the general purpose mechanism would be used, the backup threads would store only the duplicated data objects. It is therefore more efficient not to send out the duplicate data objects, but rather to keep them on the sender node. Since the operations running on stateless threads do not use any local state, these operations can be executed on any thread. If a stateless thread fails, it is removed from the thread collection. The sender node resends the data objects to another thread in the collection. The execution of the application can continue as long as at least one thread remains valid within the stateless thread collection.

The flow graph provides information about the runtime execution patterns of applications, allowing the framework to transparently select the appropriate recovery mechanism for the graph segments. For compute bound applications, the fault-tolerance overheads during normal program execution remain low thanks to the asynchronous communications that occur in parallel with computations. A detailed description of both fault-tolerance mechanisms and the associated performance overheads can be found in [11].

4   Implementing Fault-Tolerance

The following sections focus on the elements that must be taken care of by the developer of a fault-tolerant application. As an example, we use two applications: a compute farm application, where a master node distributes computation tasks onto worker nodes, and a complex application with a distributed state that is updated iteratively. These applications use the flow graphs illustrated in Figures 2 and 4 respectively. The DPS fault-tolerance mechanism is presented in two steps. The first step aims at adding fault-tolerance, allowing the application to survive multiple failures. The second step ensures an efficient reconstruction process by enabling checkpointing.

4.1   Simple Compute Farm Applications

A fault-tolerant compute farm application needs to be able to survive two types of failures: the failure of a worker node, and the failure of the master node. Since the worker threads do not store any local data, these threads can be handled by the specialized sender-based stateless thread recovery mechanism provided by DPS. Since this mechanism simply redistributes the unprocessed worker tasks to the surviving worker threads, no changes are required in the source code implementation of the application. Therefore, when the application is running, any node other than the one running the master thread can fail at any time. As long as one worker node remains active, the program execution is unaffected.

Fault-tolerance on the master thread is important, since this thread is running the split and merge operations. At least one backup thread needs to be added to the mapping of the thread collection *MasterThread*. This will allow the master thread to be reconstructed on other nodes participating in the computation, ensuring successful completion if the initial master thread fails. The backup thread is simply created by adding a list of valid backup nodes to the mapping of the master thread collection:

```
masterThread.addThread("node1+node2+node3");
```

In this example, the master thread is located on *node1* and its backup thread on *node2*. The third node *node3* will take over the role as backup if either of the other nodes fails in order to ensure support for multiple subsequent failures.

On a master node failure, the split operation is restarted from the beginning, and all processing requests are sent again. The routing function does not necessarily return constant results for a given data object when the total number of threads varies, some data objects will get routed to different nodes on re-execution, and part of the computation may possibly be performed again. Those data objects that are resent to the same nodes will be caught by a mechanism for eliminating duplicate data objects [11]. This additional reconstruction overhead can be reduced by periodically checkpointing the main thread, i.e. by replicating its current state to the backup thread as described in section 5.

4.2 Applications Storing a Distributed State

Applications that store local data within their computation threads need backup threads. For example, let us consider an application using a thread collection *computeThreads*, containing three computation threads mapped onto nodes *node1*, *node2* and *node3*. Each thread needs to have at least one backup thread. In order to ensure that the thread collection can survive failures until a single node is left, we use all nodes as backups for each thread, creating a round-robin mapping as shown in Figure 6. The proposed mapping can be obtained with the following mapping string:

```
computeThreads.addThread
  ("node1+node2+node3 node2+node3+node1 node3+node1+node2");
```

This mapping ensures that any two nodes may fail without preventing the application from completing successfully. The thread mapping strings (*"node1+ node2+node3 node2+node3+node1 node3+node1+node2"*) with round robin mapping of backup threads may be generated automatically by the DPS framework [12]. In order to ensure acceptable reconstruction times, it is again necessary to perform periodic checkpointing.

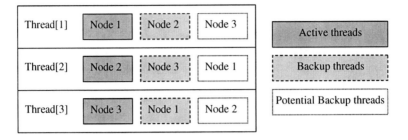

Fig. 6. Mapping of a thread collection with backup threads

5   Checkpointing Support

In order to provide support for checkpointing, long-running operations that may be suspended (split and merge operations) need some minor modifications, so as to allow them to be restarted from other points than from the beginning. Since operations are simple C++ functions, and since the language does not provide a simple means to checkpoint the current state of a function and to restart it later, the application needs to help the framework in order to obtain the desired functionality. The required modifications are independent of the general application structure, since the changes affect only individual operations. For the following discussion, we use the split and merge operations of the compute farm application (Figure 2) as example.

The first functionality that the application needs to provide is the ability to checkpoint the current state of the operation. For the split operation previously shown in section 2, the loop counter *splitIndex* needs to be made serializable, allowing the operation to be recreated from a checkpoint. Since DPS provides an automatic serialization mechanism for data objects, we reuse this mechanism for operations. Therefore, the split operation uses the automatic serialization syntax for its data members as follows:

```
class Split : public dps::SplitOperation
  <SplitInDataObject, SplitOutDataObject, MasterThread>
{
  CLASSDEF(Split)
    BASECLASS(dps::OperationBase)
  MEMBERS
    ITEM(Int32,splitIndex) // Current loop counter
  CLASSEND;
```

The second functionality that the application needs to provide is the ability to restart the operation from a saved checkpoint. DPS uses the input data object parameter of the function to distinguish between a normal call to the operation and a restarted call. When the operation is initially called during normal execution, it receives a valid non-NULL input data object. However, when it is being restarted from a checkpoint after a failure, no input data object is passed as parameter (i.e. the input data object pointer is NULL). This particular case is used to skip the initialization of the internal variables, since they have already been set up by the checkpoint:

```
public:
  // Split operation
  void execute(SplitInDataObject *in)
  {
    // If the input data object is NULL, the operation is
    // being restarted from a checkpoint. Otherwise, we need to
    // initialize our variables.
    if(in)
      splitIndex=0;
```

The content of the loop itself is kept unchanged. The update of the loop counter has been moved to a position before the call to *postDataObject*, since it is at this point that a checkpoint is taken when a checkpoint is requested. The loop condition can be checked with a *while* statement.

```
    // Loop until all output data objects have been generated
    while(splitIndex<NB_PARTS)
    {
      SplitOutDataObject *sot=new SplitOutDataObject(splitIndex);
      splitIndex++;

      postDataObject(sot);
    }
  }
```

Finally, the application needs to call the checkpointing function for the main thread collection. Since checkpointing is fully asynchronous within the DPS framework, this can be done anywhere. In the present example, we add the checkpointing request within the main loop of the Split operation. Three checkpoints are requested, one for every 25% of output data objects posted. We introduce an additional member variable *next* that indicates at which point the next checkpoint is due. This variable is checked within the loop, and checkpoints are requested accordingly. This variable also needs to be serializable like the loop counter.

```
    // Loop until all output data objects have been generated
    while(splitIndex<NB_PARTS)
    {
      // Do some periodic checkpointing in Split
      if(splitIndex>next)
      {
        next+=NB_PARTS/4;
```

```
        // This is an asynchronous call, the checkpoint will be
        // taken shortly after.
        getController()->getThreadCollection<MasterThread>
                                        ("master").checkpoint();
    }

    SplitOutDataObject *sot=new SplitOutDataObject(splitIndex);
    splitIndex++;

    postDataObject(sot);
    }
```

Calling the *checkpoint* function does not immediately create a checkpoint, but informs the framework that a checkpoint should be taken as soon as possible. Since all the threads within a thread collection are independent, they are checkpointed individually. The checkpointing process is started as soon as the currently executing operation on the current thread ends or is suspended (for example when waiting for its next input data object). When no operation is running on a thread, its state is guaranteed to be consistent. The checkpoint is then sent to the backup thread. The checkpoint is composed of the current local state of the active thread, the list of currently suspended operations as well as the list of all the data objects that have been processed since the last update. The new state replaces the previous state stored on the backup thread, and the listed data objects are removed from the backup thread's data object queue. When the checkpointing process is complete, execution resumes normally on the thread. In the above example, the checkpoint is taken on the call to *postDataObject* immediately following the call to *checkpoint*.

When checkpointing is used on this type of application, it is important to enable flow control, in order to ensure that the split operation does not post all subtasks at once. If flow control is disabled, all the checkpoints are taken at the same time after termination of the execution of the split function, making the complete process useless. With flow control enabled, the checkpoints are taken as expected, since the split operation is periodically suspended while waiting for the merge operation to catch up.

The Merge operation needs similar changes in order to ensure that the current output data object state is correctly preserved when checkpointing. The following source code describes the original merge operation before adding code for fault-tolerance:

```
class Merge : public dps::MergeOperation
    <MergeInDataObject, MergeOutDataObject >
{
    void execute(MergeInDataObject *in)
    {
        // Create output data object
        MergeOutDataObject *output=new MergeOutDataObject();
```

```
  // Wait until all the computation results have been received
  do
  {
    // Add the result contained in the input data object 'in'
    // to the output data object
  }
  while((in=waitForNextDataObject())!=NULL);

  postDataObject(output);
  }
}
```

The local state of the operation is entirely contained in the output data object, which is updated for each incoming data object in a *while* loop. Therefore, in order to enable restarting, the output data object needs to be stored within the merge operation class. In the DPS framework, the *dps::SingleRef* class is used to store a serializable pointer.

```
class Merge : public dps::MergeOperation
  <MergeInDataObject, MergeOutDataObject >
{
  CLASSDEF(Merge)
    BASECLASS(dps::OperationBase)
  MEMBERS
    // The output data object
    ITEM(dps::SingleRef<MergeOutDataObject>,output)
  CLASSEND;
```

Just like the Split operation, the Merge operation uses the state of the input data object for initialization of the output data object. The loop within the merge operation is unchanged compared with the non fault-tolerant code, since the local state is already updated before calling *waitForNextDataObject*. In the fault-tolerant case, the last operation of the flow graph is responsible for storing the result of the parallel computation, rather than posting a data object to the caller of the parallel schedule. This is necessary to ensure that the parallel application terminates even when the original master node that initiated the execution of the parallel schedule is dead. Since the merge operation is the last operation in the flow graph, the operation ends with a call to *endSession* in the DPS controller, which causes the application to terminate. Since the application terminates from within the merge operation, the output data object is never posted.

```
  void execute(MergeInDataObject *in)
  {
    // If the operation is not being restarted, initialize the
    // output data object
```

```
if(in!=NULL)
  output=new MergeOutDataObject();

// Wait until all the computation results have been received
do
{
  // Add the result from the input data object 'in' to the
  // output data object if in is not NULL
}
while((in=waitForNextDataObject())!=NULL);

// Store computation result before terminating application

getController()->endSession(true);
}
```

5.1   Serializing Thread States

For applications that store a local thread state, it is necessary to ensure that the local thread state can be copied correctly within the checkpointing process. This is achieved by using the DPS serialization mechanism. Consider the following thread with local data:

```
struct ComputeThread
{
  int data; // Single integer stored in thread
};
```

The thread is simply converted to the serializable form as follows:

```
struct ComputeThread
{
  CLASSDEF(ComputeThread)
  MEMBERS
    ITEM(int,data)  // Single integer stored in thread
  CLASSEND;
};
```

6   Conclusions and Future Work

DPS is a novel high-level environment for developing parallel applications specified as executable flow graphs. The DPS framework provides dynamic handling of resources, in particular the ability to specify the mapping of threads to nodes at runtime, and to modify this mapping during program execution. Flow graphs and updatable thread mappings are the foundation on which we build fault-tolerance.

We implement fault-tolerance by providing a hybrid recovery scheme using two compatible mechanisms for the recovery of flow graph program execution segments located on a failed node. The first general purpose mechanism relies on duplicate data objects sent to backup nodes in order to enable the reconstruction of the state of a thread upon node failure. Backup threads are kept up to date by periodical checkpointing of thread states. Upon occurrence of a failure, the current state of the threads that were on the failed node is reconstructed on the backup threads by re-executing operations. The valid execution sequence of operations is automatically deduced from the flow graph of the corresponding DPS application by applying a simple sender-based data object numbering scheme. A second specialized sender-based mechanism is used for operations that do not depend on local state information, such as graph segments comprising simple compute farms. Since no state needs to be reconstructed in case of failures, the duplicate communications are avoided. The flow graph provides information about the runtime execution patterns of applications, allowing the framework to transparently select the appropriate recovery mechanism for the graph segments. For compute bound applications, the fault-tolerance overheads during normal program execution remain low thanks to the DPS asynchronous communications that occur in parallel with computations.

The general-purpose fault-tolerance mechanism allows computation to continue as long as for each thread within every thread collection either the active thread or its backup thread remains valid. The optional compatible stateless recovery mechanism requires that at least one thread remains valid within every stateless thread collection, and that the threads hosting the surrounding split-merge pair are recoverable with the general purpose recovery mechanism.

The fault-tolerance mechanisms are not fully transparent to the application developer. However, only minor changes need to be made to the application in order to enable fault-tolerance. The required changes are due to limitations of the C++ language. Some aspects, such as checkpointing requests, are currently left to the programmer. These requests could also be performed automatically by the framework by monitoring the applications flow graph. The resulting fault tolerance scheme may then become more transparent to the application developer.

The complete DPS software package is available on the Web under the GPL license at http://dps.epfl.ch. The complete source code for the applications presented in this paper can also be found at this address.

Acknowledgements

This project has been partially funded by the Hasler Foundation, project DICS-1845.

References

1. A. Agbaria, R. Friedman, Starfish: Fault-tolerant dynamic MPI programs on clusters of workstations, 8th International Symposium on High Performance Distributed Computing (HPDC-8'99), IEEE CS Press, August 1999

2. A. Baratloo, P. Dasgupta, Z.M. Kedem, Calypso: A Novel Software System for Fault-Tolerant Parallel Procssing on Distributed Platforms, Proc. International Symposium on High-Performance Distributed Computing, pp. 122-129, 1995

3. R. Batchu, J. Neelamegam, Z. Cui, M. Beddhua, A. Skjel-lum, Y. Dandass, M. Apte, MPI/FT: Architecture and taxonomies for fault-tolerant, message-passing middleware for performance-portable parallel computing, 1st IEEE International Symposium of Cluster Computing and the Grid, Melbourne, Australia, 2001

4. B. Bhargava, S.R. Lian, Independent Checkpointing and Concurrent Rollback for Recovery - an Optimistic Approach, Proc. IEEE Symposium on Reliable Distributed Systems, pp. 3-12, 1988

5. S. Chakravorty, L.V. Kale, A fault tolerant protocol for massively parallel systems, 18th International Parallel and Dis-tributed Processing Symposium (IPDPS'04), pp. 212-219, April 2004

6. D. Das, P. Dasgupta, P.P. Das, A New Method for Transparent Fault Tolerance of Distributed Programs on a Network of Workstations Using Alternative Schedules, Proc. Conf. on Algorithms and Architectures for Parallel Processing (ICAPP'97), pp. 479-486, 1997

7. J. Dongarra, S. Otto, M. Snir, D. Walker, A message passing standard for MPP and Workstations, Communications of the ACM Vol. 39, No. 7, pp. 84-90, 1996

8. E.N. Elnozahy, L. Alvisi, Y.M. Wang, D.B. Johnson, A Survey of Rollback-Recovery Protocols in Message-Passing Systems, ACM Computing Surveys, Vol. 34, No. 3, pp. 375-408, September 2002

9. E.N. Elnozahy, W. Zwaenepoel, Manetho: Transparent Rollback-Recovery with Low Overhead, Limited Rollback and Fast Output Commit, IEEE Transactions on Computers, Vol. 41 No. 5, pp. 526-531, May 1992

10. S. Gerlach, R.D. Hersch, DPS - Dynamic Parallel Schedules, International Parallel and Distributed Processing Symposium (IPDPS'03), pp. 15-24, April 2003

11. S. Gerlach, R.D. Hersch, Fault-tolerant Parallel Applications with Dynamic Parallel Schedules, International Parallel and Distributed Processing Symposium (IPDPS'05), p. 278b, April 2005

12. S. Gerlach, DPS online documentation, http://dps.epfl.ch

13. D.B. Johnson, W. Zwaenepoel, Sender based message logging, Digest of Papers, FTCS-17, Proc. 17th Annual International Symposium on Fault-Tolerant Computing, pp. 14-19, 1987

14. J.S. Plank, Y. Kim, J.J. Dongarra, Algorithm-Based Diskless Checkpointing for Fault Tolerant Matrix Operations, FTCS-25, Proc. 25th Annual International Symposium on Fault-Tolerant Computing, pp. 351-360, 1995

15. R. Strom, S. Yemini, Optimistic recovery in distributed systems, ACM Transactions on Computer Systems, Vol. 3, No. 3, pp. 204-226, 1985

16. Y. Tamir, C.H. Sequin, Error recovery in multicomputers using global checkpoints, Proceedings of the International Conference on Parallel Processing, pp. 32-41, 1984

17. Y.M. Wang, W.K. Fuchs, Lazy Checkpoint Coordination for Bounding Rollback Propagation, Proc. 12th Symposium on Reliable Distributed Systems, pp. 78-85, October 1993

Autonomic Computing for Virtual Laboratories*

Cesare Pautasso[1], Win Bausch[2], and Gustavo Alonso[1]

[1] Department of Computer Science
ETH Zurich, 8092 Zürich, Switzerland
Tel.: +41 01 632 0879; Fax: +41 01 632 1425
pautasso@inf.ethz.ch, alonso@inf.ethz.ch
[2] AWK Group AG
Leutschenbachstrasse 45, 8050 Zürich, Switzerland
Tel.: +41 44 305 97 63; Fax: +41 44 305 95 19
win.bausch@awkgroup.ch

Abstract. Virtual laboratories can be characterized by their long-lasting, large-scale computations, where a collection of heterogeneous tools is integrated into data processing pipelines. Such virtual experiments are typically modeled as scientific workflows in order to guarantee their reproduceability. In this chapter we present JOpera, one of the first autonomic infrastructures for managing virtual laboratories. JOpera provides a sophisticated Eclipse-based graphical environment to design, monitor and debug distributed computations at a high level of abstraction. The chapter describes the architecture of the workflow execution environment, emphasizing its support for the integration of heterogeneous tools and evaluating its autonomic capabilities, both in terms of reliable execution (self-healing) and automatic performance optimization (self-tuning).

1 Introduction

More and more scientific disciplines are switching from *in vitro* to *in silico* research where natural phenomena are explored using a computer in a virtual laboratory instead of being observed in the field. On the one hand, this is due to the fact that the cost of storing observations has become lower than the cost of making them. On the other hand, scientific workflow tools [15] – such as the one described in this chapter – have been developed in order to make it easier for scientist to process and analyze such observations by composing an increasingly large number of basic analysis and simulation tools.

Although virtual laboratories are typically associated with very large amounts of data, data processing is even more critical than data management due to the sheer computational complexity involved. Given the heterogeneity and complexity of the underlying distributed execution environments and the long duration of the computations involved, it is not feasible to manually manage the lifecycle of such virtual experiments. Instead, a virtual laboratory infrastructure should

---

* This work is partly supported by grants from the *Hasler Foundation* (DISC Project No. 1820).

J. Kohlas, B. Meyer, and A. Schiper (Eds.): Dependable Systems, LNCS 4028, pp. 211–230, 2006.

automate most tasks related to the reliable and reproduceable execution of such computations. Ideally, a virtual laboratory infrastructure should provide a team of scientists with support for easily creating and efficiently running virtual experiments. Additionally, virtual laboratories are rarely designed in a top-down fashion. They typically emerge from a collection of disconnected pieces of data processing code (e.g., written in FORTRAN) and glue scripts (e.g., in PERL [1]) that are developed and maintained by individual scientists. Such an ad-hoc approach leads to systems that are difficult to modify and maintain, cannot be easily shared among researchers and involves rather primitive and unsystematic methods for running, monitoring, and steering the computations.

Considering that all of these problems are a major source of inefficiencies, it becomes clear that an organized way to store and manage information and meta-information about the entire lifecycle of a virtual experiment is critical to its success. Thus, not only high level languages and abstractions to define such computations are needed but also efficient execution tools integrated with user-friendly management and monitoring environments are required.

In this chapter we focus on how this functionality has been provided in JOpera [16], an autonomic process support system specifically tailored for virtual laboratories. The JOpera project has its roots in the BioOpera [5] project and it has been developed at the Information and Communications Systems Research Group of ETH Zurich. JOpera extends the Eclipse platform with a graphical environment where scientists can use a drag, drop and connect programming metaphor to define distributed computations out of reusable components. The resulting high-level models are then automatically compiled into Java bytecode so that they can be efficiently executed by the system. In case of virtual laboratories where a large number of computations are concurrently executed, JOpera can distribute their execution across a cluster of computers in order to provide the appropriate level of performance. Moreover, JOpera includes self-management capabilities, where the distributed engine can automatically determine its optimal configuration based on its current workload. With this, the need for manual intervention and tuning the system's performance is greatly reduced.

The rest of this chapter is organized as follows. We discuss in more detail the problems of virtual laboratories by showing some typical examples in Section 2. In order to address these challenges, scientific workflow tools such as JOpera offer a solution based on two aspects. The first one consists of a language targeted towards modeling virtual experiments at a high level of abstraction (Section 3). The second one – presented in Section 4 – lies in the middleware infrastructure supporting the execution of such a language. An evaluation of the autonomic capabilities of the system is discussed in Section 5 before concluding the chapter in Section 6.

2   Motivation

This section illustrates the issues scientists running large scale virtual experiments need to cope with. Each example represents a pattern frequently encountered in a virtual experiment. Each of these patterns has different characteristics and requires a different type of support from the virtual laboratory infrastructure.

2.1 Structured Computations

A structured computation involves a set of applications that needs to be executed in a specific order. These applications run on different operating systems and hardware platforms. They exchange data with each other through a number of input and output mechanisms (e.g., command line input parameters, input and output files, web page downloads) This data is produced at different points in time throughout the computation and may have to be converted between different formats. Programming such application may prove to be too difficult for ordinary users, if appropriate high level programming tools are not available.

In addition to design-time support, run-time support is also important. For instance, considering a distributed environment, manually taking care of routing data from task to task at the right time becomes difficult, time consuming and error-prone. Thus, data transfers should be automated, not just to improve the efficiency of the virtual experiment, but also to collect important lineage and data provenance information. The goal is to automatically log all of the necessary meta-data in order to support the correct interpretation of the results of a virtual experiment, i.e., by tracing how this was generated.

An example of this structured computation pattern can be found in the bioscience domain. Microarray technology is a promising approach to find clues concerning the function of specific genes in a cell's metabolism. The idea is to expose the cell to an artificially created stimulus (also called *condition*) and observe the cellular response in terms of the level of activity (or the *expression level*) of some genes over time. Development of appropriate computational models as well as innovation in wet lab equipment have made it possible to move elements of the microarray processing pipeline into virtual laboratories.

Such a virtual microarray experiment involves a range of data extraction, transformation and correction steps that need to be performed prior to a complex statistical analysis of the data. Figure 1 provides a high-level overview of the procedure, which is described in more detail in [3]. This microarray processing pipeline was implemented with BioOpera by integrating existing, standalone, publicly available software packages written in different programming languages and maintained by different reseach groups [5].

2.2 Embarrassingly Parallel Computations

Whereas the main challenge of the *Microarray analysis pipeline* concerns the specification of the complex interactions between a large set of heterogeneous tools, in this section we deal with the evolution of the execution environment when running long-lived computations.

An embarrassingly parallel computation consists of a set of tasks that can be processed independently of each other. This kind of computations are commonly used in a virtual laboratory setting as, given enough execution capacity,

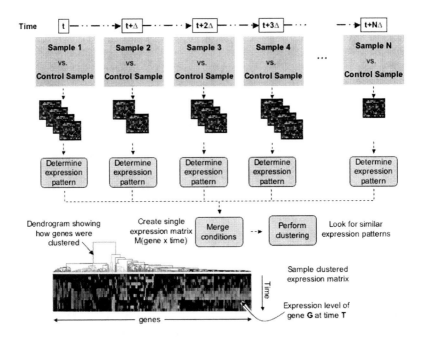

Fig. 1. Microarray analysis pipeline: from raw samples to correlated expression patterns

their execution time can be reduced by executing all tasks in parallel. However, when such a pattern is implemented without appropriate support from the virtual laboratory infrastructure, several challenges become apparent. For instance, choices need to be made concerning the granularity of the tasks, how to schedule tasks to run on the available resources (e.g., whether several tasks can share a single processor), and finally, how to handle the failure of individual tasks. Without appropriate support, the onus for such chores lies on the *user*. Not surprisingly, manually and painstakingly maintaining such computation becomes the dominant factor in the overall cost of performing such virtual experiments and does not scale to a large number of tasks running on a large number of computers.

An example of this kind of computation is a sequence alignment, a problem that lies at the heart of comparative genomics. Given an unknown set of nucleo or peptide sequences, the initial step into any inquiry concerning the evolution, structure, and function (e.g., [8,9,20]) of these biomolecules consists of the *cross-comparison* of each sequence in this set against every sequence of a reference data set such as Swiss-Prot [6] - an *All vs. All*, if the two data sets coincide. Typically, a single comparison requires seconds of CPU time, depending on the method that is being used and the length of the sequences being compared, and that the total number of pairwise sequence comparisons is in the order of billions. From this, several years of CPU time are required to perform the whole experiment. Being composed out of a number of pairwise sequence comparisons independent of each other, an All vs. All is embarrassingly easy to parallelize: each alignment can be computed independently.

Ample details concerning a month-long lifecycle of running such a computation with BioOpera can be found in [4]. Throughout the computation, processor availability has been subject to substantial unexpected and uncontrolled fluctuation. Without load balancing or job migration across machines to compensate for resource failures, utilization of the overall available computing resources is bound to be suboptimal. Also, a failure of the node coordinating the computation halts the entire computation. Dealing with these issues manually is indeed inefficient and time consuming. If a computation environment made out of hundreds of hosts is considered, it is clear that all of the previously described aspects of its execution should be controlled automatically.

2.3   Parameter-Sweep Computations

This pattern represents a combination of the ones discussed in the previous two sections. A parameter sweep computation [2] consists of applying the same algorithm to all parameter value combinations in a predefined parameter space. Since each each parameter combination can be typically processed independently, parameter sweeps are embarassingly parallel and share the requirements for a reliable and distributed execution environment. Concerning structured computations, not only a complex computation is applied to each parameter combination but also traceability needs to be guaranteed (i.e., in order to correlate which results have been produced by which input parameter values).

An example parameter sweep application to which JOpera has been successfully applied involved the simulation of protocols for wireless ad-hoc networks [21]. Communication partners in such networks are in motion with respect to each other and may leave and join the network at any time. Additionally, the network is infrastructureless. Unlike in mobile telephony, for instance, there is no fixed infrastructure that keeps track of nodes and routes data from sender to receiver. Data is directly routed through the mobile nodes and routing paths have to be recomputed as nodes move in and out of transmission range.

The objective of the experiment described here is to compare the simulated behavior of a set of resource reservation protocols under certain assumptions like congestion, network latency or node population distribution. In order to gain a complete understanding of the problem, this parameter space should be explored in its entirety. Although an individual simulation is on average relatively short, on the order of 20 seconds of CPU time, the size of the parameter space makes running the entire simulation challenging. Each simulation depends on 17 parameters, resulting in around 1.5 million independent simulations. Again, parallel execution on a cluster of computers is mandatory to ensure that the results are delivered in a reasonable amount of time.

2.4   Discussion

From the previous examples it is clear that a virtual laboratory infrastructure needs to cope with a variety of design-time and run-time problems. These involve providing good abstractions to model the structure of computations that are built by integrating heterogeneous scientific tools. However, modeling is not enough, as computations need to be reliably and efficiently executed in a distributed (and failure-prone) environment. The main features of such a virtual laboratory infrastructure can be categorized as follows:

Modeling. An easy to use, intuitive programming environment should be provided so that scientific computations can be specified at a high level of abstraction by fostering the reuse of existing tools.

Integration. Virtual laboratories must cope with heterogeneity, not only regarding data formats but also concerning the environments on which analysis tools are executed.

Distribution. Distribution is another property of virtual laboratories, as local and remote (e.g., Web-based) data sources and tools have to be accessed.

Steering. In addition to reporting their status and progress, long-running computations require support for interacting with them in order to proactively steer their execution.

Scalability. In this context, the notion of scalability needs to be extended to encompass the virtual laboratory infrastructure itself, which should scale to handle a very large number of virtual experiments.

Fault Tolerance. Given that most of today's Grid and cluster environments are failure prone, various failure masking and exception handling approaches should be in place in order to minimize the number of troubleshooting activities to be performed.

Combining all of these features and mechanisms with the appropriate self-management strategies yields an autonomic infrastructure for managing virtual laboratories as we are going to describe in the following sections.

3   Modeling Virtual Experiments with Processes

A language for modeling virtual experiments should allow scientists to model all aspects of a virtual laboratory (e.g., which tools to use, what are their dependencies, how to invoke them, where the data should be stored) in a well-defined, formalized way so that these experiments can not only be executed in a fully automatic fashion but the management of related metadata is also automated.

Thus, the main challenge in designing such a language lies in keeping the balance between two extremes. On the one hand, a risk lies in abstracting away too many details – e.g., like the data flow, typically disregarded in many business process modeling languages – that are of primary importance for modeling executable scientific computations. On the other hand, a lower-bound is defined by traditional scripting languages (e.g., PERL or PYTHON). These languages can also be used as the glue to patch together and run virtual experiments. However, they lack the necessary abstractions to deal with issues such as reuse of scientific tools and algorithms, scalable, reliable and persistent execution, simplified orchestration of distributed components, interactive monitoring and steering of computations as well as tracking lineage and data provenance meta-data.

In the following, we give an overview about the abstractions provided by JOpera's languages (Processes and Programs) and how they fit together (Binding and Flow).

3.1 Modeling the Flow with Processes

Processes can be seen as an executable blueprint of a distributed application built using a pipe-and-filter architectural style [7]. Processes model computations as a combination of heterogeneous tools which are to be executed as the computation goes through its various stages. Processes can be run once over a certain input dataset, or can also be applied over a range of input parameter values.

In JOpera, processes model the interactions between a set of programs. A JOpera process consists of a set of *tasks* linked by *data* and *control* flow dependencies. Tasks represent each step of the computation to be carried out. Executing a task involves the invocation of an external program or the call of another sub-process.

Both the data and the control flow of a process can be formally described as a graph. The edges of the control flow graph link the tasks of a process and define their partial order of execution. These edges can be labeled with boolean expressions in order to select upon which condition they are activated and thus provide support for adding alternative or multiple branches, loops and synchronization points in the control flow. The data flow edges link data parameters of tasks declaring how information is transferred from one program to the next. Processes also have input and output parameters, so that it is possible to pass information to a process when starting it and retrieving its results when it is completed. Data flow and control flow are related since tasks consuming data cannot be started before all tasks producing the required data have successfully completed their execution. Thus, when executing a process, JOpera analyzes its structure and concurrently schedules all tasks that are found to be independent. If enough computing resources are available, these tasks will be executed concurrently.

Traditionally, workflow management tools have used a visual syntax to graphically depict the flow linking the various scientific tools together into a process. This is also the approach followed in JOpera with its JOpera Visual Composition Language (JVCL). With it, both the control flow and data flow of a process can be specified using a very simple, graph-based visual notation. Nevertheless, the JOpera visual composition language supports advanced constructs (e.g., iteration, streaming, reflection, recursion, nesting, or dynamic late binding) without resorting to ad-hoc (and difficult to interpret) extensions of the visual syntax. We refer the reader to [18] for an in-depth presentation of the JVCL language.

3.2 Binding Processes with Programs

The notion of binding in JOpera defines the flexible relationship between processes (i.e., the compositions) and programs (i.e., the components). Although processes model how a virtual experiment is composed out of a set of programs, the description of the programs themselves is kept – by design – separate from the processes. This separation has several advantages. It enhances the reusability of the programs, which can be shared among different processes. Likewise, the same process can be reused by binding it with different programs.

More precisely, a binding defines what are the constraints to be satisfied by a program in order to be included in a process [19]. Such a binding can be evaluated along the entire lifecycle of a process: at design-time (early binding), at compilation-time, at deployment-time, at run-time (late and very late binding).

Given the goal of supporting an open and heterogeneous set of programs, JOpera makes very little assumptions about the mechanisms that are used to invoke their functionality. Instead JOpera provides a meta-library of component types that can be used to define programs. Programs wrap existing tools employing the most appropriate invocation mechanism both in terms of performance but also development convenience [17]. Proof of the openness of the JOpera service meta-model is provided in Table 1 where all currently supported component types are listed. Depending on the relevant aspects that should be taken into account when designing a virtual experiment, these components can be classified along the following dimensions:

Granularity. Both fine-grained (e.g., Java snippets) and coarse-grained (e.g., Web services) programs are supported by JOpera within a single process. Furthermore, the overhead of invoking each component type is proportional to its granularity. In other words, JOpera can leverage the standardized (but relatively inefficient) SOAP protocol without being constrained by it. If necessary, more efficient invocation mechanisms can still be selected to access fine-grained programs.

Local vs. Remote Invocation. At run-time, programs can be separated from a process by an increasingly large distance. For example, Java methods are invoked by a thread running within the same Java virtual machine where the process is running. Legacy UNIX applications invoked through the local operating system shell run in a separate operating system process with respect to the one running the JOpera process. Additionally, programs can represent the execution of an application on a remote host through a secure shell connection and, going even further away, jobs submitted to a resource management and scheduling system (e.g., Condor [14] or Globus [10]) to be executed on a cluster of computers in a remote Grid environment.

Data-Driven vs. Computation-Oriented. In addition to computations, programs can also be used to manage the data that is required and produced by other programs. Data-driven programs are used to model data transfers (e.g., file-staging through secure copy or GridFTP), access to persistent storage (e.g., SQL database queries), and can play the role of mediators and adapters (e.g., Java snippets or XML data transformations written in XPath, XSLT, or XQuery).

Interaction Style. In addition to synchronous (RPC-style) interactions, where a program models the complete invocation of an external tool, we have also

Table 1. Summary of the component types currently supported by JOpera

Component Type	Description
Local Computation	
UNIX Application	(UNIX) Execute a command line through the local operating system
Java Method	(JAVA) Call a local Java method
Java Snippet	(JAVA.SNIPPET) Embed a Java snippet into the process
Remote Computation	
Java Remote Method	(JAVA.RMI) Invoke a remote Java method
Web Service	(SOAP) Web service call (using raw SOAP messages)
Web Service	(WSIF) Web service call (using the WSIF framework [13])
Secure Shell	(SSH) Execute a remote command through a secure shell connection
Data Transfer	
Web Page	(HTTP) Download (or upload) a page from a web site
Secure Copy	(SCP) Transfer a file with secure copy
Database	
Database Query	(SQL) Send any SQL statement to a JDBC compliant database
Telegraph Query	(TELEGRAPH) Subscribe to a telegraph stream described by an SQL query
XML transformation	
X-Path Query	(XPATH) Query an XML document with X-Path
Style Sheet Transformation	(XSLT) Transform an XML document with an XSL transformation
Cluster/Grid computing	
Globus [10]	(GLOBUS) Submit a job to a grid managed by Globus
Condor [14]	(CONDOR) Submit a job to a cluster managed by Condor
Internal	
JOpera Echo	(ECHO) Echo a message back
JOpera Process	(OPERA) Spawn another process
JOpera API	(API) Call the API of JOpera
Human-oriented	
Workflow task	(WF) Add a new activity to a user's worklist

applied JOpera's meta-model to provide support for asynchronous interactions, where the execution of a program involves a one-way message exchange or the start (or termination) of an independently running application. In this case, data exchanges between the process and the program can occur at any time, i.e., when the program is started (input), after it has completed (output) but also during its execution (streaming).

Machine-Bound vs. Human-Oriented. Although most computational tools are usually meant to be executed in non-interactive mode, parts of a process may also explicitly include a task requiring some form of human intervention, e.g., to validate partial results and steer the process accordingly or take some manual corrective actions before the computation is carried on.

Data vs. Metadata. Reflection and introspection are also two important features of JOpera's visual composition language. With these it becomes possible, e.g., to control the execution of a process from another process, or to dynamically discover properties about the execution environment and use this information from within a process. For example, it is possible to dynamically detect how many resources are available and partition a dataset accordingly or measure the invocation time of a remote Web service to detect whether a service-level agreement has been violated.

Additional component types can be easily added to JOpera by plugging a service invocation adapter into the corresponding extension point, as we are going to show in the next section.

4   An Autonomic Infrastructure for Virtual Laboratories

The architecture of JOpera is composed of a set of Eclipse plug-ins (Figure 2). Following Eclipse's design guidelines, we have separated plug-ins responsible for the user interface (UI) from plug-ins that work with the internal process data model. Along an orthogonal dimension, we have also separated the design-time from the run-time functionality, so that, if necessary, the system can be deployed in a partial configuration (e.g., where only the run-time monitoring features are enabled). The compiler, which links the design-time to the run-time part has been developed in its own plug-in. On the run-time side, the run-time kernel provides the basic process execution infrastructure used by the compiled code. It is extended by the service invocation adapters plug-ins, which implement the mechanisms and provide support for the protocols used to invoke the various kinds of components that were described in the previous section. Finally, the API wrappers are used to expose the functionality of the kernel to clients supporting a variety of protocols.

4.1   Design-Time Tools

The JVCL model core plug-in contains the functionality used at design-time to manage the information about programs and processes described in the JOpera Visual Composition Language. This includes the ability of internalizing such information loading it from an XML serialization. This plug-in also manages an object-oriented in-memory model of the processes and programs which has been automatically produced from the corresponding schema using a generative programming approach. Clients observing the model may use its event notification facilities to be notified when parts of the model are changed, e.g., to perform some incremental validation or to update the information displayed by the corresponding UI views. This way, after each modification, the model is checked incrementally for consistency with respect to various criteria. In case a violation

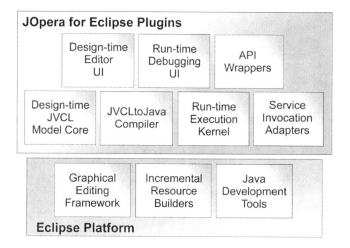

Fig. 2. JOpera is built as a set of Eclipse plugins

is detected, a specific problem (or a warning) marker is attached to the part of the model that triggered it. Such verification happens in the background, without user intervention so that errors and potential problems are reported immediately. In an agile development environment, such immediate feedback is nowadays taken for granted as it contributes to reducing the overhead of the typical compose-compile-fix development cycle and it is very important to decrease the slope of the environment's learning curve.

The editor UI plug-in contains the user-interface code that presents the content of the currently open processes to the developer. We use two different kinds of visual user interfaces to display and edit the structure of a process. List-based forms are used to choose the services to be composed and to define their interface parameters. Additionally, the control flow and data flow graphs of the processes are edited in a visual environment. Such visual editor is implemented by extending the Graphical Editing Framework (GEF) of Eclipse to use the visual syntax of the JVCL language. In addition to providing a new kind of editor, the UI plug-in reuses the existing Outline, Problems and Property views of Eclipse to display the structure of the active composition, its current error and warning markers and the attributes of its selected graph elements (Figure 3).

4.2   Run-Time Tools

Following a model-driven approach and by leveraging Eclipse's incremental resource builders, JOpera's JVCLtoJava compiler plug-in incrementally recompiles the modified composition to Java executable code whenever a process is saved. This Java code is then once more compiled by Eclipse's integrated Java compiler into bytecode. The latter is then automatically and transparently re-deployed for execution by dynamically loading it into JOpera's run-time execution kernel.

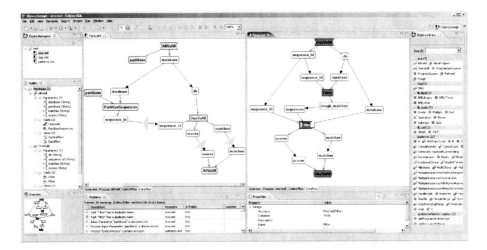

Fig. 3. JOpera: Design-time Editor and Background Model Checker

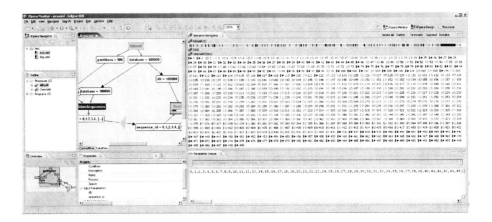

Fig. 4. JOpera: Run-time Process Monitor and Debugger

At this point, a valid, compiled composition is ready to be executed. Unlike most current model-driven environments, the progress of the execution can be followed interactively in the same environment – and most important – using the same visual syntax that was used to define it. Thus, not only JOpera features a so-called reverse model transformation, where the original visual process definition is extracted back from the compiled bytecode, but is also able to join this with the current state of the execution. This way, the visual representation is augmented at run-time with color-coded information representing the state of the execution of each of the service invocations (e.g., white for not yet executed, yellow for active, blue for finished, red representing a failure). Using the tools provided by the debugging UI plug-in (Figure 4), individual data parameters can be

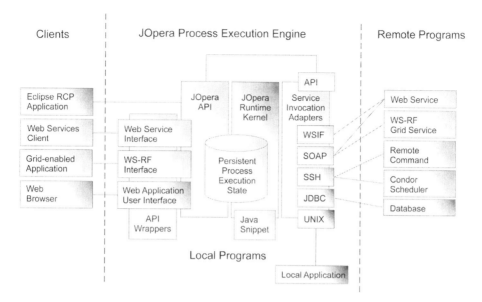

Fig. 5. Layered Architecture of the JOpera Process Execution Engine

inspected, so that – for example, in case a Web service is involved – the actual SOAP request and response messages can be displayed for debugging purposes. Similarly, in case a remote execution fails it is possible to distinguish whether the remote host could not be reached from the actual failure of the execution.

The persistent state of the execution and the navigation over the control flow graph of the process are managed by the JOpera Process Execution Engine. Figure 5 shows its various interfaces, towards clients used to access the functionality of processes and towards the local or remote programs invoked from a process. Processes are executed by the engine's run-time kernel, which delegates the interaction with different component types to a set of service invocation

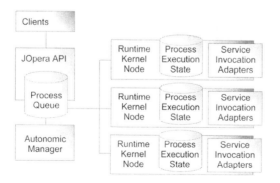

Fig. 6. Scaling the runtime kernel by replication

adapters. Its API can be accessed using a variety of means so that processes deployed in the kernel are automatically published, e.g., as Web and Grid services [12]. In this regard, JOpera can be seen as an open platform for heterogeneous   service composition since it is possible to extend the kinds of services that can be composed by adding user-defined service invocation plug-ins.

In order to handle large workloads, the run-time kernel can be distributed on a cluster of computers as shown in Figure 6. Processes submitted by clients for execution are stored into a central queue so that they can be scheduled for execution on a node of the kernel having enough free capacity. As we are going to discuss in the next section, depending on the number and characteristics of the processes to be executed, one node of the cluster may not provide sufficient execution capacity. In this case, additional nodes can be dynamically allocated to the kernel by the autonomic manager component [11].

5   Evaluation

In this section we present some experimental results on the autonomic capabilities of JOpera. They validate the architecture of the system and show that it is possible to automatically deal with a significant set of failures and, in general, changes in the execution environment (self-healing) but also react to changes in the workload to be executed (self-configuration).

5.1   Self-healing Capabilities

Dealing with Outages in the Execution Cluster. In this experiment we tested the system's ability to cope with changes in the resource set allocated

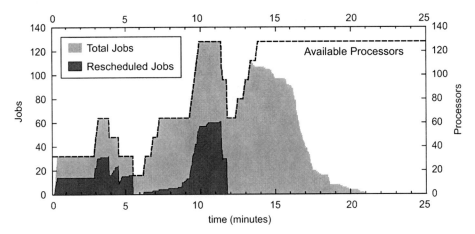

Fig. 7. Dealing with outages and cluster reconfigurations

to the execution of the All vs. All process using a reduced input data set. The workload consisted of 256 independent jobs, each requiring an average CPU time of 4 minutes.

Figure 7 shows a trace of the experiment execution using the distributed engine. The y-axis measures both the number of processors in the cluster as well as the number of jobs (each job is allocated to one processor). The dashed line represents the number of available processors. At time t, the Total line indicates the number of jobs running in the cluster. The Rescheduled Jobs line indicates how many jobs at a future point in time are going to be rescheduled due to a failure of the node where they have been running. Thus, the area under this line represent the amount of CPU time lost due to failures.

In general, Figure 7 demonstrates the ability of the kernel to adapt a running computation to the set of available processors, which has shrunk and grown many times throughout the experiment. The kernel is able to take advantage of new machines by immediately scheduling jobs on them and to reschedule lost jobs. Automatic rescheduling can be observed whenever a processor fails: the availability line drops since less processors are available for the computation. Upon such event, the kernel immediately retracts the jobs running on the failed processors to reschedule them on another node. In the graph, this is shown by the Rescheduled Jobs line closely following the number of available processors. Since a copy of the input data used by a task is stored persistently by the kernel as part of the state of the process execution, lost jobs can be recovered by sending a copy of such input data to another processor.

Kernel Recovery. Recovery of the kernel ensures that process execution resumes in a consistent state after a failure has interrupted the kernel's normal operation. In order to determine the overhead of such recovery, we measured the time taken by the various recovery steps:

1. Re-loading process instance state information from persistent storage;
2. Navigating through them in order to determine what are the tasks to be recovered;
3. Synchronizing the state of the tasks which are remotely executed.

The results of Figure 8 clearly indicate that the recovery times grow linearly with the number of tasks that were active at the time of the failure. More specifically, the most expensive operation is the loading of the instance data from the database, which takes 5 milliseconds when there are no tasks to be recovered, up to 50 seconds when loading 40 process instances composed of 100 tasks each. Since navigation is performed in main memory it is two orders of magnitude faster: less than 0.4 seconds for 4000 tasks. Synchronization with the cluster nodes is the step presenting the most time variability. This can be explained by the fact that when a recovering kernel attempts to contact a remote node to find out about the state of the task being recovered, it blocks either until the remote node responds or until the connection times out, which is the case if the remote node has failed. In addition to this timeout penalty all jobs lost due to node failures are automatically rescheduled adding to the duration of the recovery procedure.

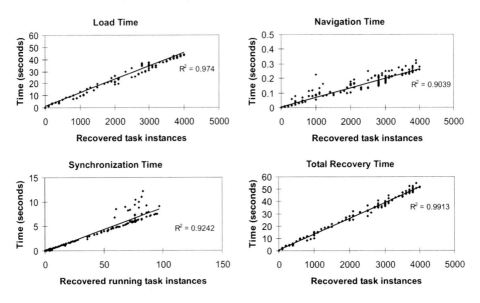

Fig. 8. Overhead of recovering a run-time kernel from persistent state

5.2   Self-configuration Capabilities

Whereas the previous section described the self-healing capabilities of the system, where the kernel can survive failures of the underlying cluster environment, in this section we explore how the kernel can automatically adapt its configuration to optimally use the available resources. First, we show that the kernel can be replicated in order to service a given workload with better performance. Second, we show that the kernel, through its autonomic manager, can automatically determine a suitable degree of replication for a given workload. To this end, we have been analyzing the effect of a replication strategy where up to 7 copies of the kernel are employed to run the parameter-sweep experiment described in Section 2.3. The process uses from 200 up to 1000 concurrent tasks to computer over an increasingly larger input dataset.

Figure 9 shows the results for the static replication strategy, where the number of replicas (x-axis) of the kernel has been manually configured to study the effect of replication on the process turnaround time (y-axis). Overall, replication has a beneficial impact on turnaround time. The system scales well, as a 5-fold increase in workload can be handled with constant time by a 7-fold increase in the number of kernel replicas. Still, for smaller workloads, it is not necessary to fully replicate the execution environment, as – due to Amdahl's law – the speedup is limited, as it can be observed for the smallest workload (200 tasks), where no improvement can be observed after 2 kernels have been used.

With this, a trade-off can be identified between minimizing the turnaround time of the processes while optimally using the available resources. Due to the potential variability of the workloads, especially if a virtual experiment has been made accessible through a Web service interface, it is important that the process

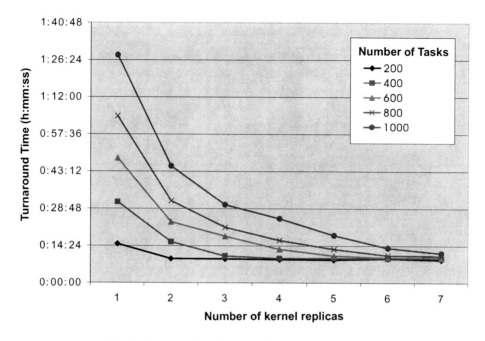

Fig. 9. Impact of replicating the kernel over a cluster

execution infrastructure is capable of automatically adjusting its configuration in response to the current workload.

Self-configuration can be achieved through an autonomic manager, which automatically adapts the degree of replication of the system to fit a specific workload. This component consists of 1) a basic resource manager, which keeps track of the nodes that can be used to run replicas of the kernel; 2) a performance monitoring component that observes the state of the system at regular intervals, detects imbalances and uses the 3) kernel reconfiguration services, to modify the number of replicas without disrupting normal system operation.

More precisely, the manager observes the aggregate number of tasks waiting to be executed by each replica as well as the number of processes waiting to be executed in the central queue (Figure 6). This value gives an indication of the backlog of the system and if it exceeds a configurable threshold, a new replica is added to the system. Conversely, if this value falls below a threshold, the replica with the least amount of work is disabled and shut down.

Figure 10 illustrates the manager's decisions by indicating when a worker has been added or removed from the computation. The x-axis shows the turnaround time, the y-axis the number of replicas involved in the computation (at least one replica is kept active at all times) and the z-axis represents different workload sizes, going from 200 tasks up to 1000 tasks.

These results show the capability of the autonomic manager to adapt the system to the workload without any human intervention. A limited amount of replicas was used to execute small workloads, whereas an increasingly larger

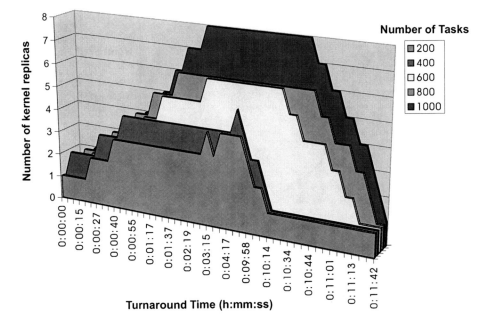

Fig. 10. Automatically adapting the number of replicas

number of replicas was used as the workload size increased. On the one hand, clients benefit from this adaptation as it keeps turnaround times low and stable in spite of different workloads. On the other hand, the virtual laboratory infrastructure can automatically adjust the amount of resources dedicated to execute the client's processes.

6   Conclusion

The paradigm shift from *in-vitro* to *in-silico* research, observed in many scientific disciplines, has resulted in the challenge of building virtual laboratory platforms. While early virtual laboratories consisted of a few applications integrated on the user interface level (e.g. in a browser), today's virtual laboratory environments evolved into a workbench supporting teams of scientists in specifying, running, monitoring and evaluating virtual experiments. Crucial to the success of such platforms is its ability to automate all aspects of a computation to the largest degree in order to make large scale computations manageable.

To this end, in this chapter we have presented the JOpera system, which brings autonomic computing techniques to meet the requirements of virtual laboratories. With it, all components (computing nodes, software tools, middleware infrastructure) that deal with the specification and the execution of a virtual experiment can be integrated using an autonomic platform. This platform combines appropriate mechanisms and strategies to 1) raise the level of abstraction at which virtual experiments can be defined, executed and debugged; 2) mask the complexity of dealing with outages in a distributed execution environment and 3) automatically tune the system's configuration for optimal performance. All in all, thanks to its autonomic computing features, JOpera is a significant step towards the goal of providing scientists with an environment that lets them concentrate on doing science while avoiding to deal with the computer science.

Acknowledgements

The authors would like to recognize the hard work of Reto Schaeppi, Andreas Bur, Oliver Deak, who greatly contributed to the BioOpera and JOpera projects.

References

1. Bioperl. http://www.bioperl.org.
2. D. Abramson, J. Giddy, and L. Kotler. High performance parametric modeling with Nimrod/G: killer application for the global grid? . In *Proceedings of the 14th International Parallel and Distributed Processing Symposium (IPDPS 2000)*, pages 520–528, Cancun, Mexico, 2000.
3. A. Alizadeh, M. Eisen, R. Davis, et al. Distinct types of diffuse large B-cell lymphoma identified by gene expression profiling. *Nature*, 403(6769):503–511, 2001.
4. G. Alonso, W. Bausch, C. Pautasso, M. Hallett, and A. Kahn. Dependable Computing in Virtual Laboratories. In *Proceedings of the 17th International Conference on Data Engineering (ICDE2001)*, pages 235–242, Heidelberg, Germany, 2001.
5. W. Bausch, C. Pautasso, R. Schaeppi, and G. Alonso. BioOpera: Cluster-aware computing. In *Proceedings of the 2002 IEEE International Conference on Cluster Computing (CLUSTER 2002)*, pages 99–106, Chicago, IL, USA, 2002.
6. B. Boeckmann, A. Bairoch, R. Apweiler, et al. The Swiss-Prot protein sequence data bank and its supplement trEMBL in 2003. *Nuc. Acids Res.*, 31:365–370, 2003.
7. F. Bushmann, R. Meunier, H. Rohnert, P. Sommerlad, and M. Stal. *A system of patterns*. Wiley, August 1996.
8. G. Cannarozzi, M. Hallett, J. Norberg, and X. Zhou. A cross-comparison of a large gene dataset. *Bioinformatics*, 16:654–655, 2000.
9. S. Chervitz. Comparison of the complete protein sets of worm and yeast: orthology and divergence. *Science*, 282:2022–2028, 1998.
10. I. Foster and C. Kesselman. Globus: A metacomputing infrastructure toolkit. *International Journal of Supercomputing Applications*, 11(2):115–128, 1997.
11. T. Heinis, C. Pautasso, and G. Alonso. Design and Evaluation of an Autonomic Workflow Engine. In *Proc. of the 2nd International Conference on Autonomic Computing*, Seattle, WA, June 2005.
12. T. Heinis, C. Pautasso, O. Deak, and G. Alonso. Publishing Persistent Grid Computations as WS Resources. In *Proc. of the 1st IEEE International Conference on e-Science and Grid Computing*, Melbourne, Australia, December 2005.
13. IBM and Apache Foundation. *Web Service Invocation Framework (WSIF)*, 2003. http://ws.apache.org/wsif/.
14. M. J. Litzkow, M. Livny, and M. W. Mutka. Condor—A Hunter of Idle Workstations. In *Proceedings of the 8th Int'l Conf. on Distributed Computing Systems*, pages 104–111, 1988.

15. B. Ludaescher and C. Goble, editors. *Special Section on Scientific Workflows*, volume 34 of *SIGMOD Record*. September 2005.
16. C. Pautasso. JOpera: Process Support for more than Web services. `http://www.jopera.org`.
17. C. Pautasso and G. Alonso. From Web Service Composition to Megaprogramming. In *Proceedings of the 5th VLDB Workshop on Technologies for E-Services (TES-04)*, pages 39–53, Toronto, Canada, August 2004.
18. C. Pautasso and G. Alonso. The JOpera Visual Composition Language. *Journal of Visual Languages and Computing*, 16(1–2):119–152, 2004.
19. C. Pautasso and G. Alonso. Flexible Binding for Reusable Composition of Web Services. In *Proceedings of the Workshop on Software Composition (SC 2005)*, Edinburgh, Scotland, April 2005.
20. B. Snel, P. Bork, and M. Muynen. Genome phylogeny based on content. *Nature Genet.*, 21:108–110, 1999.
21. P. Stuedi and G. Alonso. Connectivity in the presence of shadowing in 802.11 ad hoc networks. IEEE Wireless and Communications and Networking Conference (WCNC), 2005.

Algorithms for Failure Protection in Large IP-over-fiber and Wireless Ad Hoc Networks

Frederick Ducatelle[1], Luca Maria Gambardella[1], Maciej Kurant[2],
Hung X. Nguyen[2], and Patrick Thiran[2]

[1] Istituto Dalle Molle di Studi sull'Intelligenza Artificiale (IDSIA)
Galleria 2, CH-6928 Manno-Lugano, Switzerland
{Frederick, Luca}@idsia.ch
[2] LCA - School of Communications and Computer Science
EPFL, CH-1015 Lausanne, Switzerland
{Maciej.Kurant, Hung.Nguyen, Patrick.Thiran}@epfl.ch
icawww.epfl.ch/kurant/hasler

Abstract. We address failure location and restoration in both optical and wireless ad hoc networks. First, we show how Maximum Likelihood inference can improve failure location algorithms in the presence of false and missing alarms. Next, we present two efficient algorithms for mapping an IP network on an optical network in such a way that it is protected against failures at the optical layer. The first algorithm offers a method to formally verify the existence of a solution, contrary to all other heuristics known to date. The second algorithm is a heuristic search that takes capacity constraints in account. Both algorithms are shown to be faster by orders of magnitude than existing solutions. Finally, we develop a new routing algorithm for wireless mobile ad hoc networks, adopting ideas from the Ant Colony Optimization metaheuristic. The routing scheme can adapt to network and traffic changes and uses multipath routing and an efficient local repair mechanism to improve failure resilience.

1 Introduction

An *IP-over-fiber network* is a typical building block of the Internet's backbone. It usually belongs to a single Internet Service Provider (ISP), and is centrally monitored and managed. The physical infrastructure of an IP-over-fiber network consists of a mesh of optical fibers usually put in the ground along roads, rails, or power-lines. Currently, with the help of the Wavelength Division Multiplexing (WDM) technique, a single optical fiber can carry many signals independently. The IP links are realized as end-to-end connections routed on this mesh. The topology formed by the IP links is a result of a centralized optimization process and reflects the long term user demands. This stack is called an *IP-over-WDM* network; its topology rarely changes.

In contrast, a *wireless ad-hoc network* consists of a group of nodes that communicate with each other through wireless radio channels. There is no fixed infrastructure. Moreover, in some scenarios the nodes are mobile. There is no

J. Kohlas, B. Meyer, and A. Schiper (Eds.): Dependable Systems, LNCS 4028, pp. 231–259, 2006.
© Springer-Verlag Berlin Heidelberg 2006

centralized control or overview. There are no designated routers: nodes serve as routers for each other, and data packets are forwarded from node to node in a multi-hop fashion. Wireless ad-hoc networks are not yet widely deployed, but their first real-life applications are beginning to emerge.

Although the IP-over-WDM and wireless ad-hoc settings are quite different in nature, they share a number of problems and challenges. One of them is *failures* of network components. There are many possible sources of failures. In IP-over-WDM networks it might be a fiber cut, a failure of optical equipment (switch, router, amplifier), software errors, system misconfiguration, to name a few. In fact, in real IP backbones failures occur almost every day [1]. Moreover, due to huge capacities of optical fibers, even a single failure may result in a very significant disruption of the network functionality. In wireless ad-hoc networks the main source of failures is the instability of the wireless medium, which results in frequent failures of existing links and arrivals of new links[1]. This happens in terms of minutes [2]. The phenomenon is especially strong if we allow for mobility. Another typical problem is the limited battery power of nodes, eventually causing a node failure.

Failures often result from random events and thus are unavoidable. Therefore one of the crucial properties of a communication network is handling failures. It is twofold. First, a failure should be *located*. Since permanent and full network monitoring is resource inefficient, the network operators often limit it, at the cost of having only a partial knowledge of the present network state, such as a set of end-to-end measurements. In this setting, locating a failure becomes a nontrivial task. Second, once a failure is located, the traffic must be rerouted and the network operability *restored*. The mechanisms ensuring this should take into account all important failure scenarios and a number of physical constraints (e.g., link capacities).

In this paper we address both issues: failure location and restoration. In Section 2 we present the algorithms that can be used for failure location in IP-over-WDM and wireless networks. Next we give a number of various algorithms for failure restoration in Section 3 (optical networks) and in Section 4 (wireless ad-hoc networks). Finally, in Section 5 we conclude the paper.

2   Failure Location

When a failure occurs in the network, monitoring devices (passive or active) detect the failure and generate alarms to warn the management system. The management system then needs to infer the location of the failures based on the received alarms. The failure location task in communication networks is hindered not only by the existence of multiple possible explanations for some sets of alarms but also by corrupted alarms, which are those alarms that unexpectedly arrive at the management system when they should not (false alarms), or those that do not arrive at the management system when they should (missing alarms).

---

[1] The terms *link* and *edge*, as well as *node* and *vertex*, will be used interchangeably.

The nature of failures and available monitoring information differ significantly in IP-over-WDM and wireless networks. Each type of network therefore needs to have its own failure location methods. We present in this section two failure location algorithms that can be used to locate failures in IP-over-fiber and wireless sensor networks, respectively.

2.1   Failure Location in IP-over-WDM Networks

Failures of optical devices often manifest themselves in the degradation or loss of optical signals. Passive monitors are widely deployed in these networks to assess the signal health. When a monitor observes a significant drop in the signal quality, it sends an alarm to the management system. Alarms can be generated by devices at the optical, SDH/SONET or IP layer. A full review of the available monitoring information is provided in [3]. Failure location in IP-over-WDM networks is known to be NP-hard [4] and several algorithms have been proposed to solve this intractable problem in the literature (see [3] for a complete review of the existing failure location algorithms). Although many researchers [4] have suggested that failure location algorithms must be able to cope with alarm errors, most location algorithms today avoid this issue because of the complexity of covering all possible failures and corrupted alarms.

In optical networks, most network monitoring devices use a threshold to decide whether they should send alarms or not. For instance, an SDH device counts the number of errors it encounters in a time window and generates an alarm if the count is greater than a threshold, otherwise it remains silent [5]. Network operators have the option of trading false alarms for missing alarms and vice versa by tuning the parameters of monitoring devices. We have studied the failure location problem in an all-optical IP-over-WDM network when there are false and missing alarms in [6]. We have rigorously shown that for a network with binary alarms (alarms are either present or not), there is an asymmetry between false alarms and missing alarms. We have proven that false alarms can be corrected in polynomial time, but the correction of missing alarms is NP-hard. The correction of missing alarms is indeed equivalent to the red-blue set cover problem [7]. Because of this asymmetry, false alarms have a lesser effect on the accuracy of the diagnosis results than missing alarms do. Network operators therefore, when allowed, should set the threshold low to favor false alarms.

To handle corrupted alarms, we have proposed in [6] a polynomial time algorithm that can accurately locate failures with corrupted alarms. The algorithm takes as inputs the network topology and the positions of the monitors (this information is available in most IP-over-WDM networks). The algorithm consists of two steps. In the first step, called the Error Correction (EC) step, the algorithm uses a maximum likelihood reasoning to identify and correct the most probable set of corrupted alarms. In the second step, called the $MFAULT$ step, the algorithm then uses a set-cover heuristic to locate the faulty components with the cleaned alarms. The failure location algorithm performs well in simulated networks of real topologies as shown in Fig. 1.

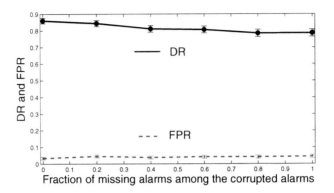

Fig. 1. Performance of the proposed failure location algorithm in the NSFNET topology [6]. The number of corrupted alarms is kept constant but the fraction of missing alarms is varied from 0 to 1, where 1 means all corrupted alarms are missing alarms. The algorithm is evaluated in terms of detection rate (DR), which is the fraction of failures that are correctly identified; and false positive rate (FPR), which is the fraction of failures that are wrongly identified. The algorithm achieves detection rates above 75% in all settings and the fewer missing alarms we have, the more accurate the algorithm is.

2.2 Failure Location in Wireless Sensor Networks

Contrary to IP-over-optical networks, qualities of wireless links vary significantly in the order of minutes [2]. In wireless sensor networks, it is not essential to monitor and locate all bad links (links with high loss rates), as the network should quickly self-organize around them. The problem occurs when all links surrounding a sensor node are lossy, because of low battery or physical obstacles. In this case, there is no other choice to access this node than to use a lossy link. The failure location task in a wireless sensor network therefore mainly concerns the identification of links that are consistently used to transport data but have bad quality. Diagnosing sensor networks is challenging because the networks cannot support much monitoring traffic and change their routing topologies frequently.

In [8] we have proposed to use only end-to-end application traffic to infer the bad performing links in sensor networks. Due to the lack of other network monitoring means, end-to-end application traffic is the most reliable source of network performance indication in wireless sensor networks. The inference of internal link properties given end-to-end observations is called network tomography. A detailed survey of the current tomography techniques is provided in [3]. In most networks end-to-end data do not provide enough information to identify the exact link loss rates but enough to identify the worst performing links.

We have introduced in [8] two inference techniques to infer lossy links in wireless sensor networks. The first algorithm (the LLIS algorithm) uses the maximum likelihood inference principle, whereas the second one (the MCMC algorithm) adopts the Bayesian principle. Both algorithms handle well noisy end-to-end data and routing changes in wireless sensor networks.

The LLIS algorithm first uses a threshold t_p to determine whether the loss rate on an end-to-end path is good or bad. After classifying all paths as good and bad, the algorithm then tries to find the smallest set of links whose badness would explain the badness of all paths in the network. The LLIS algorithm has the advantage of being simple. But, it is sensitive to estimation errors of end-to-end transmission rates and the choice of the path threshold t_p. The end-to-end transmission rates are only accurate when we have a sufficiently large number of packets. To handle the cases where there are not sufficient data to calculate the end-to-end transmission rates, we have proposed to use the second technique, namely the Bayesian inference technique [9] that is less vulnerable to end-to-end loss rates but also much more complex. The idea here is to try to generate a set of possible link loss rates that can explain the observations of end-to-end data. If the majority of the possible loss rates of a link are bad, then it is likely that the link is bad, otherwise it is good. For details of the MCMC method, please refer to [9].

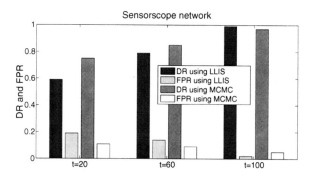

Fig. 2. Performance of the failure location algorithms (LLIS and MCMC) on the Sensorscope [10] network. We consider only links that are used to route more than t packets. As t increases, the algorithms become more accurate because of two reasons: (1) end-to-end data are more reliable, and (2) there are less errors generated by routing changes.

The performance of both inference algorithms (LLIS and MCMC) are evaluated by simulations and real network traces in [8]. Both algorithms achieve accurate failure location results with high detection and low false positive rates as shown in Fig. 2.

3   Failure Protection and Restoration in IP-over-WDM Networks

The Wavelength Division Multiplexing (WDM) technique allows the same optical fiber to carry many signals independently, each using different wavelengths (colors). In real networks the number of these signals is in the order of tens (in

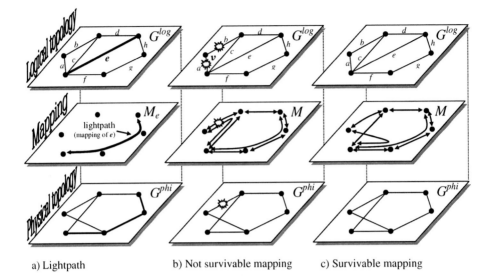

Fig. 3. IP-over-WDM network. (a) Given the physical and logical topologies, every logical edge (here e) is mapped on the physical topology as a lightpath. (b) An example of a mapping that is *not* survivable. After a failure of the indicated physical link, the logical topology becomes disconnected (the node v gets separated from the rest of the logical graph). (c) An example of a survivable mapping. One can easily check that after any single physical link failure the logical topology remains connected.

the Sprint network the maximum number is 25 [1]). Specialized labs can reach hundreds and thousands. Therefore a single failure of a physical fiber might have very significant consequences on the network, and should be carefully handled.

In an IP-over-WDM network we distinguish *two layers*: the *physical graph* is a mesh of optical fibers (edges) and optical switches (nodes). The *logical graph* is a mesh of IP connections (edges) and IP routers (nodes). Since we assume that on every optical switch lies an IP router, the sets of nodes at both layers are identical. Each logical link is mapped on the physical topology as a *lightpath* (see Fig. 3a). The set of all lightpaths defines a *mapping* of the logical graph on the physical graph. To construct a mapping, many objectives should be taken into account. One of them is the robustness to failures, or *survivability*. This issue is especially important in the IP-over-WDM architectures, where one physical link can carry many lightpaths, and thus where a single physical link failure may bring down a large number of logical links. A survey of different approaches for providing survivability of IP-over-WDM networks can be found in [3]. In this paper we consider exclusively the *IP restoration approach* that was shown to be effective and cost–efficient (see e.g., Sprint network [11]). In IP restoration, failures are detected by IP routers, and alternative routes in the logical topology are found. In order to enable this, the logical topology should remain *connected* after a failure of a physical link; this in turn may be guaranteed by an appropriate mapping of logical links on the physical topology. We call such a mapping a *survivable mapping.* In Fig. 3 we present two examples of mappings: the first one is not survivable (b) and the second one is survivable (c).

The problem of finding a survivable mapping was first defined in [12], and many algorithms solving this problem (with different variations) have been proposed since then. In general, they can be divided into two groups: exact algorithms based on Integer Linear Programming (ILP), and heuristics. The ILP solutions can be found for example in [13,14]. They lead to an unacceptably high complexity for networks of a non-trivially small size [15] (larger than a few tens of nodes). This is because the survivable mapping problem is NP-complete [16]. To avoid this prohibitive complexity, the second line of approach uses various heuristics, such as Tabu Search [12,17,18,14], Simulated Annealing [19] and others [20,21].

In this paper we describe two recent algorithms solving the survivable mapping problem: SMART [22,23] and FastSurv [24,25,26]. These algorithms are very efficient, and somewhat complementary. SMART is the fastest and the most scalable algorithm known to date. Moreover, the formal analysis of SMART [23] has led to new applications: the formal verification of the existence of a survivable mapping, and a tool tracing and repairing the vulnerable areas of the network. SMART can be applied only if we assume unlimited capacities of the physical links. In a more realistic scenario, the FastSurv algorithm shows its strengths. FastSurv can be easily adapted to any set of real-life constraints, while still being much faster and more scalable than the other heuristics known to date.

In the following subsections we present versions of the SMART and FastSurv algorithms that solve the basic survivability problem (single physical edge failures, no capacity constraints). A number of specific properties of the algorithms and their possible extensions are described in a later section.

We will use the following notation. The physical and logical topologies are represented by undirected graphs $G^{phi} = (V, P)$ and $G^{log} = (V, L)$, respectively. V is the set of vertices (common for both layers), P and L are the sets of undirected edges. Note that according to our assumption, we take $V^{phi} \equiv V^{log} \equiv V$. The mapping is represented in a form of a $|P| \times |L|$ binary matrix $M = \{m_{p,l}\}$, where $m_{p,l} = 1$ if the logical link l uses the physical link p in its mapping. A mapping M is survivable if after the failure of any single physical link $p \in P$, the logical topology G^{log} remains connected. More formally, M is survivable, if for every physical link $p \in P$ the graph

$$G_p^{log} = G^{log} \setminus \{l : m_{p,l} = 1\} \tag{1}$$

is connected.

3.1   SMART

One of the main operations in the SMART algorithm is contraction [27]. *Contracting* an edge $e \in E$ in a graph $G = (V, E)$ is deleting that edge and merging its end–nodes into one. The result is called a *contracted graph* G^{con}. We will also allow contracting a set of edges $A \subset E$. Note that the order of the edges in A does not affect the result.

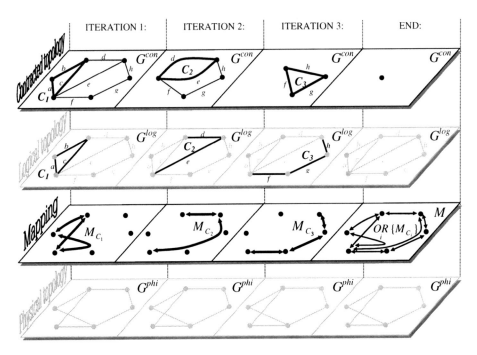

Fig. 4. Illustration of the SMART algorithm. We have four layers, from bottom to top: physical topology G^{phi}, mapping, logical topology G^{log} and contracted logical topology G^{con}. During a run of the SMART algorithm, only the contracted topology and the mapping change from one iteration to the next one. The logical and physical topologies are included only for the context; therefore they are set in grey. At each iteration a cycle C picked from the contracted topology is set in bold. This cycle is defined as a set C of logical links. (Although C is always a cycle in the contracted topology G^{con}, it does not necessarily form a cycle in the logical topology G^{log}; see e.g., Iteration 2 and 3.) Next, a disjoint mapping M_C is found for the set C. Then C is contracted in G^{con}, resulting in a new contracted logical topology G^{con} used at the subsequent iteration. Once G^{con} has converged to a single node, the underlying mapping is survivable. If there are still some unmapped logical links, they can be mapped in any way (e.g., a shortest path). Now we combine the lightpaths found in all iterations to obtain a mapping M (last column) of the entire logical topology. The mapping M is survivable.

Now we present the idea of the SMART algorithm. First choose from the logical topology G^{log} a cycle $C \subset L$ and map it *disjointly* (i.e., not using the same physical edge twice). The disjoint mapping of a logical cycle ensures that this cycle will remain connected after any single physical link failure. In other words, the cycle C is already mapped in a survivable way. Now, we contract the cycle C in the logical topology G^{log} and repeat the above procedure for the resulting graph. We iterate this operation until the contracted logical topology converges to a single node, which guarantees survivability. The example run of SMART is illustrated in Fig. 4. The pseudo-code of the SMART algorithm is:

Initialization. Contracted logical topology $G^{con} := G^{log}$.

Step 1: Pick a cycle C in G^{con}.

Step 2: Use DisjointMap (see below) to map disjointly the cycle C on the physical topology. Denote this mapping by M_C. (M_C is of the size of M, with non-zero elements appearing only in the rows corresponding to the logical edges in C)

Step 3: Contract C in G^{con}.

IF G^{con} consists of *one* node, **THEN RETURN** survivable mapping M which is a superposition of all disjoint mappings M_C found before: $M = \bigvee_i M_{C_i}$. END.

Step 4: GOTO Step 1.

DisjointMap. In Step 2 of the SMART algorithm, we have to find a disjoint mapping of the set C of logical links. The problem is equivalent to the edge-disjoint paths problem [28] that is proven to be NP-complete. Therefore we apply the following heuristic we call *DisjointMap* . Let each physical edge have a weight (these weights will be used exclusively within DisjointMap) and let this weight be initially set to one. At each iteration, map the logical links from C with shortest path. If no physical link is used more than once, a disjoint solution is found. Otherwise, the weight of each physical link used more than once is increased, and a new iteration starts.

Clearly, DisjointMap does not guarantee success. Therefore after several unsuccessful iterations it fails. In this case, the SMART algorithm cannot proceed to Step 3. Instead it comes back to Step 1 and picks another cycle; a choice of a short cycle will help the heuristic to converge rapidly. After a rare event of several consecutive failures of Step 2, the SMART algorithm quits returning the partial mapping $M = \bigvee_i M_{C_i}$ (some rows of M remain empty).

It is possible that even if the contracted graph G^{con} converges to a single node, there are still some unmapped logical links. They would form self-loops in G^{con}. We can map them in any way (e.g., with shortest path), which does not affect the survivability of the resulting full mapping.

3.2   FastSurv

FastSurv is a heuristic algorithm that works in an iterative manner. It starts from an initial mapping $M(0)$ obtained with a simple method. At each iteration t, the algorithm evaluates the current solution $M(t)$ and tries to improve it by rerouting a number of logical links.

The improvement phase is based on an observation made in [13] that a mapping is survivable if and only if no physical link is shared by all logical links belonging to a cut-set of G^{log}.[2] E.g., in Fig. 3b, logical links a and b share a physical link and cause unsurvivability because $\{a, b\}$ is a cut-set of G^{log}. In Fig. 3c, however, a, e and f share a link, but this does not cause unsurvivability because $\{a, e, f\}$ is not a cut-set of G^{log}. An exact solution method based on this

---

[2] A *cut-set* of a network is defined by a cut of the network: a cut is a partition of the set of nodes V into two sets S and $V - S$, and the cut set defined by this cut is the set of edges that have one endpoint in S and one in $V - S$.

idea (such as the ILP method of [13]) needs to take all cut-sets into account as hard constraints when constructing a mapping, which can be difficult and inefficient. In FastSurv, we use the notion of cut-sets in a heuristic way. Specifically, the algorithm keeps track of information about which pairs of logical links l_i and l_j cause unsurvivability when they are routed together over the same physical link, and which do not. If l_i and l_j form a cut-set of size two (such as $\{a, b\}$ in Fig. 3), they cause unsurvivability each time they are routed together. If l_i and l_j are part of a larger cut-set (e.g., in Fig. 3, a and e are part of the larger cut-set $\{a, c, e, f\}$), they only cause unsurvivability if all the other logical links of the same cut-set are also routed on the same link. The routing of these other logical links depends on the specific situation (the current mapping $M(t)$), which in FastSurv changes slowly from iteration to iteration since each time a number of logical links are rerouted. FastSurv updates at each iteration according to the current mapping the information about which pairs of logical links cause unsurvivability when they share a link, and uses this information to reroute logical links. This way, FastSurv can focus on the cut-sets which are important in the current situation when trying to improve the survivability of the mapping. The pseudo code for FastSurv is as follows:

Initialization. Calculate $M(0)$ and set the number of iterations t to 0.
Step 1: Evaluate $M(t)$.
Step 2: Update the information about which pairs of logical links cause unsurvivability when they share a physical link, based on the evaluation of $M(t)$.
Step 3: RETURN $M(t)$ IF $((M(t)$ is survivable) OR $(t = $ maximum number of iterations)).
Step 4: Calculate $M(t + 1)$ by rerouting logical links of $M(t)$ using the information of Step 2.
Step 5: Increase t and GOTO Step 1.

To obtain $M(0)$, the logical links are routed on G^{phi} one after the other in random order. We use shortest path routing, with the cost of a physical link p equal to the number of logical links that are already routed over p. This simple algorithm avoids that some links carry many more logical links than others, which would make them more vulnerable with respect to survivability.

In Step 1, $M(t)$ is evaluated by considering all physical links p of P individually, and investigating whether the remaining logical graph G_p^{log} (as defined in formula (1)) is connected. Physical links whose failure leaves G_p^{log} disconnected are called *unsurvivable physical links*, and the logical links that are routed over them are called *unsurvivable logical links*. The algorithm uses a binary vector $U = \{u_p\}(t)$, where $u_p(t) = 1$ if p is an unsurvivable physical link in $M(t)$ and $u_p(t) = 0$ otherwise.

The information about which pairs of logical links cause unsurvivability when they share a physical link is kept in a $|L| \times |L|$ matrix $Z = \{z_{l_i,l_j}\}$. Z is updated according to the formulas (2)-(4) below. In formula (2), $a_{l_i,l_j}(t)$ is defined as the number of times that logical links l_i and l_j share a physical link in $M(t)$, and in formula (3), $b_{l_i,l_j}(t)$ is defined as the number of times that this shared physical link is unsurvivable in $M(t)$. Dividing $b_{l_i,l_j}(t)$ by $a_{l_i,l_j}(t)$, one obtains a ratio that can be seen as an estimate (based on the experience of iteration t) of the probability that combining logical links l_i and l_j on a physical link will make that physical link unsurvivable. z_{l_i,l_j} is then defined in formula (4) as the exponential average of this probability estimate (with $\alpha = 0.2$ in the experiments).

$$a_{l_i,l_j}(t) = \sum_p m_{p,l_i}(t)m_{p,l_j}(t) \qquad \forall l_i, l_j \in L \tag{2}$$

$$b_{l_i,l_j}(t) = \sum_p u_p(t)m_{p,l_i}(t)m_{p,l_j}(t) \qquad \forall l_i, l_j \in C \tag{3}$$

$$z_{l_i,l_j} = \begin{cases} \alpha z_{l_i,l_j} + (1-\alpha)\frac{b_{l_i,l_j}(t)}{a_{l_i,l_j}(t)} & if \quad a_{l_i,l_j}(t) > 0 \\ z_{l_i,l_j} & if \quad a_{l_i,l_j}(t) = 0 \end{cases} \tag{4}$$

In Step 4, FastSurv reroutes all logical links that are unsurvivable in the current mapping (survivable logical links are left mapped as they were), using the probability estimates of Z. A shortest path algorithm is applied in which the cost of a path for a logical link l_i is the probability that l_i will be unsurvivable somewhere along its path. The probability $Prob^{l_i}_{path}$ that l_i will be unsurvivable on a path is the probability that it will be unsurvivable on at least one physical link of the path. The probability $Prob^{l_i}_p$ that l_i will be unsurvivable on a physical link p of the path is the probability that l_i will cause unsurvivability when routed together with any of the other logical links l_j which use p,[3] which is estimated in z_{l_i,l_j}. We use formula (5) to estimate $Prob^{l_i}_p$ and formula (6) to estimate $Prob^{l_i}_{path}$.

$$Prob^{l_i}_p = 1 - \prod_{l_j \text{ on } p} (1 - z_{l_i,l_j}) \tag{5}$$

$$Prob^{l_i}_{path} = 1 - \prod_{p \text{ on } path} (1 - Prob^{l_i}_p) \tag{6}$$

3.3 Time Complexity

SMART. The complexity of one iteration of SMART is dominated by the DisjointMap function in Step 2 of the algorithm. Assuming a small size of the cycles C (in order of $O(1)$), this heuristic has a complexity $O(Dijkstra)$ that is at most $O(N^2)$, where N is the number of nodes in the graph. To estimate the number of iterations before SMART converges, we note that a single iteration maps one cycle, which reduces the number of nodes by at least one. So we need at most $O(N)$ iterations. It results in a total complexity of SMART equal to $O(N^3)$.

In practice, the physical graph is sparse, i.e., has got $O(N)$ edges, which reduces the complexity of $O(Dijkstra)$ to $O(N \log N)$. Consequently, the complexity of SMART drops to $O(N^2 \log N)$.

---

[3] Other logical links can already be using p either because they were not removed after the previous iteration or because they were rerouted before l_i.

FastSurv. Each iteration of FastSurv consists of an evaluation and a number of logical link reroutings. Rerouting a single logical link has a complexity $O(Dijkstra)$ (which is maximally of $O(N^2)$) and the evaluation of survivability has a maximal complexity of $O(N^4)$ [26]. Therefore, given that the maximum number of logical links to be rerouted in one iteration is the total number of logical links, which is $O(N)$ (we follow [17], where logical networks of a fixed degree are considered), a single iteration of FastSurv has a maximal complexity of $O(N^4)$. Since the maximal number of iterations is a parameter independent of N (and usually small), the overall complexity of FastSurv is $O(N^4)$ as well.

3.4   Results

ILP Approach. In [13] the necessary and sufficient conditions for a mapping to be survivable are specified (see Subsection 3.2 for details). These conditions are injected into the Integer Linear Programming (ILP) formulation, that is used to find a survivable mapping. Then a simple relaxation (ILP-Relax) for the ILP is introduced, which substantially reduces the processing time.

We ran the SMART and FastSurv algorithms for exactly the same topologies as in [13], namely NSFNET as the physical topology and the same 300 random graphs of degree $\bar{d} = 3, 4$ and 5 as those in [13] for the logical topologies. A survivable mapping was found in *all runs* when using ILP, ILP-Relax, SMART and FastSurv approaches. Therefore it is interesting to compare the *run–times* of the algorithms. The machines were not the same, yet comparable (Sun Sparc Ultra-10 vs. Pentium 500). However, we must stress that SMART and FastSurv were implemented in pure C++, whereas ILP required a dedicated program (CPLEX), which could significantly affect the results. The run-times from [13] are reprinted in Table 1; the last two columns show the results of SMART and FastSurv. The SMART algorithm is several orders of magnitude faster than pure ILP, and about 3 orders of magnitude faster than the relaxed version of ILP. FastSurv is about one order of magnitude slower than SMART. Note that, in contrast to ILP, the degree of the logical topology hardly affects the run-time of SMART and FastSurv.

Tabu Search and Large Topologies. One of the most efficient and widely used techniques to solve a survivable mapping problem is *Tabu Search*. Our implementation of Tabu Search follows the one in [12]; we will refer to it as *Tabu97*. Since Tabu Search turned out to be substantially faster than the ILP approach (described in the previous section), we carried out the simulations

Table 1. Run-times of ILP, SMART and FastSurv

Average degree d	ILP	ILP-Relax	SMART	FastSurv
3	8.3 sec	1.3 sec	0.0028 sec	0.0117 sec
4	2 min 53 sec	1.5 sec	0.0028 sec	0.0155 sec
5	19 min 17 sec	2.0 sec	0.0029 sec	0.0166 sec

for relatively large graphs and studied the scalability of Tabu Search, FastSurv and SMART. To emulate larger real-life physical topologies we generate square lattices where each vertex is connected by an edge to its four closest neighbors only. Next a fraction f of these edges is deleted; we call them f-lattices. We keep only these f-lattices that are 2–edge–connected.[4] The parameter f ranges from 0 to 0.35. The maximal value 0.35 was chosen in such a way that even the smallest topologies could be 2–edge–connected. Since the logical graph is less regular (for instance, there is no reason why it should be planar), the logical topologies are 2-edge-connected random graphs of average vertex degree $\bar{d} = 4$. The number of vertices ranges from $N = 16$ to 900.

In Fig. 5 we present the results obtained in simulations on a Pentium 4 machine, for the three algorithms implemented in C++. In Fig. 5a we investigate the run–times of the Tabu97, FastSurv and SMART. The observed complexities of the algorithms are polynomial, with $O(N^{3.6})$ for Tabu97, $O(N^{2.8})$ for FastSurv, and $O(N^{2.4})$ for SMART[5]. These values fit in the theoretical maximal bounds that are $O(N^5)$, $O(N^4)$ and $O(N^3)$, respectively. Note that Tabu97 took about 11 hours when solving a 900 node problem, which is a lot more than the 3 minutes measured for FastSurv and the 25 seconds for SMART.

Fig. 5b is related to the *effectiveness* of the algorithms, i.e., their ability to find a survivable mapping. Although FastSurv and SMART are comparable (with a slight advantage of the former), Tabu97 is significantly worse, especially for larger topologies. It should be noted that for every N a fraction of studied topologies is impossible to be mapped in a survivable way, which makes the upper bound of the effectiveness smaller than one.

3.5 Extensions

In the previous sections we have defined the survivability problem by taking into account single physical edge failures only, and assuming no capacity or other real-life constraints. We have described and compared the versions of the SMART and FastSurv algorithms, solving this basic survivability problem. However, these algorithms have a number of useful properties that can be exploited. In that regard they turn out to differ substantially. In particular, a proper application of the SMART algorithm gives us a valuable insight into the survivability problem, whereas FastSurv can be easily extended to a setting with any set of real-life constraints (e.g., limited fiber capacities). We briefly describe some of the possible applications below.

Capacity Constraints. An optical fiber connection can only carry a limited number of different lightpaths, which is a capacity constraint for each physical

---

[4] A graph G is *k-edge-connected* if G is connected and every set of edges disconnecting G has at least k edges [27]. Clearly, 2-edge-connectivity of both physical and logical graphs is a necessary condition for the existence of a survivable mapping.

[5] The measured value of SMART complexity $O(N^{2.4})$ is larger than the theoretical bound $O(N^2 \log N)$. This is probably because the DisjointMap function often takes several (not one) iterations to converge.

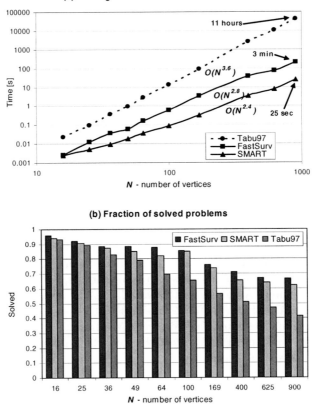

Fig. 5. Test results for Tabu97, FastSurv and SMART using logical and physical networks of increasing number of nodes (16 − 900). The logical networks are random graphs, whereas the physical networks are f-lattices, with f ranging from 0 till 0.35 with a step size of 0.05. Each data point represents an average over 1000 different test problems and over all values for f. (a) shows the run time in CPU seconds as a function of the number of nodes in a log-log scale. For each curve we indicate the exponent of its power-law fit. (b) shows the fraction of successfully mapped topologies as a function of the number of nodes.

link. Here we present an extended version of the FastSurv algorithm that can find a survivable mapping while considering the limited physical link capacities. For SMART such an extension is less straightforward due to its particular approach.

Like the basic FastSurv survivable routing algorithm, the extended FastSurv algorithm starts from an initial solution that it tries to improve in subsequent iterations. The algorithm uses two different types of iterations. *Survivability iterations* are identical to the iterations of the basic FastSurv algorithm and aim at improving survivability while relaxing the capacity constraint. *Capacity iterations* reduce the number of capacity constraint violations while relaxing the survivability goal. The algorithm alternates between a number of survivability iterations and a number of capacity iterations, and stops when it finds a mapping that is survivable and satisfies all link capacity constraints (or when a maximum number of iterations is reached).

In each capacity iteration, the algorithm tries to improve the current mapping by rerouting logical links that were routed on overfull physical links. For the rerouting, we use the shortest path routing where the cost of a physical link is equal to the number of logical links already routed over this physical link divided by the maximum capacity of the physical link, except when the number of logical links is higher than or equal to the capacity, in which case the number is not divided by the capacity. This way physical links that are full are avoided.

In a large series of tests, we have shown that the extended FastSurv algorithm outperforms tabu search in terms of solution quality and time [26]. Moreover, it is much more scalable.

Verification of the Existence of a Survivable Solution. If a heuristic fails, nothing can be claimed about the existence of a survivable mapping. To date, the only general method verifying the existence of a survivable mapping was an exhaustive search run for the *entire* logical topology G^{log}. Due to NP-completeness of the survivable mapping problem, the exhaustive approach is not realizable in practice for topologies larger than a few nodes. The SMART algorithm can substantially simplify this procedure. It turns out that it is sufficient to verify only the resulting contracted graph G^{con} (from a terminated run), instead of G^{log}. This makes the verification of the existence of a survivable mapping often possible for moderate and large topologies [23].

Tracing and Repairing the Vulnerable Areas in the Network. A second novel application of SMART is tracing the vulnerable areas in the network and pointing where new link(s) should be added to enable a survivable mapping.

Once we know that a particular pair of physical and logical topologies cannot (or can difficultly) be mapped in a survivable way, a natural question is to modify the topologies to enable such a mapping. Where should a new logical link l^{new} be added? The SMART algorithm helps us answer this question. Run SMART and wait until it terminates. Since a survivable mapping does not exist, the contracted topology G^{con} will not converge to a single node. Most probably G^{con} will shrink to a small structure (in comparison with the original logical graph G^{log}) and the algorithm will give up. Consider the graph G^{con}. Addition of the new logical link l^{new} to the logical topology results in addition of l^{new} also to G^{con}. In [23] it was shown that if l^{new} forms a self-loop in G^{con}, then its introduction will never help survivability. In other words, to enable a survivable mapping we should locate l^{new} in such a way, that it connects two different vertices in G^{con}.

The simulation results in [23] have shown that the SMART-aided introduction of a new logical link greatly helps, contrary to a completely random choice of location of this link.

Node, Span and Double Link Failures. So far we have only considered survivability with respect to single physical link failures, which are the most common type of failures in WDM networks. Here, we describe how FastSurv and SMART can be adapted to deal with more complicated failures such as span, node and double link failures. A span is a bundle of physical links that have been placed together for cost reasons (e.g., along railway and electricity lines). A single cut can break all of these physical links at once, in which case we speak of *span failure* [29]. We can also encounter *node failures* [30]; they are the consequence of a failure of equipment at nodes, such as switches. In our context a node failure is equivalent to a failure of all physical links neighboring the node. Finally, we consider *double–link failures*, i.e., independent failures of any two physical links [31]. Usually such a situation takes place when the second failure occurs before the first one is repaired.

Adapting FastSurv to deal with span failures is straightforward. Although the basic algorithm described in Subsection 3.2 kept track of which pairs of logical links cause unsurvivability when they share a link, it should now consider which pairs of logical links cause unsurvivability when they share a span. To adapt SMART we have to modify only the DisjointMap function used in Step 2 to produce *span-disjoint* mappings (instead of only link-disjoint).

The adaptation of FastSurv to deal with node failures is again not difficult: the algorithm should consider which pairs of logical links cause unsurvivability when they are routed together over the same node. Since a logical link can never be routed survivably with respect to its end nodes, logical links incident on a node should not be considered to share that node. For SMART, we make DisjointMap generate *node-disjoint* mappings.

To deal with double link failures, FastSurv should investigate survivability with respect to all pairs of physical links, and register which pairs of logical links cause unsurvivability when routed over these pairs of physical links. In the case of SMART, any logical cycle C processed by the algorithm can clearly be disconnected by a double failure. In order to enable protection against double failures we take small 3-edge-connected structures instead of this cycle, as shown in Fig. 6. Note that the contracted logical graph can have multi-edges, and so do these structures. The rest of the SMART algorithm remains unchanged. In particular the DisjointMap heuristic searches for a link-disjoint mapping, as in its original version.

Fig. 6. Examples of 3-edge-connected structures that might be used by SMART to handle double failures

3.6 Conclusion

Table 2 summarizes the efficiency and functionality of SMART and FastSurv, and compares them with ILP and Tabu97. Both algorithms are much faster and more scalable than any solution proposed to date. As for the possible extensions and particular properties, the two algorithms can be regarded as being complementary. SMART provides us with a method of formal verification of the existence of a survivable mapping and a tool tracing and repairing the vulnerable areas of the network, whereas FastSurv can be easily adapted to any set of real-life requirements such as capacity constraints.

Table 2. Comparison of the efficiency and functionalities of SMART, FastSurv, ILP and Tabu97. The question mark "?" means that the option might be possible to realize, but that, to the best of our knowledge, no one has yet done it to date.

Functionality	SMART	FastSurv	ILP	Tabu
fast and scalable	✓✓	✓	×	×
capacity and other constraints	×	✓	✓	✓
verification of a solution existence	✓	×	✓	×
node failures	✓	✓	?	?
span failures	✓	✓	?	?
multiple failures	✓	✓	?	?
tracing and repairing the vulnerable areas	✓	×	×	×

4 Failure Restoration in Mobile Ad Hoc Networks by Rerouting

Mobile Ad Hoc Networks (MANETs) [32] are wireless ad hoc networks in which all nodes are mobile. Due to this mobility, the network topology, which is formed by the wireless links established between nodes that are in each other's vicinity, is dynamic, with regular failures of existing links and arrivals of new links. Dealing with these constant changes is made more difficult by other challenges, such as the low bandwidth of the shared wireless channel, which is mainly due to the need to use inefficient decentralized mechanisms for medium access control, the limited resources of mobile devices (battery power and memory), the high error rates and signal interference in wireless communication, the lack of central control, etc.. In this setting a failure restoration problem boils down to constructing a scalable and highly adaptive routing algorithm. It should also be robust and efficient, and work in a distributed way. The abilities to deal with link failures and to take advantage of new opportunities arising from the appearance of new links are crucial.

In this section, we describe a novel routing algorithm for MANETs which is adaptive and failure resilient. It takes inspiration from Ant Colony Optimization (ACO) [33] and the related class of ACO routing algorithms [34], and uses both reactive and proactive strategies to deal with the dynamic MANET topology.

In what follows, we first give a short overview of the current state of the art in MANET routing. Next, we give an introduction to the field of ACO and ACO routing. Then we describe the working of our algorithm, and finally we provide some results from simulation tests.

4.1 MANET Routing

Over the course of the last 10 years a large number of different MANET routing protocols have been proposed (see [32,35] for overviews). All these algorithms deal with the dynamic aspects of MANETs in their own way, using reactive or proactive behavior, or a combination of both. *Reactive behavior* means that an algorithm gathers routing information in response to an event, such as the start of a data session or the failure of a link on an existing route. *Proactive behavior* means that the algorithm also gathers routing information at other times, so that it is readily available when the event happens.

In the MANET literature, the classical distinction is between table-driven, on-demand and hybrid algorithms. *Table-driven* algorithms, such as e.g. Destination-Sequenced Distance-Vector Routing (DSDV) [36], are purely proactive: all nodes try to maintain routes to all other nodes at all times. This means that they need to keep track of all topology changes, which can become difficult if there are a lot of nodes or if they are very mobile. *On-demand* algorithms, such as Ad-Hoc On-Demand Distance Vector Routing (AODV) [37] and Dynamic Source Routing (DSR) [38], are purely reactive: nodes only gather routing information when a data session to a new destination starts, or when a route that is in use fails. Reactive algorithms are generally more scalable since they greatly reduce the overhead [39], but they can suffer from oscillations in performance because they are never prepared for disruptive events. In practice, many algorithms are *hybrid algorithms* (e.g. Zone Routing Protocol (ZRP) [40]), using both proactive and reactive components in order to combine the best of both worlds.

The traditional distinction between table-driven, on-demand and hybrid protocols tells only part of the story. One can classify MANET routing algorithms along a wide range of other dimensions. An important classification with respect to the work presented here is the difference between single path and *multi-path algorithms*. Many algorithms that use more than one path between each source and destination have been proposed (see [41] for an overview). They differ in the way multiple paths are set up, maintained and used. Multiple paths can serve as a way to enhance throughput, or as a way to increase robustness to link failures by providing backup paths. A disadvantage is that more overhead is needed because more than one path needs to be maintained.

4.2 ACO and ACO Routing

ACO (Ant Colony Optimization) is a framework for optimization inspired by the mechanisms used by ant colonies to find the shortest path between their nest and a food source [33]. Ants leave behind a trail of a volatile chemical substance called *pheromone*; they also move preferentially in the direction of a higher pheromone intensity [42]. Since shorter paths can be completed quicker and more frequently by the ants, they get marked with higher pheromone intensity. These paths therefore attract more ants, which in turn increases the pheromone level. Finally, there is convergence of the majority of the ants onto the shortest path, with only a few ants continuing exploration of other paths. In ACO, artificial ants build solutions to an optimization problem guided by an artificial pheromone matrix, and update the matrix according to the quality of the solution they have constructed. ACO was first developed as a meta-heuristic for combinatorial optimization, and its first applications were for the travelling salesman problem [43]. Later, it has been applied to a whole range of different problems (see [33] for an overview).

The application of the ACO ideas to the problem of routing in wired networks led to the development of ACO routing algorithms [34], such as *Ant Based Control* (ABC) [44] and *AntNet* [45]. The main idea behind ACO routing is the acquisition of routing information through path sampling using ant agents. These lightweight agents are generated concurrently and independently by the nodes, with the task to try out a path to an assigned destination. An ant going from source s to destination d collects information about the cost of its path (e.g. end-to-end delay) and, tracing its way back from d to s, uses this information to update routing tables at intermediate nodes. The routing tables contain values indicating the relative goodness of each routing decision. The routing tables are updated by the ants and they are also used by the ants to find their way to their destination: at each node ants stochastically choose a next hop, giving higher probability to those next hops that are associated with higher goodness values. This way, the routing table entries play the role of artificial pheromone values in the ant learning process. The routing tables are therefore also called *pheromone tables*, and their entries *pheromone values*. The continuous generation of ants results in the availability at each node of a bundle of paths, each with an estimated measure of quality. These paths are used to route data packets. Like the ants, data packets are routed *stochastically*, choosing with a higher probability those links associated with higher pheromone values. This way data for a same destination are adaptively spread over *multiple paths* (but with a preference for the best paths), resulting in *load balancing*.

4.3   A Novel ACO Routing Algorithm for MANETs

ACO routing algorithms have properties that are useful for MANETs. First of all, the continuous exploration of paths provides adaptivity, which is crucial in the dynamic MANET environment. Although ACO routing algorithms for wired networks were mainly designed to provide adaptivity with respect to data load changes, the same techniques can be extended to provide adaptivity with respect to topology changes, allowing for the use of new links and adjusting routing information after link failures. Second, the use of multiple paths provides a way to both increase throughput via data load spreading and to proactively deal with link failures by providing backup paths. Finally, the fact that routing information is learned from the accumulated experience of agents that sample full paths offers robustness, in two different ways. First of all, loss of agents is not a problem: it leads to slower updates, but not to wrong information. Second, route cost estimates are based on real experiences. This is in contrast with information bootstrapping techniques used in traditional distance vector routing algorithms [46], where nodes calculate route cost estimates based on the estimates reported by neighboring nodes. Although information bootstrapping is an efficient process, it is slow to converge after changes and can easily lead to errors in dynamic environments. Sampling full paths provides extra guarantees with respect to the correctness of the information.

There are however also disadvantages for MANETs in ACO routing. Firstly, ACO routing algorithms are normally purely proactive, maintaining routing information between all pairs of nodes at all times. Following this approach, a lot of unnecessary overhead is created, making the algorithm less efficient. Also, the lack of reactive components decreases adaptivity, because no specific reactions are triggered after a disruptive event. A second important disadvantage of ACO routing algorithms is the fact that the repeated path sampling using ant agents can come into conflict with the limited bandwidth in MANETs. Moreover, the high change rate of MANETs commands a higher sampling rate to keep routing information up to date, further aggravating the problem.

Here we present *AntHocNet*, an attempt to build an efficient, adaptive and robust routing algorithm for MANETs using the design principles from ACO routing. The algorithm has a hybrid architecture, combining a reactive path setup phase, which is typical for purely reactive algorithms such as AODV [37], with proactive monitoring and exploration using sampling with ant agents. Further reactive elements are introduced for dealing with link failures: while proactive path sampling allows for the updating of information about current paths and for the finding of new paths, the use of mechanisms to reactively deal with link failures enhances direct adaptivity. A last important feature of AntHocNet is the fact that the process of path sampling using ant agents is supported by a lightweight information bootstrapping mechanism: the routing information learned by the ant agents is spread over the networks in a process we call pheromone diffusion. Although information bootstrapping is more efficient, it is less reliable and robust than ant sampling, and it is therefore used as a secondary process to guide and speed up the learning by the ants.

In what follows, we first give a general overview of the AntHocNet algorithm, and then discuss each of its components in more detail. For other, more detailed descriptions of the algorithm, we refer the interested reader to [47,48,49,50,51].

Overview of the Algorithm. In AntHocNet nodes only actively gather and maintain routing information for destinations they are currently communicating with. At the start of a communication session, the source node gathers initial routing information in a *reactive path setup* phase. During the course of the session, the source node engages in *proactive route maintenance and exploration*. To this end, it periodically sends out ant-like agents, to sample paths to the destination, very much like in ACO routing algorithms for wired networks. This basic mechanism is supported by the previously discussed *pheromone diffusion* process: the routing information obtained via repeated ant sampling is spread between the nodes of the MANET via information bootstrapping to provide secondary guidance. When a link failure is detected during the course of a session, this is dealt with using *reactive link failure mechanisms*, such as a local route repair mechanism and the spreading of failure notification messages. The use of all of these mechanisms together results in the availability of a set of multiple paths for each communication session. *Data packets are spread stochastically* over these different paths, according to the learned pheromone tables.

Pheromone Routing Tables. Like other ACO routing algorithms, AntHocNet uses the datagram model of IP networks, where paths are expressed in the form of tables kept locally at each node. A pheromone table $\mathcal{T}^i$ at node i is a matrix, where each entry $\mathcal{T}^i_{nd} \in \mathbb{R}$ of the table is an artificial pheromone value indicating the estimated goodness of going from i over neighbor n to reach destination d. Goodness is a combined measure of path end-to-end delay and number of hops. Since AntHocNet only maintains information about destinations that are active in a communication session, and since the neighbors of a node change continually, the filling of the pheromone tables is sparse and dynamic. The learned tables are used to route data packets in a stochastic forwarding process (see further).

Reactive Path Setup. When a source node s starts a communication session with a destination node d, and it does not have routing information for d available, it broadcasts a *reactive forward ant* to obtain initial information. At each node, the ant is either unicast or broadcast, depending on whether the current node has or has not routing information for d. If pheromone information is available, the ant chooses its next hop n with the probability P_{nd} which depends on the relative goodness of n as a next hop, expressed in the pheromone variable $\mathcal{T}^i_{nd}$:

$$P_{nd} = \frac{(\mathcal{T}^i_{nd})^\beta}{\sum_{j \in \mathcal{N}^i_d} (\mathcal{T}^i_{jd})^\beta}, \quad \beta \geq 1, \tag{7}$$

where $\mathcal{N}^i_d$ is the set of neighbors of i over which a path to d is known, and β is a parameter value that controls the exploratory behavior of the ants. If no pheromone information is available, the ant is broadcast. Due to subsequent broadcasts, many duplicate copies of the same ant travel to the destination. A node that receives multiple copies only accepts the first and discards the others. This way, only one path is set up initially. During the course of the communication session more paths are added via the proactive path exploration and maintenance mechanism to provide a *mesh of multiple paths* for data forwarding.

Each forward ant keeps a list $\mathcal{P} = [1, 2, \ldots, d]$ of the nodes it has visited. Upon arrival at the destination d, it is converted into a *backward ant* that travels back to the source retracing $\mathcal{P}$. At each intermediate node $i \in \mathcal{P}$ ($i < d$), the backward ant reads a locally maintained estimate $\hat{T}^i_{i+1}$ of the time it takes to reach the neighbor $i+1$ the ant is coming from. The time $\hat{T}^i_d$ it would take a data packet to reach d from i over $\mathcal{P}$ is calculated incrementally as the sum of the local estimates $\hat{T}^j_{j+1}$ gathered by the ant between i and d. A pheromone value is a goodness measure, expressed as an inverted cost, which takes into account both end-to-end delay and number of hops. It has the dimension of an inverted time. Therefore, to calculate the pheromone update value τ_d^i, we combine the estimated delay $\hat{T}_d^i$ with the number of hops to the destination h as follows:

$$\tau_d^i = \left(\frac{\hat{T}_d^i + h T_{hop}}{2} \right)^{-1}, \tag{8}$$

where T_{hop} is a fixed value representing the time to take one hop in unloaded conditions. Defining τ_d^i like this is a way to avoid possibly large oscillations in the time estimates gathered by the ants (e.g., due to local bursts of traffic) and to take into account both end-to-end delay and number of hops. The pheromone value $\mathcal{T}_{nd}^i$ is updated as follows:

$$\mathcal{T}_{nd}^i = \gamma \mathcal{T}_{nd}^i + (1 - \gamma)\tau_d^i, \quad \gamma \in [0, 1]. \tag{9}$$

Once the backward ant makes it back to the source, a full path is set up and the source can start sending data. If the backward ant does not arrive for some reason, a timer will run out at the source, and the whole process is started again.

Proactive Path Maintenance and Exploration. During the course of a session, source nodes send out *proactive forward ants* to update the information about currently used paths and to try to find new paths. They follow pheromone and update routing tables in the same way as reactive forward ants. As pointed out previously, the ant sending rate needed to keep up with the constant changes of a MANET environment is quite high, so that the process comes into conflict with the typically limited bandwidth in such networks. Moreover, to find entirely new paths, blind exploration through random walks or broadcasts would be needed, again leading to excessive bandwidth consumption. Therefore, we use a supporting process, called *pheromone diffusion*. It provides a second way of updating pheromone information about existing paths and can give information to guide exploratory behavior.

Pheromone diffusion is implemented using *hello messages*, broadcast periodically and asynchronously by the nodes. In these messages, the sending node n places a list of destinations it has information about, including for each of these destinations d the best pheromone value $\mathcal{T}_{m^*d}^n, m^* \in \mathcal{N}_d^n$, which n has available for d. A node i receiving the hello message from n first registers that n is its neighbor. Then, for each destination d listed in the message, it can derive an estimate of the goodness of going from i to d over n, combining the cost of hopping from i to n with the reported pheromone value $\mathcal{T}_{m^*d}^n$. We call the obtained estimate the *bootstrapped pheromone* variable $\mathcal{B}_{nd}^i$, since it is built up using an estimate which is non-local to i. This bootstrapped pheromone variable can in turn be forwarded in the next hello message sent out by i, giving rise to a bootstrapped pheromone field over the MANET. This way of spreading information over a network is based on information bootstrapping techniques used in dynamic programming and it is often used in traditional routing algorithms for wired networks [46]. It is an efficient process, but can be slow to converge.

For the *maintenance* of existing paths, a bootstrapped pheromone is used directly. If i already has a pheromone entry $\mathcal{T}_{nd}^i$ in its routing table for destination

d going over neighbor n, $\mathcal{B}_{nd}^i$ is treated as an update of the goodness estimate of this path, and is used directly to replace $\mathcal{T}_{nd}^i$. Due to the slow multi-step forwarding of bootstrapped pheromone in hello messages, this information does not provide the most accurate view of the current situation. However, the information is obtained via a lightweight, efficient process, and is complemented by the explicit path updating done by the ants. In this way we have two updating frequencies in the path maintenance process.

For path *exploration*, a bootstrapped pheromone is used indirectly. If i does not yet have a value for $\mathcal{T}_{nd}^i$ in its routing table, $\mathcal{B}_{nd}^i$ could indicate a possible new path from i to d over n. However, this path has never been sampled explicitly by an ant, and due to the slow convergence of the multi-step pheromone bootstrapping process it could be inaccurate, containing undetected loops or dangling links. It is therefore not used directly for data forwarding. It is seen as a sort of virtual pheromone, which needs to be tested. Proactive forward ants will use both the regular and the virtual pheromone to find their way to the destination, so that they can test the proposed new paths. This way, promising virtual pheromone is investigated, and if the investigation is successful it is turned into a regular path that can be used for data.

Reactively Dealing with Link Failures. Nodes can detect link failures when unicast transmissions fail, or when expected periodic hello messages were not received from a neighbor. When a neighbor disappears, the node takes a number of actions. First, it removes the neighbor from its neighbor table and all associated entries from its pheromone table. Next, the node broadcasts a link failure message to notify other nodes of the changed situation. The message contains a list of the destinations to which the node lost its best path, and the new best pheromone to this destination (if it still has entries for the destination). All its neighbors receive the message and update their pheromone table using the new estimates. If they in turn lost their best only path to a destination, they will broadcast a message on to their neighbors, until all concerned nodes are notified of the new situation.

If after the link failure an intermediate node is left with data packets to send but without paths to their destination, the node will start a *local route repair*. The node broadcasts a *route repair ant* that travels to the involved destination like a reactive forward ant: it follows available routing information when it can and is broadcast otherwise. One important difference is that it has a restricted number of broadcasts so that its proliferation is limited. If the local repair fails, the node broadcasts a link failure message to notify other nodes. If the source of a communication session is left with no paths to the destination, it starts a new path setup phase.

Stochastic Data Routing. Data are forwarded according to the values of the pheromone entries. Like in other ACO routing algorithms, nodes in AntHocNet *forward data stochastically*. When a node has multiple next hops for the destination d of the data, it randomly selects one of them, with probability P_{nd}. P_{nd} is calculated in the same way as for reactive forward ants, using equation (7). However, a higher value for the exponent β is used in order to avoid the least good paths. The probabilistic routing strategy leads to data load spreading according to the estimated quality of the paths. If estimates are kept up-to-date, this leads to *automatic load balancing*. When a path is clearly worse than others, it is avoided, and its congestion is relieved. Other paths get more traffic, leading to higher congestion, which makes their end-to-end delay increase. By adapting the data traffic, the nodes spread the data load evenly over the network.

4.4   Simulation Results

AntHocNet's performance was evaluated in an extensive set of simulation tests using QualNet [52]. We have studied the behavior of the algorithm under different conditions for network size, connectivity and change rate, radio channel capacity, data traffic patterns, and node mobility. Performance was measured in terms of data delivery ratio, end-to-end packet delay and delay jitter as *measures of effectiveness*, and routing overhead in number of control packets per successfully delivered data packet as *measure of efficiency*. To assess the performance of our algorithm relative to the state of the art in the field, we compare to AODV [37], which is a de facto standard algorithm and is commonly used in comparative studies. Due to space limitations, we only present a small subset of the results of these simulation tests. For the full set of experiments we again refer to [47,48,49,50,51].

For the tests reported on here, we used MANET scenarios in which 100 nodes are randomly placed in an area of $3000 \times 1000 \ m^2$. Each test lasts 900 seconds. Data traffic is generated by 20 constant bit rate (CBR) sources sending one 64-byte packet per second. Each source starts sending at a random time between 0 and 180 seconds after the start of the simulation, and keeps sending until the end. The radio range of the nodes is 300 meters, and the data rate is 2 Mbit/s. At the MAC layer we use the IEEE 802.11b DCF protocol as is common in MANET research. The nodes move according to the *random waypoint* (RWP) mobility model [38]: they choose a random destination point and a random speed, move to the chosen point with the chosen speed, and then rest at that point for a fixed amount of pause time before they choose a new destination and speed. The speed is chosen between 0 and 20 m/s. The pause time is the variable over which we compare the algorithms.

We created experiments using pause times from 0 up to 480 seconds. Higher pause times lead to slower changing environments (so less link failures), but also to sparser scenarios and hence to lower connectivity. This is because moving nodes tend to cluster around the middle of the MANET area, whereas nodes that pause are spread out randomly (see [53] for properties of the node distribution under RWP mobility). For each pause time we made 10 different test runs. The results of the tests are presented in Figs. 7 (average delay and delivery ratio) and 8 (average jitter and overhead). AntHocNet shows much better effectiveness than AODV, in terms of average delay, delivery ratio and jitter. AODV has better efficiency, measured as routing overhead, but the difference is rather small. The bad efficiency for high pause times is due to the reduced connectivity: AntHocNet has a high frequency to retry failed path setups, leading to high overhead in case source and destination are not connected.

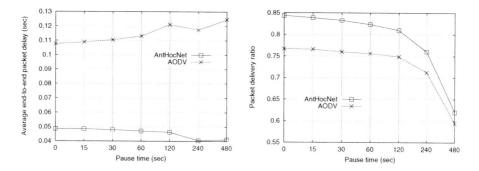

Fig. 7. Average delay and delivery ratio for increasing pause times

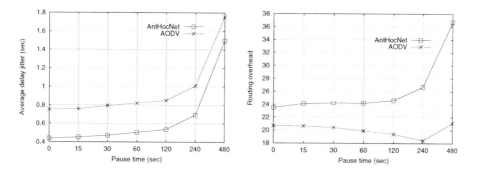

Fig. 8. Average jitter and overhead for increasing pause times

In order to illustrate the difference in adaptivity between AntHocNet and AODV, we show the detailed evolution of the end-to-end delay (rather than showing average values) over the course of a test run in which some important events take place. We use the same setup as before, but keep the pause time constant at 30 seconds, and use different data traffic patterns in order to introduce disruptive events. 10 randomly chosen sources start to send to one single destination between 100 and 110 seconds after the simulation begins, and they keep on sending until the end. After 300 seconds, 20 new sources start to send to a different single destination. 200 seconds later these stop again. All sources send four 64 byte packets per second. Fig. 9 shows, for one communication session,how the end-to-end delay, averaged per 10 seconds, evolves throughout the simulation. The arrival of 20 new sessions after 300 seconds leads to a long period of unstable behavior. The congestion caused by the increased data traffic not only leads to longer queueing times, but also to higher interference that can cause transmissions to fail. Since failed transmissions are usually treated as link failures by routing algorithms, they often trigger strong reactions. As can be seen in the figure, AntHocNet deals with this challenge in a much smoother way than AODV. After the end of the 20 sessions, at second 500, the situation stabilizes again, but faster for AntHocNet than for AODV.

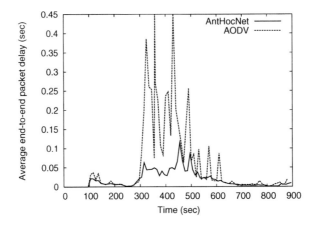

Fig. 9. Evolution of the end-to-end delay over the course of a test run

4.5   Conclusions

In this section we have described AntHocNet, a novel ACO routing algorithm for MANETs. It is a hybrid algorithm that combines reactive route setup with proactive route maintenance and exploration. The main learning mechanism based on path sampling using ant agents is supported by a lightweight information bootstrapping process. Link failures are also dealt with in a hybrid way: proactive protection is provided by the use of multiple paths, whereas reactive mechanisms like route repair and link failure notification messages are used to enhance the adaptivity in the highly mobile MANET environments. In simulation tests, we show that AntHocNet can outperform AODV in different environments, and for different evaluation measures. A detailed examination of the evolution of the algorithm's performance during the course of an experiment illustrates its adaptivity.

5   Conclusion

In this paper we have presented a number of recent algorithms for failure location and restoration in both IP-over-fiber and wireless ad-hoc networks.

For failure location we use a Maximum Likelihood inference to correct error alarms. This approach, together with a standard set-cover heuristic, turned out to handle false and missing alarms far better than the techniques proposed to date.

For failure restoration in IP-over-fiber networks we described two different algorithms, SMART and FastSurv. Both are much faster and more scalable than any solution proposed to date. Moreover, each approach has a number of possible extensions. SMART provides us with a novel method of formal verification of the existence of a survivable mapping and a tool tracing and repairing the vulnerable areas of the network, whereas FastSurv can be easily adapted to any set of real-life requirements such as capacity constraints.

In wireless ad-hoc networks the connectivity changes so quickly, that failure restoration is in fact equivalent to a highly adaptive routing algorithm. Therefore we addressed this problem separately, and proposed AntHocNet - a routing algorithm inspired by Ant Colony Optimization. AntHocNet outperforms standard algorithms in terms of efficiency and scalability.

References

1. Markopoulou, A., Iannaccone, G., Bhattacharyya, S., Chuah, C.N., Diot, C.: Characterization of Failures in an IP Backbone. Proc. of IEEE INFOCOM'04 (2004)
2. Woo, A., Tong, T., Culler, D.: Taming the underlying challenges of reliable multhop routing in sensor networks. In: The First ACM Conference on Embedded Networked Sensor Systems, Los Angeles, CA, USA (2003)
3. Kurant, M., Nguyen, H.X., Thiran, P.: Survey on Dependable IP over Fiber Networks. In: Dependable Systems: Software, Computing, Networks, eds. J. Kohlas, B. Meyer, A. Schiper, Lecture Notes in Computer Science 4028, Springer, 2006 (this volume).
4. Mas, C., Nguyen, H., Thiran, P.: Failure location in WDM networks. In: Optical WDM Networks: Past Lessons and Path Ahead. Kluwer Academic Publishers (2004)
5. ITU-T Rec. G.783. Characteristics of SDH equipment functional blocks (1997)
6. Nguyen, H.X., Thiran, P.: Failure location in all optical networks: the assymetry between false and missing alarms. In: Proceedings of ITC 19. (2005)
7. Carr, R.D., Doddi, S., Konjevod, G., Marathe, M.: On the red-blue set cover problem. In: Proceedings of Symposium on Discrete Algorithms. (2000)
8. Nguyen, H.X., Thiran, P.: Using end-to-end data to infer lossy links in sensor networks. In: To appear in the proceedings of INFOCOM 2006. (2006)
9. Padmanabhan, V.N., Qiu, L., Wang, H.J.: Server-based inference of internet performance. In: Proceedings of the IEEE INFOCOM'03, San Francisco, CA (2003)
10. Schmid, T., Dubois-Ferriere, H., Vetterli, M.: Sensorscope: Experiences with a wireless building monitoring. In: Proceedings of Workshop on Real-World Wireless Sensor Networks (REALWSN'05). (2005)
11. Iannaccone, G., Chuah, C.N., Bhattacharyya, S., Diot, C.: Feasibility of IP restoration in a tier-1 backbone. Sprint ATL Research Report Nr. RR03-ATL-030666 (2003)
12. Armitage, J., Crochat, O., Boudec, J.Y.L.: Design of a Survivable WDM Photonic Network. Proceedings of IEEE INFOCOM 97 (1997)
13. Modiano, E., Narula-Tam, A.: Survivable lightpath routing: a new approach to the design of WDM-based networks. IEEE Journal on Selected Areas in Communications 20 (2002) 800–809

14. Giroire, F., Nucci, A., Taft, N., Diot, C.: Increasing the Robustness of IP Backbones in the Absence of Optical Level Protection. Proc. of IEEE INFOCOM 2003 (2003)
15. Leonardi, E., Mellia, M., Marsan, M.A.: Algorithms for the Logical Topology Design in WDM All-Optical Networks. Optical Networks Magazine (2000)
16. Sen, A., Hao, B., Shen, B.: Survivable routing in WDM networks. In: Proceedings of the 7th International Symposium on Computers and Communications (ISCC). (2002)
17. Crochat, O., Boudec, J.Y.L.: Design Protection for WDM Optical Networks. IEEE Journal of Selected Areas in Communication **16** (1998) 1158–1165
18. Nucci, A., Sansò, B., Crainic, T., Leonardi, E., Marsan, M.A.: Design of Fault-Tolerant Logical Topologies in Wavelength-Routed Optical IP Networks. Proc. of IEEE Globecom 2001 (2001)
19. Fumagalli, A., Valcarenghi, L.: IP Restoration vs. WDM Protection: Is There an Optimal Choice? IEEE Network (2000)
20. Sahasrabuddhe, L., Ramamurthy, S., Mukherjee, B.: Fault management in IP-Over-WDM Networks: WDM Protection vs. IP Restoration. IEEE Journal on Selected Areas in Communications **20** (2002)
21. Sasaki, G.H., Su, C.F., Blight, D.: Simple layout algorithms to maintain network connectivity under faults. In Proceedings of the 2000 Annual Allerton Conference (2000)
22. Kurant, M., Thiran, P.: Survivable Mapping Algorithm by Ring Trimming (SMART) for large IP-over-WDM networks. Proc. of BroadNets 2004 (2004)
23. Kurant, M., Thiran, P.: On Survivable Routing of Mesh Topologies in IP-over-WDM Networks. Proc. of Infocom'05 (2005)
24. Ducatelle, F., Gambardella, L.: A scalable algorithm for survivable routing in IP-over-WDM networks. In: Proceedings of the First Annual International Conference on Broadband Networks (BroadNets). (2004)
25. Ducatelle, F., Gambardella, L.: Fastsurv: A new efficient local search algorithm for survivable routing in WDM networks. In: Proceedings of Annual IEEE Global Telecommunications Conference (Globecom). (2004)
26. Ducatelle, F., Gambardella, L.: Survivable routing in IP-over-WDM networks: An efficient and scalable local search algorithm. Optical Switching and Networking (2005) To appear.
27. Gross, J., Yellen, J.: Graph Theory and its Applications. CRC Press, 1999 (1999)
28. Frank, A.: Packing paths, circuits and cuts - a survey (in Paths, Flows and VLSI-Layout). Springer, Berlin, 1990 (1990)
29. Li, G., Doverspike, B., Kalmanek, C.: Fiber Span Failure Protection in Mesh Optical Networks. Optical Networks Magazine **3** (2002) 21–31
30. Kim, S., Lumetta, S.: Addressing node failures in all-optical networks. Journal of Optical Networking **1** (2002) 154–163
31. Choi, H., Subramaniam, S., Choi, H.A.: On Double-Link Failure Recovery in WDM Optical Networks. Proc. of IEEE INFOCOM'02 (2002)
32. Royer, E., Toh, C.K.: A review of current routing protocols for ad hoc mobile wireless networks. IEEE Personal Communications (1999)
33. Dorigo, M., Di Caro, G., Gambardella, L.M.: Ant algorithms for discrete optimization. Artificial Life **5** (1999) 137–172
34. Di Caro, G.: Ant Colony Optimization and its application to adaptive routing in telecommunication networks. PhD thesis, Faculté des Sciences Appliquées, Université Libre de Bruxelles, Brussels, Belgium (2004)
35. Abolhasan, M., Wysocki, T., Dutkiewicz, E.: A review of routing protocols for mobile ad hoc networks. Ad Hoc Networks **2** (2004) 1–22

36. Perkins, C., Bhagwat, P.: Highly dynamic destination-sequenced distance-vector routing (DSDV) for mobile computers. In: ACM SIGCOMM'94 Conference on Communications Architectures, Protocols and Applications. (1994)

37. Perkins, C., Royer, E.: Ad-hoc on-demand distance vector routing. In: Proc. of the 2nd IEEE Workshop on Mobile Computing Systems and Applications. (1999)

38. Johnson, D., Maltz, D.: Dynamic Source Routing in Ad Hoc Wireless Networks. In: Mobile Computing. Kluwer (1996) 153–181

39. Broch, J., Maltz, D., Johnson, D., Hu, Y.C., Jetcheva, J.: A performance comparison of multi-hop wireless ad hoc network routing protocols. In: Proc. of the 4th Annual ACM/IEEE Int. Conf. on Mobile Computing and Networking (MobiCom98). (1998)

40. Haas, Z.: A new routing protocol for the reconfigurable wireless networks. In: Proc. of the IEEE Int. Conf. on Universal Personal Communications. (1997)

41. Mueller, S., Tsang, R., Ghosal, D.: Multipath routing in mobile ad hoc networks: Issues and challenges. In: Performance Tools and Applications to Networked Systems. Volume 2965 of LNCS. Springer-Verlag (2004)

42. Camazine, S., Deneubourg, J.L., Franks, N.R., Sneyd, J., Theraulaz, G., Bonabeau, E.: Self-Organization in Biological Systems. Princeton University Press (2001)

43. Dorigo, M., Maniezzo, V., Colorni, A.: The ant system: Optimization by a colony of cooperating agents. IEEE Transactions on Systems, Man, and Cybernetics–Part B **26** (1996) 29–41

44. Schoonderwoerd, R., Holland, O., Bruten, J., Rothkrantz, L.: Ant-based load balancing in telecommunications networks. Adaptive Behavior **5** (1996) 169–207

45. Di Caro, G., Dorigo, M.: AntNet: Distributed stigmergetic control for communications networks. J. of Artificial Intelligence Research **9** (1998) 317–365

46. Bertsekas, D., Gallager, R.: Data Networks. Prentice–Hall, Englewood Cliffs, NJ, USA (1992)

47. Di Caro, G., Ducatelle, F., Gambardella, L.: AntHocNet: an ant-based hybrid routing algorithm for mobile ad hoc networks. In: Proceedings of Parallel Problem Solving from Nature (PPSN VIII). LNCS, Springer-Verlag (2004)

48. Ducatelle, F., Di Caro, G., Gambardella, L.: Ant agents for hybrid multipath routing in mobile ad hoc networks. In: Proceedings of The Second Annual Conference on Wireless On demand Network Systems and Services (WONSS). (2005)

49. Di Caro, G., Ducatelle, F., Gambardella, L.: Swarm intelligence for routing in mobile ad hoc networks. In: Proceedings of the 2005 IEEE Swarm Intelligence Symposium (SIS). (2005)

50. Di Caro, G., Ducatelle, F., Gambardella, L.: AntHocNet: an adaptive nature-inspired algorithm for routing in mobile ad hoc networks. European Transactions on Telecommunications **16** (2005)

51. Ducatelle, F., Di Caro, G., Gambardella, L.: Using ant agents to combine reactive and proactive strategies for routing in mobile ad hoc networks. International Journal of Computational Intelligence and Applications (IJCIA) (2005) To appear.

52. Scalable Network Technologies, Inc. Culver City, CA, USA: Qualnet Simulator, Version 3.6. (2003) http://stargate.ornl.gov/trb/tft.html.

53. Bettstetter, C., Resta, G., Santi, P.: The node distribution of the random waypoint mobility model for wireless ad hoc networks. IEEE Transactions on Mobile Computing **2** (2003) 257–269

Robustness of the Internet at the Topology and Routing Level*

Thomas Erlebach[1], Alexander Hall[2], Linda Moonen[3], Alessandro Panconesi[4], Frits Spieksma[3], and Danica Vukadinović[5]

[1] Department of Computer Science, University of Leicester, England
t.erlebach@mcs.le.ac.uk
[2] Department of Computer Science, ETH Zürich, Switzerland
alex.hall@inf.ethz.ch
[3] Department of Applied Economics, Katholieke Universiteit Leuven, Belgium
{linda.moonen, frits.spieksma}@econ.kuleuven.be
[4] DSI – Università La Sapienza, Rome, Italy
ale@dsi.uniroma1.it
[5] Computer Engineering and Networks Laboratory (TIK), Department of
Information Technology and Electrical Engineering, ETH Zürich, Switzerland
vukadin@tik.ee.ethz.ch

Abstract. Classical measures of network robustness are the number of
disjoint paths between two nodes and the size of a smallest cut separating
them. In the Internet, the paths that traffic can take are constrained by
the routing policies of the individual autonomous systems (ASs). These
policies mainly depend on the economic relationships between ASs, e.g.,
customer-provider or peer-to-peer. Paths that are consistent with these
policies can be modeled as valley-free paths. We give an overview of
existing approaches to the inference of AS relationships, and we survey
recent results concerning the problem of computing a maximum number
of disjoint valley-free paths between two given nodes, and the problem of
computing a smallest set of nodes whose removal disconnects two given
nodes with respect to all valley-free paths. For both problems, we discuss
NP-hardness and inapproximability results, approximation algorithms,
and exact algorithms based on branch-and-bound techniques. We also
summarize experimental findings that have been obtained with these
algorithms in a comparison of different graph models of the AS-level
Internet with respect to robustness properties.

1 Introduction

A substantial part of today's communication takes place over the Internet. Therefore, the robustness of the Internet is an issue of fundamental importance. A classical method for assessing the robustness of a network is to model the network

---
* Research partially supported by Hasler Foundation in DICS-project 1838, and by the
European Commission in the 5th Framework Programme under contract IST-2001-
32007 (APPOL II) and in the 6th Framework Programme under contract 001907
(DELIS), with funding in Switzerland provided by SBF.

J. Kohlas, B. Meyer, and A. Schiper (Eds.): Dependable Systems, LNCS 4028, pp. 260–274, 2006.
© Springer-Verlag Berlin Heidelberg 2006

topology as a graph and compute the number of vertex-disjoint or edge-disjoint paths between pairs of nodes, or to compute the sizes of vertex cuts or edge cuts. This method has been used to analyze the robustness of the Internet as well. For example, the number of vertex- and edge-disjoint paths is computed for an undirected model of the Internet topology on the level of autonomous systems (ASs) as well as for the topology of one Internet Service Provider in [27]. Here, the undirected model of the AS-level Internet consists of an undirected graph that has an undirected edge between two ASs if there is at least one physical link between them. Such a model is also referred to as an (undirected) *AS graph*. It turns out, however, that the way traffic is routed in the Internet is not captured accurately if standard models of graphs and paths are used. This is due to the routing policies that restrict the paths along which traffic can flow; these routing policies depend mainly on the economic relationships between ASs. Therefore, it becomes necessary to incorporate the effects of routing policies into the network model considered; this is achieved by the *valley-free path model*.

In this paper, we give a short overview of different methods that have been used to infer the relationships between ASs, and we survey recent algorithmic results on the generalization of classical robustness measures to the valley-free path model. While these robustness measures can be computed efficiently in the standard graph model using network flow techniques (see, e.g., [2]), it turns out that the generalization to the valley-free path model makes them computationally more difficult.

We discuss complexity and inapproximability results as well as efficient approximation algorithms with provable performance guarantees that have been presented in [10,11]. Furthermore, we outline exact algorithms presented in [12] that make it possible to obtain optimal results on Internet graphs of realistic size in reasonable time. We also summarize some of the experimental findings of [12], which are concerned with vertex-disjoint paths and vertex cuts in the valley-free path model computed with these algorithms for real Internet graphs.

We consider the Internet on the level of ASs. An AS is a subnetwork under separate administrative control. Individual ASs can consist of tens to thousands of routers and hosts. Two ASs that are connected by at least one physical link exchange routing information using the Border Gateway Protocol (BGP).

As a prerequisite for a robustness analysis of the Internet, it is necessary to understand the routes along which traffic can be sent. Each AS uses a local routing policy that determines which routes are announced to which neighboring ASs. For commercial reasons, details about these policies are not publicly available. This makes it difficult to create an accurate model that can be used in the analysis of the robustness of the Internet.

Information about the types of commercial agreements between ASs can be found in [17,18,4]. The economic relationships between ASs have a significant impact on Internet routing. For example, the routing policies arising from these economic relationships have been shown to be a contributing factor in BGP path inflation [15,25,26] and slow route convergence [20]. Therefore, an undirected graph model of the Internet that does not incorporate the effects of routing policies is too simplistic. On the other hand, it would be infeasible to include all aspects of the many different commercial agreements in the model. Therefore, Gao [14] proposed a classification of AS relationships into three main categories: customer-provider relationships, peer-to-peer relationships, and sibling relationships.

If two ASs are in a *customer-provider* relationship, the provider announces all its routes (i.e., the set of all paths from that provider to some destination that are stored in its routing table) to the customer, but the customer announces to the provider only its own routes (i.e., routes with a destination inside its own AS) and routes of its customers. Roughly speaking, this implies that the customer can send traffic for arbitrary destinations to the provider, but the provider can send traffic to the customer only if the destination is in the customer's AS or in an AS that is itself a customer of the customer. This policy is used because customers do not want to forward traffic from one provider to another provider. If two ASs are in a *peer-to-peer* relationship, they exchange their own routes and routes of their customers, but not routes of their providers or other peers. If they are *siblings*, they exchange all their routes. Sibling relationships typically exist between different ASs owned by the same company.

It was observed by Gao [14] that valid paths between ASs follow a particular structure: no path contains more than one peer-to-peer relationship, and once a provider-customer or peer-to-peer relationship is encountered on the path, no customer-provider relationship can follow. If we imagine providers at a higher level than their customers and peers at the same level, the allowed types of paths are "only up," "only down," and "first up and then down." Valid paths can have only one "peak" (which can consist of a single AS or of two ASs connected by a peer-to-peer relationship) and they must not contain "valleys." Therefore, such paths are called *valley-free paths* [14]. A formal definition of valley-free paths will be given in Section 3. In the remainder of this paper, we will use the terms "valley-free path" and "valid path" interchangeably.

Since information about economic relationships between ASs is not publicly available, several heuristic algorithms have been proposed for inferring these relationships from BGP routing table information [14,24,8,9]. However, it is not clear how accurate the relationship classifications produced by these algorithms are. Thus, it is an interesting question how the models produced by these algorithms differ from each other, especially with respect to robustness properties.

1.1 Outline

The remainder of this survey is structured as follows. In Section 2, we give a brief overview of existing approaches dealing with the inference of AS relationships. In Section 3, we give formal definitions of the valley-free path model and the disjoint paths and cut problems considered in later sections. Section 4 gives an overview of the complexity and approximation results for disjoint valid paths and minimum valid cuts from [10,11]. In Section 5, we explain the primal-dual formulation of the problem proposed in [12], and we outline the exact algorithms for the computation of disjoint valid paths and of minimum valid cuts that are presented in [12]. In Section 6, we summarize some of the experimental findings that have been obtained in [12] concerning the number of vertex-disjoint valid paths and the sizes of minimum cuts in four different graph models with inferred relationships and in the undirected model. We give our conclusions in Section 7.

2   Inference of AS Relationships

As it is necessary to know the economic relationships between ASs in order to model the effects of routing policies on the paths traffic can take in the Internet, several researchers have considered the problem of inferring AS relationships from other information. In particular, the BGP tables provided by the University of Oregon Route Views project [23] are often used as input. These tables contain a large number of BGP paths, i.e., sequences of ASs that represent paths from a source AS to a destination AS.

Gao [14] was the first to propose a heuristic algorithm for inferring AS relationships. Her algorithm uses BGP paths as input and can be sketched as follows. For each BGP path, the AS with largest degree (in the undirected AS graph) is taken to be the top provider of the path. Pairs of consecutive ASs before the top provider are assumed to have a customer-provider relationship, and pairs of consecutive ASs after the top provider are assumed to have a provider-customer relationship. Pairs that are assigned a customer-provider and a provider-customer relationship in this way (this happens if the pair occurs on two paths in such a way that it is assigned one relationship via the first path and a different relationship via the second path) are reclassified as siblings. Finally, a heuristic method is used to classify some edges incident to the top providers of BGP paths as peer-to-peer edges. An implementation of Gao's algorithm is available from [13].

Further work on the inference of AS relationships is presented by Subramanian et al. [24]. They formalize the inference problem as the optimization problem of giving an orientation to the edges of an undirected AS graph with the goal of maximizing the number of paths in the given BGP tables that become valid for this orientation. This problem is called the Type-of-Relationship (ToR) problem. They leave its complexity as an open question. They also present a heuristic algorithm for the inference of AS relationships. Their algorithm exploits the structure of partial views of the AS graph seen from different locations in the Internet. For each location, BGP paths from that location (AS) to a number of other ASs are used to construct a local graph. By repeated pruning of leaf vertices in that local graph, rank numbers are assigned to each AS in such a way that larger ranks correspond to a perceived higher level of the AS. As this procedure is repeated for all available locations, each AS receives a vector of ranks. Finally, an edge is classified as a peer-to-peer relationship if the rank vectors of its endpoints are equal in many components, and as a customer-provider relationship if the number of components of the rank vector that have a smaller value for the first AS is much larger than the number of components with a smaller value for the second AS. Some edges are left unclassified by this approach, and it is meaningful to consider them as sibling edges. Relationship classifications produced with the algorithm of [24] are available from [1].

Independently, Di Battista et al. [8] and Erlebach et al. [9] have resolved the open question of [24] and proved that the ToR problem is $\mathcal{NP}$-hard. Furthermore, in [9] an inference algorithm is proposed that translates the problem into a maximum satisfiability problem with two literals per clause (MAX 2SAT) and then applies a known MAX 2SAT approximation algorithm. The truth assignment given by the MAX 2SAT algorithm is converted into an AS relationship classification for the original problem. The classification produced by their algorithm uses only customer-provider edges. In [8], another inference algorithm is presented that also exploits the relationship of the inference problem to the 2SAT problem, but in a different way: The algorithm creates a 2SAT instance that is satisfiable if and only if there is an orientation of the undirected AS graph that makes all given paths valid. As such an orientation does not exist in general, the algorithm repeatedly applies a heuristic procedure that removes paths from the input until the resulting 2SAT instance is satisfiable. The satisfying assignment then gives a classification of most edges of the undirected AS graph as customer-provider relationships, but leaves some relationships undetermined. The software bgpSat implementing the algorithm of [8] is available at [7].

Rimondini et al. [22] compare the algorithms from [24] and [8]. They study the relationships that are found by the same algorithm on data sets for different dates (*stability analysis*) and compare the classifications found by the two algorithms on the same data set (*algorithm independence analysis*). They find that the classifications produced by both algorithms are stable and very similar.

Xia and Gao [30] use BGP community attribute data and IRR (Internet Routing Registry) databases to obtain accurate information about the relationships for a certain subset of AS pairs. Then they use this *partial information* to check the correctness of the relationship classifications produced by the algorithms from [14] and [24]. They find that both algorithms achieve a very good overall accuracy, but perform poorly with respect to peer-to-peer relationships: only about 25% (about 49%) of the peer-to-peer relationships covered by the partial information are classified correctly by the algorithm from [24] (from [14]). Motivated by this shortcoming of existing algorithms, they propose a new algorithm that uses the partial information as a starting point. Based on the partial information, the algorithm filters out BGP paths that cannot be valley-free and uses inference rules to determine the classifications of additional edges that are implied by the starting set. Edges that remain unclassified are then treated with the algorithm from [14]. They conclude that their new algorithm outperforms the existing algorithms with respect to the achieved accuracy, especially concerning peer-to-peer edges.

3   ToR Graphs, Valid Cuts, and Disjoint Valid Paths

The AS relationships discussed in Section 1 can be represented in a graph model as follows [12]: The vertices of the graph are the ASs. The graph is a *mixed graph*, i.e. it can contain directed and undirected edges. If there is at least one physical link between two ASs x and y, their corresponding vertices are connected in one of the following three ways: If x and y are in a peer-to-peer relationship, there is an undirected edge $\{x, y\}$. If x is a customer of y, there is a directed edge (x, y). If x and y are siblings, there is a directed edge (x, y) as well as a directed edge (y, x). A graph constructed in this way is called a *ToR graph*, as the problem of classifying the relationships between ASs is called the Type-of-Relationship (ToR) problem in [24,8,9].

The following definition of valid paths captures the notion of "valley-free" paths arising from BGP routing policies. A path $p = v_1, v_2, \ldots, v_r$ from v_1 to v_r in a ToR graph $G = (V, E)$ is called *valid* if it satisfies one of the following two conditions [14,12]:

- The path consists of a sequence of sibling edges or customer-provider edges in forward direction, followed by a sequence of sibling edges or customer-provider edges in reverse direction. Formally, this means that there exists j, $1 \leq j \leq r$, such that $(v_i, v_{i+1}) \in E$ for $1 \leq i \leq j - 1$ and $(v_i, v_{i-1}) \in E$ for $j + 1 \leq i \leq r$.
- The path consists of a sequence of sibling edges or customer-provider edges in forward direction, followed by a single peer-to-peer edge, followed by a sequence of sibling edges or customer-provider edges in reverse direction. Formally, this means that there exists j, $1 \leq j \leq r$, such that $(v_i, v_{i+1}) \in E$ for $1 \leq i \leq j - 1$, $\{v_j, v_{j+1}\} \in E$, and $(v_i, v_{i-1}) \in E$ for $j + 2 \leq i \leq r$.

Otherwise, a path is called *invalid*. From now on, when we refer to paths in a ToR graph, we mean valid paths. A path from s to t is also called an *s-t path*.

If $p = v_1, v_2, \ldots, v_r$ is a valid path, we imagine p as consisting of a *forward part* and a *backward part*. If p contains an undirected edge $\{v_j, v_{j+1}\}$, the initial part of p up to v_j is the forward part, and the rest of p, starting with v_{j+1}, is the backward part. If p does not contain an undirected edge, the backward part begins with the first customer-provider edge that is traversed in reverse direction. Intuitively, the forward part goes "up" in the Internet hierarchy and the backward part goes "down."

As we are interested in robustness, where the traditional metrics are cut size and number of disjoint paths, we now present suitable adaptations of these concepts to the valley-free path model. Let $s, t \in V$ be two distinct vertices in a ToR graph $G = (V, E)$. A set $C \subseteq V \setminus \{s, t\}$ is a *valid s-t-cut* if there is no valid path from s to t in $G - C$. A smallest such set C is called a *min valid s-t-cut*. Two valid s-t-paths are called *vertex-disjoint* (or simply *disjoint*) if the only vertices that they have in common are s and t. The optimization problems that we are interested in are those of computing minimum size cuts and maximum size sets of disjoint paths: the min valid s-t-cut problem and the max disjoint valid s-t-paths problem.

An approximation algorithm A for an optimization problem Π is a polynomial algorithm that always outputs a feasible solution (we consider only instances where a feasible solution always exists). A is a ρ-approximation algorithm (has approximation ratio ρ) if the objective value of the solution that it outputs is at most a factor of ρ away from the optimal solution, for every problem instance.

In a ToR graph, two ASs with at least one physical link between them are connected by a single edge (or a single pair of edges, in the case of siblings). If we work with this graph model, computing edge cuts or edge-disjoint paths would not be very meaningful; for example, cutting a single edge of the ToR graph might correspond to cutting many links of the real Internet, so a small edge cut in the ToR graph does not imply a small robustness in the real network. For this reason, we only consider vertex cuts and vertex-disjoint paths in this survey. We refer to [10,11] for approximation and complexity results concerning edge cuts and edge-disjoint paths.

4   Complexity and Approximation Results

In this section, we discuss complexity and approximation results from [10,11] for disjoint paths and minimum cuts in the valley-free path model. First, note that it is easy to see that a peer-to-peer edge (undirected edge) between A and B can be replaced by two customer-provider edges from A to X and from B to X, where X is a new node, without affecting the solutions to the min valid s-t-cut problem and the max disjoint valid s-t-paths problem. Similarly, it is easy to see that a pair of directed edges representing a sibling relationship can be replaced by a small subgraph consisting only of customer-provider edges. See Fig. 1 for an illustration. Therefore, without loss of generality, in this section we consider a model with only customer-provider edges.

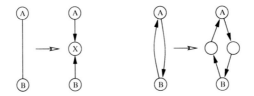

Fig. 1. Peer-to-peer relationships (left) and sibling relationships (right) can be replaced by customer-provider relationships

4.1   The Two-Layer Model

First, we introduce the *two-layer model* that leads to a relaxation of flows and cuts in ToR graphs [11]. From a ToR graph $G = (V, E)$ and $s, t \in V$ we construct a *two-layer model* H, which is a directed graph, in the following way. First, create two copies of the graph G, called the *lower* and the *upper layer*. Reverse all edge directions in the upper layer, and connect each node v in the lower layer with a directed edge to the corresponding copy of v, denoted v', in the upper layer. Finally, merge the two s-nodes (of lower and upper layer) and also the two t-nodes, and remove the incoming edges of s and the outgoing edges of t.

A valid path $p = v_1, \ldots, v_r$ in G with $v_1 = s$ and $v_r = t$ corresponds to a directed path in H in the following way: The forward part of p is routed in the lower layer, then there is a possible transition to the upper layer with a (v, v') type edge, and finally the backward part of p is routed in the upper layer. If p has only a forward or only a backward part, the corresponding path in H uses only one of the two layers. See Fig. 2 for an illustration.

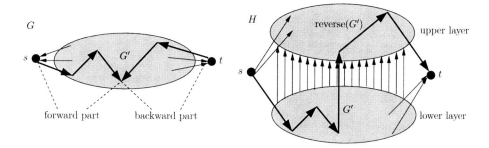

Fig. 2. Path in ToR graph G and corresponding path in the two-layer model H [11]. G' denotes $G - \{s, t\}$.

Two paths in H that correspond to disjoint valid paths in G are also disjoint, but two disjoint paths in H do not necessarily give disjoint valid paths in G: One path might use a node in one layer and the other path the counterpart in the other layer, giving two valid path that both go through the same node of G.

From a valid s-t-cut C_G in G one can easily construct an s-t-cut in H of cardinality $2|C_G|$: It suffices to take both copies of the nodes in C_G. On the other hand, s-t-cuts in H do not necessarily have the property that a node v is in the cut if and only if also its counterpart v' is in the cut.

4.2   Min Valid s-t-Cut

The min valid s-t-cut problem was shown to be *NP*-hard and *APX*-hard in [10,11]. The *APX*-hardness result implies that there is a constant $\rho > 1$ such that it is not possible to find a ρ-approximation algorithm for the min valid s-t-cut problem unless $P = NP$ [3].

Given a ToR graph $G = (V, E)$ and $s, t \in V$ (where we assume that there is no direct edge in G between s and t, because otherwise a valid s-t-cut does not exist), the min valid s-t-cut approximation algorithm proposed in [11] works as follows: First, the two-layer model H is constructed. Then, a min s-t-cut C_H in H is computed, using a min s-t-cut algorithm for standard directed graphs. Note that the min s-t-cut problem can be solved in polynomial time for standard directed graphs [2]. Finally, a valid s-t-cut C_G in G is constructed by including all nodes of which at least one copy is contained in C_H.

It is easy to see that $|C_G| \leq |C_H|$ holds and C_G is a valid s-t-cut in G. Furthermore, the cardinality of C_H is at most twice the cardinality of the optimum valid s-t-cut in G, yielding the following theorem.

Theorem 1 (Erlebach et al. [11]). *There is a 2-approximation algorithm for the min valid s-t-cut problem in ToR graphs.*

4.3 Max Disjoint Valid s-t-Paths

It was shown in [11] that finding the maximum number of disjoint valid s-t paths for given vertices s and t in a ToR graph $G = (V, E)$ is NP-hard. Moreover, the number of paths is inapproximable within a factor $2 - \varepsilon$ for any $\varepsilon > 0$, unless P equals NP, and it is even NP-hard to decide if there are at least two disjoint valid paths between s and t.

We proceed to describe the approximation algorithm presented in [11]. First, let us introduce some terminology. If the forward part of a valid s-t path p_1 intersects the backward part of a path p_2 at a node v, this is called a *crossing* at v. If two valid s-t paths cross at v, they can be *recombined* at the crossing to form a new path, consisting of the initial part of p_1: $s, \ldots, v$ and the final part of p_2: $v, \ldots, t$.

The algorithm works as follows. First, the two-layer model H is constructed, and a maximum cardinality set $\mathcal{P}_H$ of vertex-disjoint s-t-paths in H is computed using standard methods based on network flow [2]. Let $\mathcal{P}_G$ be the set of valid s-t-paths in G that correspond to the paths in $\mathcal{P}_H$. Note that the paths in $\mathcal{P}_G$ are not necessarily vertex-disjoint, since the forward part of one path can intersect the backward part of another path. Now the idea is to recombine the forward parts and the backward parts so as to obtain a set of disjoint valid s-t-paths in the end. To achieve this, the algorithm repeatedly selects a path p whose forward part has not yet been recombined and has at least one remaining crossing. If the first crossing on that forward part is at node v, the path p is recombined with the path p' whose backward part contains v. Crossings preceding v on the backward part of p' are discarded, and if p' was previously recombined with another path p'', the status of the forward part of p'' reverts back to "not yet recombined." The process is repeated until each forward part is either recombined or has no remaining crossing. The set of recombined paths is output as the solution.

It is shown in [11] that the algorithm runs in polynomial time and the set of paths output by the algorithm is vertex-disjoint. The analysis of the approximation ratio of the algorithm can be sketched as follows. Assume that k is the optimal number of paths. Clearly, $|\mathcal{P}_G| \geq k$. In the end, for each path p in $\mathcal{P}_G$ at least one of its two parts, the forward part or the backward part, must have been recombined. Thus, at least $|\mathcal{P}_G|/2 \geq k/2$ disjoint valid s-t paths are found. This gives the following theorem.

Theorem 2 (Erlebach et al. [11]). *There is a 2-approximation algorithm for the max disjoint valid s-t-paths problem.*

4.4 On the Gap Between Disjoint Paths and Minimum Cuts

In the standard model of paths in directed or undirected graphs, Menger's theorem states that the maximum number of disjoint s-t-paths is equal to the size of a minimum s-t-cut (provided that there is no direct edge from s to t). It is shown in [11] that for the valley-free path model there is always a valid s-t-cut that is at most twice as large as the maximum number of vertex-disjoint valid s-t-paths. An example showing that the bound of 2 is tight is given in Fig. 3.

In this example, the size of a minimum valid s-t-cut is 2, while the maximum number of disjoint valid s-t-paths is 1.

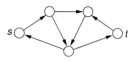

Fig. 3. ToR graph demonstrating a gap of 2 between disjoint paths and cuts [11]

4.5   Max Disjoint Valid s-t-Paths in DAGs

We briefly discuss the problem of computing disjoint valid paths in directed acyclic graphs. This is motivated by the consideration that in a strictly hierarchical network, one would obtain ToR graphs that are acyclic. For acyclic graphs, finding the maximum number of disjoint valid s-t-paths was proved to be *NP*-hard in [10,11]. While it is *NP*-hard to decide whether there are two disjoint valid paths from s to t in a general ToR graph, it was shown in [10,11] that this decision problem can be solved in polynomial time for any constant number of paths in acyclic graphs.

5   Exact Algorithms

In this section, we first review the integer programming formulations given in [12] for the max disjoint valid s-t-paths problem and for the min valid s-t-cut problem, and then outline the exact algorithms proposed in [12] for these problems.

The max disjoint valid s-t-paths problem and the min valid s-t-cut problem can be formulated as integer linear programs in a straightforward way. Let $\mathcal{P}$ be the set of all valid s-t paths, and let $\mathcal{V}_p$ be the set of all vertices (except s and t) contained in a path $p \in \mathcal{P}$. The integer linear program for the max disjoint valid s-t-paths problem uses a 0–1 variable x_p for each valid path p, indicating whether the path is used or not, and looks as follows:

$$\text{(P)   Maximize} \sum_{p \in \mathcal{P}} x_p \tag{1}$$

$$s.t. \sum_{p:v \in \mathcal{V}_p} x_p \leq 1 \quad \forall v \in V \setminus \{s, t\} \tag{2}$$

$$x_p \in \{0, 1\} \quad \forall p \in \mathcal{P} \tag{3}$$

The objective function (1) counts the number of s-t-paths that are part of the solution. Constraints (2) ensure that each vertex can be contained in at most one path.

The min valid s-t-cut problem can be formulated as an integer linear program using a 0–1 variable y_v for every $v \in V \setminus \{s,t\}$ that indicates whether v is taken in the cut or not:

$$\text{(D)} \quad \text{Minimize} \quad \sum_{v \in V \setminus \{s,t\}} y_v \tag{4}$$

$$s.t. \quad \sum_{v \in V_p} y_v \geq 1 \qquad \forall p \in \mathcal{P} \tag{5}$$

$$y_v \in \{0,1\} \qquad \forall v \in V \setminus \{s,t\} \tag{6}$$

As observed in [12], the LP-relaxations of (P) and (D), i.e., the linear programs in which the variables x_p and y_v can take arbitrary values in the interval $[0,1]$, constitute a primal-dual pair of linear programs.

Formulation (P) has exponentially many variables (since the number of valid s-t paths can be exponential in the number of vertices), and, correspondingly, formulation (D) has exponentially many constraints. Nevertheless, it is shown in [12] that optimal solutions to the LP-relaxations of (P) and (D) can be computed in polynomial time without explicitly constructing the linear programs, since the separation problem [16] for (D) can be solved using a shortest-path computation in the two-layer model with suitable edge weights. Furthermore, it is described in [12] how the LP-relaxation of (P) can be solved in practice using column generation, or that of (D) using a cutting-plane approach. However, the optimal solutions to the LP-relaxations can be fractional (i.e., the variables can have values strictly between 0 and 1), and a branch-and-bound approach must be employed to arrive at optimal integral solutions.

In [12], two exact algorithms for the max disjoint valid s-t-paths problem are proposed. The first one is a branch-and-price algorithm [5,28] based on the integer programming formulation (1)-(3). It solves the LP-relaxation of (P) using column generation. If the obtained solution is fractional, it identifies a fractional vertex, i.e., a vertex v at least three of whose incident edges are used by fractional paths, and then creates a branch for each possible way of deleting all but two of the incident edges of v (the two edges that are not deleted must be such that they can be used consecutively on a valid path). In this way, no integral solution is excluded, and moreover v cannot be a fractional vertex in any of the branches. Implemented in a branch-and-bound framework, this approach yields an optimal integral solution to (P).

The second algorithm is a pure branch-and-bound algorithm that does not solve the LP-relaxation of (P). Instead, it uses the two-layer model H as a relaxation of (P). The algorithm computes a largest set $\mathcal{P}_H$ of vertex-disjoint paths in H. If the obtained paths are also vertex-disjoint in G, they represent an optimal solution. If they are not vertex-disjoint, there must be a vertex v such that both copies of v are used by the paths in $\mathcal{P}_H$. In this case, two branches are created using suitable modifications of H: In one branch, v can only be used in the upper layer, and in the other branch, v can only be used in the lower layer (or for a transition from lower to upper layer). Again, no integral solution is excluded, and the algorithm computes an optimal integral solution to (P).

The exact algorithm for the min valid s-t-cut problem from [12] can be outlined as follows. The algorithm solves the LP-relaxation of (D) using a cutting-plane approach. If the optimal solution to the LP-relaxation is fractional, a vertex v with y_v-value strictly between 0 and 1 is selected, and two branches are created: The constraint $y_v = 0$ is added to the LP-relaxation in one branch, and the constraint $y_v = 1$ in the other. Implementing this in a branch-and-bound framework, one obtains optimal integral solutions to (D).

6   Experimental Results

In this section we briefly summarize some of the experimental results described in [12]. Internet graphs from five different dates between April 2001 and February 2004 are considered. Undirected graph models for the five dates are constructed using BGP table information available from the University of Oregon Route Views project [23]. They are referred to as *undirected BGP graphs*. Four different ToR graphs are constructed for each date from the undirected BGP graph using the AS relationship classification algorithms of [9,8,24,14]. As all four algorithms are heuristics, they typically output different relationship classifications. Nevertheless, about 90% of all edges are classified in the same way by different algorithms [12].

In [12], 47 representative ASs are selected, and all computations are carried out for all 1,081 pairs among these ASs. The selected ASs are geographically well spread and contain various types of ASs: bigger and smaller Internet Service Providers, telecom nodes (e.g. Japanese and Belgian telecom), well-connected universities and research centers (e.g. University of Stanford, University of Oregon, and National Center for Supercomputing Applications), exchange points (e.g. London and Hongkong Internet Exchange), etc.

As described in [12], the algorithms have been implemented in C++ using CPLEX 9.0 [19] to solve linear programs and the LEDA library [21] to process graphs. For all computations, several preprocessing methods have been applied to the graph input data. In particular, vertices with degree 1 were pruned, leaving graphs with up to 11,000 vertices and 30,000 edges for the main computations.

The two exact algorithms for the max disjoint valid s-t-paths problem described in Section 5 have been used in [12] to calculate the maximum number of vertex-disjoint paths for all pairs among the selected 47 ASs. The conclusion is that both algorithms perform well on the average: The majority of problem instances are solved in a few seconds of computation time. The branch-and-bound algorithm was faster than the branch-and-price algorithm in over 70% of the instances, but its running-times displayed a higher variability, and on some instances it could not be run to completion. Furthermore, it usually needed a larger number of branching nodes. The min valid s-t-cut algorithm described in Section 5 has also been implemented and evaluated experimentally in [12]. Its performance was even better than that of the disjoint paths algorithms, with an average running-time under 2 seconds per AS pair. Furthermore, it was shown in [12] that the approximation algorithms discussed in Section 4 run very fast on the ToR graphs used in the experiments (less than one second of computation time per AS pair). The approximation algorithms mostly give solutions that are optimal or at most one away from the optimum.

The minimum valid cut sizes and the numbers of disjoint valid paths computed by the exact algorithms for the ToR graphs were compared to the corresponding quantities in the undirected BGP graphs in [12]. It turns out that the numbers for all four types of ToR graphs are similar and significantly smaller than for the undirected BGP graphs. For more than 70% of all pairs, the number of disjoint paths (and the minimum cut size) is at least 1.5 times as large in the undirected BGP graphs as in the ToR graphs, and for approximately 44%, these values in the undirected BGP graphs are at least twice as large as in the ToR graphs. While the values for the different ToR graphs are similar, it is observed in [12] that, generally, graphs produced with the algorithm from [8] have the highest values and graphs produced with the algorithm from [24] have the lowest values. The average number of disjoint paths was between 7.4 and 8.1 in the different ToR graphs (with a maximum of 65), and about 13.5 in the undirected BGP graphs (with a maximum of 107). The values for the cut sizes are very similar, as it was found that the number of disjoint paths and the cut size was the same for most of the AS pairs in the ToR graphs, although these quantities could be a factor of two apart in general ToR graphs.

The trends over time of the number of disjoint paths and the cut sizes were also analyzed in [12]. One interesting observation is that from January 2003 to February 2004, about 70% of the AS pairs display increasing connectivity in the undirected BGP graph, but only about 50% of the pairs do so in the four ToR graphs.

7   Conclusions

We have given a survey of recent results concerning disjoint valid s-t-paths and valid s-t-cuts in the valley-free path model. These problems arise in the analysis of the AS topology of the Internet if commonly used routing policies are taken into account. The size of a minimum valid s-t-cut can be viewed as a reasonable measure of the robustness of the Internet connection between ASs s and t. The minimum cut size indicates the number of ASs that must fail in order to completely disconnect s and t. Therefore, the discussed concepts and algorithms could be useful for network administrators who want to assess the quality of their network's connection to the Internet.

After giving an overview of existing approaches to the inference of AS relationships, we have surveyed the exact and approximation algorithms from [10,11,12] and summarized the experimental results of [12] obtained from the computation of disjoint valid paths and valid cuts in four different types of graphs with inferred AS relationships (ToR graphs) and in undirected BGP graphs. The exact algorithms require a small amount of computation time to find optimal values, and the approximation algorithms run very fast and give solutions close to optimal. The algorithms and experimental findings make it possible to quantify the differences in connectivity between ToR graphs and the traditional undirected model of the Internet, which ignores routing policies. The use of ToR graphs instead of undirected graphs is essential for Internet analysis and simulations that are concerned with connectivity properties, e.g. in studies concerning topological robustness or multi-path routing.

From a theoretical perspective, the problems we have considered may be seen as instances of a more general family of problems where paths in the graph must obey certain restrictions. One example of such a restriction is given by oriented paths (paths containing at least one directed edge) in mixed graphs, as considered by Wanke and Kötter [29]. Another example is given by paths in graphs with labeled edges where a path is valid only if the sequence of its edge labels forms a word from a given formal language; shortest-path problems for this type of restriction are studied by Barrett et al. [6] in the context of transportation problems. It would be interesting to study the max disjoint s-t-paths problem and min s-t-cut problem in such a setting.

References

1. S. Agarwal, L. Subramanian, J. Rexford, and R.H. Katz. Characterizing the Internet hierarchy from multiple vantage points, project web-page, 2002–2003. http://www.cs.berkeley.edu/~sagarwal/research/BGP-hierarchy/.
2. A. Ahuja, T. Magnanti, and J. Orlin. *Network Flows: Theory, Algorithms, and Applications*. Prentice-Hall, Englewood Cliffs, N.J., 1993.
3. G. Ausiello, P. Crescenzi, G. Gambosi, V. Kann, A. Marchetti-Spaccamela, and M. Protasi. *Complexity and Approximation. Combinatorial Optimization Problems and their Approximability Properties*. Springer, Berlin, 1999.
4. P. Baake and T. Wichmann. On the economics of Internet peering. *Netnomics*, 1(1), 1999.
5. C. Barnhart, E. Johnson, G. Nemhauser, M. Savelsbergh, and P. Vance. Branch-and-price: Column generation for solving huge integer programs. *Operations Research*, 46(3):316–329, 1998.
6. C. L. Barrett, R. Jacob, and M. Marathe. Formal language constrained path problems. *SIAM J. Comput.*, 30(3):809–837, 2000.
7. G. Di Battista, M. Patrignani, and M. Pizzonia. Computing the types of the relationships between Autonomous Systems, project web-page. http://www.dia.uniroma3.it/~compunet/relationships/.
8. G. Di Battista, M. Patrignani, and M. Pizzonia. Computing the types of the relationships between autonomous systems. In *Proceedings of INFOCOM'03*, 2003.
9. T. Erlebach, A. Hall, and T. Schank. Classifying customer-provider relationships in the Internet. In *Proceedings of the IASTED International Conference on Communications and Computer Networks*, pages 538–545, 2002.
10. T. Erlebach, A. Hall, A. Panconesi, and D. Vukadinović. Cuts and disjoint paths in the valley-free path model. TIK-Report 180, Computer Engineering and Networks Laboratory (TIK), ETH Zürich, 2003. Available electronically at ftp://ftp.tik.ee.ethz.ch/pub/publications/TIK-Report180.pdf.

11. T. Erlebach, A. Hall, A. Panconesi, and D. Vukadinović. Cuts and disjoint paths in the valley-free path model of Internet BGP routing. In *Proceedings of the First Workshop on Combinatorial and Algorithmic Aspects of Networking* (CAAN'04), LNCS 3405, pages 49–62, Springer-Verlag, 2005.

12. T. Erlebach, L.S. Moonen, F.C.R. Spieksma, and D. Vukadinović. Connectivity measures for Internet topologies. DTEW Research Report 0550, Katholieke Universiteit Leuven, Leuven, Belgium, 2005.

13. D.R. Figueiredo, Z. Ge, and S. Jaiswal. Logical relationship inference program (implementation of algorithms from [14]). http://www-net.cs.umass.edu/~ratton/AS/.

14. L. Gao. On inferring Autonomous System relationships in the Internet. *IEEE/ACM Transactions on Networking*, 9(6):733–745, 2001.

15. L. Gao and F. Wang. The extent of AS path inflation by routing policies. In *Proceedings of IEEE Global Internet Symposium 2002*, 2002.

16. M. Grötschel, L. Lovász, and A. Schrijver. *Geometric algorithms and combinatorial optimization*. Springer-Berlin, 1988.

17. G. Huston. Interconnection, peering and settlements—Part I. *Internet Protocol Journal*, 2(1):2–16, March 1999.

18. G. Huston. Interconnection, peering and settlements—Part II. *Internet Protocol Journal*, 2(2):2–23, June 1999.

19. ILOG CPLEX Optimizer, version 9.0. http://www.ilog.com/products/cplex/.

20. C. Labovitz, A. Ahuja, R. Wattenhofer, and S. Venkatachary. The impact of Internet policy and topology on delayed routing convergence. In *Proceedings of INFOCOM'01*, 2001.

21. Library of efficient data types and algorithms (LEDA). http://www.algorithmic-solutions.com/enleda.htm.

22. M. Rimondini, M. Pizzonia, G. Di Battista, and M. Patrignani. Algorithms for the Inference of the Commercial Relationships between Autonomous Systems: Results Analysis and Model Validation. In *Proceedings of IPS 2004, International Workshop on Inter-domain Performance and Simulation*, 2004.

23. Route Views project web-site, University of Oregon. http://www.routeviews.org.

24. L. Subramanian, S. Agarwal, J. Rexford, and R. Katz. Characterizing the Interenet hierarchy from multiple vantage points. In *Proceedings of INFOCOM'02*, 2002.

25. H. Tangmunarunkit, R. Govindan, and S. Shenker. Internet path inflation due to policy routing. In *Proceedings of SPIE ITCom'01*, 2001.

26. H. Tangmunarunkit, R. Govindan, S. Shenker, and D. Estrin. The impact of routing policy on Internet paths. In *Proceedings of INFOCOM'01*, 2001.

27. R. Teixeira, K. Marzullo, S. Savage, and G. Voelker. Characterizing and measuring path diversity of Internet topologies. In *Proceedings of ACM SIGMETRICS 2003*, 2003.

28. F. Vanderbeck and L.A. Wolsey. An exact algorithm for IP column generation. *Operations Research Letters*, 19:151–159, 1996.

29. E. Wanke and R. Kötter. Oriented paths in mixed graphs. In *Proceedings of the 15th International Symposium on Algorithms and Computation* (ISAAC'04), LNCS 3341, pages 629–643, Springer-Verlag, 2004.

30. J. Xia and L. Gao. On the Evaluation of AS Relationship Inferences. In *Proceedings of IEEE Global Communications Conference (GLOBECOM 2004)*, 2004.

Dependable Peer-to-Peer Systems Withstanding Dynamic Adversarial Churn

Keno Albrecht, Fabian Kuhn, and Roger Wattenhofer

ETH Zurich, Computer Engineering and Networks Laboratory,
CH-8092 Zurich, Switzerland
{albrecht, kuhn, wattenhofer}@tik.ee.ethz.ch

Abstract. The most essential difference between classical distributed data structures and peer-to-peer systems is the dynamic behavior of the latter. Unlike traditional systems which consist of a fixed set of machines of which a few might occasionally fail in some way, peer-to-peer systems are characterized by continuous joins and leaves at a high rate (called churn). We address this dynamism in two ways. We present a general information aggregation method which can be used to implement deterministic join and leave protocols which keep the network in a well-balanced state. We also use the information aggregation algorithm together with a primitive called token distribution to obtain a general way of constructing efficient peer-to-peer systems which are resilient to dynamic, adversarial joins and leaves. In each time step, an adversary is allowed to insert and delete a bounded number of arbitrary peers. The system adapts to this churn by rearranging peers or adjusting the topology whenever necessary.

1 Introduction

Storing and handling data in an efficient way lie at the heart of any data-driven computing system. Compared to a traditional client/server approach, decentralized peer-to-peer (P2P) systems have the advantage to be more reliable, available, and efficient because there is no single point of failure and because the load is distributed to many machines. P2P systems are based on common desktop machines ("peers"), distributed over a large-scale network such as the Internet. These peers share and manage data that is conventionally stored on a central server. Usually, peers are under the control of individual users who turn their machines on or off at any time. Such peers join and leave the P2P system at high rates ("churn"), a problem that is not existent in orthodox distributed systems. In other words, a P2P system consists of unreliable components only. Nevertheless, the P2P system should provide a reliable and efficient service.

The growing popularity of real-world P2P systems has spawned a thriving research community. The focus of most research is the development of an efficient lookup operation: given a search key, a peer responsible for the key must be identified. This operation is related to hashing and is therefore sometimes also known as distributed hashing in conjunction with a distributed hash table (DHT).

J. Kohlas, B. Meyer, and A. Schiper (Eds.): Dependable Systems, LNCS 4028, pp. 275–294, 2006.
© Springer-Verlag Berlin Heidelberg 2006

Following the seminal work of Plaxton et al. [26], an assortment of variants of P2P systems and distributed hashing algorithms have been proposed in the literature, such as CAN [28], Chord [32], Tapestry [36], or Kademlia [22].[1] Generally, these systems assign overlay identifiers (IDs) to peers. The IDs are used to organize peers in different topologies (or overlay networks), such as ring, tree, or hypercube topologies. Furthermore, the lookup operation is performed by routing on the topology to a peer with an ID that is "nearest" to a given key.

An important lingering problem is how overlay IDs are assigned to peers. Since a P2P system is completely decentralized and highly dynamic, present solutions often assign the overlay IDs randomly: a newly joining ("bootstrapping") peer connects to an arbitrary peer in the P2P system and chooses a random overlay ID, e.g. by hashing its own IP address. Similarly to a lookup operation, the newly joining peer is routed to its place—determined by the chosen overlay ID—in the P2P system and connects to its neighbors.

It is often argued that random overlay ID assignment will balance the keys well. This is not quite true; in fact, a balls-into-bins analysis will reveal that there is a logarithmic imbalance factor [7]. In other words, with high probability a highly loaded peer stores a factor of $\Theta(\log n)$ more keys than a peer with average load.

In the first part of this paper, we propose an abstract distributed aggregation service for P2P networks. The service allows to (approximately) calculate the value of system-wide variables, such as the number of peers in the system. But it can also be applied to a broader application area, such such as system monitoring, e.g. the "health" of a system [35], or publish/subscribe mechanisms, e.g. how many peers are interested in some topic. Although we describe this service for tree topologies only, our approach directly translates to several other topologies as well.

Using this service, we present a non-randomized join algorithm (and therefore the assignment of overlay IDs), which leads to well-balanced P2P systems. Based on the depth of the tree, which is calculated by our aggregation mechanism, the algorithm determines the largest "gap" in the overlay ID space in which a newly joining peer is inserted.

In the second part of the paper, we go a step further and develop a system which is able to handle dynamic joins and leaves. Using the information aggregation scheme of the first part, we always have a current estimate on the total number of peers in the system which allows us to adapt the topology of the network appropriately.

Most P2P systems in the literature are analyzed against an adversary who can crash a functionally bounded number of random peers. After crashing a few peers the system is given sufficient time to recover again. Our scheme significantly differs from this in two major aspects. First, we assume that joins and leaves occur in a worst-case manner. We think of an adversary which can remove and

---

[1] A variety of applications have been proposed to be run on top of a P2P system, including file sharing tools [8,12], file systems [10,23,11], and spam filter systems [4,37].

add a bounded number of peers. The adversary cannot be fooled by any kind of randomness. It can choose which peers to crash and how peers join. Note that we use the term "adversary" to model worst-case behavior. We do not consider Byzantine faults. Second, the adversary does not have to wait until the system is recovered before it crashes the next batch of peers. Instead, the adversary can constantly crash peers while the system is trying to stay alive. Indeed, our system is *never fully repaired* but *always fully functional*. In particular, our system is resilient against an adversary which continuously attacks the "weakest part" of the system. Such an adversary could for example insert a crawler into the P2P system, learn the topology of the system, and then repeatedly crash selected peers, in an attempt to partition the P2P network. Our system counters such an adversary by continuously moving the remaining or newly joining peers towards the sparse areas.

Clearly, we can not allow our adversary to have unlimited capabilities. In particular, in any constant time interval, the adversary can at most add and/or remove $\Theta(\log n)$ peers, n being the total number of peers presently in the system. Since the peer degree—or the *routing state* per peer—is also in $O(\log n)$, this is asymptotically optimal: If the adversary was allowed to remove as many peers as the the peer degree, it would be able to disconnect a peer completely from the system by crashing all the peer's neighbors. Our model covers an adversary which repeatedly takes down machines by a distributed denial of service attack, but only a bounded number of machines at each point in time. Our system is *synchronous* and we assume messages to be delivered timely, that is, in at most constant time between any pair of operational peers. It would be possible to adapt the system for an asynchronous environment; in this case, the propagation delay of the slowest message defines the notion of time which is needed for the adversarial model.

In principle, our P2P system could be based on almost any of the common P2P topologies [19]. To obtain a system which is as simple as possible, we decided to use a hypercube as the basic structure of our scheme. Each peer is part of a distinct hypercube node; each hypercube node consists of $\Theta(\log n)$ peers. Peers have connections to other peers of their hypercube node and to peers of the neighboring hypercube nodes. In the case of joins or leaves, some of the peers have to change to another hypercube node such that up to constant factors, all hypercube nodes own the same number of peers at all times. If the total number of peers grows or shrinks above or below a certain threshold, the dimension of the hypercube is increased or decreased by one, respectively.

The balancing of peers among the hypercube nodes can be seen as a dynamic token distribution problem [24] on the hypercube. Each node of a graph (hypercube) has a certain number of tokens, the goal is to distribute the tokens along the edges of the graph such that all nodes end up with the same or almost the same number of tokens. While tokens are moved around, an adversary constantly inserts and deletes tokens. Our P2P system builds on two basic components: i) an algorithm which performs the described dynamic token distribution and ii) an information aggregation algorithm which is used to estimate the number of peers in the system and to adapt the dimension accordingly.

Based on the described structure, we get a fully scalable, efficient P2P system which tolerates $O(\log n)$ worst-case joins and/or crashes per constant time interval. As in other P2P systems, peers have $O(\log n)$ neighbors, and the usual operations (e.g. search) take time $O(\log n)$. The main contribution of the paper, however, is to propose and study a model which allows for dynamic adversarial churn. Our basic algorithms (dynamic token distribution and information aggregation) can also be applied to other P2P topologies [19], they can even be used for P2P systems that go beyond distributed hash tables (DHT).

The remainder of the paper is organized as follows. We give a summary of relevant related work in Section 2. Section 3 introduces our information aggregation service and show how it can be used to obtain a deterministic join algorithm. In Section 4, we describe our P2P system which is resilient to dynamic, adversarial churn.

2   Related Work

A plethora of different overlay networks with various interesting technical properties have been proposed over the last years (e.g. [1,3,5,6,16,18,21,26,28,32,36]). There is generally a tradeoff between the number of hops it takes to lookup a specific key and the size of the routing table maintained on every node. For instance, with high probability, Chord [32] guarantees $O(\log n)$ hops and maintains a routing table with $O(\log n)$ entries, while in Kelips [15] lookups are resolved in constant time but this involves $O(\sqrt{n})$ of memory space.

Algorithms for the clever assignment of IDs to joining peers are primarily used to achieve load balancing. At a high level, the idea of employing system information, such as provided by our aggregation scheme, in order to assign IDs to joining peers can be found, in a local scope though, in CAN [28]. CAN proposes a join algorithm in which the joining peer chooses a random ID, and the peer responsible for this ID returns another ID that would split the most loaded peer among itself and all its neighbors.

In Chord [32], multiple *virtual nodes* are mapped to each physical peer to overcome the logarithmic imbalance factor. That is, each peer is (virtually) inserted $O(\log n)$ times with unrelated identifiers into the Chord ring. Rao et al. [27] explore different algorithms to re-arrange load among virtual servers. Simulation results show that it is possible to reach up to 95% of the optimal load balancing. While virtual nodes are primarily used to balance key/data item pairs among peers, our approach can easily be adapted to match other criteria, such as the number of requests per peer, the total disk space available, or even combinations thereof. On the other hand, our join algorithm could be combined with virtual nodes.

Byers et al. [7] applied the "power of two choices"-paradigm to reduce the logarithmic imbalance to a factor of $\log \log n / \log d + O(1)$, where $d \geq 2$ is the number of different hash functions. Among d peers, the least loaded one is chosen to store an item, while the others only redirect to it. In contrast, our approach neither needs to store additional (redirect) information per item nor does it lengthen the search path.

The Astrolabe system [33] is a distributed information management system, which the authors describe as a decentralized hierarchical database. Astrolabe employs an aggregation technique that is similar to the one presented in this paper, although more powerful using a SQL-like query style. In comparison to our work, Astrolabe as well as its follow up work Willow [34] are presented as new stand-alone systems, whereas our aggregation scheme is intended to be integrated into existing P2P systems, such as Kademlia [22] or Chord [32]. An aggregation scheme which is based on gossiping techniques can be found in [17].

Zhang et al. [35] introduced another infrastructure providing system meta information. In this approach, a "Self-Organized Meta Data Overlay" (SOMO) tree is built and maintained on top of an arbitrary DHT, such as CAN [28]. The tree grows and shrinks dynamically as the system size changes. All the information is aggregated bottom up along this tree, and disseminated down again. Since SOMO implements a hierarchical approach, it can be used in a plug-in like fashion independently of the underlying P2P topology. Although this offers a variety of features, it can be criticized from a "pure P2P mindset," as done by the authors themselves. In some sense, our aggregation mechanism provides SOMO functionality in a downright P2P style, with zero message overhead. Furthermore, we consider the deterministic assignment of SOMO's root node a drawback. Although in the case of failures, another node automatically takes over the responsibility of the SOMO root node, with permanent—probably malicious—failures of the changing root node, the SOMO service is at risk. Since our approach operates on the regular P2P topology, it does not have a single point of failure. Therefore, it provides reliable information even in malicious environments.

Due to the nature of P2P systems, fault-tolerance has been a prime issue from the beginning. The systems usually tolerate a large number of random faults. However after crashing a few peers the systems are given sufficient time to recover again. From an experimental point of view, churn has been studied in [29], where practical design tradeoffs in the implementation of existing P2P networks are considered.

Resilience to worst-case failures has been studied in [13,30]. They propose a system where, w.h.p., $(1 - \varepsilon)$-fractions of peers and data survive the adversarial deletion of up to half of all nodes. Unlike in our work the failure model is static. Moreover, if the total number of peers changes by a constant factor, the whole structure has to be rebuilt from scratch.

Scalability and resilience to worst-case joins and leaves has been addressed by Abraham et al. in [2]. The focus lies on maintaining a balanced network rather than on fault-tolerance in the presence of concurrent faults. In contrast to our paper, whenever a join or leave happens, the network has some time to adapt.

The only paper which explicitly treats arbitrarily concurrent worst-case joins and leaves is by Li et al. [20]. The main difference to our work is that Li et al. consider a completely asynchronous model where messages can be arbitrarily delayed. The stronger communication model is compensated by a weaker failure model. It is assumed that peers do not crash. Leaving peers execute an appropriate "exit" protocol and do not leave before the system allows this; crashes are not allowed.

3   Distributed Aggregation Service

The *Distributed Aggregation Service* is an abstract decentralized service which provides approximate[2] information about a P2P system.

The service is built on top of the regular P2P structure. We present our results for "tree" topology P2P systems, such as Kademlia [22]. But the basic idea can be applied to several other topologies as well.

For completeness, we give a quick overview on a Kademlia-like tree topology. Each peer is assigned a unique overlay identifier, a binary bit string. This ID specifies the "domain space" of the peer; a peer is responsible for storing all keys that are within its domain space. In particular, a key is stored by the peer whose bit string matches the longest prefix of the key. A peer p with the bit string $b_1b_2\ldots b_k$ keeps contact with k other peers—its "neighbors." Neighbor p_i $(i = 1,\ldots,k)$ of peer p features a similar bit string as peer p; in particular, all the first $(i-1)$ bits are the same as the bits of peer p, and the bit i itself is inverted. Note that various systems handle the remaining bits differently; this difference is not relevant in this paper.

The basic idea of our aggregation service is now as follows: a peer p with the bit string $b_1b_2\ldots b_k$ is considered to be an "expert" on all the sub domains of all the prefixes of its bit string, that is, for $b_1b_2\ldots b_i$, $i = 0,\ldots,k$. The expert knowledge is constructed inductively through information exchange with the neighbor peers. The peer p is by definition an expert about its own sub domain $b_1b_2\ldots b_k$. Also, the peer p can deduce the state in sub domain $b_1b_2\ldots b_i$ by aggregating its own knowledge on sub domain $b_1b_2\ldots b_{i+1}$, which is available by induction, with the knowledge provided by neighbor peer p_{i+1} about sub domain $b_1b_2\ldots \overline{b_{i+1}}$. In the end, peer p can deduce the state of the whole P2P system, which is equivalent to the sub domain of the empty prefix.

For illustration, we give an example: we use our aggregation service to learn the total number of peers in the P2P system. We assume to have a stable P2P system, as shown in Figure 1.

We describe our example from the perspective of peer p with the bit string 001 (see Figure 2). Peers (periodically) exchange sub domain information with their neighbors. In particular, peer p sends the information that there is one peer in sub domain 001 to neighbor peer p_3 (with ID 000), and in exchange learns that there is one peer in sub domain 000 from neighbor p_3. Literally summing up one and one, peer p deduces that there are 2 peers with prefix 00. Similarly, on the next higher level, peer p exchanges information with neighbor peer p_2

---

[2] The exact up-to-date state of the whole system cannot be known. This would be equivalent to consensus in an asynchronous and dynamic distributed system, which is well known to be impossible [14].

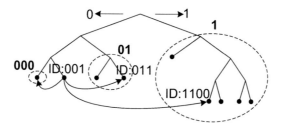

Fig. 1. A sample illustration of sub domains. Dashed circles indicate the partitioning of the system into sub domains for peer 001.

(ID 011) to learn that there are 2 peers with prefix 01. This sums up to a total of 4 peers with prefix 0. In a last step, peer p learns from neighbor peer p_1 (ID 1100) that there are 5 peers with prefix 1.

Since there are 4 peers with prefix 0 and 5 peers with prefix 1, peer p knows that there is a total of 9 peers in the P2P system. Note that our aggregation mechanism runs simultaneously at every peer, and, therefore, provides information in a bottom-up aggregated manner at every peer.

The accuracy of our aggregation service depends on the message propagation mechanisms of the implementation. In a static system, that is, without peers joining or leaving, the service provides exact information without message overhead. In a dynamic system, however, more accuracy requires more frequent message exchange between neighbors. A good tradeoff is to *piggyback* aggregation information on top of ordinary messages and generate new messages only if the traffic is generally low.

Besides computing the total number of peers in the system, our aggregation scheme can deliver a wide range of information, such as the average up-time of peers, the total amount of bytes stored in the system, or, as we show in the next section, the minimal depth of a peer in the tree structure.

3.1   Join Algorithm

The insertion of new peers is an essential and challenging operation in a P2P system. In this section, we introduce a join algorithm as an example application using information provided by our aggregation service describe in Section 3.

For our join algorithm, we employ the *minimal depth service*. The *depth* of a peer is defined as the length of its bit string. Note that we use bit strings of variable length. If the bit strings would be of fixed length, the depth of a peer is the length of the so far assigned prefix of its bit string.

The minimal depth service works as follows (we consider the example given in Figures 1 and 2 again): peer p with ID 001 wants to know in which sub domain a peer with minimal depth can be found. From its neighboring peer p_3 (ID 000) it knows that the minimal depth is 3, and so deduces that with prefix 00 the minimal depth is 3, since both the sub domain of p_3 and p have the same minimal depth. In the next inductive step, through information exchanged with neighbor

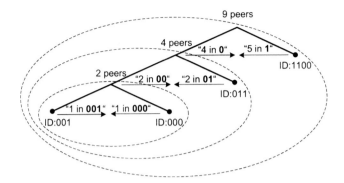

Fig. 2. Illustration of the messages exchanged by peer p (ID 001) for the example given in Figure 1

p_2 (ID 01), peer p learns that the minimal depth in the sub domain of p_2 is 3 as well. In a last step, peer p gets to know from neighbor p_1 (ID 1100) that the minimal depth in its sub domain is 2. Thus, the overall minimal depth is 2, and the aggregation service provides peer p with this result.

Generally, using the *depth join algorithm (DJ)*, each peer can deduce the minimal depth of its sub domains. A new peer (*joiner*) is first routed through the P2P system to sub domains with the smallest minimal depth and then assigned an overlay ID. At every peer passed, one bit of the bit string of the joiner is fixed; this guarantees termination. If a peer (*inserter*) cannot route the joiner any further, it becomes responsible for inserting the new peer. The inserter assigns the joiner its own bit string plus a 1, and appends a 0 to its own bit string, thus splitting its domain space in half. In our example, the joiner would be routed to the peer with ID 10, which splits its current domain space in half, inserts the new peer with ID 101 into the system, and chooses the ID 100 as its own. Afterwards, the tree is balanced with a minimal depth of 3.

It is worth mentioning that the number of peers in a certain sub domain is not a good criterion for inserting new peers. Consider Figure 1 again. A newly joining peer is inserted on the left half of the tree, that is with prefix 0, because the sub domain with prefix 0 is sparser. Since the most loaded peer (ID 10) remains at depth 2, this does not reduce the imbalance in the P2P system. Therefore, we chose the minimal depth as our criterion for inserting peers.

Note that our join approach can also adapt to other criteria than the depth of a node, such as the average number of requests per node, the available disk space or cpu time, or even combinations thereof. Moreover, it can be used with other load balancing strategies, such as load-stealing or load-shedding as described in [7].

As an additional feature, our join algorithm also works against attackers: a malicious adversary might attack a random join system by simply taking out all the peers of a sparse sub domain, making that sub domain even sparser, and raising the load of the remaining peers in the sub domain. Our non-randomized solution will constantly guide newly joining peers towards the sub domain with smallest minimal depth, filling the gaps of the peers that left.

4   Dynamic Adversarial Churn

Compared to classic distributed systems, a major characteristic of P2P systems is their high dynamism. Whereas in classic systems—except for occasional failures—the set of network nodes is fixed, in P2P systems, typically new peers join and leave all the time. In the second part of the paper, we describe a P2P system which can cope with such a highly dynamic situation. We describe a distributed protocol which maintains a simulated hypercube in the presence of an adversary which constantly adds and removes peers. The goal of the maintenance algorithm is twofold. It guarantees that each node always contains at least one peer which stores the node's data. Further, it adapts the hypercube dimension to the total number of peers in the system. This is achieved by two basic components. First, we present a dynamic token distribution algorithm for the hypercube. Based on the information aggregation scheme of Section 3, we then describe a protocol which allows the nodes of the system to coordinate dimension changes of the hypercube. Section 4 is organized as follows. After specifying our communication model in Section 4.1, the token distribution and information aggregation protocols are described in Sections 4.2 and 4.3, respectively. The two components are then put together in Sections 4.4–4.6. Thereby, Section 4.4 defines the overlay topology of our P2P system and Section 4.5 provides a detailed description of the algorithm maintaining the given topology. To obtain a simpler algorithm and a more readable proof, we describe a system with peer degree $O(\log^2 n)$ in Section 4.4 and 4.5. In Section 4.6, we outline how to obtain a system with peer degree $O(\log n)$ while asymptotically preserving all desired properties.

4.1   Model

We consider the *synchronous message passing model* where time is divided into rounds. In every round, each peer can send a message to all its neighbors and receive the messages from all neighbors. Additionally, we have an adversary $\mathcal{A}(J, L, \lambda)$ which may perform J arbitrary joins and L arbitrary leaves (crashes) in each interval of λ rounds.

We assume that a joining peer π_1 contacts an arbitrary peer π_2 which already belongs to the system; π_2 then triggers the necessary actions for π_1's integration. A peer may be contacted by several joining peers simultaneously. In contrast to other systems where peers have to do some finalizing operations before leaving, we consider the more general case where peers depart or crash without notice.

4.2   Dynamic Token Distribution

The problem of distributing peers uniformly throughout a hypercube is a special instance of a *token distribution problem*, first introduced by Peleg and Upfal [24]. The problem has its origins in the area of load balancing, where the workload is modeled by a number of *tokens* or jobs of unit size; the main objective is to distribute the total load equally among the processors. Such load balancing problems arise in a number of parallel and distributed applications including job scheduling in operating systems, packet routing, large-scale differential equations and parallel finite element methods. More applications can be found in [31].

Formally, the goal of a token distribution algorithm is to minimize the maximum difference of tokens at any two nodes, denoted by the *discrepancy* ϕ. This problem has been studied intensively; however, most of the research is about the *static variant* of the problem, where given an arbitrary initial token distribution, the goal is to redistribute these tokens uniformly. In the *dynamic variant* on the other hand, the load is dynamic, that is, tokens may arrive and depart *during* the execution of the token distribution algorithm. In our case, peers may join and leave the simulated hypercube at arbitrary times, so the emphasis lies on the dynamic token distribution problem on a d-dimensional hypercube topology.

We use two variants of the token distribution problem: In the *fractional token distribution*, tokens are arbitrarily divisible, whereas in the *integer token distribution* tokens can only move as a whole. In our case, tokens represent peers and are inherently integer. However, it turns out that the study of the fractional model is useful for the analysis of the integer model.

We use a token distribution algorithm which is based on the *dimension exchange method* [9,25]. Basically, the algorithm cycles continuously over the d dimensions of the hypercube. In step s, where $i = s \bmod d$, every node $u = \beta_0...\beta_i...\beta_{d-1}$ having a tokens balances its tokens with its adjacent node in dimension i, $v = \beta_0...\overline{\beta_i}...\beta_{d-1}$, having b tokens, such that both nodes end up with $\frac{a+b}{2}$ tokens in the fractional token distribution. On the other hand, if the tokens are integer, one node is assigned $\lceil \frac{a+b}{2} \rceil$ tokens and the other one gets $\lfloor \frac{a+b}{2} \rfloor$ tokens.

It has been pointed out in [9] that the described algorithm yields a perfect discrepancy $\phi = 0$ after d steps for the static fractional token distribution. In [25], it has been shown that in the worst case, $\phi = d$ after d steps in the static integer token distribution.

In the following, the dynamic integer token distribution problem is studied, where a "token adversary" $\mathcal{A}(J, L, 1)$ adds at most J and removes at most L tokens at the beginning of each step. In particular, we will show that if the initial distribution is perfect, i.e., $\phi = 0$, our algorithm maintains the invariant $\phi \leq 2J + 2L + d$ at every moment of time.

For the dynamic fractional token distribution, the tokens inserted and deleted at different times can be treated independently and be superposed. Therefore, the following lemma holds.

Lemma 1. *For the dynamic fractional token distribution, the number of tokens at a node depends only on the token insertions and deletions of the last d steps and on the total number of tokens in the system.*

Proof. Assume that a total amount of T tokens are distributed in two different ways on the d-dimensional hypercube. According to [9], each node has exactly $\frac{T}{2^d}$ tokens after d steps in the absence of an adversary. On the other hand, the token insertions and removals of the adversary that happen in-between can be treated as an independent superposition, as the corresponding operations are all linear.   □

We can now bound the discrepancy of the integer token distribution algorithm by comparing it with the fractional problem.

Lemma 2. *Let v be a node of the hypercube. Let $\tau_v(t)$ and $\tau_{v,f}(t)$ denote the number of tokens at v for the integer and fractional token distribution algorithms at time t, respectively. We have $\forall t : |\tau_v(t) - \tau_{v,f}(t)| \leq \frac{d}{2}$.*

Proof. For $t = 0$, we have $\tau_v(t) = \tau_{v,f}(t)$. For symmetry reasons, it is sufficient to show the upper bound $\tau_v(t) \leq \tau_{v,f}(t) + \frac{d}{2}$. We first prove by induction that $\tau_v(t) \leq \tau_{v,f}(t) + \frac{t}{2}$ at time t.

For the induction step, we consider two neighbors u and v which exchange tokens. We have

$$\tau_v(t+1) \leq \left\lceil \frac{\tau_v(t) + \tau_u(t)}{2} \right\rceil \leq \left\lceil \frac{\lfloor \tau_{v,f}(t) + \frac{t}{2}\rfloor + \lfloor \tau_{u,f}(t) + \frac{t}{2}\rfloor}{2} \right\rceil$$
$$\leq \frac{\lfloor \tau_{v,f}(t) + \frac{t}{2}\rfloor + \lfloor \tau_{u,f}(t) + \frac{t}{2}\rfloor}{2} + \frac{1}{2} \leq \tau_{v,f}(t+1) + \frac{t+1}{2}.$$

The second inequality follows from the induction hypothesis and the fact that $\tau_v(t)$ and $\tau_u(t)$ are integers. Note that adding or removing tokens has no influence on the difference between τ_v and $\tau_{v,f}$ because it modifies τ_v and $\tau_{v,f}$ in the same way.

So far, we have seen that the number of integer tokens can deviate from the number of fractional tokens by at most $\frac{d}{2}$ after the first d steps. In order to show that this holds for all times t, we consider a fractional token distribution problem $\hat{\tau}_{v,f}$ for which $\hat{\tau}_{v,f}(t-d) = \tau_v(t-d)$. Using the above argument, we have $\tau_v(t-d) \leq \hat{\tau}_{v,f}(t)$ and by Lemma 1, we get $\hat{\tau}_{v,f}(t) = \tau_{v,f}(t)$. This concludes the proof. $\square$

Lemma 3. *In the presence of an adversary $\mathcal{A}(J, L, 1)$, it always holds that the integer discrepancy $\phi \leq 2J + 2L + d$.*

Proof. We show that the *fractional* discrepancy ϕ_f is bounded by $2J + 2L$. Since Lemma 2 implies that for the integer discrepancy ϕ_i it holds that $\phi_i - \phi_f \leq d$, the claim follows. Let $J_t \leq J$ and $L_t \leq L$ be the insertions and deletions that happen at the beginning of step t. First, we consider the case of joins only, i.e., $L_t = 0$. Assume that all J_t tokens are inserted at node $v = \beta_0...\beta_i...\beta_{d-1}$ where $i = t \bmod d$. In the upcoming paragraph, all indices are implicitly modulo d. In step t, according to the token distribution algorithm, v keeps $J_t/2$ tokens and sends $J_t/2$ to node $u = \beta_0...\overline{\beta_i}...\beta_{d-1}$. In step $t+1$, $J_t/4$ are sent to nodes $\beta_0...\beta_i\overline{\beta_{i+1}}...\beta_{d-1}$ and $\beta_0...\overline{\beta_i}\overline{\beta_{i+1}}...\beta_{d-1}$, and so on. Thus, after step $t + d - 1$, every node in the d-dimensional hypercube has the same share of $\frac{J_t}{2^d}$ tokens from that insertion. We conclude that a node can have at most all insertions of this step, half of the insertions of the last step, a quarter of all insertions two steps ago and so on:

$$\underbrace{J_t + \frac{J_{t-1}}{2} + \frac{J_{t-2}}{4} + \ldots + \frac{J_{t-(d-1)}}{2^{d-1}}}_{< 2J} + \underbrace{\frac{J_{t-d}}{2^d} + \frac{J_{t-(d+1)}}{2^d} + \frac{J_{t-(d+2)}}{2^d} + \ldots}_{\text{shared by all nodes}}$$

Since $J_{t-i} \leq J$ for $i = 0, 1, 2, \ldots$, we have $\phi_f \leq 2J$. For the case of only token deletions, the same argument can be applied, yielding a discrepancy of at most $2L$. Finally, if there are both insertions and deletions which do not cancel out each other, we have $\phi_f \leq 2J + 2L$. $\qquad\square$

4.3 Information Aggregation

When the total number of peers in the d-dimensional hypercube system exceeds a certain threshold, all nodes $\beta_0 \ldots \beta_{d-1}$ have to split into two new nodes $\beta_0 \ldots \beta_{d-1}0$ and $\beta_0 \ldots \beta_{d-1}1$, yielding a $(d+1)$-dimensional hypercube. Analogously, if the number of peers falls beyond a certain threshold, nodes $\beta_0 \ldots \beta_{d-2}0$ and $\beta_0 \ldots \beta_{d-2}1$ have to merge their peers into a single node $\beta_0 \ldots \beta_{d-2}$, yielding a $(d-1)$-dimensional hypercube. Using the ideas introduced in Section 3, we present an algorithm which provides the same estimated number of peers in the system to all nodes in every step allowing all nodes to split or merge synchronously, that is, in the same step. The description is again made in terms of *tokens* rather than peers.

Assume that in order to compute the total number of tokens in a d-dimensional hypercube, each node $v = \beta_0 \ldots \beta_{d-1}$ maintains an array $\Gamma_v[0, \ldots, d]$, where $\Gamma_v[i]$ for $i \in \{0, \ldots, d\}$ stores the estimated number of tokens in the sub-cube consisting of the nodes sharing v's prefix $\beta_0 \ldots \beta_{d-1-i}$. Further, assume that at the beginning of each step, an adversary inserts and removes an arbitrary number of tokens at arbitrary nodes. Each node $v = \beta_0 \ldots \beta_{d-1-i} \ldots \beta_{d-1}$ then calculates the new array $\Gamma_v'[0, \ldots, d]$. For this, v sends $\Gamma_v[i]$ to its adjacent node $u = \beta_0 \ldots \overline{\beta_{d-1-i}} \ldots \beta_{d-1}$, for $i \in \{0, \ldots, d-1\}$. Then, $\Gamma_v'[0]$ is set to the new number of tokens at v which is the only node with prefix $\beta_0 \ldots \beta_{d-1}$. For $i \in \{1, \ldots, d\}$, the new estimated number of tokens in the prefix domain $\beta_0 \ldots \beta_{d-1-(i+1)}$ is given by the total number of tokens in the domain $\beta_0 \ldots \beta_{d-1-i}$ plus the total number of tokens in domain $\beta_0 \ldots \overline{\beta_{d-1-i}}$ provided by node u, that is, $\Gamma_v'[i+1] := \Gamma_v[i] + \Gamma_u[i]$.

Lemma 4. *Consider two arbitrary nodes v_1 and v_2 of the d-dimensional hypercube. Our algorithm guarantees that $\Gamma_{v_1}[d] = \Gamma_{v_2}[d]$ at all times t. Moreover, it holds that this value is the correct total number of tokens in the system at time $t - d$.*

Proof. We prove by induction that at time $t + k$, all nodes sharing the prefix $\beta_0 \ldots \beta_{d-1-k}$ for $k \in \{0, \ldots, d\}$ store the same value $\Gamma_v[k]$ which represents the correct state of that sub-domain in step t. Because there is only one node with prefix $\beta_0 \ldots \beta_{d-1}$, the lemma is clear for $k = 0$. By the induction hypothesis, all nodes v with prefix $\beta_0 \ldots \beta_{d-1-(k+1)} \beta_{d-1-k}$ share the same value $\Gamma_v[k]$ which corresponds to the state of the system k steps earlier, and the same holds for all nodes u with prefix $\beta_0 \ldots \beta_{d-1-(k+1)} \overline{\beta_{d-1-k}}$. In step $k+1$, all these nodes having the same prefix $\beta_0 \ldots \beta_{d-1-(k+1)}$ obviously store the same value $\Gamma_v'[k+1] = \Gamma_u'[k+1] = \Gamma_v[k] + \Gamma_u[k]$. $\qquad\square$

4.4   Simulated Hypercube

Based on the components presented in the previous sections, both the topology and the maintenance algorithm will now be described in detail. Given an adversary $\mathcal{A}(d+1, d+1, 6)$ which inserts and removes at most $d+1$ peers in any time interval of 6 rounds we present a system for which 1) the out-degree of every peer is bounded by $\Theta(\log^2 n)$ where n is the total number of peers in the system, 2) the network diameter is bounded by $\Theta(\log n)$, and 3) every node of the simulated hypercube has always at least one peer which stores its data items, so no data item will ever be lost.

We start with a description of the overlay topology. As already mentioned, the peers are organized to simulate a d-dimensional hypercube, where the hypercube's nodes are represented by a group of peers. A data item with identifier id is stored at the node whose identifier matches the first d bits of the hash-value of id.

The peers of each node v are divided into a *core* $\mathcal{C}_v$ of at most $2d+3$ peers and a *periphery* $\mathcal{P}_v$ consisting of the remaining peers; all peers within the same node are completely connected (*intra-connections*). Moreover, every peer is connected to all *core* peers of the neighboring nodes (*inter-connections*). Figure 3 shows an example for $d = 2$.

The data items belonging to node v are replicated on all core peers, while the peripheral peers are used for the balancing between the nodes according to the peer distribution algorithm and do not store any data items. The partition into core and periphery has the advantage that the peers which move between nodes do not have to replace the data of the old node by the data of the new nodes in most cases.

4.5   6-Round (Maintenance) Algorithm

The *6-round (maintenance) algorithm* maintains the simulated hypercube topology described in the previous section given an adversary $\mathcal{A}(d+1, d+1, 6)$. In

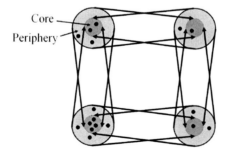

Fig. 3. A simulated 2-dimensional hypercube with four nodes, each consisting of a core and a periphery. All peers within the same node are completely connected to each other, and additionally, all peers of a node are connected to all core peers of the neighboring nodes. Only the core peers store data items, while the peripheral peers may move between the nodes to balance biased adversarial changes.

particular, it ensures that 1) every node has at least one core peer all the times and hence no data is lost; 2) each node always has $\Theta(d)$ peers (the number of peers turns out to be between $3d + 10$ and $45d + 86$); 3) only peripheral peers are moved between nodes, thus the unnecessary copying of data is avoided.

In the following, we refer to a complete execution of all six rounds (ROUND 1 – ROUND 6) of the maintenance algorithm as a *phase*. Basically, the 6-round algorithm balances the peers across one dimension in every phase according to the token distribution algorithm as described in Section 4.2; additionally, the total number of peers in the system is computed with respect to an earlier state of the system by the information aggregation algorithm of Section 4.3 to expand or shrink the hypercube if the total number of peers exceeds or falls below a certain threshold. In our system, we use the lower threshold $LT = 8d + 16$ and the upper threshold $UT = 40d + 80$ for the total number of peers *per node on average*.[3]

While peers may join and leave the system at arbitrary times, the 6-round algorithm considers the (accumulated) changes only once per phase. That is, a snapshot of the system is made in ROUND 1; ROUNDS 2 – 6 then ignore the changes that might have happened in the meantime and depend solely on the snapshot at the beginning of the phase.

ROUND 1

Outline: Each node v makes a snapshot of the currently active peers, denoted by the ID set $\mathcal{S}_v$. The later rounds will only be based on these sets.

Sent Messages: Each peer of a node v sends a packet with its own ID and the (potentially empty) ID set of its joiners to all adjacent peers *within* v.

ROUND 2

Outline: Based on the snapshot of ROUND 1, the core peers of a node v know the total number of peers in the node, $size(v) := |\mathcal{S}_v|$. This information is needed for the peer distribution algorithm (see Section 4.2) and for the estimation of the total number of peers in the system (see Section 4.3).

Local Computations: The core peers compute $size(v) := |\mathcal{S}_v|$.

Sent Messages: Each peer informs its joiners about $\mathcal{S}_v$. The core peers $\mathcal{C}_v$ additionally send the number $size(v)$ to their neighboring core $\mathcal{C}_u$, where node u is v's neighbor in dimension i (the node with which v has to balance its peers in this phase). The core also exchanges the new estimated total number of peers in its domains with the corresponding adjacent cores (according to the algorithm presented in Section 4.3).

ROUND 3

Outline: At the beginning of this round, every peer within a node v knows $\mathcal{S}_v$, and the transfer for the peer distribution algorithm can be prepared. Let v again be an arbitrary node and u its adjacent node in dimension i. We assume

---

[3] Note that since we consider the threshold *on average*, and since these values are provided with a delay of d phases in a d-dimensional hypercube (see Lemma 4), the number of peers at an individual node may lie outside $[LT, UT]$.

that $size(v) > size(u)$; the case where $size(v) \leq size(u)$ is analogous and not described further here. The ID set $\mathcal{T}$ of peers that have to move from node v to node u are the $\frac{size(v)-size(u)}{2}$ (arbitrarily rounded) peers in the periphery $\mathcal{P}_v$ having the smallest identifiers.

Local Computations: The peers in each node v compute the new periphery $\mathcal{P}_v := \mathcal{S}_v \setminus \mathcal{C}_v$. The core remains the same.

Sent Messages: All cores forward the information about the new estimated total number of peers in the system to their peripheral peers. Moreover, the core of the larger node $\mathcal{C}_v$ sends the identifiers of the peers that need to be transferred $\mathcal{T}$ to $\mathcal{C}_u$, and the number $\frac{size(v)-size(u)}{2}$ to the new periphery $\mathcal{P}_v$.

Round 4

Outline: The transfer for the peer distribution algorithm is continued. Moreover, this round prepares the dimension reduction if necessary.

Sent Messages: The core $\mathcal{C}_u$ informs the peers in $\mathcal{T}$ about all neighboring cores $\mathcal{C}_{u_j}$, where u_j is the neighbor of u in dimension j for $j \in \{0, \ldots, d-1\}$, about $\mathcal{C}_u$ itself, about $\mathcal{S}_u$ and about its peripheral peers $\mathcal{P}_u$. Moreover, $\mathcal{C}_u$ informs its own periphery $\mathcal{P}_u$ about the newcomers $\mathcal{T}$.

If the estimated total number of peers in the system is beyond the threshold, the core peers of a node $\bar{v}$ which will be reduced send their data items plus the identifiers of all their peripheral peers (with respect to the situation *after* the transfer) to the core of their adjacent node $\underline{v}$.

Round 5

Outline: This round finishes the peer distribution, establishes the new peripheries, and prepares the building of a new core. If the hypercube has to grow in this phase, the nodes start to split, and vice versa if the hypercube is going to shrink.

Local Computations: Given the number $\frac{size(v)-size(u)}{2}$, the peripheral peers $\mathcal{P}_v$ can compute the set $\mathcal{T}$ selecting the $\frac{size(v)-size(u)}{2}$ smallest elements in $\mathcal{P}_v$. From this, the new periphery $\mathcal{P}_v := \mathcal{P}_v \setminus \mathcal{T}$ is computed. Analogously, the peers in node u (including $\mathcal{T}$) can compute the new periphery $\mathcal{P}_u := \mathcal{P}_u \cup \mathcal{T}$.

Then, all peers of each node v calculate the new core $\mathcal{C}_v^{new}$: It consists of the peers of the old core which have still been alive in Round 1, i.e., $\mathcal{C}_v^{old} := \mathcal{C}_v \cap \mathcal{S}_v$, plus the $2d + 3 - |\mathcal{C}_v \cap \mathcal{S}_v|$ smallest IDs in the new periphery $\mathcal{P}_v$, denoted by $\mathcal{C}_v^\triangle$. Hence, the new core is given by $\mathcal{C}_v^{new} := \mathcal{C}_v^{old} \cup \mathcal{C}_v^\triangle$, and the new periphery by $\mathcal{P}_v^{new} := \mathcal{P}_v \setminus \mathcal{C}_v^\triangle$.

If the hypercube has to grow in this phase, the smallest $2d + 3$ peers in the new periphery $\mathcal{P}_{\underline{v}}^{new}$ become the new core of the expanded node, $\mathcal{C}_{\bar{v}}$. Half of the remaining peripheral peers, the ones with the smaller identifiers, build the new periphery $\mathcal{P}_{\bar{v}}$, and the other half becomes $\mathcal{P}_{\underline{v}}$. All these operations can be computed locally by every peer.

Sent Messages: The old core $\mathcal{C}_v^{old}$ informs all its neighboring nodes (i.e., their old cores) about the new core $\mathcal{C}_v^{new}$. Moreover, $\mathcal{C}_v^{old}$ sends its data items to the peers in $\mathcal{C}_v^\triangle$.

If the hypercube is about to grow, $\mathcal{C}_{\underline{v}}^{old}$ sends the necessary data items to the core peers of the new node, $\mathcal{C}_{\overline{v}}$. Moreover, $\mathcal{C}_{\underline{v}}^{old}$ informs its neighboring (old) cores about the IDs of its expanded core $\mathcal{C}_{\overline{v}}$.

If the hypercube is about to shrink, all cores $\mathcal{C}_{\underline{v}}^{old}$ inform their periphery about the peers arriving from the expanded node and the peers in the expanded node about the new core $\mathcal{C}_{\underline{v}}^{new}$ and its periphery. $\mathcal{C}_{\underline{v}}^{old}$ copies also the data items of $\mathcal{C}_{\overline{v}}^{old}$ to the peers $\mathcal{C}_{\underline{v}}^{\Delta}$.

Round 6

Outline: Building the new cores and accomplishing the dimension change if necessary.

Local Computations: If the hypercube has been reduced, every peer can now compute the new periphery $\mathcal{P}_v$.

Sent Messages: The old core $\mathcal{C}_v^{old}$ forwards the information about the new neighboring cores to the peers $\mathcal{C}_v^{\Delta} \cup \mathcal{P}_v$.

If the hypercube has grown, $\mathcal{C}_{\underline{v}}^{old}$ forwards the expanded cores of its neighboring nodes to *all* peers in its expanded node $\overline{v}$. Note that his requires that $\mathcal{C}_{\underline{v}}^{old}$ remembers the peripheral peers that have been transferred to $\overline{v}$ in Round 5.

Theorem 1. *Given an adversary $\mathcal{A}(d+1, d+1, 6)$ which inserts and removes at most $d+1$ peers per phase, the described 6-round algorithm ensures that 1) every node always has at least one core peer and hence no data is lost; 2) each node has between $3d + 10$ and $45d + 86$ peers, yielding a logarithmic network diameter; 3) only peripheral peers are moved between nodes, thus the unnecessary copying of data is avoided.*

Proof. We first consider a simpler system without the separation into core and periphery, where the maintenance algorithm simply runs the peer distribution algorithm and the information aggregation algorithm to count the total number of peers in the system, and expands or reduces the hypercube with respect to the thresholds $LT = 8d + 16$ and $UT = 40d + 80$ presented above. Moreover, assume that these operations are performed in quiet phases, where the adversary may remove at most $d + 1$ and add at most $d + 1$ peers only in-between.

For this simpler system, it holds that every node in the simulated d-dimensional hypercube has at least $3d + 10$ and at most $45d + 86$ peers at every moment of time. Moreover, after the hypercube has changed its dimension from d_{old} to d_{new}, the dimension will remain stable for at least $2d_{new} + 1$ phases. We will now prove these properties.

We consider the cases where the average number of peers per node μ falls beyond the lower threshold $8d_{old} + 16$ or exceeds the upper threshold $40d_{old} + 80$ in turn. Note that such an event will lead to a dimension change with a delay of d_{old} phases only, see Lemma 4. We prove that after the change, $\mu \in \{8d_{new} + 16, \ldots, 40d_{new} + 80\}$ for at least $d_{new} + 1$ phases. The dimension remains stable for at least $2d_{new} + 1$ phases which implies—together with Lemma 3—that the discrepancy before the next change is limited by $2(d_{new}+1)+2(d_{new}+1)+d_{new} = 5d_{new} + 4$.

Case $\mu < 8d + 16$: At time $t - d_{old}$, it held that $\mu < 8d_{old} + 16$ while at time $t - d_{old} - 1$ we had $\mu \geq 8d_{old} + 16$. In $d_{old} + 1$ phases, there are at most $(d_{old} + 1)(d_{old} + 1) = d_{old}^2 + 2d_{old} + 1$ leaves, so $\mu \geq 8d_{old} + 16 - \frac{d_{old}^2 + 2d_{old} + 1}{2^{d_{old}}} > 8d_{old} + 14$ before merging. Clearly, there must be a node with more than $8d_{old} + 14$ peers, hence, given the discrepancy of $5d_{old} + 4$ (see Lemma 3), every node has more than $3d_{old} + 10$ peers before merging.

What about the maximum? At time $t - d_{old}$, $\mu < 8d_{old} + 16$, and there have been at most $d_{old}(d_{old} + 1)$ joins in d_{old} steps, so $\mu < 8d_{old} + 16 + \frac{d_{old}(d_{old} + 1)}{2^{d_{old}}} < 8d_{old} + 18$ before merging, and $\mu < 16d_{old} + 36$ afterwards. The maximum node has less than $21d_{new} + 61$ peers.

Next, we show that $\mu \geq 8d_{new} + 16$ for the next $d_{new} + 1$ phases after a reduction. At time $t - d_{old} - 1$, $\mu \geq 8d_{old} + 16 = 8d_{new} + 24$. The reduction doubles the average number of peers per node, so $\mu \geq 16d_{new} + 48$. Further, there are at most $(d_{old} + 1)(d_{old} + 1) + (d_{new} + 1)(d_{new} + 1) = 2d_{new}^2 + 6d_{new} + 5$ leaves in the meantime, so $\mu \geq 16d_{new} + 48 - \frac{2d_{new}^2 + 6d_{new} + 5}{2^{d_{new}}} > 16d_{new} + 41 > 8d_{new} + 16$.

Finally, $\mu \leq 40d_{new} + 80$ for $d_{new} + 1$ phases. At time $t - d_{old}$, $\mu < 8d_{new} + 24$, so $\mu < 16d_{new} + 48$ after the reduction. There are at most $d_{old}(d_{old} + 1) + (d_{new} + 1)(d_{new} + 1) = 2d_{new}^2 + 5d_{new} + 3$ joins, so $\mu < 16d_{new} + 48 + \frac{2d_{new}^2 + 5d_{new} + 3}{2^{d_{new}}} < 16d_{new} + 54 < 40d_{new} + 80$.

Case $\mu > 40d + 80$: At time $t - d_{old}$, $\mu > 40d_{old} + 80 = 40d_{new} + 40$, so $\mu > 20d_{new} + 20$ after splitting; there are at most $d_{old}(d_{old} + 1) = d_{new}^2 - d_{new}$ leaves in d_{old} steps, so $\mu > 20d_{new} + 20 - \frac{d_{new}^2 - d_{new}}{2^{d_{new}}} > 20d_{new} + 19$. According to Lemma 3, the minimum node has more than $15d_{new} + 15$ peers after splitting. At time $t - d_{old} - 1$, $\mu \leq 40d_{old} + 80$, and there are at most $(d_{old} + 1)(d_{old} + 1) = d_{old}^2 + 2d_{old} + 1$ joins. So before splitting, $\mu \leq 40d_{old} + 80 + \frac{d_{old}^2 + 2d_{old} + 1}{2^{d_{old}}} < 40d_{old} + 82$, and the maximum node has at most $45d_{old} + 86$ peers.

Next, we show that $\mu \geq 8d_{new} + 16$ for the next $d_{new} + 1$ phases after the expansion. At time $t - d_{old}$, $\mu > 40d_{old} + 80 = 40d_{new} + 40$, so $\mu > 20d_{new} + 20$ after the expansion. Moreover, there are at most $d_{old}(d_{old} + 1) + (d_{new} + 1)(d_{new} + 1) = 2d_{new}^2 + d_{new} + 1$ leaves, and $\mu > 20d_{new} + 20 - \frac{2d_{new}^2 + d_{new} + 1}{2^{d_{new}}} > 20d_{new} + 17 \geq 8d_{new} + 16$. Finally, $\mu \leq 40d_{new} + 80$ for the next $d_{new} + 1$ steps: At time $t - d_{old} - 1$, $\mu \leq 40d_{old} + 80 = 40d_{new} + 40$, so $\mu \leq 20d_{new} + 20$ after the expansion; moreover, there are at most $(d_{old} + 1)(d_{old} + 1) + (d_{new} + 1)(d_{new} + 1) = 2d_{new}^2 + 2d_{new} + 1$ joins, so $\mu \leq 20d_{new} + 20 + \frac{2d_{new}^2 + 2d_{new} + 1}{2^{d_{new}}} < 20d_{new} + 24 < 40d_{new} + 80$.

In our real system, repairing takes six rounds and runs *concurrently* to the adversary. However, as all operations in the whole phase are based upon the state of ROUND 1, a phase can be considered as running uninterruptedly, that is, as if the adversary inserted $d + 1$ and removed $d + 1$ peers only *between* the phases. Thus, the properties shown above also hold in our system. However, we additionally have to postulate that there is always at least one *core peer*. We know that it is always possible to select $2d + 3$ core peers in ROUND 5 with respect to the state of ROUND 1. These peers have to survive until ROUND 6 of the next phase, so for twelve normal rounds in total; however, as the adversary

$\mathcal{A}_{adv}(d + 1, d + 1, 6)$ may remove at most $2d + 2$ peers in twelve rounds, this clearly holds.

Finally, we show that there are indeed enough peripheral peers in ROUND 3 such that core peers do not have to change the node for the peer distribution, that is: In ROUND 3, it holds that $|\mathcal{P}_v| > \frac{size(v) - size(u)}{2}$. From the considerations made above, we know that $size(v) \geq 3d + 10$ and $size(u) \geq 3d + 10$. As v has at most $2d + 3$ core peers, we have $|\mathcal{P}_v| \geq size(v) - (2d + 3) \geq size(v) - size(u) > \frac{size(v) - size(u)}{2}$. □

4.6 Reducing the Degrees

In order to enhance clarity, we described a scheme which is as simple as possible. In this section, we briefly outline the necessary changes which allow to reduce the peer degree from $O(\log^2 n)$ to $O(\log n)$.

The reason for the high peer degree are the connections between adjacent nodes of the underlying hypercube. Each peer of a given hypercube node is connected to a logarithmic number of peers in each neighboring hypercube node. It is clear that in order to significantly reduce the peer degrees, we have to replace the complete bipartite graphs between cores and peripheries of adjacent hypercube nodes by a sparser structure. It can be shown that connectivity can still be guaranteed if we choose a sparse graph where every peer is connected to only one core peer of each adjacent hypercube node and where every core peer has only a constant number of connections to each adjacent hypercube node. We will need a few more rounds in the maintenance algorithm because sending a message from a hypercube node to all peers of an adjacent hypercube node now takes two rounds instead of one round. If all constants are chosen carefully, it can be shown that we obtain a system with peer degree $O(\log n)$ and diameter $O(\log n)$. The system tolerates $O(\log n)$ worst-case joins and leaves per time unit.

References

1. K. Aberer. P-Grid: A Self-Organizing Access Structure for P2P Information Systems. In *Proc. 9th Int. Conference on Cooperative Information Systems (CoopIS)*, pages 179–194, 2001.
2. I. Abraham, B. Awerbuch, Y. Azar, Y. Bartal, D. Malkhi, and E. Pavlov. A Generic Scheme for Building Overlay Networks in Adversarial Scenarios. In *Proc. 17th Int. Symp. on Parallel and Distributed Processing (IPDPS)*, page 40.2, 2003.
3. I. Abraham, D. Malkhi, and O. Dobzinski. LAND: Stretch $(1 + \varepsilon)$ Locality-Aware Networks for DHTs. In *Proc. 15th Ann. ACM-SIAM Symp. on Discrete Algorithms (SODA)*, pages 550–559, 2004.
4. K. Albrecht, N. Burri, and R. Wattenhofer. Spamato – An Extendable Spam Filter System. In *Proceedings of 2nd Conference on Email and Anti-Spam (CEAS)*, 2005.
5. J. Aspnes and G. Shah. Skip Graphs. In *Proc. 14th Ann. ACM-SIAM Symp. on Discrete Algorithms (SODA)*, pages 384–393, 2003.
6. B. Awerbuch and C. Scheideler. The Hyperring: A Low-Congestion Deterministic Data Structure for Distributed Environments. In *Proc. 15th Ann. ACM-SIAM Symp. on Discrete Algorithms (SODA)*, pages 318–327, 2004.

7. J. Byers, J. Considine, and M. Mitzenmacher. Simple Load Balancing for Distributed Hash Tables. In *Proceedings of 2nd International Workshop on Peer-to-Peer Systems (IPTPS)*, 2003.
8. B. Cohen. Incentives Build Robustness in BitTorrent. In *Proceedings of 1st Workshop on the Economics of Peer-to-Peer Systems*, 2003.
9. G. Cybenko. Dynamic Load Balancing for Distributed Memory Multiprocessors. *Journal on Parallel Distributed Computing*, 7:279–301, 1989.
10. F. Dabek, M. F. Kaashoek, D. Karger, R. Morris, and I. Stoica. Wide-area cooperative storage with CFS. In *Proceedings of the 18th ACM Symposium on Operating Systems Principles (SOSP)*, 2001.
11. P. Druschel and A. Rowstron. PAST: A Large-Scale, Persistent Peer-to-Peer Storage Utility. In *Proceedings of 8th Workshop on Hot Topics in Operating Systems (HotOS)*, 2001.
12. eDonkey. http://www.edonkey2000.com/.
13. A. Fiat and J. Saia. Censorship Resistant Peer-to-Peer Content Addressable Networks. In *Proc. 13th Symp. on Discrete Algorithms (SODA)*, 2002.
14. M. J. Fischer, N. A. Lynch, and M. S. Paterson. Impossibility of distributed consensus with one faulty process. *Journal of the ACM*, 32(2):374–382, 1985.
15. I. Gupta, K. Birman, P. Linga, A. Demers, and R. van Renesse. Kelips: Building an Efficient and Stable P2P DHT Through Increased Memory and Background Overhead. In *Proceedings of 2nd International Workshop on Peer-to-Peer Systems (IPTPS)*, 2003.
16. N. J. A. Harvey, M. B. Jones, S. Saroiu, M. Theimer, and A. Wolman. SkipNet: A Scalable Overlay Network with Practical Locality Properties. In *Proc. 4th USENIX Symp. on Internet Technologies and Systems (USITS)*, 2003.
17. M. Jelasity, A. Montresor, and O. Babaoglu. Gossip-based aggregation in large dynamic networks. *ACM Transactions on Computer Systems*, 23(3):219–252, 2005.
18. J. Kubiatowicz, D. Bindel, Y. Chen, P. Eaton, D. Geels, R. Gummadi, S. Rhea, H. Weatherspoon, W. Weimer, C. Wells, and B. Zhao. OceanStore: An Architecture for Global-scale Persistent Storage. In *Proc. of ACM ASPLOS*, November 2000.
19. F. Kuhn, S. Schmid, J. Smit, and R. Wattenhofer. Constructing robust dynamic peer-to-peer systems. Technical report, ETH Zurich, 2005. TIK Report 216.
20. X. Li, J. Misra, and C. G. Plaxton. Active and Concurrent Topology Maintenance. In *Proc. 18th Ann. Conference on Distributed Computing (DISC)*, 2004.
21. D. Malkhi, M. Naor, and D. Ratajczak. Viceroy: A Scalable and Dynamic Emulation of the Butterfly. In *Proc. 21st Ann. Symp. on Principles of Distributed Computing (PODC)*, pages 183–192, 2002.
22. P. Maymounkov and D. Mazieres. Kademlia: A Peer-to-peer Information System Based on the XOR Metric. In *Proceedings of 1st International Workshop on Peer-to-Peer Systems (IPTPS)*, 2002.
23. A. Muthitacharoen, R. Morris, T. M. Gil, and B. Chen. Ivy: A Read/Write Peer-to-Peer File System. In *Proceedings of 5th Symposium on Operating Systems Design and Implementation (OSDI)*, 2002.
24. D. Peleg and E. Upfal. The Token Distribution Problem. *SIAM Journal on Computing*, 18(2):229–243, 1989.
25. C. G. Plaxton. Load Balancing, Selection and Sorting on the Hypercube. In *Proc. 1st Ann. ACM Symp. on Parallel Algorithms and Architectures (SPAA)*, pages 64–73, 1989.
26. C. G. Plaxton, R. Rajaraman, and A. W. Richa. Accessing Nearby Copies of Replicated Objects in a Distributed Environment. In *Proc. 9th Ann. ACM Symp. on Parallel Algorithms and Architectures (SPAA)*, pages 311–320, 1997.

27. A. Rao, K. Lakshminarayanan, S. Surana, R. Karp, and I. Stoica. Load Balancing in Structured P2P Systems. In *Proceedings of 2nd International Workshop on Peer-to-Peer Systems (IPTPS)*, 2003.

28. S. Ratnasamy, P. Francis, M. Handley, R. Karp, and S. Shenker. A Scalable Content Addressable Network. In *Proc. of ACM SIGCOMM 2001*, 2001.

29. S. Rhea, D. Geels, T. Roscoe, and J. Kubiatowicz. Handling Churn in a DHT. In *Proc. USENIX Ann. Technical Conference*, 2004.

30. J. Saia, A. Fiat, S. Gribble, A. Karlin, and S. Saroiu. Dynamically Fault-Tolerant Content Addressable Networks. In *Proc. 1st Int. Workshop on Peer-to-Peer Systems (IPTPS)*, 2002.

31. B. A. Shirazi, K. M. Kavi, and A. R. Hurson. *Scheduling and Load Balancing in Parallel and Distributed Systems*. IEEE Computer Science Press, 1995.

32. I. Stoica, R. Morris, D. Karger, M. F. Kaashoek, and H. Balakrishnan. Chord: A Scalable Peer-to-peer Lookup Service for Internet Applications. In *Proc. ACM SIGCOMM Conference*, 2001.

33. R. Van Renesse, K. P. Birman, and W. Vogels. Astrolabe: A Robust and Scalable Technology for Distributed System Monitoring, Management, and Data Mining. *ACM Transactions on Computing Systems*, 21(2):164–206, 2003.

34. R. van Renesse and A. Bozdog. Willow: DHT, Aggregation, and Publish/Subscribe in One Protocol. In *Proc. 3rd Int. Workshop on Peer-To-Peer Systems (IPTPS)*, 2004.

35. Z. Zhang, S.-M. Shi, and J. Zhu. SOMO: Self-Organized Metadata Overlay for Resource Management in P2P DHT. In *Proceedings of 2nd International Workshop on Peer-to-Peer Systems (IPTPS)*, 2003.

36. B. Y. Zhao, L. Huang, J. Stribling, A. D. Joseph, and J. D. Kubiatowicz. Tapestry: A Resilient Global-scale Overlay for Service Deployment. *IEEE Journal on Selected Areas in Communications*, 22(1), 2004.

37. F. Zhou, L. Zhuang, B. Y. Zhao, L. Huang, A. D. Joseph, and J. D. Kubiatowicz. Approximate Object Location and Spam Filtering on Peer-to-peer Systems. In *Proceedings of 4ht ACM/IFIP/USENIX International Middleware Conference (Middleware)*, 2003.

Author Index

Lecture Notes in Computer Science

For information about Vols. 1–3999

please contact your bookseller or Springer

Vol. 4048: L. Goble, J.-J.C.. Meyer (Eds.), Deontic Logic and Artificial Normative Systems. X, 273 pages. 2006. (Sublibrary LNAI).

Vol. 4047: M. Robshaw (Ed.), Fast Software Encryption. XI, 434 pages. 2006.

Vol. 4046: S.M. Astley, M. Brady, C. Rose, R. Zwiggelaar (Eds.), Digital Mammography. XVI, 654 pages. 2006.

Vol. 4045: D. Barker-Plummer, R. Cox, N. Swoboda (Eds.), Diagrammatic Representation and Inference. XII, 301 pages. 2006. (Sublibrary LNAI).

Vol. 4044: P. Abrahamsson, M. Marchesi, G. Succi (Eds.), Extreme Programming and Agile Processes in Software Engineering. XII, 230 pages. 2006.

Vol. 4043: A.S. Atzeni, A. Lioy (Eds.), Public Key Infrastructure. XI, 261 pages. 2006.

Vol. 4042: D. Bell, J. Hong (Eds.), Flexible and Efficient Information Handling. XVI, 296 pages. 2006.

Vol. 4041: S.-W. Cheng, C.K. Poon (Eds.), Algorithmic Aspects in Information and Management. XI, 395 pages. 2006.

Vol. 4040: R. Reulke, U. Eckardt, B. Flach, U. Knauer, K. Polthier (Eds.), Combinatorial Image Analysis. XII, 482 pages. 2006.

Vol. 4039: M. Morisio (Ed.), Reuse of Off-the-Shelf Components. XIII, 444 pages. 2006.

Vol. 4038: P. Ciancarini, H. Wiklicky (Eds.), Coordination Models and Languages. VIII, 299 pages. 2006.

Vol. 4037: R. Gorrieri, H. Wehrheim (Eds.), Formal Methods for Open Object-Based Distributed Systems. XVII, 474 pages. 2006.

Vol. 4036: O. H. Ibarra, Z. Dang (Eds.), Developments in Language Theory. XII, 456 pages. 2006.

Vol. 4035: T. Nishita, Q. Peng, H.-P. Seidel (Eds.), Advances in Computer Graphics. XX, 771 pages. 2006.

Vol. 4034: J. Münch, M. Vierimaa (Eds.), Product-Focused Software Process Improvement. XVII, 474 pages. 2006.

Vol. 4033: B. Stiller, P. Reichl, B. Tuffin (Eds.), Performability Has its Price. X, 103 pages. 2006.

Vol. 4032: O. Etzion, T. Kuflik, A. Motro (Eds.), Next Generation Information Technologies and Systems. XIII, 365 pages. 2006.

Vol. 4031: M. Ali, R. Dapoigny (Eds.), Advances in Applied Artificial Intelligence. XXIII, 1353 pages. 2006. (Sublibrary LNAI).

Vol. 4029: L. Rutkowski, R. Tadeusiewicz, L.A. Zadeh, J. Zurada (Eds.), Artificial Intelligence and Soft Computing – ICAISC 2006. XXI, 1235 pages. 2006. (Sublibrary LNAI).

Vol. 4028: J. Kohlas, B. Meyer, A. Schiper (Eds.), Dependable Systems: Software, Computing, Networks. XII, 295 pages. 2006.

Vol. 4027: H.L. Larsen, G. Pasi, D. Ortiz-Arroyo, T. Andreasen, H. Christiansen (Eds.), Flexible Query Answering Systems. XVIII, 714 pages. 2006. (Sublibrary LNAI).

Vol. 4026: P.B. Gibbons, T. Abdelzaher, J. Aspnes, R. Rao (Eds.), Distributed Computing in Sensor Systems. XIV, 566 pages. 2006.

Vol. 4025: F. Eliassen, A. Montresor (Eds.), Distributed Applications and Interoperable Systems. XI, 355 pages. 2006.

Vol. 4024: S. Donatelli, P. S. Thiagarajan (Eds.), Petri Nets and Other Models of Concurrency - ICATPN 2006. XI, 441 pages. 2006.

Vol. 4021: E. André, L. Dybkjær, W. Minker, H. Neumann, M. Weber (Eds.), Perception and Interactive Technologies. XI, 217 pages. 2006. (Sublibrary LNAI).

Vol. 4020: A. Bredenfeld, A. Jacoff, I. Noda, Y. Takahashi (Eds.), RoboCup 2005: Robot Soccer World Cup IX. XVII, 727 pages. 2006. (Sublibrary LNAI).

Vol. 4019: M. Johnson, V. Vene (Eds.), Algebraic Methodology and Software Technology. XI, 389 pages. 2006.

Vol. 4018: V. Wade, H. Ashman, B. Smyth (Eds.), Adaptive Hypermedia and Adaptive Web-Based Systems. XVI, 474 pages. 2006.

Vol. 4017: S. Vassiliadis, S. Wong, T.D. Hämäläinen (Eds.), Embedded Computer Systems: Architectures, Modeling, and Simulation. XV, 492 pages. 2006.

Vol. 4016: J.X. Yu, M. Kitsuregawa, H.V. Leong (Eds.), Advances in Web-Age Information Management. XVII, 606 pages. 2006.

Vol. 4014: T. Uustalu (Ed.), Mathematics of Program Construction. X, 455 pages. 2006.

Vol. 4013: L. Lamontagne, M. Marchand (Eds.), Advances in Artificial Intelligence. XIII, 564 pages. 2006. (Sublibrary LNAI).

Vol. 4012: T. Washio, A. Sakurai, K. Nakajima, H. Takeda, S. Tojo, M. Yokoo (Eds.), New Frontiers in Artificial Intelligence. XIII, 484 pages. 2006. (Sublibrary LNAI).

Vol. 4011: Y. Sure, J. Domingue (Eds.), The Semantic Web: Research and Applications. XIX, 726 pages. 2006.

Vol. 4010: S. Dunne, B. Stoddart (Eds.), Unifying Theories of Programming. VIII, 257 pages. 2006.

Vol. 4009: M. Lewenstein, G. Valiente (Eds.), Combinatorial Pattern Matching. XII, 414 pages. 2006.

Vol. 4008: J.C. Augusto, C.D. Nugent (Eds.), Designing Smart Homes. XI, 183 pages. 2006. (Sublibrary LNAI).

Vol. 4007: C. Àlvarez, M. Serna (Eds.), Experimental Algorithms. XI, 329 pages. 2006.

Vol. 4006: L.M. Pinho, M. González Harbour (Eds.), Reliable Software Technologies – Ada-Europe 2006. XII, 241 pages. 2006.

Vol. 4005: G. Lugosi, H.U. Simon (Eds.), Learning Theory. XI, 656 pages. 2006. (Sublibrary LNAI).

Vol. 4004: S. Vaudenay (Ed.), Advances in Cryptology - EUROCRYPT 2006. XIV, 613 pages. 2006.

Vol. 4003: Y. Koucheryavy, J. Harju, V.B. Iversen (Eds.), Next Generation Teletraffic and Wired/Wireless Advanced Networking. XVI, 582 pages. 2006.

Vol. 4001: E. Dubois, K. Pohl (Eds.), Advanced Information Systems Engineering. XVI, 560 pages. 2006.